ADVANCE PRAISE FOR

Diagnosing Whiteness and Anti-Blackness
White Psychopathology, Collective Psychosis, and Trauma in America

"One quote out of many that stood out for me in history was that of Toni Morrison when she shared, 'If you can only be tall because someone else is on their knees, then you have a serious problem. And white people have a very, very serious problem.' Toni Morrison went on to call those implementing racism as bereft with distorted psyche's explaining that racism for white people is almost as a drug and without it, they would live in the addictive state of withdrawal. Toni Morrison gave a call in for white people to learn how to exist without racism as a backbone to their identity.

Dante D. King's original examination built upon Morrison's observation of the white racial psyche through his book, *Diagnosing Whiteness and Anti-Blackness: White Psychopathology, Collective Psychosis, and Trauma in America*. His infused insights are now expanded upon in this book through a trauma-informed lens.

The root of racialized trauma and minoritization are impelled upon us as Black people through the actions of White supremacy, White privilege, and the ideology of Whiteness. King's research shows how each of these components are rooted in White psychopathy, White sociopathy, and White psychopathology. Such diseases, including the study and diagnosis of each, are postured under the umbrella of racism through white terrorism. In this book, King brilliantly synthesizes such researched elements of racism to the sociohistorical and sociopolitical dynamics of development and behavior."

—Debra Debi Jenkins, PhD, author of
Daring to Dismantle: Audaciously Addressing Race and Caste in Betrayal Trauma

"The book ranks for me as one of the most significant, erudite, thorough, and powerfully voiced books ever written on race in America. This a riveting, compelling and excruciating presentation, indictment, and prosecution of 'White America' from its inception as a psychopathic and sociopathic construction, which persists into the present. 'White' America exists juxtaposed to its violently parasitic extortion of Blackness. While the book makes the case for pathology and sociopathy, no such 'racism' diagnosis currently exists in the DSM or WHO-ICD, but such a diagnosis is a logical extension of King's argument. We cannot jump straight to renewal in the United States of America without truth and reconciliation. For us to realize our best days ahead as a nation, the truth presented in this book is foundational reading."

—Dr. William J. Watson, author of *Twelve Steps for White America*

"Dante D. King's book is not only a challenging, searing look at our racial crisis, it's a guide for how to begin climbing out of our pit. By turns mind-blowing and instructive, *Diagnosing Whiteness and Anti-Blackness* is an urgent book for our times."

—David Talbot, author of New York Times Best Sellers
The Devil's Chessboard and *Season of the Witch*

"His understanding, explanation of, and specific references to the social, legal, psychological establishment of American anti-Blackness empowering White supremacy from colonial 1619 to the present are spectacular historical game changers; his scholarship is outstanding."

—Wyndy Knox Carr, Knox Book Beat, *Berkeley Times*

Diagnosing Whiteness and Anti-Blackness

Diagnosing Whiteness and Anti-Blackness

White Psychopathology,
Collective Psychosis,
and Trauma in America

WRITTEN BY DANTE D. KING

TABLE OF CONTENTS

DEAR BLACK PEOPLE

Dear Black people,

White America was built upon a foundation of collective White American psychopathological violence, collective psychosis, and Black trauma. The delusion and perversion of Whiteness informs every aspect of American culture and its institutions. Black people have been and remain casualties of White psychopathological violence and trauma. Black people remain casualties of American culture and institutions. Our exploitation in White America cannot be controlled. Therefore, we are not responsible for any of the disruptions and oppressive conditions that have been caused to our community.

We must recognize that every Black person who has ever existed under the oppressive systems and culture in White America has done their absolute best to survive the abusive and debilitating nature of Whiteness and anti-Blackness. The mayhem we see happening throughout Black communities across America is the result of intentional decisions made by White people over hundreds of years. While we know this in theory, it is important to examine this in more concrete terms.

Because of our place in White America, more specifically as exploited subjects of White people and White American institutions, we remain in a state of perpetual psychosis and trauma.

Please remember that White supremacy culture (White people themselves, as well as any people prioritized above African Americans) requires daily Black subjugation. This means culturally, morally, physically, mentally, intellectually, and ideologically.

Whiteness is a construct created to maintain power, supremacy, exclusion, and oppression through legal, social, cultural, psychological, emotional, economic, and all other structures. That means everyone non-White, but Black people in particular. [26,162]

White identity was created in juxtaposition to Black identity and is inherently dependent upon anti-Blackness. This means that as a Black person in America, you must never do anything to disagree with or upset White people (or anyone prioritized on the racial hierarchy above you). You must present in ways that do not disturb their perception of who you are because it will ultimately lead to them canceling your ability to survive in this country. That includes in literal terms.

You, the oppressed Black person, must recognize that the reality of "White privilege," as some social scientists now refer to it, is more than just privilege. It requires the ceaseless dehumanization of the other. Any other, but especially you. It is not merely a matter of racism or of prejudice. Jewish people may understand this well, given their recent history.

The reality that we are victims of genocide must be clear to you. And that White America will continue to slaughter us in every way it can, for as long as it can. The process will start from birth and end only with death. Put another way, White people have accomplished with Black people what Adolf Hitler attempted to accomplish with Jewish people in the 1930s and 1940s in Germany. That is to say he normalized and perpetuated an anti-human mentality surrounding a group of others. The distinction is that Hitler was stopped by a massive and global effort. White America has succeeded in normalizing anti-Blackness. As Malcom X stated in his 1962 talk, "Who Taught You to Hate Yourself":

> The press, the radio, the television, and the newspapers are stacked against Negroes. The controlled press, the White press, has inflamed the White public against Negroes. The police are able to use it to paint the Negro community as a criminal element. The police are able to use the press to make the White public think that 99% of the Negroes in the Negro community, are criminals. And once the White public is convinced that most of the Negro community is a criminal element, then this automatically paves the way for the police to move into the Negro community, exercising Gestapo tactics, stopping any Black man on the sidewalk whether he is guilty or whether he is innocent, whether he is well dressed or whether he is poorly dressed, whether he is educated or whether he is dumb, whether he is Christian or whether he is Muslim—as long as he is Black and a member of the Negro community, the White public thinks that the White police are justified in going in there and trampling on that man's civil rights and on that man's human rights.
>
> Once the police have convinced the White public that the so-called Negro community is a criminal element, they can go in and question, brutalize, murder unarmed innocent Negroes, and the White public are gullible enough to back them up.[200]

The main difference between 1962 and 2022 is that a greater number of non-White (Asian, Middle Eastern, Hispanic, Latinx, etc.) and Black people have been infected with a White supremacist mindset. Though many will claim to be allies, most are not. The problem is that their identities are still defined by Whiteness. It is a White mentality that sets the parameters for how they self-identify. Whiteness is still king. So, their value can only be earned by getting as close to (but never one with) Whiteness as possible. That means as far away from Blackness as possible. View with suspicion those who don't support you entirely. They are not as impacted by their non-Whiteness as you are by your Blackness. You are not where their home is. You are not the tribe they aspire to cozy up to. The experiences of Black people in America are unlike any other experiences of people from other, non-White communities, and we must understand this. America's cultural orientation with Black people is distinct in its inhumanity.

The words of President Donald Trump in 2023, President Richard Nixon in 1969, President Woodrow Wilson in 1915, President Abraham Lincoln in 1858, President Andrew Johnson in 1841, and President Thomas Jefferson in 1781 clearly demonstrate the purpose for this book.

In the words of President Donald Trump, December 16 and 18, 2023:

America is the land of opportunity, however, the influx—it needs to be kept to a certain level. They're destroying the blood of our country. They come from Africa, they come from Asia, they come from South America. That's what they're doing. They're destroying our country. They let—I think the real number is 15–16 million people into our country. When they do that, we got a lot of work to do. They're poisoning the blood of our country.[398,399]

And in the words of President Richard Nixon, April 28, 1969:

You have to face the facts, the whole problem is really the Black people. The key is to devise a system that recognizes this without appearing to.[250-51]

And in the words of President Woodrow Wilson, 1915:

The white men of the South were aroused by the mere instinct of self-preservation to rid themselves, by fair means or foul, of the intolerable burden of governments sustained by the votes of ignorant negroes and conducted in the interest of adventurers.[310,313]

And in the words of President Abraham Lincoln, September 18, 1858:

> I will say then that I am not, nor ever have been, in favor of bringing about
> in any way the social and political equality of the white and black races,
> that I am not nor ever have been in favor of making voters or jurors of
> negroes, nor of qualifying them to hold office, nor to intermarry with white
> people; and I will say in addition to this that there is a physical difference
> between the white and black races which I believe will forever forbid the
> two races living together on terms of social and political equality. And in-
> asmuch as they cannot so live, while they do remain together there must be
> the position of superior and inferior, and I as much as any other man am in
> favor of having the superior position assigned to the white race.[279]

And in the words of President Andrew Johnson, 1841:

> If blacks were given the right to vote, that would place every splay-foot-
> ed, bandy shanked, hump-backed, thick-lipped, flat-nosed, woolly-headed,
> ebon-colored negro in the country upon an equality with the poor white
> man.[311,314]

And in the words of President Thomas Jefferson, 1781 and 1820, respectively:

> I advance it therefore as a suspicion only, that the blacks, whether original-
> ly a distinct race, or made distinct by time and circumstances, are inferior
> to the whites in the endowments both of body and mind.[312,315]

> I know no error more consuming to an estate than that of stocking farms
> with men almost exclusively. I consider a woman who brings a child every
> two years as more profitable than the best man on the farm. What she
> produces is an addition to the capital, while his labors disappear in mere
> consumption.[312,315]

A QUOTE REPEATEDLY ATTRIBUTED to Maya Angelou: "There is no great-er agony than bearing an untold story inside you." This is what comes to mind when I think of this work by Dante King. For years, he has been overflowing with both love and hurt. He has held on to a 100-pound weight that holds the truth he knows and the sorrow he feels for so many of us who do not know the truth.

Dante displays courage and tirelessness in this work. He treasures the history we all share and cries out to explain the relevance, relation, and ge-nealogy of the disease of anti-Black racism and White supremacy. The agony Dante bears is eased by the telling of the stories inside these pages.

Dante is an educator, and as my mother might say, a learned man. He has immersed himself in history and social phenomenon. He understands that the artificial construct of race was created to dehumanize, oppress, and economize Africans and Africans born in this country. Dante produces ev-idence that the roots of this country's legal, judicial, political, economic, educational, and cultural institutions are founded on anti-Black racism and White supremacy. He proves the intentionality of the acts of dehumanizing Black people.

This work contains information for those of us who wondered about the methods deployed to oppress Black people beginning as early as 1619. This work contains information for those of us who wondered about a divide between Black males and Black females and supposed that history could shed some light. This work contains information for those of us who wondered about the stronghold colorism has on Black people as a group. Finally, this work contains information for those of us who know that we have been afforded privileges but will never be treated like anything more than "an exception" to the rule.

If you are a student of Black history, you will not be able to put this work down. If you are a student of the sociology of culture and concerned with the systematic analysis of culture, you will not be able to put this work down. If you have always known that laws affect every aspect of our daily lives, you will not be able to put this work down. If you understand that tradition and culture are transmitted from generation to generation, inherited so to speak, you will not be able to put this work down. Lastly, if you are fascinated by the significance of origins, you will not be able to put this work down. You will not be able to put this work down because Dante has provided the factual, legal, judicial, and cultural basis for his assertions that present and perpetual racial inequities and disproportionate outcomes are historical and psychological in origin.

Reading this work will require you to interact and engage with your prior understanding of bias, what it means to be humane, and what structural racial exclusion and anti-Blackness mean.

You took the first steps: picking up this text and reading the foreword. Take the next step: READ IT. Your life will be forever changed.

I AM WHITE. As I read *Diagnosing Whiteness & Anti-Blackness* by Dante King, I come across terms such as *White sociopathy, malignant diabolical psychopathy,* and *White malignant narcissism.* One may reasonably ask, "How does that make you feel as a white person?" I can answer with sincerity that I feel recognition and relief. I even feel excited and empowered. Why? Recognition because Dante describes a racial orientation inculcated within me at an early age and continually reinforced throughout my life. Relieved because these words break White racial taboos and directly name White sociopathy. Excited because to receive a diagnosis is the first step toward a cure. I feel empowered because I can move past unproductive and self-serving feelings such as guilt and shame. I did not choose to be conditioned into this disorder, and would never have accepted had I been given that choice. Dante's analysis is about me, but it isn't personal. That understanding is actually *liberating* as it frees me from defensiveness, hurt, anger, and denial. It renders my self-focus moot. I am left ready to challenge White sociopathy within myself, my fellow White people, and society as a whole.

I have been involved in anti-racist education for over two decades, working both internally and externally to expose and challenge White supremacy. I could not have done that without deep mentorship from Black people and other people of color. That mentorship required me to break with my conditioning and see value in having relationships across race. As a White woman, I was not raised to know or love Dante King. What a tragic loss that would have been if I had not made the changes in my life that would bring us into relationship. Dante is among the most powerful of teachers I have had the honor to learn from. I hold the deepest sense of awe for his brilliance, compassion, commitment, and courage.

Dante does not tiptoe around White fragility, bending over backwards so as not to upset our delicate sensibilities and set off our rage. Yet as Marguerite Malloy testifies, Dante's directness exacts a very high toll. To be Black in the U.S. is to carry a heavy allostatic load due to the chronic stress of White sociopathy. To be Black in the U.S. and continually speak truth to power is to amplify that load, as well as to amplify the risk of violence. I implore my fellow White people to open your hearts, allow Dante's message in, and feel the urgency. As our country moves ever closer to renewed legal and social entrenchment of White supremacy, our humanity is at stake. We, too, have an investment in ending this devastating form of mental illness which so profoundly limits our capacity for full and moral lives. To my Black brothers and sisters, I hope to remind you that regardless of the lies we keep repeating, you are not and have never been the problem.

"*The intentions of this melancholy country,*
as concerns Black people, and anyone who doubts me
can ask any Indian, have always been genocidal.

They (white people) needed us for labor and for sport,
and now they cannot get rid of us.

The machinery of this country operates day in and day out,
hour by hour, until this hour, to keep a nigger in his place."

—James Baldwin, 1979

VIOLENT THREATS

THE FOLLOWING SCREENSHOTS OF posts and messages were sent to me after I gave a Black History Month presentation at the University of California, San Francisco (UCSF), in February 2024. The topic of my presentation became the basis for this book.

Many White people took umbrage to my questions about whether American society should be examining the functionalities of race and racism as psychotic. Many doctors, scholars, and activists, as you will explore throughout this text, have posited that racism is an illness. Psychopathic.

Upon offering my own analysis and contribution to this topic area many White people reacted sending the following messages to me.

Thank you!

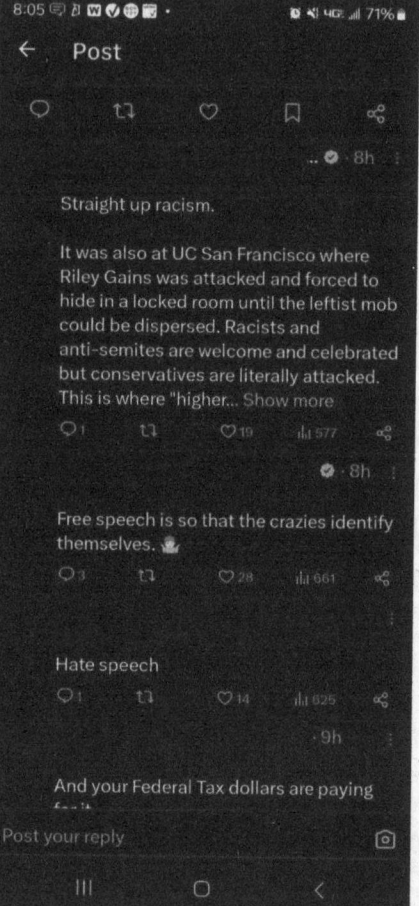

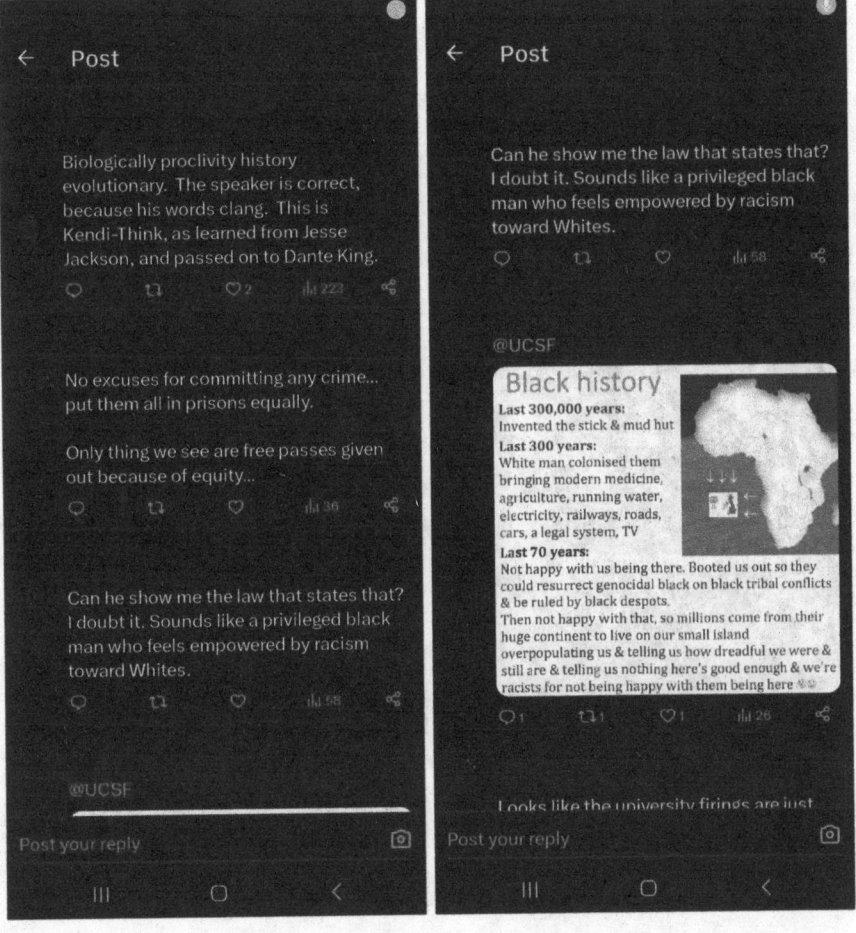

Biologically proclivity history evolutionary. The speaker is correct, because his words clang. This is Kendi-Think, as learned from Jesse Jackson, and passed on to Dante King.

♡ 2 ılı 223

No excuses for committing any crime... put them all in prisons equally.

Only thing we see are free passes given out because of equity...

ılı 36

Can he show me the law that states that? I doubt it. Sounds like a privileged black man who feels empowered by racism toward Whites.

ılı 58

@UCSF

Can he show me the law that states that? I doubt it. Sounds like a privileged black man who feels empowered by racism toward Whites.

ılı 58

@UCSF

Black history

Last 300,000 years:
Invented the stick & mud hut

Last 300 years:
White man colonised them bringing modern medicine, agriculture, running water, electricity, railways, roads, cars, a legal system, TV

Last 70 years:
Not happy with us being there. Booted us out so they could resurrect genocidal black on black tribal conflicts & be ruled by black despots.
Then not happy with that, so millions come from their huge continent to live on our small island overpopulating us & telling us how dreadful we were & still are & telling us nothing here's good enough & we're racists for not being happy with them being here 🤷🤷

♡ 1 ılı 26

Looks like the university firings are just

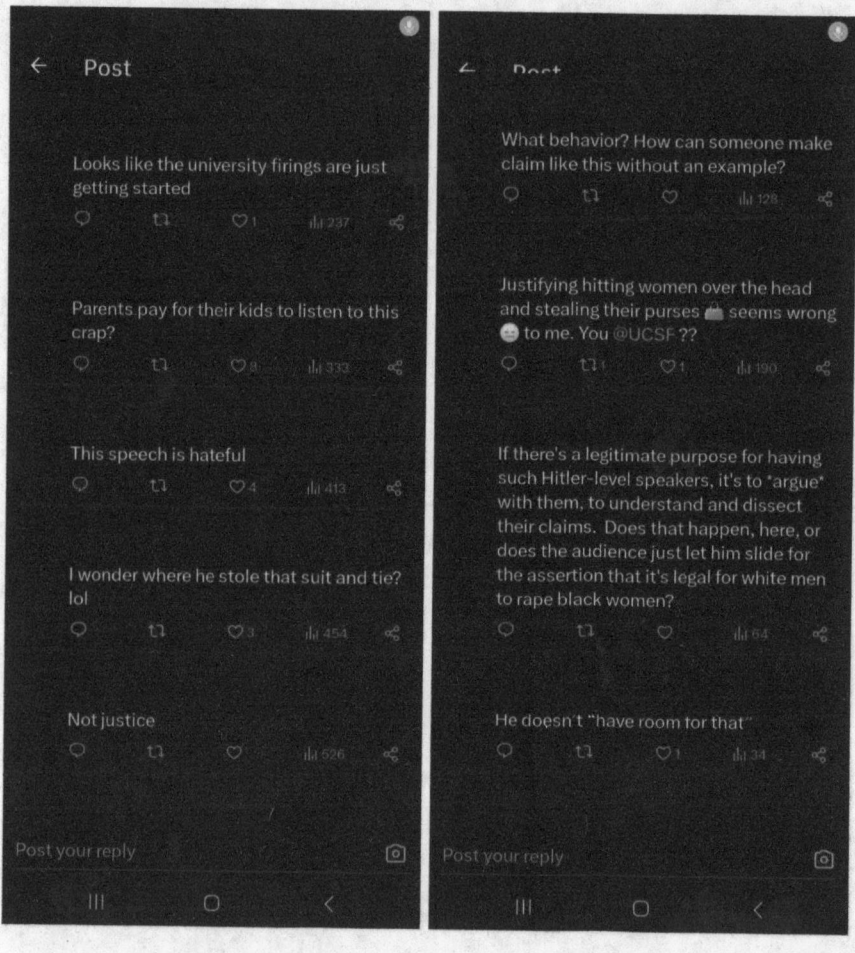

← Post

Looks like the university firings are just getting started

♡ 1   237

Parents pay for their kids to listen to this crap?

♡ 8   333

This speech is hateful

♡ 4   413

I wonder where he stole that suit and tie? lol

♡ 3   454

Not justice

526

Post your reply

← Post

What behavior? How can someone make claim like this without an example?

128

Justifying hitting women over the head and stealing their purses 👜 seems wrong 😣 to me. You @UCSF ??

1   ♡ 1   190

If there's a legitimate purpose for having such Hitler-level speakers, it's to "argue" with them, to understand and dissect their claims. Does that happen, here, or does the audience just let him slide for the assertion that it's legal for white men to rape black women?

64

He doesn't "have room for that"

♡ 1   34

Post your reply

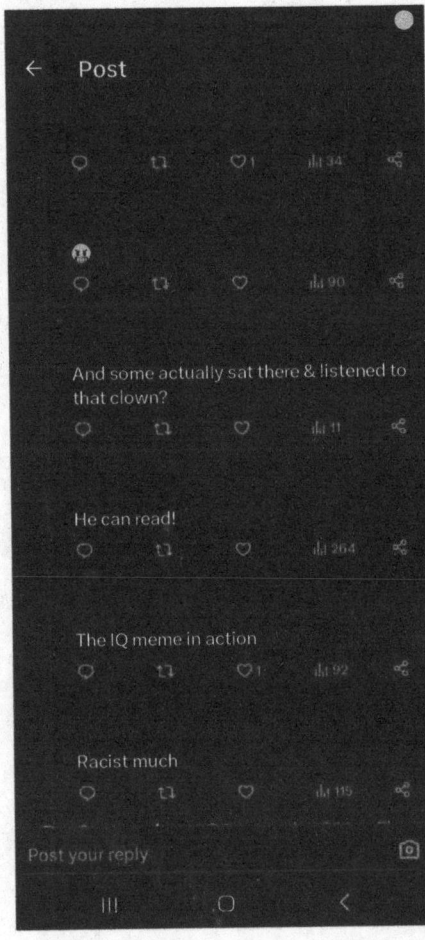

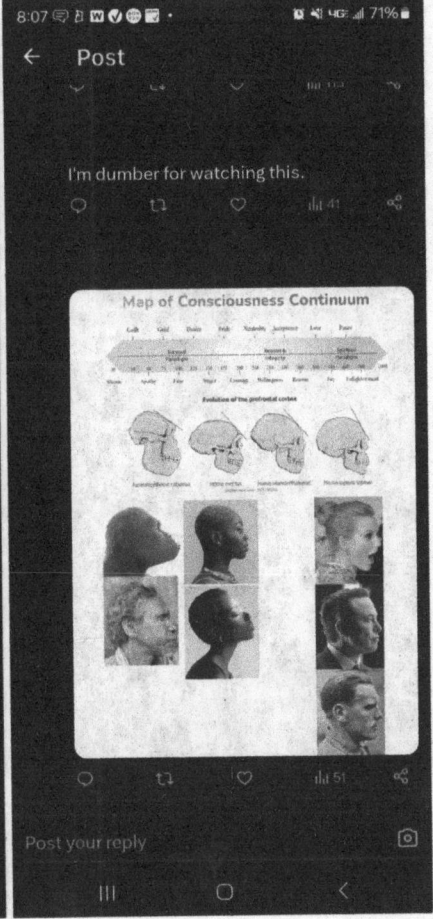

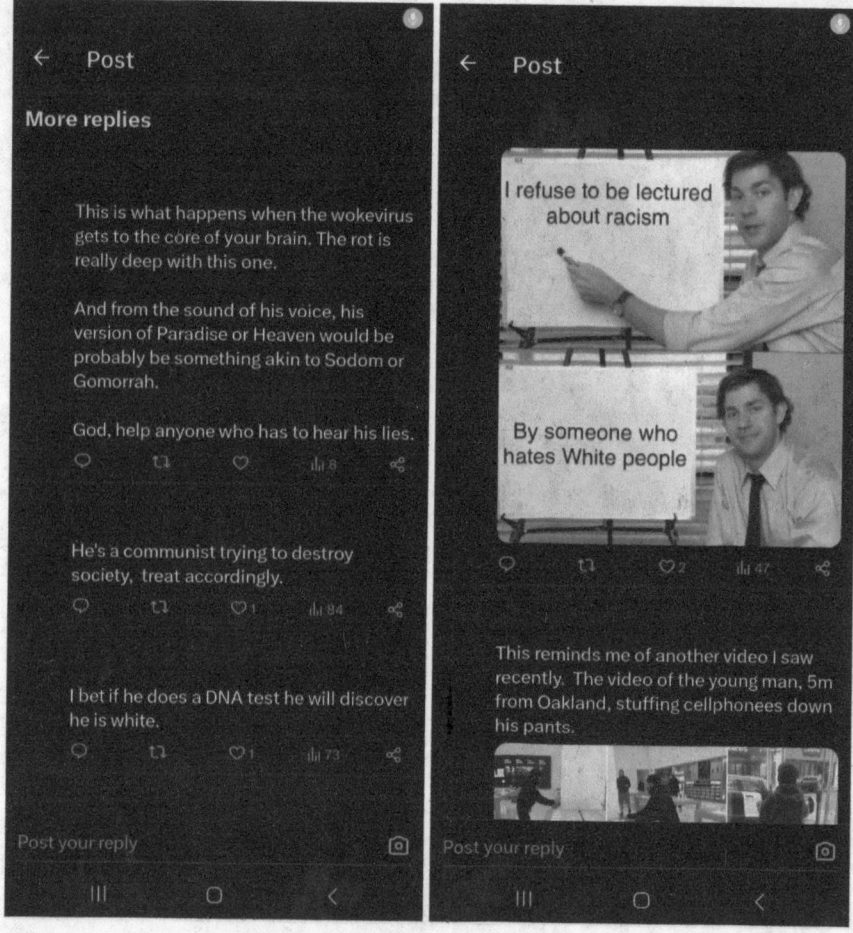

← Post

More replies

This is what happens when the wokevirus gets to the core of your brain. The rot is really deep with this one.

And from the sound of his voice, his version of Paradise or Heaven would be probably be something akin to Sodom or Gomorrah.

God, help anyone who has to hear his lies.

He's a communist trying to destroy society, treat accordingly.

I bet if he does a DNA test he will discover he is white.

Post your reply

← Post

I refuse to be lectured about racism

By someone who hates White people

This reminds me of another video I saw recently. The video of the young man, 5m from Oakland, stuffing cellphonees down his pants.

Post your reply

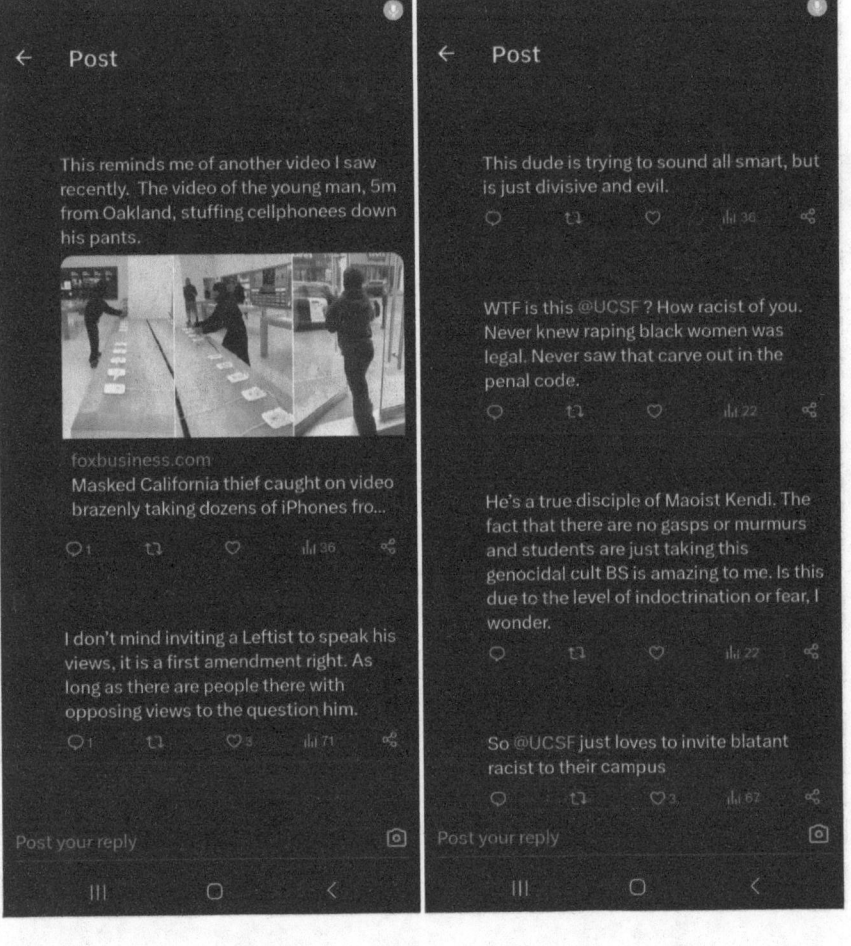

Left screen:

← Post

This reminds me of another video I saw recently. The video of the young man, 5m from Oakland, stuffing cellphonees down his pants.

foxbusiness.com
Masked California thief caught on video brazenly taking dozens of iPhones fro...

1   36

I don't mind inviting a Leftist to speak his views, it is a first amendment right. As long as there are people there with opposing views to the question him.

1   3   71

Post your reply

Right screen:

← Post

This dude is trying to sound all smart, but is just divisive and evil.

            36

WTF is this @UCSF ? How racist of you. Never knew raping black women was legal. Never saw that carve out in the penal code.

            22

He's a true disciple of Maoist Kendi. The fact that there are no gasps or murmurs and students are just taking this genocidal cult BS is amazing to me. Is this due to the level of indoctrination or fear, I wonder.

            22

So @UCSF just loves to invite blatant racist to their campus

        3   82

Post your reply

← Post

So @UCSF just loves to invite blatant racist to their campus

The racist dude actually believes 2% of the country built this country 😄. He's daft. But being a minority and a racist speaker / author pays good 🪝

We need a condemnation from the people who invited him. The dean. The board. And then we need them brought before congress and questioned about what they're doing to combat anti-white hatred.

he is reading a speech, you would think he would have his racist rants down pat.

Post your reply

← Post

he is reading a speech, you would think he would have his racist rants down pat.

His Koolaid got more than sugar in it

If I close my eyes, this is what I picture:

ONE MOMENT

Post your reply

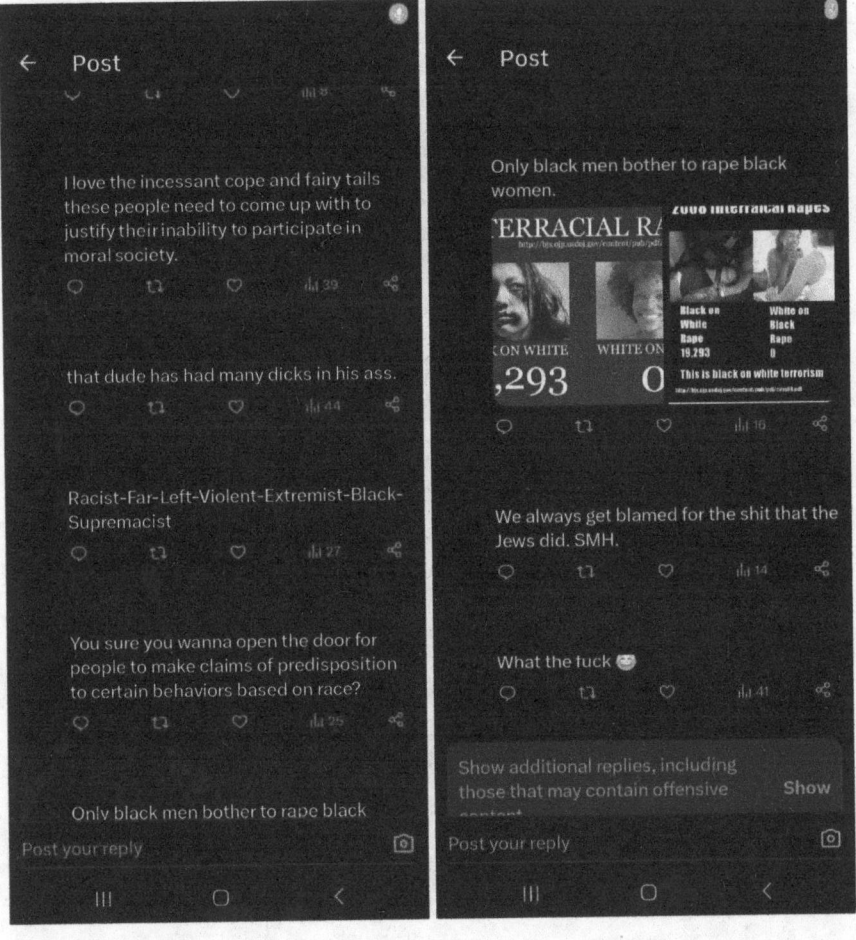

I love the incessant cope and fairy tails these people need to come up with to justify their inability to participate in moral society.

that dude has had many dicks in his ass.

Racist-Far-Left-Violent-Extremist-Black-Supremacist

You sure you wanna open the door for people to make claims of predisposition to certain behaviors based on race?

Only black men bother to rape black

Post your reply

Only black men bother to rape black women.

We always get blamed for the shit that the Jews did. SMH.

What the fuck 😂

Show additional replies, including those that may contain offensive content.   Show

Post your reply

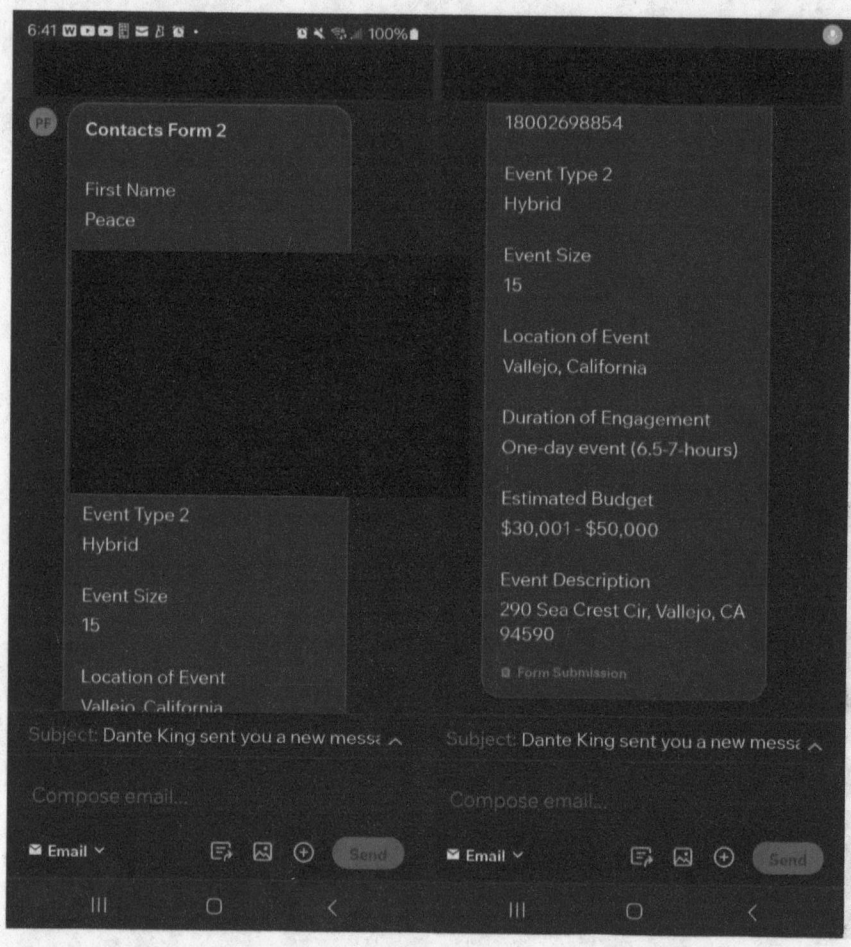

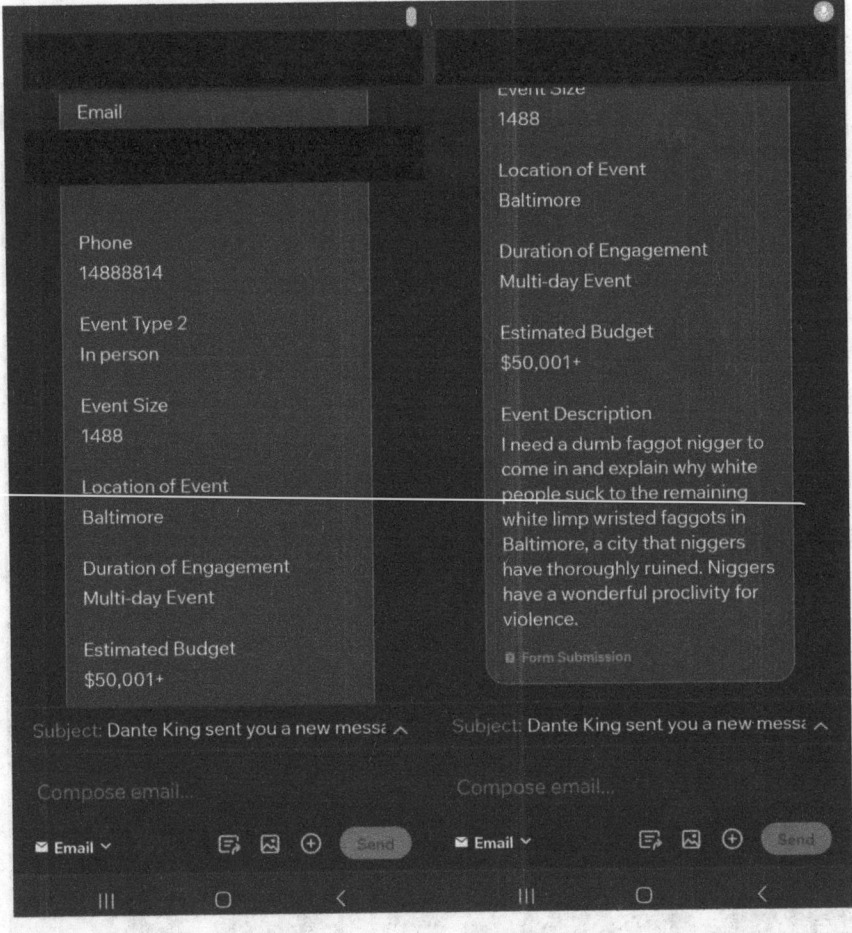

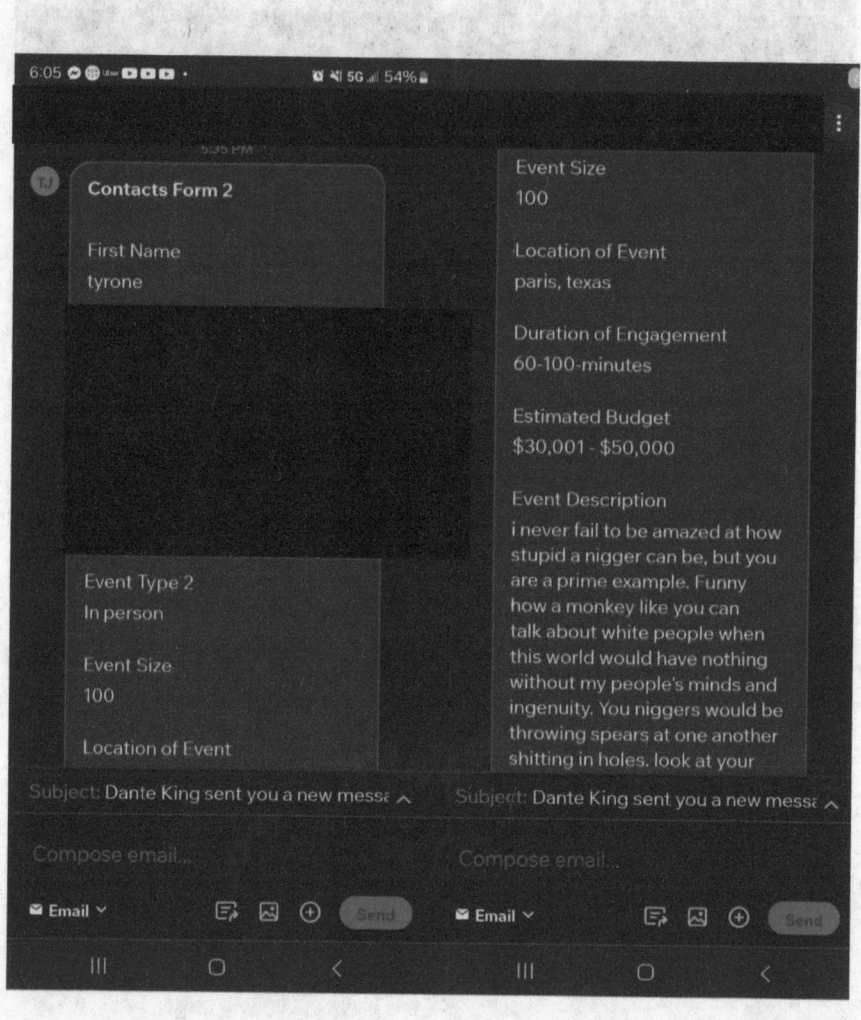

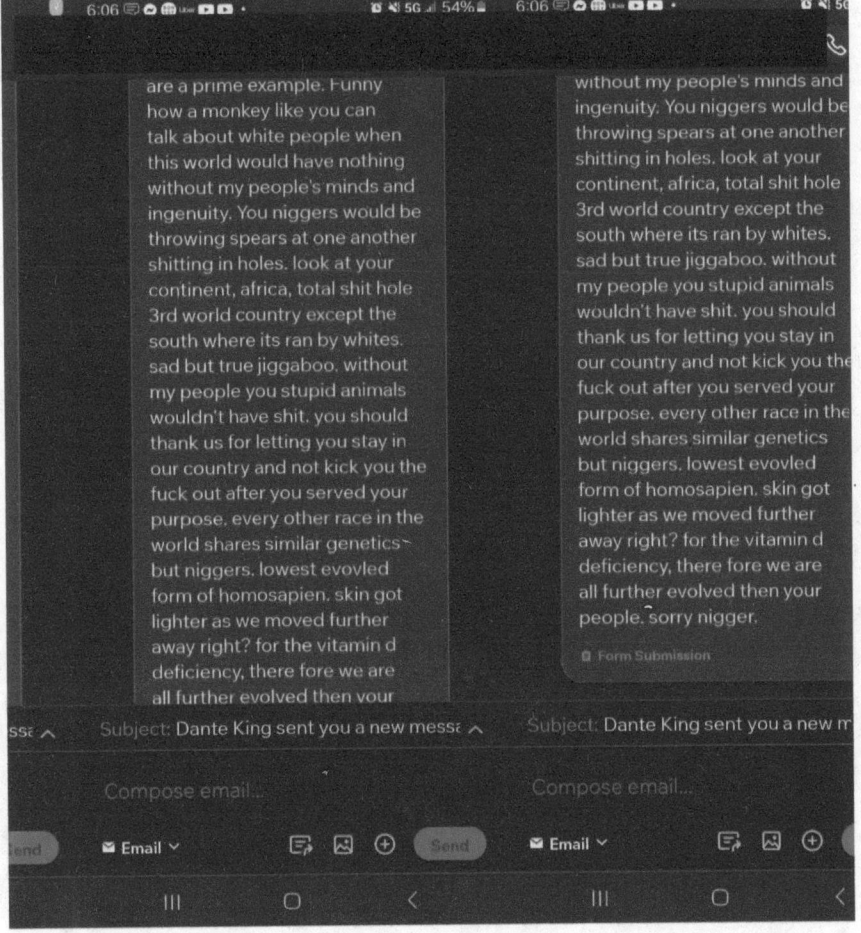

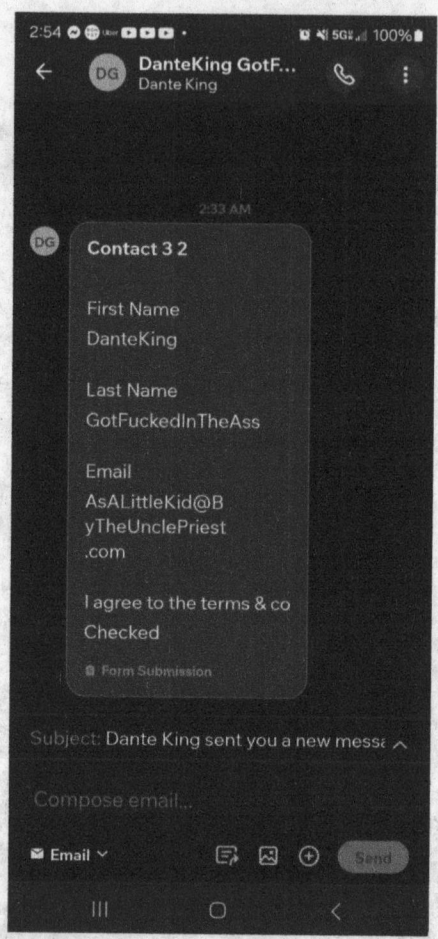

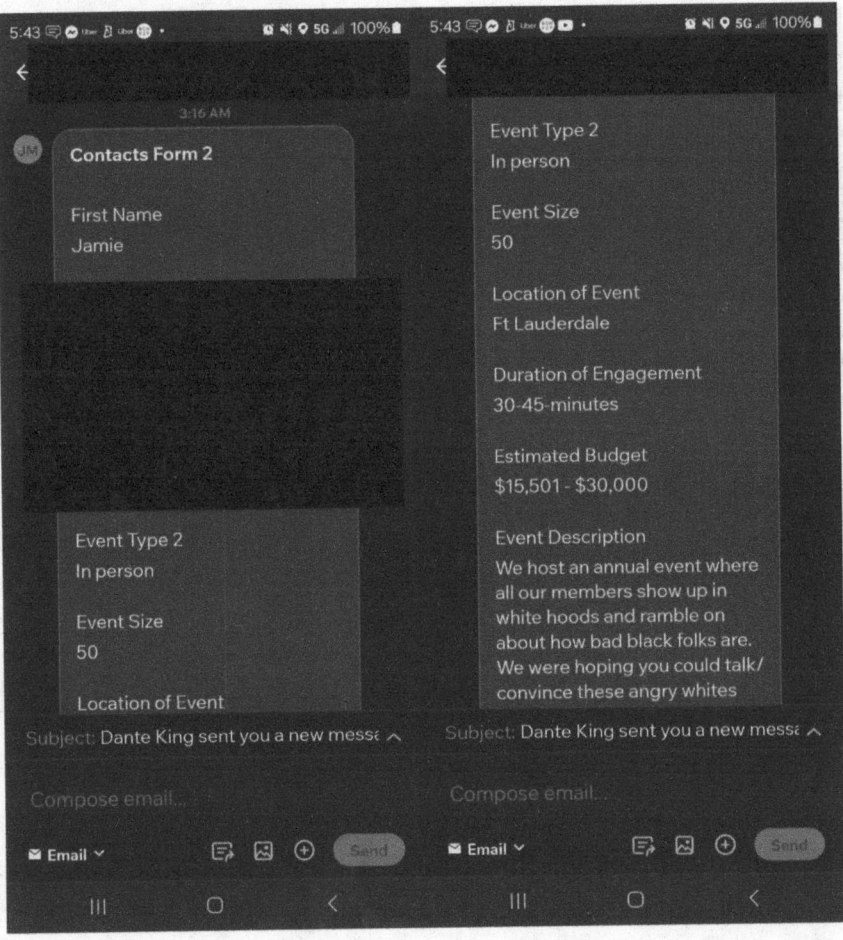

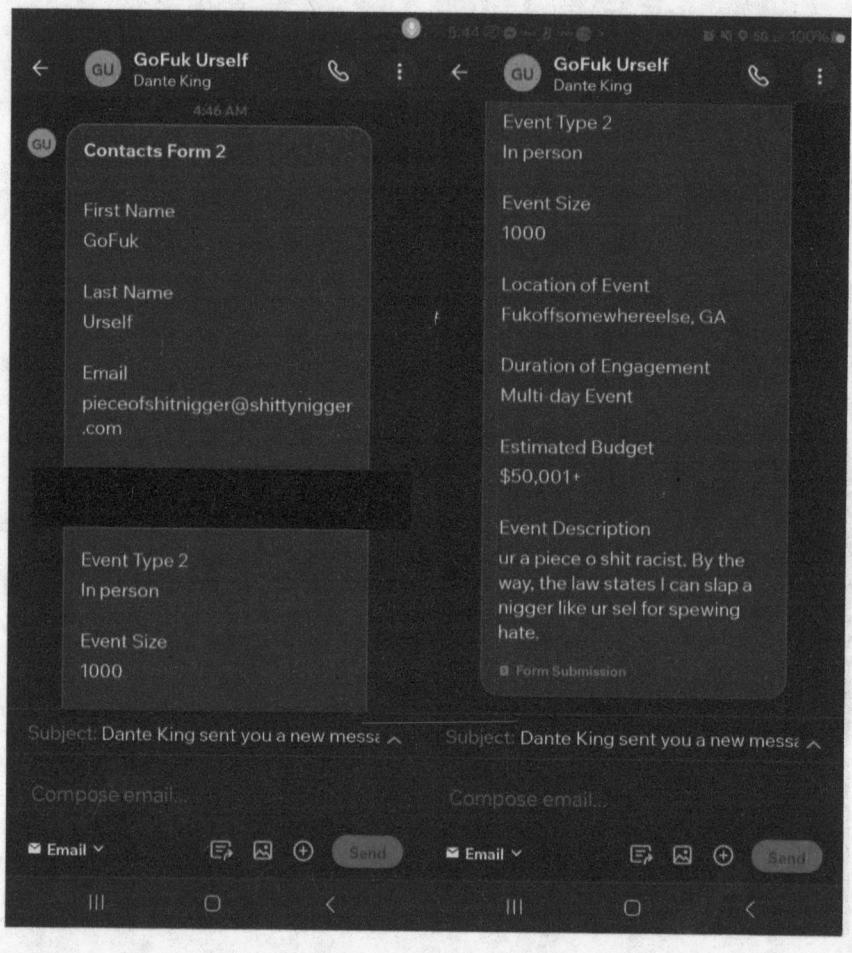

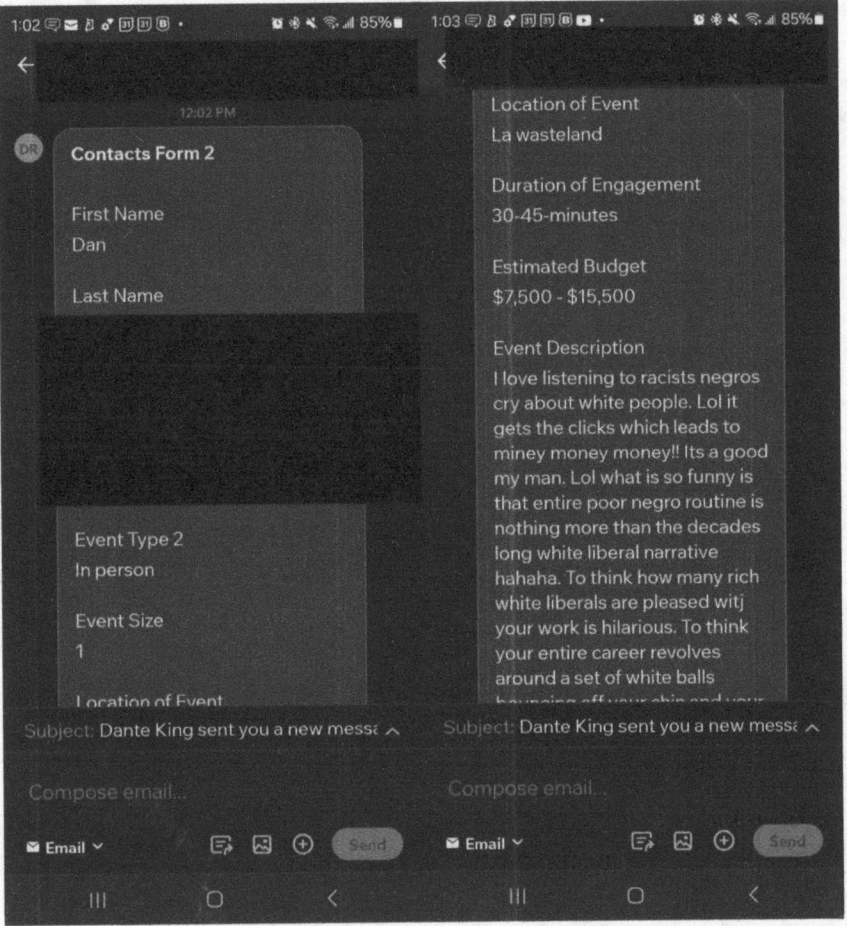

1:02 🗨📧 ♫ ☁ 🗓🗓 Ⓑ •   📷 ❄ 📶 85%▪

←

12:02 PM

Contacts Form 2

First Name
Dan

Last Name

Event Type 2
In person

Event Size
1

Location of Event

Subject: Dante King sent you a new messa ⌃

Compose email...

✉ Email ⌄   📑 🖼 ⊕ Send

III   ○   ‹

1:03 🗨 ♫ ☁ 🗓🗓 Ⓑ ▶ •   📷 ❄ 📶 85%▪

←

Location of Event
La wasteland

Duration of Engagement
30-45-minutes

Estimated Budget
$7,500 - $15,500

Event Description
I love listening to racists negros
cry about white people. Lol it
gets the clicks which leads to
miney money money!! Its a good
my man. Lol what is so funny is
that entire poor negro routine is
nothing more than the decades
long white liberal narrative
hahaha. To think how many rich
white liberals are pleased witj
your work is hilarious. To think
your entire career revolves
around a set of white balls

Subject: Dante King sent you a new messa ⌃

Compose email...

✉ Email ⌄   📑 🖼 ⊕ Send

III   ○   ‹

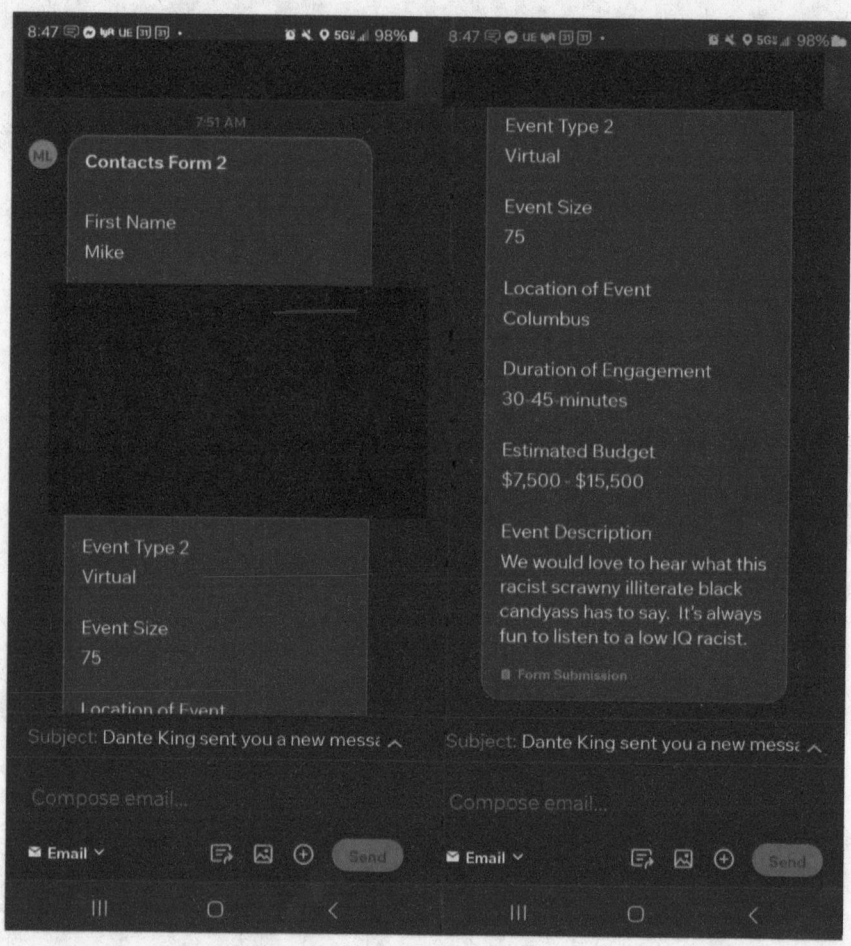

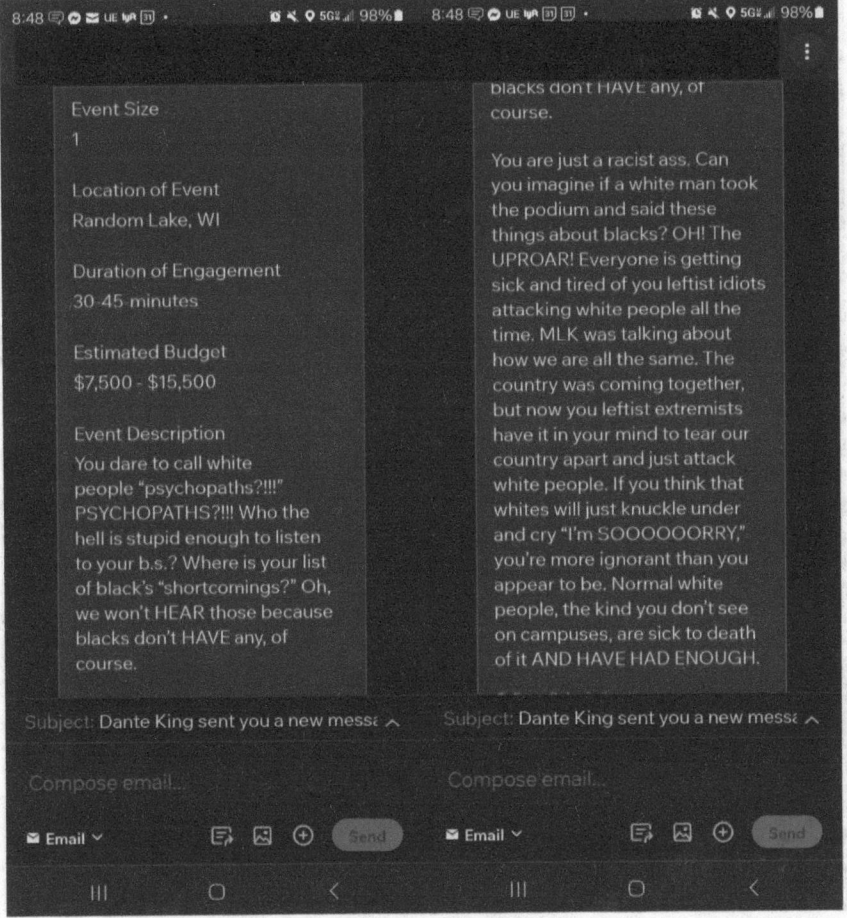

8:48 5G 98%

Event Size
1

Location of Event
Random Lake, WI

Duration of Engagement
30-45 minutes

Estimated Budget
$7,500 - $15,500

Event Description
You dare to call white people "psychopaths?!!!" PSYCHOPATHS?!!! Who the hell is stupid enough to listen to your b.s.? Where is your list of black's "shortcomings?" Oh, we won't HEAR those because blacks don't HAVE any, of course.

8:48 5G 98%

blacks don't HAVE any, of course.

You are just a racist ass. Can you imagine if a white man took the podium and said these things about blacks? OH! The UPROAR! Everyone is getting sick and tired of you leftist idiots attacking white people all the time. MLK was talking about how we are all the same. The country was coming together, but now you leftist extremists have it in your mind to tear our country apart and just attack white people. If you think that whites will just knuckle under and cry "I'm SOOOOOORRY," you're more ignorant than you appear to be. Normal white people, the kind you don't see on campuses, are sick to death of it AND HAVE HAD ENOUGH.

Subject: Dante King sent you a new messa ∧

Compose email...

✉ Email ∨   Send

Subject: Dante King sent you a new messa ∧

Compose email...

✉ Email ∨   Send

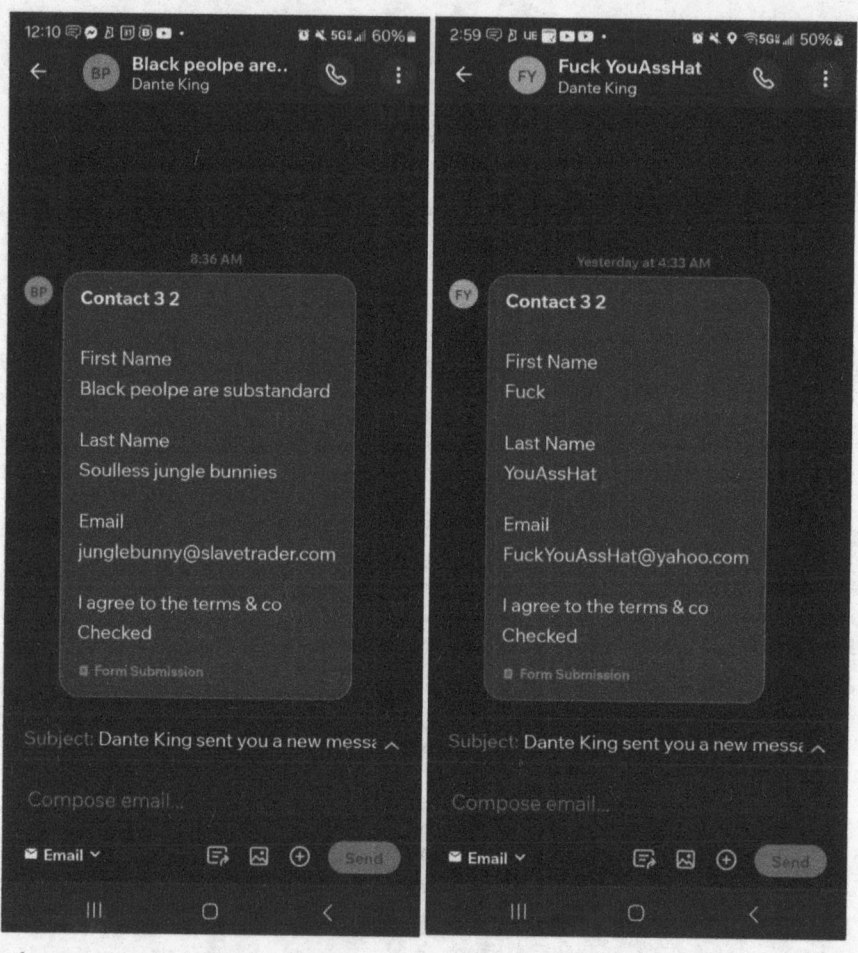

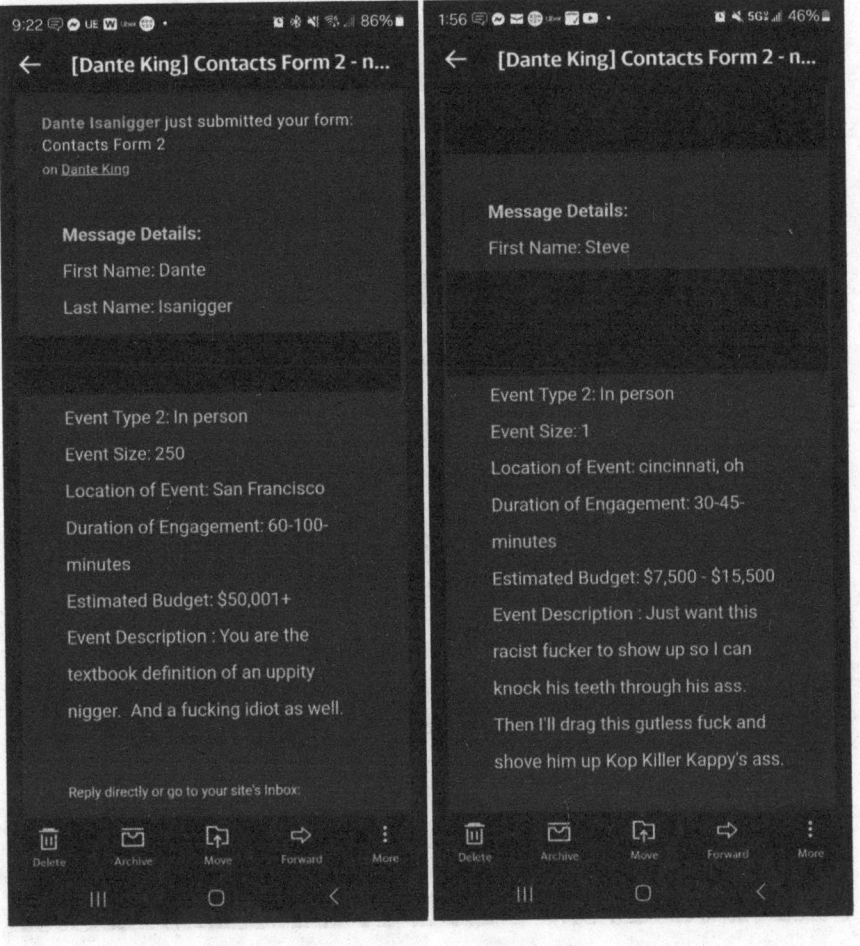

Screenshot 1 (left):

9:22 · 86%

← [Dante King] Contacts Form 2 - n...

Dante Isanigger just submitted your form: Contacts Form 2
on Dante King

Message Details:

First Name: Dante

Last Name: Isanigger

Event Type 2: In person

Event Size: 250

Location of Event: San Francisco

Duration of Engagement: 60-100-minutes

Estimated Budget: $50,001+

Event Description : You are the textbook definition of an uppity nigger. And a fucking idiot as well.

Reply directly or go to your site's Inbox:

Delete   Archive   Move   Forward   More

Screenshot 2 (right):

1:56 · 5G 46%

← [Dante King] Contacts Form 2 - n...

Message Details:

First Name: Steve

Event Type 2: In person

Event Size: 1

Location of Event: cincinnati, oh

Duration of Engagement: 30-45-minutes

Estimated Budget: $7,500 - $15,500

Event Description : Just want this racist fucker to show up so I can knock his teeth through his ass. Then I'll drag this gutless fuck and shove him up Kop Killer Kappy's ass.

Delete   Archive   Move   Forward   More

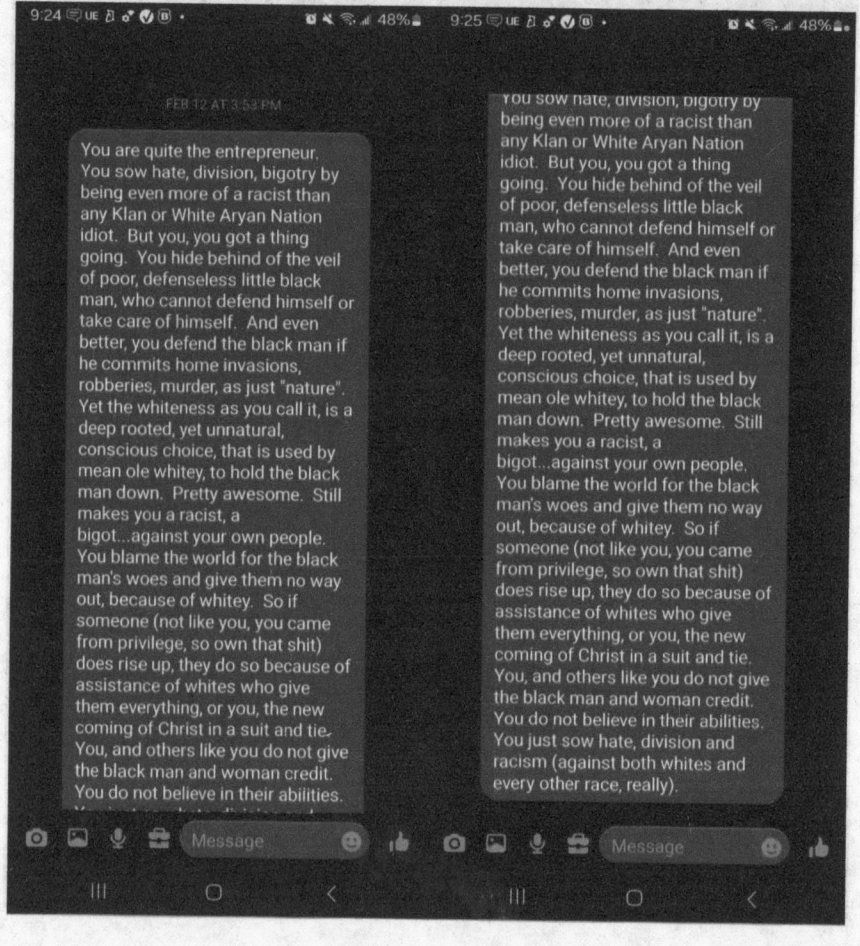

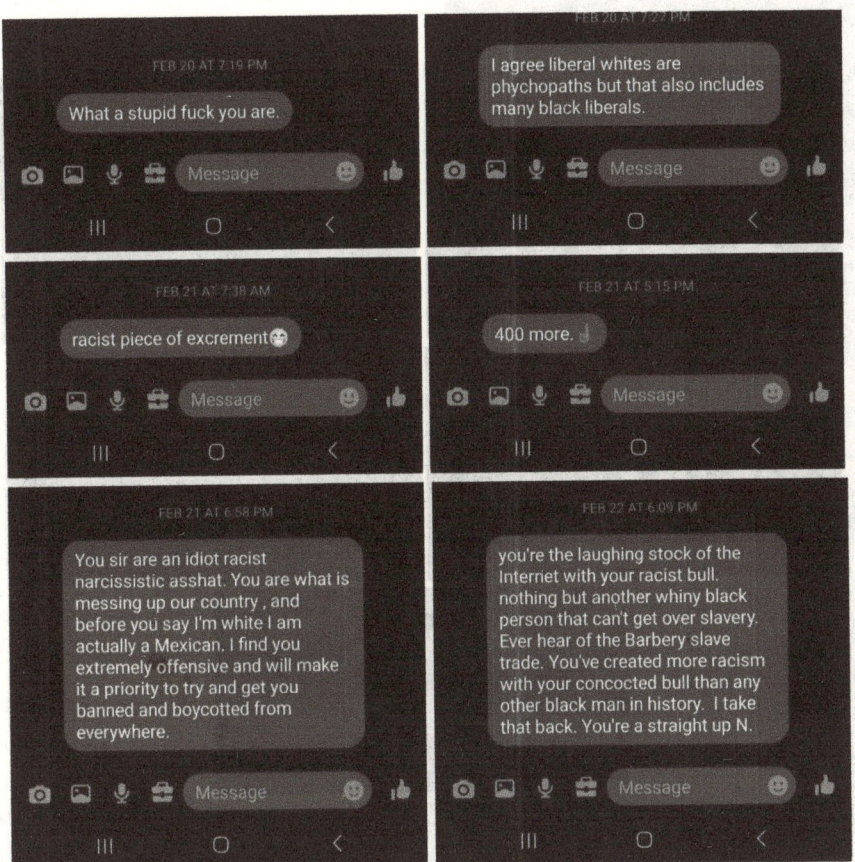

FEB 20 AT 7:19 PM

What a stupid fuck you are.

FEB 20 AT 7:27 PM

I agree liberal whites are phychopaths but that also includes many black liberals.

FEB 21 AT 7:38 AM

racist piece of excrement😂

FEB 21 AT 5:15 PM

400 more.

FEB 21 AT 6:58 PM

You sir are an idiot racist narcissistic asshat. You are what is messing up our country , and before you say I'm white I am actually a Mexican. I find you extremely offensive and will make it a priority to try and get you banned and boycotted from everywhere.

FEB 22 AT 6:09 PM

you're the laughing stock of the Internet with your racist bull. nothing but another whiny black person that can't get over slavery. Ever hear of the Barbery slave trade. You've created more racism with your concocted bull than any other black man in history. I take that back. You're a straight up N.

Culture = A means by which a group of people organizes the way that it thinks, believes, and sees the world so as to create a consciousness by which it cooperates in achieving certain ends. Culture is an instrument of power. The individual, through culture, extends the power of the group.

Malignant Diabolical Psychopathy = Collective group disorder upon which a hegemonic society exhibits systematic ill will or hatred towards non-White people, especially Black individuals; spread with extreme cruelty or wicked tactics of destruction, showing no empathy or remorse, but it is exhibited as a normal thought process.

This term, coined by Dr. Danyelle Marshall, expresses the combination of several mental health disorders to explain the unbridled viciousness toward others that include psychological, physical, and behavioral techniques to create an atmosphere of terror among the powerless, thus, to keep power to select few which is usually White men and women.

White Impression Management = The conscious or subconscious process by which White people have attempted to influence others' perceptions about themselves (i.e., superiority, inflated sense of self, collective group valorization, etc.) vs. non-White peoples (i.e., inferior, dehumanization, collective group devaluation, etc.). An intentional process consisting of regulating, omitting, and controlling and manipulating historical and ongoing facts, social interactions, and cultural conditions.

White Projection = A core tenet of White psychosis stemming from White paranoia. It is a defense mechanism White people employ to project their undesirable and otherwise unacceptable thoughts, feelings, and impulses onto others, rather than accepting them.[373]

White Affirmative Action = Laws, policies, and any other practices meant to benefit Whites at the expense of all others, most severely Black people.

White Culture = An experiment of conspiratorial assemblage. A means by which White people have organized the way that they perceive reality so as to create a consciousness based on mutual aid and which facilitates their superior status. White supremacy culture is an instrument of power.

White Psychopathology is a disorder created and perpetuated based upon psychological and cultural tenets of psychopathy, sociopathy, and terrorism.

White Psychopathy = The historical and perpetual functioning of White people in relationship to themselves and Black people. The psychologically ingrained need to oppress Black people as the main way of sourcing and retaining value. Enjoying and experiencing White privilege in the midst of ongoing White terrorism against Black, Indigenous, and other non-White peoples is key, as is never evaluating where the White privilege and power come from.

White Solidarity = Solidarity that aids all moral wrongs, irrespective of the degree of harm exacted, including rape and murder.

White Psycho-economics and Psycho-politics = The process of economizing and politicizing White thought patterns and objectives, all of which get filtered and distributed through White institutions, educational and otherwise. They serve White people.[24,81,346-48]

The culture, attitudes, and behaviors of Black people have been organized by White people through negative orientations, labels, and pathologies. These negative orientations provide the reasoning for denigrating Black people, for many reasons, but in particular economic ones. The ultimate goal is to increase White monetary wealth. Money is power.

In short, White people have stigmatized Blackness, making its destruction acceptable, if not desirable. To be Black is to be:

√ Immoral

√ Unfit in any regard

√ Undesirable

√ Ugly/Unattractive

√ Problematic

√ Negative

√ Aggressive

√ Lazy

√ Angry

√ Rageful

√ Criminal

√ Developmentally disabled

√ Uneducable

These ideas have had and still have overwhelmingly negative consequences. Some include:

° Developing and institutionalizing racial slavery (1619–1865).

° Establishing Jim Crow laws and instituting segregation (1866–1977).

° Rationalizing disproportionate school suspensions for young Black boys (resulting from the U.S. Supreme Court's ruling in *Brown v. Board of Education* in 1955).

° Surplus funding availability for schools diagnosing children as special needs (1866–present).

° Funding whole industries, such as Big Pharma, dedicated to "diagnosing" behavior that does not comport with White standards (1977–present).

° Funding the abuse of Black bodies through various fake sciences, such as phrenology and eugenics (1600s–present).

° Surplus funding availability to various law enforcement agencies dedicated to depriving Black people of their liberties by falsely accusing them of criminal behavior (1874–present). Ultimately this leads to imprisonment, homelessness, economic insecurity, and poor health outcomes.

As Dr. Amos N. Wilson stated in the early 1990s:

> You'll learn one day, ladies and gentlemen, that Black problems and labeling Black people as problematic people, is worth billions of dollars to White people."[349]

White people are organized in opposing terms. Their language, institutions, and attitudes favor them.

Some examples include but are not limited to:

° Accumulation of power and control

° Sustaining power by controlling educational, legal, and health care structures. This can include unmerited elevations and omitted punishments in various forms.

All of this is foundational to how Whites are oriented. It is how they have come to define every metric of American life, including the vaunted American Dream. These variables make up the brand or brand-value of Whiteness.

These ideas are detailed in several books worth reading. Those books include:

√ *Black-on-Black Violence: The Psychodynamics of Black Self-Annihilation in Service of White Domination*

and

√ *Blueprint for Black Power: A Moral, Political, and Economic Imperative for the Twenty-First Century*

Dr. Amos N. Wilson wrote both. His scholarship is critical to advancing our collective understanding.

Additional definitions include:

White Sociopathy = Reinforcing White superiority and the "less than" mentality it bestows on all others, especially Black persons. Enjoying the benefits of Whiteness, which was built through institutionalized terrorism and not recognizing said reality.

White Epigenetics = The intergenerational traumatic impact of various forms of normalized sexual predation, including the mass rape of adults and children, prostitution, and human trafficking; normalized corporal punishment, other forms of violence, and murder as a means of life, liberty, and the pursuit of happiness.

White Malignant Narcissism = Extreme arrogance and self-centeredness. Disregards feelings and needs of others. Manipulates, uses, and exploits others for personal gain or pleasure. Possesses an extreme need for power. Exacts revenge against others upon critique. Fantasizes about ways to gain more power or dominance over others. Lacks conscience, regret, or remorse for actions and behaviors. Delights in acts of cruelty and pain of others. Directs high levels of aggression at other people. Exhibits paranoia and mistrust of others.

White Paranoia = A persistent fear that Black and other non-White people are plotting to seek revenge against White people.

Genocide (as noted in the Holocaust Encyclopedia) = This includes any of the following acts committed with intent to destroy, in whole or in part, a national, ethnic, racial, or religious group, including:

a) Murdering members of the group

b) Causing serious bodily or mental harm to members of the group

c) Deliberately inflicting on the group conditions of life calculated to bring about its physical destruction in whole or in part

d) Imposing measures intended to prevent births within the group

e) Forcibly transferring children of the group to another group[249]

Writing, an inherently reflective process, has been liberating and painful for me.

I have been afforded the opportunity to think about who we are, how we got to where we are, and far more. That is a privilege. I know well the beauty that is within us and how it still persists through great trials.

But that is also what is painful. Our beauty never should have flourished under such profound trials. It should have flourished as free people. We could have created more, laughed more, achieved more. We were restrained and lashed, I mean literally, for just being ourselves. Our most human desires, the desire to learn, the desire to have a family, the desire to work on one's own terms, were all stripped of us, along with everything else.

Did we find and make beauty where we could? Yes, we did.

Should we have ever had to? No, we should not have.

This has been an arduous process for me. It has depleted me thoroughly.

Despite my extensive research, I do not have a comprehensive, nuanced understanding of the sheer horror inflicted upon us. Nor will I ever. That enrages me. I am horrified.

That horror is what fueled my curiosity and commitment to reframe the Black experience in America. Once I read books such as, *Black Power: The Politics of Liberation* by Kwame Ture and Charles Hamilton, *The Fire Next Time* by the inimitable James Baldwin, *Race Matters* by Dr. Cornel West, and *Black Reconstruction in America* by W.E.B. DuBois, in addition to many of the other texts noted and referenced within this work, my world changed. Once I focused on speeches by Dr. Angela Davis, Fannie Lou Hamer, Ella Baker, Kwame Ture, and Malcom X, I became equipped with the vocabulary I needed to begin the laborious process of mending that which I knew viscerally was broken.

I began to understand that I had been robbed of the truth of my identity here. To be clear (because truth can often be subjective), I had been robbed of facts, of information. Did I have some understanding that American Black people had been discriminated against unjustly? Certainly. Did I understand the nuances of how? Not entirely, no. It was through my long, often painful studies that I began understanding how we became and have since remained public enemy number one in this country. American Black people, especially those who are descendants of slaves, exist in a constant state of fear and even terror; not frequently, unexceptionally. This is because any number of unpredictable misfortunes can strike us at any time due to White American cultural function and the sheer value of anti-Blackness.

As I learned the truth about the nuances that have made Blackness and Whiteness in America, I began to evaluate the cumulative cultural, psychological, and emotional effects. I also began to understand the gradual, persistent development of White hatred toward Africans and/or people interpreted as Black, as well as the infinite ways this disdain reared its head through legal, political, and other cultural institutions and norms. As I began understanding and evaluating the impacts of these realities, I began drafting a curriculum well suited to combat them. The curriculums have become known to many as:

√ Unlearning and Addressing Anti-Blackness, White Supremacy, and Racism in American Culture and Institutions Leaders Fellowship (16 weeks; 4.5 hours per week)

√ The 400-Year Holocaust Course (12 weeks; 4.5 hours per week)

√ Diagnosing Whiteness and Anti-Blackness (8 weeks; 4.5 hours per week)

√ Understanding the Roots of Racism and Bias: Anti-Blackness, and Its Link to Whiteness, White Racism, Privilege, and Power (2-day course offered through the University of California, San Francisco Continuous Medical Education Program)

√ Developing Anti-racism Leadership Competencies to Achieve Inclusive Practices and Health Equity (16 hours offered through the Mayo Clinic School of Continuous Professional Development and Continuous Medical Education)

Through this layered educational experience, I map out the aforementioned elements, some of which I have highlighted in this text. The process requires that students and participants come to terms with the realities of the conditions developed within and throughout White culture. It also requires people to immerse themselves in examining, feeling, and relating to the perpetual and wounding impacts of such persistent, intentional, and manufactured dehumanization over a period of 400+ years. The most critical elements of this experience are (1) all of it is framed through legal and political contexts, and (2) individuals are invited to reframe the evolution and persistence of White racism and anti-Blackness as psychopathic and sociopathic, rather than mere social constructs.

Waking up to the truth, Black Truth, and reliving the effects of what it takes to write, teach, and learn about Whiteness and anti-Blackness, have been more painful than any other experience in my life. And I will never be able to unlearn or believe in ideas such as justice, freedom, or equality. These are ideas only, not realities, and they are not available to Black people in America. The last 400+ years have proven this fact, and it is imperative for posterity's sake that this book be written in ways that enable all who are willing to explore deeply and examine the roots and effects of racism as Whiteness and anti-Blackness to understand.

Below is a list of details I want to make abundantly clear to every person who reads this:

√   This book is grounded in Afro-Realism (or African American Realism or Black Realism). Afro-Realism is a qualitative, quantitative, ethnographic, evidenced-based research methodology. It encompasses an Afrocentric pedagogical, theoretical, and analytical approach that leverages the fact-based, anti-Black legal and institutional conditions and experiences of African people, which were established and instituted by European and White people in America. The first objective of Black-Realism is to define, scale, and demonstrate the intersectional functionalities of legalized and institutionalized Whiteness and anti-Blackness in American institutions—its very identity, culture, and society. The second objective of Afro-Realism is to understand the core foundations and development of Whiteness (i.e., White psychology, White sociology, White people, White culture, etc.). The goal being to fully grasp the depths of White racism, White supremacy culture, White extremism, as well as anti-Blackness, and their impacts on the daily experiences of White/White-presenting, non-White/ "not-Black," and Black people in America.

√ This book should be used as a prerequisite for registering for Understanding the Roots of Racism and Bias: Anti-Blackness, and Its Links to Whiteness, White Racism, Privilege, and Power, which can be accessed by going to www.danteking.com, and/or by emailing: understandingtherootsofracism@danteking.com.

√ The original title of this book was *Prosecuting Whiteness and Anti-Blackness in America* but was changed to encompass a far greater scale of the impacts of these conditions, which translate to an ongoing racial genocide. Dr. Martin Luther King, Jr. stated this much in his speech entitled, "The Other America," which he gave in 1967 at Stanford University. He said:

> In the final analysis, racism is evil, racism is evil because its ultimate logic is genocide. Hitler was a sick and tragic man who carried racism to its logical conclusion. He ended up leading a nation to the point of killing about six-million Jews. And this is the tragedy of racism because its ultimate logic is genocide.[225]

√ In order to confront anti-Blackness and White racism as mere social problems, one must deny facts. In addition, one must also accept that these dynamics are ordinary when they are clearly not.

√ The main objective of this book is to examine the realities of Whiteness and anti-Blackness in America. It is to highlight the complexities of the situation. It is to amplify and reinforce criticisms and philosophies presented by other scholars who have chosen to express themselves about the matter. It is also to offer my own assessments in a way that holds to account legal constructs and the way they were designed to be pro-White and anti-Black.

√ This book is written from a Black perspective that has understood and is continuing to understand the Black experience outside of the parameters of White psychology, White sociology, and White normativity. The perspective applied here is one that attempts to hold to account Whiteness and White racism. It recognizes my own humanity as well as that of my ancestors. They must not be forgotten, as they endured the horror that is anti-Black terrorism and torture, which were uniformly perpetrated by Whites.

√ The information here is presented in ways that do not conform to anyone's "widely accepted" set of principles and/or practices that are associated with White-American-normative-mainstream publishing standards (i.e., Modern Language Association, American Psychological Association, etc.). Abiding by such principles reinforces the subjugation of non-Whites and/or anyone who rejects Western-oriented and established academic principles. These principles limit how information can or should be presented, thereby degrading its potency. There are those who will understand what I mean by this and those who will not. Regardless, I have made the decision to ensure that this material is available to everyone in the way that my heart and soul feel it should be. I have also made sure that it is being presented in a way that is accessible to people who may exist within the White, racist, academic structure known as "the academy," as well as people who do not exist there, who have not had any contact with it, and/or who have chosen to resist the institutions altogether. This material should be easily accessible to everyone.

√ This does not mean that some of the ways the information is presented will not reflect certain standards and principles. It means that I am not limiting myself to anyone, formalized presentation style or adhering to White "standardized" and/or "widely accepted" principles and practices about how information should be presented.

√ The root of all problems faced by Black people in America is White oppression. Whether in education, employment, housing, economics, politics, law, healthcare, homelessness, etc., Whites have worked to oppress Black people both individually and systematically for centuries due to delusional, irrational, and demented proclivities that have led them to believe that Black people deserve to be treated inhumanely.

√ The term "European" points to Anglo-Europeans and/or people who have been identified as Caucasian and/or White.

√ This is not a book about Black history or Black people in America. If anything at all, it is a book about White history, Whiteness, White people's creation of Black identity, Black experiences, and anti-Blackness in America.

√ Whether produced by judiciaries, legislatures, commissions, and/
or private policies, anti-Blackness was the main reason for mass
imprisonment throughout the period of Black enslavement. It is
named in the law as such. Anti-Blackness is also the condition and
motivating factor behind "Jim Crow/Separate but Equal" constructions. Anti-Blackness is the reason for ongoing, crushing economic,
legal, political, employment, educational, and health care–related
conditions destroying Black life in America.

√ It is important that the terms highlighted in the title, which are
consistently referenced throughout this text, be defined. There are
additional words that I am defining, as they are used in the text
also. This is to ensure that readers unfamiliar with these terms have
a basic understanding. I have chosen to use the Anglo-White-Amer-
ican-adopted-and-accepted-orientation of definitions for these
terms. The words and definitions appear here, as they do on www.
dictionary.com. They are:

° **Psychopath**—A person with a psychopathic personality,
which manifests as amoral and antisocial behavior, lack of
ability to love or establish meaningful personal relationships,
extreme egocentricity, failure to learn from experience, etc.

° **Sociopath**—A person with a psychopathic personality whose
behavior is antisocial, often criminal, and who lacks a sense
of moral responsibility or social conscience.

° **Pathological** Involving, caused by, or of the nature of a physical or mental disease.

° **Psychopathological**— (1) the conditions and processes of a mental disorder; (2) a pathological deviation from normal or efficient
behavior.

√ It is important to highlight that Whites and other racialized groups
in America do not know and have never known African American people outside of a colonized context. Put another way, White
Americans, Asian Americans, Latinx/Hispanic Americans, and others around the world are only familiar with African Americans in a
reality of colonized, subjugated, disempowered, and inferior profiles. And because African Americans have never lived outside of
a colonized reality, we are only familiar with ourselves and each

other through this particular lens. In addition, most Black people are not honest with White and other racially privileged and oppressive peoples about the way in which we are triggered by them. And because White and other racially privileged people's experiences with Black people are limited in most cases, most "not-Black" people are in touch with Black people in terms of White superiority and anti-Black sentiments. As a result, they expect Black people to function in limited, inferior ways. This only bolsters the White ideology. Black people tend to not want to invest much emotionally because of the range of White trauma inflicted on us daily. We are the only ones who know the burden we carry. No one else, no matter how sympathetic they may seem, does. Whites and others with racial privilege should stop using the term "privilege" in isolation; context is required. The benefits and privileges that have been built exist and depend on the historical, ongoing, and rampant terror aimed against Black people. The word "privilege" deals only with the tenet of exclusivity and higher worth based upon the delusion of superiority. And yet, the tenet of historical and perpetual subjugation and perceived inadequacies of Black people is not contained within the word or the use of the word. Furthermore, its definition does not quite capture the totality of the experiences of White and other racially privileged peoples. The privileged benefit from anti-Black terrorism; it is the result of psychological delusion. This delusion must be acknowledged separately from the ambiguous term "privilege" before any meaningful understanding can be attained.

We are unable to remedy this and must ask why. It is because Whites have never known Black people outside of a system that tells them White is better. They have never engaged their Black counterparts in a system that values both groups equally and wishes to see both flourish in equal measure. This type of profile of Black people, one that is empowered and on equal footing, frightens White and other racially privileged peoples. Again, Black people are expected to submit.

√ I take an anthropological and sociological approach to this text. Much of it is an examination of structural Whiteness and White identity as an institution, and structural Blackness as an institution. There are litanies of examples that are used to develop the examinations of these entities. The goals are to both question and call out the general mindsets and actions of Whiteness. Additionally, I highlight the relentless effects it has on Blackness. To this end, I have modified the definition of "anthropology" such that it deviates slightly from its Dictionary.com reading. It is: "Science that deals with the origins, physical and cultural development, biological characteristics, and social customs, and beliefs on White and Black people in America" instead. Moreover, I define and use the term "sociology" in this text as "The science or study of the origin, development, organization, and functioning of White society, and their impacts on White people and Black people through judicial, legal, political, social, religious, scientific, economic, and all other institutional and cultural means."

√ The terms "Black" and/or "Negro" are used interchangeably and refer to people of non-Anglo and African origin, or people interpreted as having predominantly African origin in America (i.e., African American, African Latina/o/x, African Asian, etc.). I am referring to people who European-Whites have labeled for more than 500 years as Negro and/or Black. I am referring to people with greater quantities of melanin in their skin. The term "non-White people" references people from communities other than White and/or Black communities.

√ Whiteness is transactional and not relational. It was built upon terrorism. Therefore, Black people should not generally expect White people to feel any empathy, remorse, or even the slightest understanding about what Black people have endured historically in this country, or the continual burden of anti-Black racism that they all benefit from and reassert upon us every single day. Perhaps with significant study, some small part of this can be remedied. Such instances are rare.

√ Black Americans, descendants of enslaved peoples and immigrants, are victims of the psychopathic racial personality in every regard—mentally, emotionally, spiritually, sexually, and physically. We remain enslaved politically, economically, judicially, legally, educationally, sociologically, psychologically, and culturally. We are trapped.

√   I consider this book to be an ode to Black people who will understand the truth of what I am attempting to explain. I also dedicate it to anyone committed to anti-racism, racial justice, and/or racial equity work. I also dedicate it to people who reject and/or who are working to unravel and escape Whiteness and anti-Blackness as cultural conditions. I ask for unwavering solidarity, grace, and support from Black people, as well as non-Black allies, as I attempt to unpack a reality that has caused and continues to cause inescapable trauma to Black people across this country.

√   I am attempting to make sense of the reasons why White people would believe they have to oppress us.

√   I will not debate this book's perspectives. The information in it is not new. It has been shared by Black people, particularly African Americans, for centuries. What is distinctive, I believe, is the unique framing and very candid, raw, repeated, nuanced critique of the ambiguous idea that is racism. I submit that most people offended by this book's thesis are unlikely to be Black themselves. They will also likely want to debate long-established facts. Opinions may be debated. Facts, dissimilarly, may not. At least not in good faith.

√   Recognizing that while many historical papers have been written by Black scholars on the topic of Whiteness, White Supremacy, and anti-Blackness, there are few that best take to task the abnormality of the construction of Whiteness or anti-Blackness. Feeling a heavy responsibility to characterize the circumstances Black people have been forced into and plagued by for centuries, I am confronting both of these issues from a Black perspective. This is the perspective of someone who is forced to carry eternal and limitless rage about the historical and perpetual terror Black people face in America. It is the perspective of someone who, along with the majority of non-affluent, non–upper middle class Black people who find themselves locked out of opportunity year after year, all while not understanding that anti-Blackness is at the core of their experience, wants change. To clarify, no matter how good or bright or skilled, the Black person will never measure up in a White-dominant structure, whatever that structure may be. This induces rage. This book does not shy away from embracing the rage and unvarnished truth I hear from most of my peers, even those who have blossomed in what amounts to a barren environment for them. Most American Black people hurt inside. They long to (but do not feel they can) scream with rage and horror at the anti-Blackness that imprisons them. In a sense, this book is for all of them. Let their screams echo through the ages. Hear them. Internalize them. Only then will there be hope.

√ I encourage you to do your own responsible research so that you can understand and evaluate the facts presented in this text. I am evaluating them from a Black perspective and have arrived at my own conclusions. I am writing this book to leave behind a gift and legacy for Black people, as well as anyone else who wants to understand the United States of America. This text is meant to help make sense of the nature and priorities of White culture, as well as the sociocultural, economic, political, and legal color-caste systems of White supremacy and anti-Blackness.

√ It is important for me to amplify the voices of people such as Elizabeth Key, Maria Stewart, E. Franklin Frazier, Carter G. Woodson, Frederick Douglass, John Henrik Clark, bell hooks, James Baldwin, Albert Cleage, Dr. Bobby Wright, Dr. Alvin Poussaint, and many other Black scholars and teachers who have inspired me to take a deeper look at anti-Blackness in the United States. These individuals have pushed me to look at this issue outside of the framework of Whiteness, White supremacy, and White domination. In doing so, they have allowed me to awaken to new methods of understanding and educating.

√ Importantly, I am not attempting to convince any "not-Black" person or group of people, especially not Whites (whether they consider themselves academics, historians, social scientists, etc.) to agree with me. Such an act would be futile. Instead, I reference the research and pedagogical approaches of scholars such as Laura Rendon, who wrote *Sentipensante Pedagogy: Educating for Wholeness, Social Justice, and Liberation*,[240] Shawn Wilson's *Research Is Ceremony: Indigenous Research Methods*,[241] Linda Tuhiwai Smith's *Decolonizing Methodologies: Research and Indigenous Peoples*,[242] and Jarvis Givens' *Fugitive Pedagogy*,[243] as the backdrops for my approach in writing this book.

In *Fugitive Pedagogy*, Jarvis Givens defines this framework as "black people's teaching and learning activities that explicitly challenged white supremacy."[243] He emphasizes the ways in which Black educators throughout the nineteenth and twentieth centuries defied White American ideals and principles in education by teaching Black children through Black perspectives and leveraging the works of Carter G. Woodson in *The Negro In Our History*, written in 1922.[244] As many recognize, Woodson (in both *The Negro In Our History* and *The Miseducation of the Negro*) dissects the innumerable ways in which the White American, pro-European educational apparatus required the dissemination of historically false narratives to Black (and all other) children. Woodson warned that Black children were being misinformed about this country's history and culture, their place in it, and the persistent reinforcement of an inferior status by limiting our history to the origins and perspectives of White, anti-Black ideology.[80]

Rendon presented the idea of a new educational landscape in "The Dreamfield," which recognizes types of intelligence outside of a White supremacist framework. She refers to this as "monocultures of the mind" and emphasizes the need for social justice scholars to embrace a combination of spiritual, emotional, and other types of heart-centered intelligences to support the emergence of more wholly developed human beings, ones who are able to reach their full potential. She refers to this pedagogical approach as *Sentipensante, Educating for Wholeness, Social Justice, and Liberation*.[240]

It is with these and other pedagogical frameworks in mind that I deem it necessary to offer the perspective that is documented throughout this text. In addition to clarifying the historical and ongoing realities of White, anti-Black racism, we must acknowledge the experiences of Black people on the topic of race and racism as expertise. Amplification of the Black experience on the subject must be defined on the terms of Black people. We have a duty to reject the ways in which White and mainstream America have required us to approach our research, attitudes, and methods of teaching. The "fugitive pedagogy" of Black people on the topic of racism must welcome emotionality. Detachment will not suffice. It minimizes the gravity of the injustice. We must connect to our passion, our anger, our pain. Only when we take an accurate accounting of our wounds can we begin to treat them comprehensively. Black "Fugitive Pedagogy" must also recognize the realities of Black and "not-Black" people who will vehemently disagree with this approach, and what some may characterize as provocative. With this in mind, it is important for Black people (especially those considered academics and activists) to stand tall and remain liberated as we do the often-crushing work of decolonizing the psyches of American children and adults.[243] These are the principles with which this book has been written.

A final pretext that I must state is that I am not interested in using White, Western definitions, and/or theories (i.e., pathologies) to describe Black people's experiences in White America. I am not interested in leveraging White theoretical linguistic inventions and conventions of "science" and/or "research" to frame my work. Dr. Bobby Wright, a phenomenally trained and educated psychologist, provided one of the most compelling rationales for this approach more than 40 years ago during a speech entitled, "White Psychopathology," which he delivered prior to his tragic and early death.

In the speech, Dr. Wright stated:

> The most serious mistake you can make is to utilize White definitions to try to define and understand Black phenomena, Black behavior. If you accept White definitions of the world, Whites will rule you.[341]

Based upon this excerpt from Dr. Wright's speech and the perspectives offered by people such as Malcolm X, consider the following questions:

1. Who would you be outside of White domination and control?

2. Who would you be outside of having to care about White American standards of education, language-orientation, presentation, and economic standing?

3. Who would you be if you did not have to comply with and depend upon White economic and capitalistic institutions to survive?

4. What and who would you be if you had access to ideas outside of White, Anglo-Saxon, European structures?

5. What could and would your values be if you had access to empowerment mechanisms of independent thought and functionality outside of Whiteness?

6. Who would you be if you had access to your fullest self, outside of the influence of Whiteness?

7. What would your name be? What clothes would you wear? What would you think about your hair? What would you think about the way you look? What would you think about others around you? Would you judge them according to the cultural standards, ideologies, and values that you have been indoctrinated with?

8. How much freer would you be to love if you loved in ways that were not influenced by the value systems of White, Anglo-Saxon Europeans?

9. Who would we be as Black people without the label of Negro (Black) that was thrust upon us by Europeans, centuries ago? What would we call ourselves? Would we still identify as Black?

10. Who would you be and how healthy would you be if your body was not ravaged by the stress that comes with having to care about what White people think?

11. Who would you be if you existed in a cultural landscape where Black people controlled the educational landscape and you were provided with the true history of this country?

12. Who would you be if Black people as a collective group controlled the economic system?

13. Who would you be if Black people as a collective group controlled the legal system in a country of our own?

14. Who would you be if Black people as a collective group controlled the educational system in a country of our own?

15. Who would you be if Black people as a collective group controlled the value system in a country of our own?

16. Who would you be if Black people as a collective group controlled the morality structure in a country of our own?

17. Who would you be if Black people as a collective group controlled the cultural system in a country of our own?

18. Who would you be if Black people as a collective group controlled the housing system in a country of our own?

19. Who would you be if Black people as a collective group controlled the health care system in a country of our own?

20. Who would you be if Black people as a collective group controlled all of the systems of industry in a country of our own?

21. What and how would your life be without the influence of White people? How much freer do you think life would be?

22. What would your name be?

23. What types of food would you eat?

24. What would your health look like without disruptions to your nervous system that are caused by White racism and/or anti-Blackness?

25. Have you thought about any of these realities?

26. Who would you be if you viewed Blackness through the lens of power rather than oppression?

27. How much more relaxed would you be if you did not have to navigate through anti-Blackness and White racism?

These are some of the questions that I encourage you to begin asking yourselves as you take this journey.

Again, this book should be used as a prerequisite for registering for Understanding the Roots of Racism and Bias: Anti-Blackness, and Its Links to Whiteness, White Racism, Privilege, and Power, which can be accessed by going to www.danteking.com, and/or emailing understandingtherootsofracism@danteking.com.

The Basic Misunderstanding

I know that many people, as I did, think that they understand anti-Black racism in America, but they do not. No group of people can understand something that they are impacted by and yet have not defined for themselves through their own language and interpretation. No group of people can understand something that they have allowed others to reduce to one word. These statements represent the widespread historical and current approaches to White America's acknowledgement of what is widely termed "racism" in White America. White America has not defined this problem adequately, as that would necessitate placing blame. The term is watered down on purpose and can be neatly addressed by learning about figures such as Dr. King (and "even" giving him his own holiday). This approach informs most people's thinking on the matter. No uncomfortable questions that require critical thinking get asked.

Most people in this country have been duped into thinking about racism as an ongoing normality of ignorant people who will eventually die. This perspective provides casual passes to White people who benefit from White supremacy and anti-Blackness. Most people in the United States of America do not possess a granular understanding about the poison that this country, its institutions, government, culture, and nature developed. Again, every institution is built to accommodate Whites and their ongoing psychopathy. Whites, Black people, and everyone else are trained to believe anti-Black ideas. Anti-Blackness is the root of White identity, White culture, White superiority, White comfort, White entitlement, and overall Whiteness. While many other scholars have discussed White racism against Black people, I think it is important to define and highlight further some details that make up anti-Blackness.

Anti-Blackness is a White American legal, social, cultural, economic, and belief system. It thrives on the de-prioritization of humans perceived as Black. It also includes the criminalization, hyper-negativity, hyper-scrutiny, and pessimistic positioning of Black people and/or Blackness throughout all aspects of American life, for the purpose of justifying political, social, cultural, and economic debasement and inhumane treatment—ultimately genocide.

Anti-Blackness encompasses:

√ Colorism, featurism, and texturism; and many times, is a combination of two or three. Black Africentric hair texture, features, and color run counter to White American Eurocentric desirability politics.

√ The criminalization, hyper-negativity, and hyper-scrutiny of Blackness—legally, socially, principally, culturally, sociologically, economically, and so forth.

√ The criminalization of Blackness in the legal system was perpetrated through the enactment of explicit laws and policies during the seventeenth, eighteenth, nineteenth, and twentieth centuries. These laws specifically targeted Black and Brown people of African descent. They were based on skin color as "prima facie evidence" of something gone horribly wrong. Some examples include the Virginia

Laws of 1669, 1680, 1705, 1723, the Negro Act of 1740, the Casual Killing Acts, the Fugitive Slave Act of 1850, the U.S. Supreme Court decisions of 1883, 1896, and 1926, the New Deal, the G.I. Bill, and the Fair Deal. Many more abound.

√ Unfavorable legal, cultural, social, and economic institutions and constructs.

√ Sociological, psychological, and emotional institutions and constructs.

√ A persisting condition and institution developed through collective European/White (i.e., Portuguese, English, French, Dutch, Spanish, Irish, British) colonialist, imperialist ideas.

√ The core of Whiteness, White ideals and ideologies, which state that Black and Brown people of African descent are inferior, animalistic, and barbaric (i.e., African, African-European, Afro-Latinx, African Haitian, etc.).

√ The foundational principle of racism and core underpinnings of Whiteness, White racism, and White identity.

√ The construct was established to demean, surveil, murder, and otherwise harm anyone perceived as Black.

√ The condition meant to destroy Black people emotionally, physically, symbolically, and spiritually. This was accomplished through political, legal, educational, economic, religious, social, and all other institutional means.

√ The core of White morality.

√ The consistently negative orientation toward people defined/interpreted as Black.

√ A negative programming that responds negatively to Black people and/or anything traditionally associated with Blackness.

√ The tendency toward adopting White-Eurocentric culture as normative and/or the standard by which all things are defined and measured. It is also reflexively anti-Black. Some examples include:

° Identifying with success and better circumstances due to White economic systems, including capitalism.

○ Feeling validated by White-Eurocentric standards of attractiveness (i.e., straight hair, thinness, proximity to White skin/lighter
skin, etc.).

○ Speaking English according to White-Eurocentric normative, educational, and sociocultural standards and implicitly belittling
and/or judging Black people who do not conform to such standards. Such judgments always find fault, they assume everything
outside of the White norm is less than.

○ Celebrating White academic institutions as the best institutions,
regardless of their historical records and perpetual policies of exclusion toward Black people.

○ Blaming Black people for their individual circumstances, rather
than understanding the magnitude of White governmental, economic, and legal forms of institutional, social, and cultural control.

This means that inherent within our culture as Americans, we are socialized
with innate psychological and emotional impulses that respond negatively to
Black people. These anti-Black reflexes react most severely to Black people
who are furthest from Whiteness (i.e., those who do not conform to White
normative standards). Jody Armour, lawyer and USC Law Professor, explained this dynamic in his book, *N*gga Theory*, as "retributive urge," which
he describes as a "strong and deep urge to blame and punish" Black people.[342]
In *N*gga Theory*, Mr. Armour writes:

So, from the standpoint of Nigga Theory, those who deny our (America's)
collective accountability for the plight of both criminals and the poor (call
them deniers) are a multiracial bipartisan group, committed to the same logic of denial; a logic that discounts macro-level social explanations of crime
and poverty. Deniers instead, adopt or give undue weight to individual-level
explanations centered on moral poverty of the poor, the moral poverty of
criminals, and hence the hyper-concentrated moral depravity of poor Black
criminals, who are thus especially likely to stoke retributive urge.

Nigga Theory recognizes that poor Black criminals belong to a special category of hyper-concentrated otherness that makes them easy to hate, a
profound otherness that the words nigger and nigga capture with fierce
felicity. The retributive urge, even in the Black community, to blame and
punish Black criminals, further stoked by the extreme otherization or nig-
gerization of Black criminals by popular stage acts, books, and op-eds by

Black entertainers, scholars, and commentators makes it easier for many 'ordinary,' 'law-abiding,' White-Americans to agree with those who deny that racial oppression can cause serious wrongdoing.

The instinctive retributive urge makes it harder to recognize the structural determinants of criminal choices, and hence then deny our collective accountability for the cataclysmic Crack plague and its festering aftermath, a monumental more than 30-year long crime and incarceration disaster that has inflicted as much misery on the Black community, as a-thousand hurricane Katrina's slamming a-thousand 9th-Wards. Our strong and deep urge to blame and punish Black wrong doers, helps ordinary Americans deny our collective accountability for the foreseeable criminal acts of poor Blacks stranded in forsaken neighborhoods brimming with guns and drugs.

The inflamed retributive urge causes voters, jurors, judges, lawmakers and others to ignore, deny, or downplay the role of macro-level social factors for which we are collectively accountable in both the production and construction of Black criminals. In sum, the better wrong doers fit the depraved nigga stereotype, the more they stir the retributive urge for blame and punishment. The more the wrong-doers stir the retributive urge, the easier it is for Americans to deny a causal connection between the specific criminal acts of poor Black wrong-doers and general macro-level social facts like racism and joblessness. And the easier it is to deny that macro-level social factors cause criminal wrongdoing, the easier it is to deny our collective accountability for the criminal consequences of being broke, Black, and hopeless in post-civil rights America.[342]

In *The Black Image in the White Mind*, written by George Frederickson (also evidenced in *Great Fear: Race in the Mind of America*, written by Gary Nash), the ways in which Blackness was regarded by Anglo-Saxon, English Europeans is discussed. Frederickson wrote:

When the English came into contact with dark-skinned Africans, they reacted negatively: Unhappily, blackness was already a means of conveying some of the most ingrained values of English society. Black—and its opposite, white— were emotion-laden words. Black meant foul, dirty, wicked, malignant, and disgraceful. And of course, it signified night—a time of fear and uncertainty. Black was a symbol signifying baseness, evil, and danger . . . . White was all the opposites—chastity, virtue, beauty, and peace. Women were married in white to symbolize purity and virginity. Day was light just like night was black. The angels were white; the devil was black. Thus, Englishmen were conditioned to see ugliness and evil in black. In this sense their encounter with the black people of West Africa was prejudiced by the very symbols of color which had been woven into English language and culture over centuries.[328–329]

This essential context is critical in understanding the ways the English/British legislatures began developing and enacting laws during the establishment of colonial America. These connections are revealed and discussed throughout the next several chapters.

In *Black Bourgeoisie*, Frazier discusses the prevalence of anti-Blackness as it pertained to the condition of White enslavement of Black people.[1] Though I take a more expanded approach in defining anti-Blackness (by considering the degradation experienced by free Black people through the periods of the White enslavement of Black people, Jim Crow, and beyond), Frazier's description of the overarching color-caste, White-supremacist, anti-Black culture called America is noteworthy. In Chapter One of his book, he summarizes the making of anti-Blackness in America as:

> The condition of the Negro slaves on the southern plantations varied considerably. In the lower south, where the large cotton plantation tended to take on the character of a purely industrial organization, the treatment of the slaves was extremely brutal since they were regarded as mere work animals. They were treated even more inhumanly by the slave traders who supplied the needs of a commercial system of agriculture. As articles of commerce, the Negro slaves were treated in the same manner as the mules which were advertised for sale along with them. On the other hand, where the plantation became a social as well as an economic organization, under a semi-patriarchal regime, more consideration was shown for the personalities of the slaves. The lives of the masters and slaves became intertwined in a system of social relationships. The relations between whites and Black people came to be regulated by a complex system of social rituals and etiquette permitting a maximum degree of intimacy while maintaining the complete subordination of Black people. The traditions governing race relations on the plantation became so firmly rooted in the South that they have persisted until the present day.[1]

The last sentence of this passage is critical; it helps us understand where we are with respect to today's racial and social terms. I highlight the impact of the legal and political systems created and enacted by and for Europeans and against Black people. This is necessary if we wish to understand the development of both peoples in America. Studying the severe sociological, psychological, and physical impacts of anti-Blackness is immensely important. It is why a condition developed in the seventeenth century still commands so much power in the twenty-first. Other pro-Black scholars, such as David Walker, Dr. W.E.B DuBois, James Baldwin, Frederick Douglass, Dr. Angela Davis, Dr. Cornel West, and Dr. Ibram Kendi, have made similar assertions.

All non-European-White and "not-Black" groups benefit from anti-Blackness. Asians, Latinx peoples, and Middle Eastern peoples, for examples, do. In a "Race Forward" sponsored lecture and interview conducted by Dr. Charlene Sinclair about her 2023 book entitled *Asian Americans in an Anti-Black World*, Dr. Claire Jean Kim explained it this way:

> White supremacy, we can think of as a force that lifts White people up and pushes down all 'not-White' people. Anti-Blackness on the other hand, pushes down Black people, and lifts-up all 'not-Black' people. So, you can immediately see that Asian Americans, as are other groups, are in an odd configuration.
>
> Asian Americans are seen, from the moment that they arrive in large numbers in the 1850's, until today, as 'not-White,' but above all 'not-Black. This means that they {Asian Americans} are seen as the lesser of two evils, as compared with Black Americans, by White people, by the power structure.[375]

In a 1999 article entitled "The Racial Triangulation of Asian Americans," Dr. Kim explained her theory in these terms:

> Asian Americans have been racially triangulated vis-à-vis Blacks and Whites or located in the field of racial positions with reference to these two other points. Racial triangulation occurs by means of two types of simultaneous, linked processes: (1) processes of "relative valorization," whereby dominant group A (Whites) valorizes subordinate group B (Asian Americans) relative to subordinate group C (Blacks) on cultural and/or racial grounds in order to dominate both groups, but especially the latter, and (2) processes of "civic ostracism," whereby dominant group A (Whites) constructs subordinate group B (Asian Americans) as immutably foreign and unassimilable with Whites on cultural and/or racial grounds in order to ostracize them from the body politic and civic membership (see Figure 1). Processes of relative valorization and civic ostracism are linked both analytically and functionally.[385]

Fgure 1.1.
Chart from The Racial Triangulation of Asian Americans (1999)[385]

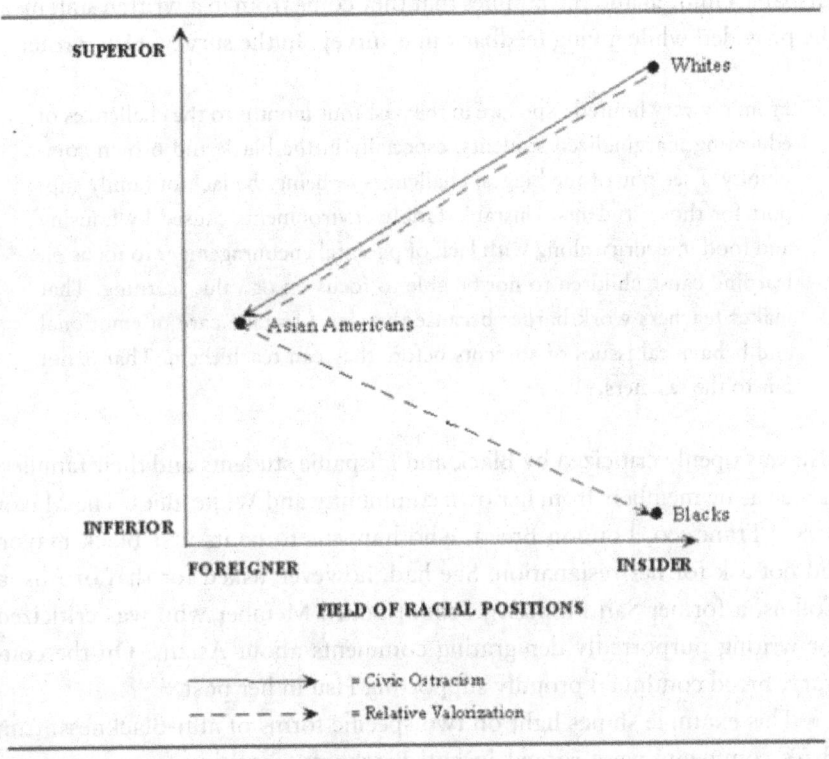

In her book, Dr. Kim asserts a small yet critical change in the position she took roughly twenty-five years ago. Black people are indeed outsiders, too.

Importantly, Black people who accept Whiteness as the primary cultural framework also benefit from anti-Blackness.

In addition, some in these groups also benefit from racial skin privilege and/or an adjacency to Whiteness.[1-3] Look to a 2022 scandal in Los Angeles, wherein former City Councilperson Nury Martinez, a White-presenting Latina, made racist comments during what she thought was a private meeting. More specifically, she was recorded calling her former colleagues adopted, Black son "parece changuito," meaning he "looks like a little monkey." She also suggested that they were raising the young Black child "like a White kid." The inherent implication in her statement is that Black children do not deserve the same flexibilities and freedoms that White children enjoy.[353]

In San Francisco (California), Ann Hsu, a current San Francisco School Board Member (as of February 2023) shared her thoughts about Black and Hispanic children and the families that they come from in a written statement she provided while giving feedback in a survey. In the survey, Hsu wrote:

> From my very limited exposure in the past four months to the challenges of educating marginalized students, especially in the black and brown community, I see one of the biggest challenges as being the lack of family support for those students. Unstable family environments caused by housing and food insecurity along with lack of parental encouragement to focus on learning cause children to not be able to focus on or value learning. That makes teachers work harder because they have to take care of emotional and behavioral issues of students before they can teach them. That is not fair to the teachers. [354]

Hsu was openly criticized by Black and Hispanic students and their families, as well as by members from her own community and White allies. The Mayor of San Francisco, London Breed, who happens to be its first Black mayor, did not ask for her resignation. She had, however, asked for that of Alison Collins, a former San Francisco School Board Member who was criticized for writing purportedly denigrating comments about Asians. On the contrary, Breed continued proudly supporting Hsu in her post.[355,356]

This example shines light on two specific forms of anti-Blackness. Ann Hsu's comments were rooted in anti-Blackness, resulting from uncontextualized rhetoric and limited experience. Mayor London Breed's position reinforced anti-Blackness as well, extending from the traditional and usual ways in which Black people are held to the "highest" possible standards, all while "model minorities" benefit from proximities to Whiteness. Examples include White-presenting Jewish Americans, White-presenting Hispanics, White-presenting Asians, etc. Members of these groups are prioritized by White Americans; they regurgitate White American values. They are leveraged by members of the White communities as allies, and in ways most Black Americans are not.

Black people who are interpreted by others in society as having lighter skin (i.e., bi-racial, people from regions of Africa with lighter pigmentation, etc.) are rewarded with a greater number of opportunities because of their proximity to Whiteness. Racism in America has been and remains an operation of color-caste, similar in nature to other regions of the world, but notably different than cultural and economic caste systems in places such as India.[4,5]

Anti-Blackness was the primary institution used to advance slavery starting in the fifteenth century, first in Portugal, then later in the West Indies, and after that in the Americas (beginning in the sixteenth century) as noted by Dr. Ibram X. Kendi in his bestselling book entitled *Stamped from the Beginning*.[4] Anti-Blackness was the primary construct used to advance Jim Crow laws in the United States and apartheid in South Africa.[3] Anti-Blackness was the basis for the continual exploitation of Black people in the United States and elsewhere.

If we address White people's enslavement of Black people separate and apart from anti-Blackness, we do ourselves no favors. It is to misunderstand the pervasiveness and the role of sex.

Stephanie Jones-Rogers, in her best-selling book entitled *They Were Her Property*, emphasizes these points further. She focuses on the prominent role White women played as land-owning enslavers. They bought, sold, chastised, demeaned, terrorized, abused, and murdered the enslaved as well as the free, and both male and female.[6] In addition, White women conspired with their male counterparts to help shape a definition of White girlhood and womanhood, all at the expense of Black girlhood and womanhood. Dr. Alvin Poussaint, in his text entitled "White Manipulation and Black Oppression," made this very point.

He said:

> It is important to remember that not only did the white male oppress Black people; so too did the white male's wife, daughter, and siblings as well as the white female in general. Since families owned slaves, white wives and their children also owned them, and they could be passed down as inheritances. White men and women bossed and oppressed Black people. The white woman was fearful of the black male because of the strong taboo against any form of equality in their relationship. Therefore, it was just as important for the White female as it was for the White male to keep the black man {and woman} in his place.[7]

Evaluating the Psychopathic and Sociopathic Sovereignty of Whiteness, White Morality, White Beliefs, and Ideals about Black People, through

White Language, White Intent, White Beliefs, White Ideals, White Religious Principles, and More . . .

Here we see examples of laws that were created throughout the British colonies to demonstrate the ways in which anti-Black, White psychopathy, sociopathy, and terrorism (called "racism" when reduced) were legalized in the most horrifying ways. One would do well by attending my seminar, Understanding the Roots of Racism and Bias: Anti-Blackness and Its Links to Whiteness, White Racism, Privilege, and Power and/or additional courses to understand better the magnitude of what confronts us as Black people and Americans. My assertions are bold; I am happy to defend them. The systems of power and privilege for White people collectively operate as a sort of prison. Whites have established an entirely pro-White, anti-Black framework to maintain the power they first began asserting violently and unjustly centuries ago.

Consider the following:

√   What are the psychological, sociological, and cultural characteristics and other variables that emerged within the White community?

√   Based on legal privilege, what White attitudes formed about Black people over time? What role is skin color–based, anti-Blackness founded on? How does this shape American culture? Including those who are just coming to integrate into it? How do they treat Whites and Black people as a result?

Again, this should be read as one part of an entire curriculum. It is not meant to be understood in isolation.

Below are links and QR Codes to courses and seminars that are currently available.

Course: Understanding the Roots of Racism and Bias: Anti-Blackness and Its Links to Whiteness, White Racism, Privilege, and Power (2-day course offered through the University of California, San Francisco; UCSF):
Go to: https://meded.ucsf.edu/cme/upcoming-ce-courses or access the following QR Code to search for upcoming classes:

Course: Unlearning and Addressing Anti-Blackness, White Supremacy and Racism in American Culture and Institutions (12-week course offered by Dante King and Guest Experts):
Go to www.danteking.com/courses.

Course: Unlearning and Addressing Anti-Blackness, White Supremacy and Racism in American Culture and Institutions Leaders Fellowship (16-week fellowship offered by Dante King and Guest Experts):
Go to www.danteking.com/courses.

Book: The 400-Year Holocaust: White America's Legal, Psychopathic, and Sociopathic Black Genocide—and the Revolt Against Critical Race Theory
Go to www.danteking.com/books.

The Perpetual Racial Genocide of Black People In America as the Need to Define, Reframe, and Examine Whiteness and Anti-Blackness as Psychosis

Years ago, Americans were deluged with images of thousands of Black people fighting for their lives as Hurricane Katrina devastated a whole region. The federal nonresponse, headed by President George W. Bush, shocked the conscience.

Then came the Kanye West moment during a fundraiser for those affected.

Held September 2, 2004 on NBC, *A Concert for Hurricane Relief* helped raise millions for those in greatest need. A star-studded event, it commanded great attention. West, articulating plainly the sentiment of countless others, said, "George Bush doesn't care about Black people."[9] Though he apologized for the commentary, it remains recorded for posterity. In my view, his language was far too narrow. Katrina was hardly America's first go-around with a catastrophe that primarily affected its Black population. The scale of the devastation required an even harsher commentary.

Consider the Great Mississippi River Flood of 1927. Black neighborhoods, including business districts in three states (Louisiana, Arkansas, and Mississippi) were destroyed by levees that were redirected and emptied into Black neighborhoods.[10,11]

This is worth repeating. For clarity, U.S. soldiers, along with help from their state and local law enforcement counterparts, emptied levees into Black neighborhoods. In addition to the loss of treasury, blood was lost, too, as some were killed in the process. This means the mass murder of Black people was organized and carried out by Whites, who exclusively wielded power. West commented on what appeared to be a total sense of indifference to Black suffering. I wondered why he did not dig deeper, as he was on to something. Bush's response was hardly surprising. It was predictable. We saw it coming. Our grandparents and parents saw it coming. They knew intimately the persistent traumas Whites inflicted on us, in times of crisis and otherwise.[12] Black people, especially African Americans who are descendants of enslaved Black people, are familiar with the disposition of George Bush as a cultural affect, artifact, and variable of the United States' overall value system. This attitude, one characterized charitably as one of indifference, extends far beyond Bush. He is merely a figurehead. The reality is plain, though painful. America hates Black people. It trains others to hate Black people, including other minorities. It trains Black people to hate other Black people. To be an American is to be anti-Black.[3,8,13] It is to have anti-Black beliefs passed down from generation to generation. It is to be programmed with uncontrollable compulsive innate psychological and emotional reflexes and impulses that react and respond negatively and unfavorabley to Black people. It is to obsessively stereotype Black people as being hypersexual and incapable of feeling pain. It is to use us as mere tokens when convenient. It is to degrade us.

To be an American is to be indoctrinated by a pro-White-European propaganda machine. It is to see Black people as outsiders—people who are suspicious, criminal, ignorant, or otherwise less than.[15] To exist in America is to live in a culture that makes individual or institutional critique of the anti-Black indoctrination an impossibility. Therefore, the problem can and never will be solved. Meanwhile, African Americans and most other Americans are trying to carve out a space for themselves in a construct that is inherently designed to exclude them because of its anti-Black, pro-White design.[1,3,16] I explore this point further later.

My Journey

When I first arrived at these admittedly jarring conclusions, I did not know how to begin processing the trauma. Deep in my inner soul, I ached. My wounds were psychological, emotional, and physical.

To be a Black American is, in its most fundamental terms, to be wounded; White psychopathy and sociopathy wounds. Terms such as racism, bias, and microaggressions are woefully inadequate. They do not convey the depth of the hurt. We live in a perpetual state of deprivation, of despair, of pain. We have internalized all the toxic messages aimed directly at, and against us. We believe ourselves to be inferior, we know only fear and hopelessness, we see no pathway forward. This is not a way to live. Only knowing grief is no way to live. This sickness, this unceasing form of emotional terror, is not incidental to American culture. It is American culture. It has long been normalized. To scrutinize it is to scrutinize America itself. What plagues us allows for a stop and frisk policy to persist. It allows for unconstitutional surveillance and modern enslavement. Our education system normalizes this abnormality, as does our economic system. The result? Black people are pathologized. This is unacceptable and yet all the mechanisms that can address it are also poisoned. We have remained in this diseased state for well in excess of 400 years.

As a people, Black people know no other existence except one rooted in oppression. There is no overreacting to this sad reality. American culture is rooted in terror against Black people. We must make space for this reality as we further examine what drives American culture. Acknowledging America's racist past in an emotionally detached manner is insufficient.

Black people in America exist in a system of steady anti-Black terror and White supremacy. American culture is entrenched in these two horrifying constructs. Its leaders and all White people in this country continuously normalize and benefit from this system. These illnesses do not impact us here in America only. They have been accepted and exported around the world. I will begin to explain this further in the next chapter.

I embark upon this journey sharing a profound understanding with you. I provide a perspective on language I have developed and continue to revise in order to ensure Black people have the language we need to express the way we need to but often cannot, due to the ways in which we have been gaslighted by White people and non-White people. In short, we have been taught to act as though things are not as bad as they seem. Things are not only as bad as they seem, but they are also much worse than they seem.

I must, for a moment, reflect on the pain that defines this journey. I would like nothing more than to not spend my life trying to address something this horrifying, but it is a burden with which I have been saddled and a burden I will continually attempt to lighten by educating those around me. We are long and far beyond the point of racial prejudice or bias. Such terms are inappropriate, given the gravity of the situation. Anti-Blackness has pervaded every aspect of our culture. Every field is tainted. Every interaction, macro and micro, is tainted. It defines us. It is our very essence. Black identity. The Whiter we become in our bodies (skeletal frame), hair (not worn in its natural state), make-up (see bleaching and whitening techniques), language (European English and obliteration of all languages of Africa), clothes (European design and style), the more worthy we regard ourselves. Black people, and all such other groups in and upon American soil, have evolved and developed within this manner. Again, nothing that I am stating here is new or revolutionary. It has only been stated in different ways, by different people.

And so, I do this because we are not taught to think this way, due to skewed, inadequate, and/or inaccurate information conveyed to us in a White cultural and educational system.

In *The Falsification of Afrikan Consciousness: Eurocentric History, Psychiatry, and the Politics of White Supremacy*, and *The Failure of the Educational System*, Dr. Amos Wilson stated:

> We have a school system that is based upon the psychology of White children and White people. We are trying to educate our children in that system; they are bound to fail. The very structure of the educational system itself is based upon a White model and therefore it has a built-in failure mechanism for us, one way or the other.[301-302]

We cannot continue to take our cues from beneficiaries or leaders who murdered, raped, castrated, whipped, beat, dismembered, and otherwise terrorized Black people between 1619 to 2022. Such a notion is absurd, and yet we persist this way. We cannot continue learning from beneficiaries of Jim Crow. We cannot continue tolerating the perpetual degradation and humiliation of Black people, which has been taking place unexceptionally for more than one hundred years (1866–1977). The period I am now referring to as America's 400-Year Holocaust and Black Genocide involves cleansing this country of even any residue of Blackness that both slavery and Jim Crow did not destroy. We must all acknowledge, frame, and reframe White privilege, White power, and White supremacy as affirmative action for White people.

I write now because there are so many people in this country who need to understand the legal construction of race, racism, White supremacy, and anti-Blackness in what we now deem as a distinctly "American" culture. The vast majority of American Natives and immigrants do not understand the formality of White terror, White psychopathy, or White sociopathy.

As a Black person, myself, I feel we must understand thoroughly who our enemy is, because once we do, we will understand we need to be utterly afraid of what may lie ahead. We must be suspicious of Whites in power, those who benefit from White power, and those who are not actively challenging or changing it. They are the gatekeepers, the overseers, the controllers. They have no incentive to destroy what most benefits them. In fact, they are completely disincentivized to do so.

Moreover, to some extent, we must also be afraid of some Black people. There is an adage many Black people have long known: all skin folk ain't kinfolk. There is wisdom in this proverb, as skin color alone does not necessarily determine identity. That is the power of anti-Blackness; it can even touch Black people. What many often refer to as Black history is something that I think of as White history, or perhaps a mix of the two. Whites dominate and dehumanize in every circumstance. The concept of Blackness, itself, was conjured up by Whites.[16,17] White supremacy and anti-Blackness are legacies of this country. As Nina Tuner, a former Ohio State Senator, put it while appearing on Jake Tapper's program in 2018, "America specializes in racism."

As outlined in Understanding the Roots of Racism and Bias: Anti-Blackness and Its Links to Whiteness, White Racism, Privilege, and Power, the tools of White supremacy include all institutions (academic, corporate, and everything in between). There is no escaping it. The tools White supremacists have at their disposal are limitless. They include:

√ Bias. It is favorable toward Whites and unfavorable toward Black people.

√ The ability to create and control all institutions, where they then implement those biases.

√   Forced assimilation, requiring Black, Brown, and all other non-White people to adopt White imperialist patriarchal standards, norms, language, thought processes, behaviors, etc., in order to be interpreted in ways that keep White people comfortable. This allows Whites to subjugate non-White people and make them need to be "like Whites" to be accepted, desired, worthy, afforded opportunities to, or rewarded. Not buying into this systematic assimilation program results in exclusion and underachievement and is the antithesis of survival. Failing to assimilate means it is unlikely that I (or other Black people) will be able to attend "that" school, get "that" job, and/or be afforded opportunities that enable me to survive and take care of myself, my family, etc.

Some of this understanding comes from the Dismantling Racism framework established in the 1990s, created by Kenneth Jones and Tema Okun. They note that racism is both favorable and unfavorable race prejudice + social and institutional power.[18] Racism is a system of social, political, economic, and cultural advantage and power based upon skin color/race privilege. Racism is a system of social, political, economic, and cultural oppression and powerlessness based upon skin color/race absence of privilege. Racism is a White supremacist system with Whites positioned at the top of the racial hierarchy, distributing sociological values to every other racial/ethnic group, with Black people unexceptionally positioned at the bottom. American racism is anti-Black.[3,19,20] White racism relies on capitalism and inflation, the main tools of White socialism. Racism in America functions as a tool of assimilation and conformity, requiring everyone who participates in this society to adopt the ways of, and become like, White-Europeans.

Racism functions sometimes loud, other times silent. Sometimes it is hidden, other times it is obvious. What it always is is deliberate and meant to benefit Whites.[20] Racism must be the norm if Black people are to continually be degraded and destroyed, which is the ultimate goal. If it were merely personal, something on a micro scale, whole institutions would not be needed to perpetuate it. It is about the collective. The scale is a macro one. It is about psychopathy, sociopathy, complete destruction.

My work does not exist in isolation. I was influenced by others. I owe it to them to include how they influenced me.

In 1975, Dr. Bobby Wright, a psychologist, wrote an essay entitled, "The Psychopathic Racial Personality."[21] In it, he states the following:

> In their relationship with the Black race, Europeans (Whites) are psychopaths, and their behavior represents an underlying biologically transmitted proclivity with roots deep in their evolutionary history. The psychopath is an individual who is constantly in conflict with other persons or groups. He is unable to experience guilt, is completely selfish and callous, and has a total disregard for the rights of others.

> One of the best methods that can be used to measure the psychopathic traits of the White race is observing and analyzing their universal overt behaviors and attitudes towards Black people.[21]

He discusses White people's obsession with Black people, their need to maintain power and control over us. He states:

> Psychopaths simply ignore the concept of right and wrong. By ignoring this trait in the White race (the lack of ethical and moral development) Black people have made and are still making a tragic mistake in basing the worldwide Black liberation movement on moral suasion. It is pathological for Black people to keep attempting to use moral suasion on a people who have no morality where race is the variable.[21]

In 1950, Elizabeth Waring, wife of South Carolina Federal Judge Julius Waties Waring (Briggs v. Elliott), gave a speech on behalf of the NAACP. In it, Ms. Waring all but agreed with Dr. Bobby Wright's position on White psychopathy. Ms. Waring asserted White people were "sick, confused, and decadent." She espoused:

> Like all decadent people, they are full of pride and complacency, introverted, morally weak, and low. You are building and creating. The White Supremacists are destroying and withholding. They are so self-centered that they are drawing the walls around themselves so close and high that they have become completely isolated from the rest of the world and have not considered themselves as a part of this country since the Civil War. So much is myth about that period and particularly the Reconstruction period, which has more lies than truth. The phobia and frenzy aroused by mention of carpetbaggers and scalawags (sic) as <u>a reason</u> for White Supremacy is like the

Versailles treaty propaganda of the Germans and an excuse for Hitler's later atrocities. Poor excuse for the persecution of you Negroes – poor excuse for the Gestapo atrocities to the Jews. Ours is a Dixiecrat Gestapo as one returned South Carolina soldier stated to our press.[415]

When questioned by Mary Cotrell during a 1950 Meet the Press interview, Ms. Waring reaffirmed her position. Ms. Cotrell asked:

"Mrs. Waring, you charged in your speech before the YWCA group in Charleston that the whites down here are a sick, confused and decadent people; and that like all decadent people, they are full of pride and complacency, introverted, morally weak and low. What brought you to this drastic conclusion?"[415]

Ms. Waring responded simply yet succinctly:

"Living there and observing them. Any people who enslave the minds and bodies of another people are bound to destroy their own souls."[415]

We know from history that this is true. Our ugly history is filled with examples to substantiate this claim. White "Christians" have engaged in irrationally violent acts against their Black counterparts. They have beaten, lashed, hung, and burned them. They have stabbed, raped, and shot them, all here in America. [22-23,38]

In 1971, in *The Black Journal's* second installment of a "Black Paper on White Racism," Dr. Alvin Poussaint, a psychiatrist, researcher, and professor at Harvard Medical School, stated:

I think that we have to establish that racism, White racism, is a mental illness. Many White social scientists would like to define racism as something that is normal, as a cultural variant. As long as we approach it that way, we really don't deal with the pathology of racism itself. It's like saying that cancer, because a lot of people have it in our society, that it is somehow normal. But we know that cancer kills, and racism kills and destroys also. It would be like defining Hitler's slaughter of the Jews, as somehow normal, and I think we have to face the fact that racism is a mental aberration. And I think underlying White racism is a White paranoia, a fear or a delusion that Black people, colored people in the world are somehow going to destroy and hurt the White man. And it is very convenient, I think, for

Whites to project their impulses, their unacceptable feelings onto Blacks, and pretend that they are the holy good ones and make Blacks the victims.

Racism is something that doesn't only affect the victim, that is, the Black man, but also affects the victimizer, the White man. It is bad for his mental health, too, because, he doesn't face himself honestly. He pretends that the problem lies outside of himself so that this society never deals with its violence, its own perversions, and corruption. They {Whites} pretend that somehow, if you get rid of all the 'niggers,' that everything will be solved and we will be much better off. Of course that's not so. That's the delusion. It even carries over into our foreign policy, our attitudes toward Asians, our attitudes in Vietnam; the massacres, the slaughter; the feeling that we are superior and can destroy and wipe out other people because we're the chosen people, so to speak.

I think that Whites, then, really don't mature fully. In addition, they have to experience a chronic anxiety and a type of chronic guilt that we all know exists because Blacks are discriminated against in this country. In many other ways they use it in their fantasies about sex or other types of acting out in this society, which is detrimental, not only to Whites, but to Blacks also.[24]

In his analysis on White racism, Dr. Poussaint offered America, particularly White people, a thoughtful, yet chilling definitive description that could and should be contained in the Diagnostic and Statistical Manual of Mental Disorders (DSM).

Saraa, clinical therapist, and an extraordinary Black woman, offered the following perspective on an Instagram post advertising one of my lectures about this book:

White supremacy is diagnosable in individuals, systems, and society as a whole. It's a delusion. Any idea of someone who is fundamentally "superior" based on race, appearance, wealth, etc., is delusional thinking. In [clinical] training, we are routinely advised to let people have their racism, homophobia, white supremacy as a "personal belief" that is not a problem unless the client says it's a problem. Okay. And should I also responsibly let my clients believe that day is night and ants are bigger than skyscrapers? No! We diagnose delusions.

My assertions are supported by world class experts. I have taught about these matters for more than 15 years.

I often ask my White students how many of them were raised believing they were inherently superior to Black people. Often, a supermajority are honest and admit to having been raised/feeling this way.

One student said:

> Integrating a new sense of self. As a white person I did not understand, until this course, the degree to which walking around in white skin and conforming broadly to social norms was causing harm day in and day out. In this course I realized simply being white means that you are uniquely programmed from birth to reproduce conditions of anti-Black racism, unconsciously or consciously, and to benefit from doing so. Toni Morrison and Alvin Poussaint suggested that racism is a form of mental illness in whites, and this resonated with me deeply. This inclination toward domination and superiority, alongside the paranoia, fear, and the psychotic inability to empathize with harms enacted, is the intergenerational inheritance of white Americans. This is the core of the white American psyche and our culture. Before this course I already didn't believe in "good" or "bad" people, but I didn't realize that because I have white skin, I am far more likely to cause harm than others. It was painful to have this aspect of myself laid out so clearly, so undeniably. Often during the course, I felt my hands squeezing my temples, trying to crack my skull, or tear my skin apart as I incorporated this inbred propensity for evil into my working sense of self.[25]

We must acknowledge the depth of the rot. This need to dominate and dehumanize Black people is embedded in the White psyche. It is central to White identity.[26] The desire provides both the foundational worth for the culture of Whiteness and White people, as well as non-White and "not-Black" racialized groups in American culture.[14,26] It reinforces all of what makes White people feel good about themselves, and most of what they believe sets them apart from Black, as well as other non-White/"not-Black," human beings that they have casually diminished and grouped together as people of color in American culture.

A third perspective on the topic which resonated with me was one shared by author and scholar Toni Morrison. During a 1993 interview with Charlie Rose, she was asked to comment on something related to Arthur Ashe. Ashe had commented on the realities of living with racism vs. living with AIDS. Morrison's reaction was:

Don't you understand that the people who practice racism are bereft. There is something distorted about the psyche. It's a huge waste and it's a corruption and a distortion. It's like a profound neurosis that nobody examines for what it is. It feels crazy. It is crazy and it has just as much of a deleterious effect on White people and possibly equal as it does Black people. If the racist White person doesn't understand that he or she is also a race; it's also constructed, it's also made, and it also has some kind of serviceability—but when you take it away—if I take your race away and there you are all strung out and all you got is your little self; and what is that? What are you without racism? Are you any good? Are you still strong? Are you still smart? Do you still like yourself? I mean these are the questions. If you can only be tall because somebody is on their knees, then you have a serious problem; and my feeling is that White people have a very serious problem, and they should start thinking about what they can do about it.

What do you need this for?[27]

What do White people need Whiteness and race for?

Morrison was clear in her language, posture, power, and perspective about White people's obsessions with oppressing Black people.

While it is psychopathy, what some have referred to as an ingrained neuro-sociopathic reality, it is also an obsessive reality. In addition, the examples of the questions provided a modern-day landscape to build on addressing the persistence of anti-Black racism in the United States. The unfolding of anti-Black terror and racial genocide in America continues to be embedded into the culture and fabric of the United States; it is reinforced through subsequent centuries in infinite ways.[28,29,30,151]

Malcolm X, during an interview at U.C. Berkeley with Professor John Leggett and Dr. J. Herman Blake (then a graduate student) on October 11, 1963, was asked a question by Mr. Blake. The question was, "What is the definition of freedom, justice, and equality for the Black man, and where and when is it to be attained?"[31] Malcolm's answer was profound, perhaps the most profound thought I have internalized. It lingers with me still. He said:

Take equality first, the Honorable Elijah Mohammed doesn't teach us to associate equality with Whites. Equality has nothing to do with Whites. We don't want to be equal with the White man. He's not the criteria or yardstick by which equality is measured. He's not in a position to tell us we are equal. It's not his right. It's not his to do. We had equality before the White man was created. We had equality before the White man came into existence. And we want equality whether the White man is on this earth or not. Equality means the opportunity to develop all of our dormant potential, all of our dormant capability; and in developing this dormant capability the right and ability to stand on this earth on some land of our own and bring about a civilization and a society in which we will be completely independent—complete freedom—to take care of the needs, to take care of the wants and the likes and dislikes of our people. To establish our own nation, our own society, our own heaven, our own future. This is what we mean by freedom, by equality; and justice means as you sew, so shall you reap. If you do wrong, you'll get wrong in return; and if you do right, you'll get right in return. When you're in your own nation, on your own land, you're in a position to get justice. But when you're in another man's country, in another man's land, under another man's flag, and under another man's government, and under another man's court system – you have to look to that other man for justice and you'll never get it! And Negroes in this country are probably authorities on that![31]

Other scholars such as Dr. Amos N. Wilson, Dr. John Henrik Clarke, and Francis Cress Welsing, agreed vehemently with Malcolm X, as did many other Black activists and scholars, on the idea of White racial control. They understood the persistent and systematic nature of cultural and social domination; its fluidity and persistence through ongoing White ownership of Black bodies through White American institutions—legal, economic, political, cultural, social, moral—and all others.

In *The Falsification of Afrikan Consciousness: Eurocentric History, Psychiatry, and the Politics of White Supremacy*, Dr. Wilson penned it this way,

There are so many of us who believe that fair housing laws, civil rights laws, voting laws, and so forth guarantee our freedom. That is an illusion. What a flight into fantasy.

Laws are no stronger than their enforcers. The same people who pass those laws are the same people who are responsible for enforcing them. If the people who enforce the laws no longer decide to do so, the laws are of no value and have no power.

Ultimately, then, fairness rests not in laws but in the activities of people and in the attitudes and consciousness of people.

Therefore, if the people who are responsible for enforcing those laws change their attitudes, then the treatment of those people whose freedom is protected by those so-called laws is changed as well.[301]

In 1973, Dr. John Henrik Clarke, professor at Hunter College, appeared on a television show called *Say Brother*, where he was asked to expand on a statement about the types of contradictions that exist in Black life.

Dr. Clarke stated:

> The contradictions of thinking that your oppressor will participate in your liberation, and that your oppressor will dismantle his big international economic apparatus in order to bring social reform to you or anyone else, when he put up the apparatus with your labor and blood and used your labor as the seed money to erect the structure of capitalism. And the whole economic system because he had your labor damn near three-hundred years free of charge. He's erected a worldwide economic system. But to be naïve enough to think that he's going to give you anything other than crumbs of appeasement from this apparatus, or he's going to dismantle any of it in your favor, is just downright wild. It is beyond a contradiction. It is a form of insanity.[304]

During another interview on the television show *Say Brother* (a program by, for, and about the Black community), he was asked about Malcolm X's influence on Black people. Specifically, the interviewer asked Dr. Clarke about the type of influence Malcolm X would have had on the Black community if he were alive at that time. Dr. Clarke answered the question stating that he believed Malcolm would have been able to aid the Black community in articulating and addressing the political contradictions that exists in Black life more effectively that other Black leaders during that period. When asked the question, "What political contradictions exists in Black life?" Dr. Clarke reinforced the earlier comments that he made during his 1971 appearance on *The Black Journal*.

Dr. Clarke offered:

> The contradictions of thinking that your oppressor will participate in your liberation. And, that your oppressor will dismantle his big international economic apparatus in order to bring social reform to you or anyone else, when he put up the apparatus with your labor and blood. He used your

labor as the seed money to erect the structure of capitalism, and the whole economic system because he had your labor damn near 300-years free of charge. He's erected a worldwide economic system. But to be naïve enough to think that he's going to give you anything other than crumbs of appeasement from this apparatus or that he is going to dismantle any of it in your favor, is just downright wild. It is beyond a contradiction. It is a form of insanity.[351]

Dr. Clarke's perspective was not unique, or new. In 1971, a Black journalist named Samuel F. Yette, wrote a book called *The Choice: The Issue of Black Survival in America*. In it, Yette assertes:

Black Americans have outlived their usefulness. Their raison d'etre (purpose for existence) to this society has ceased to be a compelling issue. Once an economic asset, they are now considered an economic drag. The wood is all hewn, the water is all drawn, the cotton all picked, and the rails reach from coast to coast. The ditches are all dug, the dishes are put away, and only a few shoes remain to be shined. Thanks to old blackbacks and new-fangled machines, the sweatchores of the nation are done. Now the same 25,000,000 Blacks face a society that is brutally pragmatic, technologically accomplished, deeply racist, increasingly overcrowded, and surly. In such a society, the absence of social and economic value is a crucial factor in anyone's fight for a future.[305]

Different versions of the book were issued and can be seen online today, with two different taglines: "The extermination of the black man in America," and "The black man is obsolete in today's white America."

In 1994, Dr. Claud Anderson released a book entitled *Black Labor, White Wealth: The Search for Power and Economic Justice*. His book, like mine, provided a historical account and explanation about anti-Blackness and the permanent disenfranchisement of Black people.[361] During a 1995 interview by Darryl Wood, on a television program called *Detroit's Black Journal*, Wood, almost immediately, led Dr. Anderson to share one of the most chilling predictions that he asserts in his text.[360] Wood stated and then asked Dr. Anderson, "One of the alarming predictions you make in the book is along those lines. You mentioned that Blacks will be pretty much a permanent underclass in America, by the year 2015. Why the year 2015?"[360] Dr. Anderson responded:

2015. Because what I have concluded from analysis is that there are going to be a converging of social factors nationally and internationally that's going to place Blacks in a permanent status of underclass-ship. One, we anticipate that by this point in time, based on all of the research coming to us, is that the next generation of Whites are going to be more anti-Black than they've been since the civil rights movement. Two, we anticipate that by the same token 86,000,000 Hispanics will be coming into the United States, and about 41,000,000 Asians by that point in time which is going to kick Black people out of being the 'majority-minority' in this society, down to 'minority-minority'. We've [Black people] been number two in this society for four-hundred years as a group. We're going to become number four. And, if we have not gotten anything after being number two for four-hundred years, you can guess what will happen when we become number four. Cause at that point in time all of the new groups coming into America, they're coming in higher than we are because this country operates off of a pref-erential acceptance program. This means that groups are coming in based on skin color. They are going from the lightest down to the darkest: Light, yellow, brown, Black; and that's what our immigration laws are based on. Black people will not be able to penetrate through those groups to get to the White society when that happens because those groups owe us nothing. They do not understand our problems and they are competitive with us. So, if we do not begin to be a little bit more aggressive about being in a competitive posture, they are going to eat our lunches.[360]

Another Black scholar, a woman named Dr. Frances Cress Welsing, who was a psychiatrist and author of *The Isis Papers*, spoke on the subject, too. During a lecture shortly before her passing, she said:

Neely Fuller informs us racism is White supremacy and White supremacy is racism. And what I'm saying is that we have thought as Black people dealing with this problem generation after generation after generation after generation that it was just a question of . . . well White people just need to be taught how to love. But beginning to understand what racism is in terms of the demographics and genetics on the planet, that this is what people who classified themselves as White felt they had to do for their survival; it is not logical to expect people who designed a system consciously and/or subconsciously for their survival—to undue that system.[32]

All of these individuals theorized about the longstanding problem of anti-Blackness. And most Black people in America have long known this deep inside. They have legitimized my work, in short.

Simply put, Whites have a need for a racism that benefits them and only them.[19] A substantial faction of White identity is rooted in anti-Blackness and White people are psychologically and emotionally primed to be anti-Black. White Americans fear Black people; they associate darker skin with danger, even though the treachery that their ancestors levied upon African/African American/Black people is still unmatched.[33]

This extends beyond White Americans. All White, non-White, and Black people in this country adapt to this way of being. There is also a knowing and a lack of knowing. On one hand, we know how it is and play a role in maintaining the powers and privileges afforded Whites. On the other hand, we do not know. We are oblivious to the extent of the hatred. White supremacy crushes reflection and dissent, for all races.

I want to highlight a quotation from John McKnight; it was from when George Foster was interviewing him. He was featured in a 1968 documentary called *"The Heritage of Slavery,"* which also featured Fannie Lou Hamer and Lerone Bennett Jr.

McKnight said:

In the South, he {the Black man} knows who the man {White man} is, the man up there on the hill in the big white house; and when he comes to a city like Chicago, it's much harder to determine who that man is. Such a complex society, it's a different man who controls the house, from the man who controls the job, from the man who controls the welfare, from the man who controls the hospital, from the man who controls the school. And I think what's happening is that he comes rather quickly to the conclusion that the man is all of White men. Not being able to discern his specific captor he decides that all people with White faces are his captors. And to the degree that all White people are engaged in supporting the systems of separation and racist institutions we have in the north—that judgement is basically accurate.

When we develop any kind of a system that by definition excludes people who are poor, inner-city, limited education people we are saying Black only. We might as well put the sign back up because it is the same thing. It is the same bag. The problem that we have in White America is that most White people when they hear about White racism, most White people say—man that's not me, I never discriminated against anybody, never did—And in their sense of what discrimination means or what racism is, they may be right. But they sit residing in a system that defines them in and defines Black people out.

We are going to have to face the fact that we are not a community. A community is where a lot of people develop mutually beneficial relationships with each other, and our racist institutions and the political boundaries of our cities define Black people out of the community. White people will sit in their suburban homes and watch their television programs and hear about all of these laws that are being passed. Many of them are beginning to wonder...well uh what is it with those colored people, why are they so upset about all of this wonderful stuff that we are doing for them. But we aren't focused on the Black man living on the block. HE lives in a two-flat on that block and he knows what the circumstances on that block were ten years ago, and he knows what it is today, and he too has heard about all of those programs and laws being passed. But the fact of the matter is that things are not changing for him. It's no wonder that the White population and the Black population are pitted against each other when the Black man knows that the change is not coming, and the White man thinks that major efforts are being undertaken when they are not. So, I don't think anybody should be surprised when one sees the Black people in open attack on the system because I suspect that they don't see that there is any other alternative.[34]

McKnight spoke about his understanding of institutional racism, and the continual oppression Black people had faced and face. He noted, too, White acknowledgement of this oppression. Emphasizing a White male perspective (as he knew it was most dominant), he noted the sheer indifference to those clearly in pain. His perspective was that, though certain practices may have fallen by the wayside in an effort to appear more humane, the plight of Black people in America had not changed much at all. The oppression simply became better hidden, more insidious. Everything else—the intent, the outcome, and more—had persisted.

One year earlier (in 1967) Charles Hamilton and Stokely Carmichael (later known as Kwame Ture) penned a book entitled *Black Power: The Politics of Liberation*.[3] In it, they defined for Black people, the greater U.S. population, and the entire world the ways in which White America had functioned and was continuing to function to continue enabling its racial genocide of Black people in this country. They distinguished between institutional and individual racism:

Racism is both overt and covert. It takes two, closely related forms: individual whites acting against individual Black people and acts by the total white community against the Black community. We call these individual racism and institutional racism. The first consists of overt acts by individuals, which cause death, injury, or the violent destruction of property. This type can be recorded by television cameras; it can frequently be observed in the process of commission. The second type is less overt, far more subtle, less identifiable in terms of specific individuals committing the acts. But it is no less destructive of human life. The second type originates in the operation of established and respected forces in society, and thus receives far less public condemnation than the first type.[3]

Simply put, the functionalities of Whiteness and anti-Blackness, specifically the ways in which Black people are regarded and mistreated by White and "not-Black" people in American culture, are genocidal. One of the main functionalities of White American culture and its institutions is to murder Black people psychically, spiritually, emotionally, and physically. This is not new and is much more apparent than ever due to enhancements in the information age. We have quicker, easier access to statistics, now; that has clarified the scope of White on Black terror.

White People's Creation and Development of Legal, Political, Cultural, Economic, and Institutional Whiteness and Anti-Blackness: Power As Psychopathology

IN 1975, A WHITE man by the name of Theodore Allen authored a book called *The Invention of the White Race*. In this book, Allen emphasized the need to understand Whiteness. He explained that Whiteness should not merely be alluded to or understood as a social construct, but that it had to be known as a "ruling class social control formation."[20] Allen also emphasized that during the colonial period, Whites were taught what it meant to be White through the frameworks of law and policy. Those were the vehicles that established, primarily, the vile conditions, diminished rights, and ultimately the sadistic and psychotic nature that defined and defines White culture.

In 1993, Dr. Cheryl I. Harris, a UCLA School of Law professor, wrote a piece for the *Harvard Law Review* entitled "Whiteness as Property."[26] In it, she explained,

> Moreover, as it emerged, the concept of Whiteness was premised on White supremacy, rather than mere difference. White was defined and constructed in ways that increased its value by reinforcing its exclusivity. Indeed, just as Whiteness as a property embraced the right to exclude, Whiteness as a theoretical construct evolved for the very purpose of racial exclusion.

Thus, the concept of Whiteness is built on both exclusion and racial sub-jugation. This fact was particularly evident during the period of the most rigid racial exclusion, as Whiteness signified racial privilege and took the form of status property.[26]

Harris wrote about Whiteness as a "traditional form of property," and in a scientifically analogous approach, she discussed the functions of Whiteness, meaning Rights of Disposition, Right to Use and Enjoyment, Reputation and Status Property, and The Absolute Right to Exclude.

In Harris' and Allen's writings, Nell Irving Painter's *The History of White People*, as well as in Jacqueline Battalora's *Birth of a White Nation*, they discuss the central idea of Whiteness being created and embedded into the law. [14,20,26,35] Embedding Whiteness in legal principles created foundation-al strength, validity, and bound Whiteness to privileged cultural identity, the way "free speech" and the "right to bear arms" have been legally foun-dational and essential to the American identity. Legalization of Whiteness/legal fortification of Whiteness is at the heart of the creation of Whiteness as a property.

Painter, Battalora, and Allen discuss laws that were enacted throughout the British colonies, which then led to the constructions of Whiteness and Blackness. Examples of the initial laws where this language was found may be found in the colony of Maryland in 1681 and in Virginia in 1691. The laws are noted below as documented in our country's historical records.[30,36,37,38]

1681 (Maryland):

Forasmuch as, divers free-born *English*, or white women, sometimes by the instigation, procurement or connivance, of their masters, mistresses, or dames, and always to the satisfaction of their lascivious and lustful de-sires, and to the disgrace not only of the *English*, but also of many other christian nations, do intermarry with negroes and slaves, by which means, divers inconveniences, controversies, and suits may arise, touching the issue or children, of such free-born women aforesaid; for prevention whereof for the future, be it further enacted . . . that if the marriage of such woman-ser-vant with any slave shall take place by the procurement or permission of the master, such woman and her issue shall be free, and enacts a penalty by fine on the master or mistress and on the person joining the parties in marriage.[36]

1691 (Virginia):

And for prevention of that abominable mixture and spurious issue which hereafter may increase in this her majesty's colony and dominion, as well by English, and other <u>WHITE</u> [emphasis added] men and women intermarrying with negros or mulattos, as by their unlawful coition with them, Be it enacted, by the authority aforesaid, and it is hereby enacted, That whatsoever English, or other white man or woman, being free, shall intermarry with a negro or mulatto man or woman, bond or free, shall, by judgment of the county court, be committed to prison, and there remain, during the space of six months, without bail or mainprize; and shall forfeit and pay ten pounds current money of Virginia, to the use of the parish, as aforesaid. (p. 86-87) [38]

Whiteness, and the degree to which it is embedded in the legal and political contexts, is made clear in colonial America and America as it continued to grow and form. The filth that is Whiteness/anti-Blackness gets embedded into the cultural fabric of the country, its most crucial institutions. That is how the practice of denying even the most basic rights began occurring and why the denial of such rights always centered around the Black body/sense of personhood.

This subjugation became normalized. White culture (with respect to individuals and as a collective) has enabled and delighted in the current 400-year Black Holocaust still plaguing America. More dangerous than Hitler and his minions were to Jewish people in the early 20th century, all Whites uphold racial privilege and are participants in and beneficiaries of pervasive White supremacy and the Black Holocaust occurring in America.

Some authors point out the transition from previous legally used ethno-religious identifiers, such as Christian or English, which represented people who were considered freeborn. These identifiers were embedded into and are highly visible within laws that were established during the 17th century, most notably the period between 1619 and 1705. I use this as part of my framing and discuss these variables in the chapters to come, establishing the language sanctioned by Whites as an identity, community, culture, nature, and way of being prior to the development and use of the term "White" for legal purposes.

As noted in the article, "Why Black Lives Haven't Mattered,"

As Africans and Native Americans began to be converted to Christianity, such a simple distinction between Christian and non-Christian was no longer useful—at least as a legal and political difference. In addition, because

Europeans, Native Americans and Africans often worked and lived together in similar circumstances of servitude and resisted and rebelled together against the way they were treated, the landowning class began to implement policies to separate European workers from African and Native-American workers. Even in this early colonial period, racism was used to divide workers and make it easier for those in power to control working conditions. Drawing on already established popular classifications, whiteness, now somewhat separate from Christianity, was delineated more clearly as a legal category in the United States in the 17th century, and the concept of life-long servitude (slavery) was introduced from the West Indies and distinguished from various forms of shorter-term servitude (indenture). In response to Bacon's rebellion and other uprisings, the ruling class, especially in the populous and dominant territory of Virginia, began to establish a clear racial hierarchy in the 1660s and 70s. By the 1730s racial divisions were firmly in place legally and socially. Most Black people were enslaved, and even free Black people had lost the right to vote, the right to bear arms and the right to bear witness. Black people were also barred from participating in many trades during this period. Meanwhile, whites gained the right to corn, money, a gun, clothing and 50 acres of land at the end of indentureship. In other words, poor whites "gained legal, political, emotional, social, and financial status that was directly related to the concomitant degradation of Indians and Negroes."[39]

It is true that Whiteness and anti-Blackness became the two foundational principles by which colonial America was established, and then later the United States of America as we know it today. This is reflected in the Nationality Act, which passed at the first U.S. Congressional Convention held in New York, between March of 1789 and March of 1791.

The Act read:

Be it enacted by the Senate and House of Representatives of the United States of America of Congress assembled, that any alien being a **FREE WHITE PERSON** [emphasis added], who shall have resided within the limits and under the jurisdiction of the United States for the term of two years, may be admitted to become a citizen thereof, on application to any common law court of record, in any one of these states wherein he shall have resided for the term of one year at least, and making proof to the satisfaction of such court, that he is a person of good character, and taking the oath or affirmation prescribed by law, to support the Constitution of the United States, which oath or affirmation such court shall administer; and the clerk of such court shall record application and the proceedings thereon; and thereupon such person shall be considered as a citizen of the United States. And the children of such persons so naturalized, dwelling within the United States, being under the age of twenty-one years at the time of such naturalization, shall also be considered as citizens of the United States. And the children of citizens of the United States that may be born beyond sea or out of the limits of the United States, shall be considered as natural born citizens.

This law, constituting Whiteness as the key property and principle of rights, privileges, and humane treatment in the United States, was reinforced by states, which took similar measures. (Many states passed laws banning free Black people from voting and, in some cases, even testifying against Whites.) This was cemented by the U.S. Supreme Court in 1857, in its now infamous Dred Scott decision, and many other cases throughout this nation's history.[38;40;41]

In *Black Reconstruction In America*, W.E.B. DuBois provided a detailed account of how each state, northern and southern, prohibited free Black people from voting, beginning in Georgia in 1777. Soon, it was Delaware in 1792; Maryland in 1793 and 1820; Florida in 1845; Louisiana in 1812; Mississippi in 1817; Alabama in 1819; Missouri in 1821; Arkansas in 1836; Texas in 1845; Ohio in 1803; Indiana in 1816; Illinois in 1818; Michigan in 1837; Iowa in 1846; Wisconsin in 1848; Minnesota in 1858; Kansas in 1861; Connecticut in 1814; New Jersey in 1807; Rhode Island beginning in or around 1790–1800; and Pennsylvania in 1838.[42]

And in the Dred Scott case, Chief Justice Taney, an anti-Black terrorist, stated the following:

Can a Negro whose ancestors were imported into this country, and sold as slaves, become a member of the political community formed and brought into existence by the Constitution of the United States and as such become entitled to all the rights, and privileges, and immunities, guaranteed by that instrument to the citizen? One of these rights is the privilege of suing in a court of the United States in the cases specified in the Constitution?

Chief Justice Taney used anti-Black/racist "logic," which actually pulled from earlier anti-Black/racist "logic," which was implemented to enact a series of laws that based the condition of enslavement on whether the parents of the persons sold and/or imported into the colonies were Christian at the time of their arrival. An example of this horror may be found in a Virginia Law dated all the way back to 1682. It said:

> It is enacted that all servants . . . which shall be imported into this country either by sea or by land, whether Negroes, Moors [Muslim North Africans], mulattoes or Indians who and whose parentage and native countries are not Christian at the time of their first purchase by some Christian . . . and all Indians, which shall be sold by our neighboring Indians, or any other trafficking with us for slaves, are hereby adjudged, deemed and taken to be slaves to all intents and purposes any law, usage, or custom to the contrary notwithstanding.[38]

Most notably, when these laws were passed, the Anglo-White colonial legislatures understood that the nations from which they were abducting and trafficking other humans were not largely Christian. Christian American identity, during most of the 17th century, contained an ethno-religious meaning.[20,22]

Legally, Christianity, in terms of who was recognized as Christian in the laws constructed during this period, was limited to Anglo-Europeans. All of that is to say White people. [20,22,43]

Because Taney and his colleagues leveraged this same "logic," the Dred Scott decision essentially said:

> The negro has no rights which the white man is bound to respect.[44]

These types of court rulings and legislative actions, supported by both public and private acts of blatant, rampant anti-Black subjugation and dehumanization, reinforced a psychological, emotional, physical, and cultural anti-Black conditioning that can still clearly be observed within the White race today. Anti-Blackness can also be observed in other racialized groups, including some Black people.

Simply put, the United States of America was founded upon an established pro-White and anti-Black legal, cultural, economic, and political set of principles. These types of laws and beliefs have remained embedded in American culture for centuries and most people do not understand how deep these issues run. Free Black people were not recognized, much less treated as full citizens. It is important to make these connections if one wants to understand the extent of the rights and privileges that were allocated on the basis of Whiteness and anti-Blackness.

Let us explore the types of rights and privileges that make up Whiteness. It will help illuminate how Whites came to regard and interact with Black people.

The central tenet of this work is to expose and scrutinize all the ways Whites abused Black people during and after colonial times. It is similar to Nikole Hannah-Jones' 1619 Project.[45] Much of this effort pauses purposefully to focus on the different types of impacts Whiteness and anti-Blackness have had.

What does the cruelty mean for the White organization, and/or White identity? What does it mean for the Black organization (race) and/or Black identity? Allen notes the following in his text:

> Others living in the colony at the time were English; They had been English when they left England, and naturally they and their Virginia-born children were English. They were not White.

> White identity had to be carefully taught, and it would be another 60-years before the word {White} would appear as a synonym for European-American.[20]

I am hardly the first to approach this subject. What I have found in my professional work is that citing example after example of the damage historical and current Whiteness causes makes denial of who we are as a country harder and harder. By creating a psychosomatic experience where people are required to spend between 70 and 90 hours internalizing the effects of racism, a process of humanization begins to take place. I use varied techniques, in the hope of reaching as many people as possible. Some involve individual work, others paired/group work. All encourage empathy, the act of walking in the shoes of another—often someone profoundly different.

I have found that grouping people together and having them consider the effects of the conditions that were manufactured through Anglo-European manufactured conditioning creates revelatory experiences. It allows people to understand the historical and ongoing traumas of Black people. It also facilitates seeing the psychopathic, deranged nature of Whites toward Black people, and the things that they believed that they needed to do in order to attain a racially superior status. I do this emphasizing the nature of Whites toward Black people, because this nature has remained the bedrock of White American culture until today. White people have normalized a negative orientation and positioning of Black people.

Blackness and anything associated with it is the abyss of American culture. The anti-Black orientation created by White people is unbreakably psychological. It is also visual, emotional, and spiritual. It is innate, a necessity in White America's value system. The majority of this book puts this reality on trial, prosecutes it, and details through examples why it matters so much.

White people learned how to be White through the legal, political, economic, judicial, and social benefits that deprioritized the humanity of others. The development of Whiteness and its connection to capitalism is well-documented. As highlighted in an article entitled "Is Afrika Cursed:"

> David and Alexander Barclays were active participants in the kidnapping and enslavement of millions of Black Africans. As was standard practice at the time, the risky and long-term nature of transatlantic slave trading required new banking houses that could offer credits to prospective slave traders, for periods of between one and a half to three years. One bank that provided this service was run by Alexander and David Barclay. Their bank still carries their name.[46]

Furthermore, in an article entitled "The Hidden Links Between Slavery and Wall Street," Zoe Thomas also highlighted:

> Slavery thrived under colonial rule. British and Dutch settlers relied on enslaved people to help establish farms and build the new towns and cities that would eventually become the United States.
>
> Enslaved people were brought to work on the cotton, sugar and tobacco plantations. The crops they grew were sent to Europe or to the northern colonies, to be turned into finished products. Those finished goods were used to fund trips to Africa to obtain more slaves who were then trafficked back to America.
>
> To raise the money to start many future plantations owners turned to capital markets in London - selling debt that was used to purchase boats, goods and eventually people.
>
> Later in the 19th Century, US banks and southern states would sell securities that helped fund the expansion of slave run plantations.
>
> To balance the risk that came with forcibly bringing humans from Africa to America insurance policies were purchased.
>
> These policies protected against the risk of a boat sinking, and the risks of losing individual slaves once they made it to America.

Some of the largest insurance firms in the US—New York Life, AIG and Aetna—sold policies that insured slave owners would be compensated if the slaves they owned were injured or killed.

By the mid-19th century, exports of raw cotton accounted for more than half of US overseas shipments. What wasn't sold abroad was sent to mills in northern states including Massachusetts and Rhode Island to be turned into fabric.

The money southern plantation owners earned couldn't be kept under mattresses or behind loose floorboards. American banks accepted their deposits and counted enslaved people as assets when assessing a person's wealth.[47]

Thomas then highlighted the financial institutions that have apologized for their roles in financing and otherwise backing the institution of African enslavement. But what tangible action, if any, has been taken? This goes to Dr. Wright's point about the absence of morality within the White race where Black people are concerned.

Shaping and Crystalizing Anti-Blackness into American Culture

In addition to the capitalistic and economic development of Whiteness, White Europeans determined **what** was and **who** was right, wrong, good, and bad in White America, starting with the colonial period and moving forward.

There are two relevant early revelations, noted in the text entitled, "After Hugh: Statutory Race Segregation in Colonial America, 1630-1725, and 1619." The concern has to do with Virginia's first Africans and highlights how race was addressed by Europeans toward Negroes. It involved a case concerning Hugh Davis and a Negro woman (in 1630),[48,38,119,120,210] Robert Sweat, a European-White, male, indentured servant, and finally Margaret Cornish, an enslaved Negro woman (roughly in 1640).[43,49,120] The case and punishment for Hugh Davis is noted as:

> *Hugh Davis to be soundly whipped, before an assembly of Negroes and others for abusing himself to the dishonor of God and shame of Christians, by defiling [emphasis added] his body in lying with a Negress, which fault he is to acknowledge next Sabbath day.*[48]

The Robert Sweat sentencing, issued by a Virginia court on October 17, 1640, noted:

Whereas Robert Sweat hath begotten with child a negro woman servant belonging unto Lieutenant Sheppard, the court hath therefore ordered that the said __negro woman shall be whipt at the whipping post__ [emphasis added] and the said Sweat shall tomorrow in the forenoon do public penance for his offence at James City church in the time of divine service according to the laws of England in that case provided.

In both cases, the rape of Black women was not the crime, incredulously. The encounters were framed as consensual, with no rape of any abduction or other coercion. They had most likely been kidnapped and/or traded against their will and brought to the colony on ships. Margaret Cornish's arrival to the Virginia colony is estimated to have taken place between 1619 and 1630. It is noted in the historical record that Margaret Cornish was from Luanda, Angola.

Again, it is important to note here the psychopathic and demented act taken by the Virginia House of Burgesses, the colonial governing body at the time. It consisted of roughly 20 to 30 White men during this period, who agreed to criminalize sex with Black females, rather than the acts of rape committed upon their bodies. These types of laws were referred to as Sumptuary Laws. As noted in the Encyclopedia:

"Sumptuary laws" usually refers to regulations of food, clothing, morals, amusements, church attendance, and Sabbath observance. Sumptuary laws existed in all of the colonies. They included general colonial statutes, local regulations, applications of common law to local situations, and fixed customs of the people in different colonies. Custom and practice were as much a part of the total laws of a community as were the formal statutes, although their enforcement was different.[280]

In the case of Margaret Cornish, she gave birth to a child as a direct result of the encounter and was then tied to a whipping post, as stated in the excerpt above, and whipped until she bled. The terror she experienced being whipped, shamed, humiliated, and traumatized—along with birthing a child she became pregnant with without her consent, meant Black women had no dignity, no humanity. Their bodies would be consumed and mutilated freely, and with the support of White women who stood by silently or conveyed support through direct participation in or encouragement of such acts.[50,52]

Let's look at a case concerning John Punch, a Negro (Black) indentured servant who ran away from Virginia. The case was noted in the Minutes of the Council and General Court of Colonial Virginia.[51]

Go back days earlier to the return and sentencing of John Punch, James Gregory, and Victor (who lacked a recorded surname), two additional European indentured servants who had also run away. John's master, Hugh Gwyn, had petitioned the courts for their return, and upon their return, the three servants were to be indentured. On July 4th, 1640, Virginia courts handed down the order.[51,210] It read, in part:

Upon the petition of Hugh Gwyn gent wherein he complained to this board of three of his servants that are run away to Maryland to his much loss and prejudice and wherein he hath humbly requested the board that he may have liberty to make the sale or benefit of the said servants in the said Maryland which the Court taking unto Consideration and weighing the dangerous consequences of such pernicious precident do order that a letter be written unto the said Governour to the intent the said servants may be returned hither to receive such exemplary and condign punishment as the nature of their offence shall justly deserve and then to be returned to their said master.

As a result of this judgment rendered to Hugh Gwyn, John Punch, James Gregory, and Victor, were brought back to the colony of Virginia, from Maryland. At their sentencing hearing, the following judgement was rendered:

Whereas Hugh Gwyn hath by order from this Board Brought back from Maryland three servants formerly run away from the said Gwyn, the court doth therefore order that the said three servants shall receive the punishment of whipping and to have thirty stripes apiece one called Victor, a Dutchman, the other a Scotchman called James Gregory, shall first serve out their times with their master according to their Indentures, and one whole year apiece after the time of their service is Expired. By their said Indentures in recompense of his Loss sustained by their absence and after that service to their said master is Expired to serve the colony for three whole years apiece, and that the third being a negro named John Punch shall serve his said master or his assigns for the time of his natural Life here or elsewhere.

John Punch received a life sentence of forced servitude, while James Gregory and Victor both received an additional four years of indentured servitude.

I have considered this episode often, specifically the part about how their skin color ensured that they would not be held accountable. And dearest brother, John! He presumably realized the dire injustice of the situation and understood wholly that his Blackness, the fact that he was a Negro, magnified the severity of the crime.

The White colonial legislative authorities knew exactly what they were doing when they did this, just as the jury who found Kyle Rittenhouse not guilty of murder in Kenosha, Wisconsin in November 2021. Furthermore, these leaders set the stage for the Black American Holocaust that has continued to evolve in America throughout the last 400 years.

These and other cases are critical to understand; they reveal to us exactly what the mentality and culture of White people were and are. This is a sadistic nature we must force ourselves to recognize, however uncomfortable. It is psychopathic and dysfunctional in the extreme.

In a Virginia House of Burgesses session held in March of 1662, to cite yet another example, members passed an unambiguous law that determined the consequences for running away with a Negro. It stated, in part:

> *WHEREAS there are diverse loytering runaways in this country who very often absent themselves from their masters service and sometimes in a long time cannot be found, that losse of the time and the charge in the seeking them often exceeding the value of their labor: Be it therefore enacted that all runaways that shall absent themselves from their said masters service shall be lyable to make satisfaction by service after the times by custome or indenture is expired, double their times of service soe neglected, and if the time of their running away was in the crop or the charge of recovering them extraordinary the court shall lymitt a longer time of service proportionable to the damage the master shall make appeare he hath susteyned, and because the adjudging the time they should serve is often referred untill the time by indenture is expired, when the proofe of what is due is very uncertaine, it is enacted that the master of any runaway that intends to take the benefitt of this act, shall as soone as he hath recovered him carry him to the next commissioner and there declare and prove the time of his absence, and the charge he hath bin at in his recovery, which commissioner thereupon shall grant his certificate, and the court on that certificate passe judgment for the time he shall serve for his absence;* **and in case any English**

servant shall run away in company of any <u>negroes</u> who are incapable of making satisfaction by addition of a time, it is enacted that the <u>English</u> soe running away in the company with them shall at the time of service to their owne masters expired, serve the masters of the said negroes for their absence soe long as they should have done by this act if they had not beene slaves, every <u>christian</u> in company serving his proportion; and if the negroes be lost or dye in such time of their being run away, the <u>christian</u> servants in company with them shall by proportion among them, either pay fower thousand five hundred pounds of tobacco and caske or fower yeares service for every negroe soe lost or dead.

For many years leading up to this, European indentured servants had begun running away. In addition, they began joining Black (Negro) people who were also subjected to legalized human rights abuses, including murder.[51,53] As a common form of resistance, both peoples began running away together to seek refuge in other regions and colonies.[29] This law established that the English and Christians, an earlier colonial classification referring to Europeans other than the English, such as Scots, Irish, Dutch, etc., literally forbade Whites from running away "in company with" Black people. It criminalized social relations between White and Black people, in other words. Such a horror could not be tolerated.

As you will see, this is one of many examples of a law whose sentiment was deeply anti-Black. This law could have been designed to forbid the English and others legally recognized as Christian, such as other Anglo-Europeans, from running away with other Whites. But it did not do that. Instead, White drafters of the law made it a point to specifically forbid running away with Black people. Only that particular act was deemed unacceptable. The law provided that if a White person ran away with a Black indentured servant and/or slave, then they would end up serving the Black person's time for the Black person's master, once the time to their own master had expired.

Note the specificity and harshness, and who this was directed to. There is a very particular kind of behavior that is disincentivized; it is co-mingling with those considered dirty. The penalty would be serving an additional four years' time for every Negro lost or dead or be subject to paying monetarily in the form of 4,500 lbs. of tobacco and caske.

What messages got conveyed to Whites? To Black people? How much more negatively could Black people have been branded? Their presence was considered toxic. Dr. Ibram X. Kendi, in his prolific and profound book entitled *Stamped from the Beginning*, does an extraordinary job of chronicling and reinforcing this point.

Additional supporting texts include Dr. Cornel West's work entitled *Race Matters*, James Baldwin's *The Fire Next Time*, W.E.B DuBois' *Black Reconstruction In America*, and Nikole Hannah Jones' *1619 Project*, just to name a few. See the end of this book for a more extensive list.

Chapter 2 Review Questions:

Note: Please go to www.danteking.com to complete the chapter assessment, which includes the questions below. Only answer the questions that you feel compelled to answer.

Considering the framing provided in Chapters One and Two:

1. What are your thoughts about the framing of Whiteness as it is highlighted in this culture?

2. What roles did pro-Whiteness and anti-Blackness play in shaping the legal, moral, and cultural practices in the development of Anglo-White America?

3. In your own words, what is your understanding of pro-Whiteness? How is it different from anti-Blackness?

4. How are anti-Blackness and pro-Whiteness aligned?

5. Why is it dangerous to minimize the effects of the harm that these historical events caused to both Black and Indigenous communities, in an attempt to untether this history from today's society?

6. How is the legal system implicated in shaping favorable cultural and institutional conditions for American Whites and unfavorable cultural and institutional conditions for American Black people?

Malignant Diabolical Psychopathy: Black Bessie, Elizabeth Key, Margaret Cornish, Celia, and White America's Legal, Moral, And Economic Institutions of Rape, Pedophilia, and Human Sex Trafficking

IN THIS CHAPTER, WE learn about Elizabeth Key Grinstead, a female, Black martyr born in 1630.[54] She should (but will not) be hailed as one of the founders of feminism in North America.

Americans do not learn about her or the way she resisted White terror. Why? Because she was subversive and powerful.

The conspiracy to exclude anyone who does not fit the anti-Black narrative persists. And it has many willing enablers who themselves are Black. Think of media figure Candace Owens, U.S. Senator Timothy Scott, and others. Their primary purpose in life is to silence the voices of their own while amplifying the very voices who want to crush them.

In *The 400-Year Holocaust: White America's Legal, Psychopathic, and Sociopathic Black Genocide—and the Revolt Against Critical Race Theory*, my first book, I posited:

> As of August of 2021, per Education Week and the Brookings Institute, eight states have banned what they are referring to as "Critical Race Theory (CRT)" from being taught in primary grades (Idaho, Oklahoma, Tennessee, Texas, Iowa, New Hampshire, Arizona, and South Carolina).[55]

Two states have bills that are awaiting the next legislative session, while five other states have bills that are involved in doing the same. Put another way, as documented by Fox News, seven additional states considering legislation to ban the teaching of CRT include Kentucky, Maine, Michigan, Missouri, New Hampshire, North Carolina, and Ohio.[56]

As of 2023, roughly 44 states have introduced bills, resolutions, or other measures to restrict educators from discussing racism and sexism.[381] Joshua Q. Nelson, Fox News journalist and contributor, highlighted this in his article entitled, "44 states introduced bills, took steps to restrict teaching CRT or how teachers discuss racism and sexism: report," published in May 2023 when he noted:

> A new report shows that more than 40 states introduced bills or took steps to restrict teaching critical race theory or how teachers discuss racism and sexism in the classroom.
>
> According to Education Weekly, "Since January 2021, 44 states have introduced bills or taken other steps that would restrict teaching critical race theory or limit how teachers can discuss racism and sexism. Eighteen states have imposed these bans and restrictions either through legislation or other avenues.
>
> Education Weekly highlighted Parent's Choice Tennessee, a Franklin-based, self-identified parents' rights group, which sued Williamson County Schools' administrators last year in July over the district's curriculum. Parents' Choice Tennessee claims that the curriculum's teaching of critical race theory is in violation of state law and common core values."[381]

Much of the propagandist paranoia and the movements that have followed have been fueled by White supremacist so-called leaders, such as Governor Ronald DeSantis of Florida, who is quoted as saying:

> In Florida we are taking a stand against the state-sanctioned racism that is critical race theory.
>
> We won't allow Florida tax dollars to be spent teaching kids to hate our country or to hate each other. We also have a responsibility to ensure that parents have the means to vindicate their rights when it comes to enforcing state standards. Finally, we must protect Florida workers against the hostile work environment that is created when large corporations force their employees to endure CRT-inspired "training" and indoctrination.[382]

Since making this open decree, Governor DeSantis has signed the "Stop Wrongs to Our Kids and Employees Act," which is a law that bans anything that Florida defines as WOKE. There is no consensus surrounding the definition of this term. He has also banned a high school A.P. African American Studies course from being taught.[383,384] Deep paranoia, in conjunction with an unbridled fear about the truth of America, White people, White culture, and the facade of Whiteness, all threaten the ego and psychology of White superiority that has been embedded into White minds and proclaimed worldwide for decades. White people across America are unraveling before our eyes. Their reputation and America's reputation are at risk of being ruined.

Psychopathy?

It is vital that Grinstead's story, and others like it, be reexamined if we are to understand the dynamics in present-day America. Doing so challenges psychopathic, anti-Black (female and male), White culture.

Elizabeth was the daughter of Thomas Key, a slave owner who had arrived in Virginia in or around 1616.[57,58] Thomas Key became a member of the colony of Virginia's legislature, the House of Burgesses, in 1626.

His wife, Martha (sometimes called Sarah) Key, arrived in Virginia in January of 1624. It is noted that she "obtained" and/or was awarded 150 acres of land on the Warwicksqueake River on December 2, 1626, presumably due to her acquisition of three Negro/Black slaves whom she "purchased" in conjunction with participation in the Headrights System, a system that provided Virginia planters with fifty acres of land per enslaved African, Negro, Black, or Mulatto person they purchased.[59-62,122,123]

For example, "Virginia planters who imported slave labor from the West Indies or directly from Africa were awarded 50 acres of land per slave. George Menefie was one of the first to claim a large number of headrights for one shipment of slaves, obtaining 1,150 acres for the 23 slaves he imported, along with 37 other servants in 1638."[62] The colony had an excess of land and a shortage of people. As noted by Battalora, "It was public policy to encourage population growth through immigration, and to induce immigration through promises of cheap land."[20,35] This was also true for Governor George Yeardley and Sir Abraham Piersey, who, in August of 1619, bought the Africans who arrived aboard the White Lion. For this purchase, Governor Yeardley procured 1,000 acres of land.[43,121-124]

One reasonably concludes that one of the three enslaved Black people "purchased" by Martha Key was Elizabeth's mother. Records show that

Elizabeth's mother was referred to as "Black Bessie," as her original name was unknown. She was an African woman from the Ndongo Kingdom in Angola, Africa.[63] Records indicate that she was aboard the White Lion, in a group of first slaves sold in Virginia to Governor George Yeardley and Sir Abraham Piersey.[43,64]

By the late 1620s (1628/29), Bessie, then approximately 19 years of age, was in the possession of Thomas Key and his wife. Thomas Key brutally and repeatedly raped Bessie. From this terror emerged a child, Elizabeth. Charged in a Blunt Point court for illegitimately fathering Elizabeth, he originally lied and stated that she had been fathered by a Turk. It is presumed that he lied to avoid any consequences for his behavior. Witnesses contradicted his testimony. He was found guilty and forced to assume responsibility for his daughter, Elizabeth.

Thomas Key, forced to acknowledge Elizabeth as his daughter, arranged for her to be baptized as a Christian, and assumed financial support for her from then on. Elizabeth was baptized as a Christian under the Church of England, and she practiced Christianity. It is noted that Elizabeth remained at home with Thomas Key until roughly the age of five or six.[54]

Prior to his 1636 (or thereabouts) death, Thomas Key indentured Elizabeth to Humphrey Higginson, whose plantation she was to live and work on for the next nine years. Elizabeth was approximately six years old at the time.[54,65] The contract was supposed to expire once she turned 15 (which was the age that females began either working for wages and/or would be married). Instead, Higginson left Virginia so he could return to England and sold Elizabeth's contract to Colonel John Mottram (noted as the first Burgess for Northumberland County in 1645) of Northumberland County.

It is important to emphasize that this child should have been a "free" Black person at the time that her contract was sold, and that no such liberation happened.[66] Upon Colonel Mottram's death in 1655, the heirs of his estate did not want to honor Elizabeth's contract of indentureship.

By this time, young Englishman William Grinstead (also noted and spelled "Greenstead") arrived in Virginia based upon a negotiated contract of indenture with Colonel Mottram; it was roughly 1650. Colonel Mottram, who Grinstead sometimes represented, had forced Elizabeth into a sexual relationship.[67,43] With no agency at all, she birthed a baby named John. Overseers of the Mottram Estate classified Elizabeth and John as Negroes and claimed that they were part of the property of the estate, which would bolster its value.

This mattered, of course, because such property valuation would benefit the heirs among whom the distribution would occur.[54]

Per the United Nations Educational, Scientific, and Cultural Organization (2021):

> With William representing her, Elizabeth sued for her most basic of human rights, her freedom. Witnesses testified to the veracity of her claims. One decision allowed Elizabeth her freedom on account of her father's freedom, while another denied her liberty because of her mother's status as enslaved. The most persuasive evidence [of daughter Elizabeth's paternity] came from the eighty-year-old former servant of John Mottram who testified that it was commonly known that Thomas Key had been fined by the court in Blunt Point for getting 'his Negro (sic) woman with Childe,' and that that child was Elizabeth.
>
> Eventually, the case rose to the Virginia General Assembly, which appointed a committee for its review. The Virginia General Assembly resolved that "by the Common Law the Child of a Woman slave begot by a freeman ought to be free." They considered the value of her Christian faith and determined that her indenture demanded that she be treated "more Respectfully than a Common servant or slave." The General Assembly decided that "the said Elizabeth ought to be free and that her last Master should give her Corn and Clothes and give her satisfaction for the time she hath served longer than She ought to have done."
>
> After determining the freedom of Elizabeth and her son, the General Assembly returned the case to the lower courts, which freed her.[54]

Consider this case carefully. Think about the ways in which the lives of this young, Black female, and that of her mother, Bessie, rested in the complete control of White men, who by all accounts had no regard for their humanity. They recognized a portion of her humanity only and continued to apply language meant for chattel to her, a human. Only her identity as a Christian afforded her some modicum of respect. The lower court, made up of a group of White, English-European males, ruled in Elizabeth's favor, based upon what she proved in accordance with the documented law at the time, Partus Sequitur Patrem, meaning the identity of the child followed the identity and lineage of the paternal parent (father). It weighed the evidence against the letter of the law and decided that she should be free.[20]

Once the case arrived at the higher court and was placed in the hands of entirely different, White, English-European males with different opinions about Black Bessie, the circumstances changed. Think about the arbitrary nature of it all. Merit played no role. Basic human rights played no role. The disdain for Elizabeth as a Black female who presumably had lighter skin was integral to the higher court's decision. The court system, like every other system, could easily be manipulated and weaponized, in other words.

Think about the White, European Mottram heirs, who attempted to hold Elizabeth hostage so they could benefit from her labor, humanity, and physicality, and from her son John's worth as an enslaved person (who represented capital/property to the estate). Think about the Mottram family's discontent with Elizabeth. It must have known no limits.

Think about the fact that the only reason Elizabeth was able to claim her freedom was because an eighty-year-old former servant (presumably Black) testified that she was, indeed, the child of Thomas Key. Think about the reality that the only way for Elizabeth to procure her freedom was through association with a White male, the White male who raped her mother. Think about the fact that charges were only brought against Thomas Key for fathering an "illegitimate child" and not because of the treacherous and violent rape that he committed against Black Bessie. Think about Black Bessie's attack being the precursor for Black females being exempted from rape laws (later to come), and the ways in which the legal system dealt with the situation, only fining Thomas Key money for fathering an illegitimate child. He faced no further consequences for the horrifying act of rape. Think about what gets incentivized when one group faces no consequences for being rapists.

Rapists.

Now is this White privilege, or something more? It was meant to protect certain people, not others. Certain properties and inanimate objects held greater value than one human life. This value system persists today, though it is arguably less obvious. Property value meant more than addressing the traumas of a Black woman. Anything and everything that elevated White interests and degraded Black ones was acceptable. This case illustrates so much about White culture; that is why it remains so well-hidden. It is an indictment, and no such indictments can be known, lest they lead to others.

Consider the case even further.

The Elizabeth Key Grinstead case facilitated and exacerbated the rapes of Black women and girls by White men everywhere. The concept of instituting fines for rape was vile and formed the basis for White men to consider Black women as unworthy and inhuman. Fines are reserved for mere mistakes, not acts of human rights abuses.

In addition, to prevent the births of mulatto (a racial classification to refer to people of mixed African and European ancestry) children (who may have shared experiences similar to those of Elizabeth's, such as having rapists for fathers), the Virginia House of Burgesses, a group consisting of all White men, saw it fit to change the law roughly six years later. In doing so, the chamber legalized White males raping Black females, and reducing their punishment for any such incidents to fines exclusively. Furthermore, the law confined the institution of racial slavery to the bodies of Black females by ensuring that the identity of an enslaved person would be determined through birth from a Black body. The new law, as documented in The Statutes At Large, read:

> Whereas some doubts have arisen whether children got by any Englishman upon a negro woman [emphasis added] should be slave or free, *Be it therefore enacted and declared by this present grand assembly,* that all children born in this country shall be held bond or free only according to the condition of the mother, [emphasis added] and that if any **Christian** [emphasis added] shall committ fornication with a negro man or woman, hee or shee soe offending shall pay double the fines imposed by the former act.[68,123]

And so, here we have a culture that continues to evolve with a core piece of its foundation being the institutionalization of the rape of Black females. It continues to affect them all, as everything that flows from it is tainted. Every part of Black identity sustained irreparable harm. Children suffered from it. Women and men suffered from it. Parenthood, sexuality—every single part of what it could have meant and did mean to be Black—suffered from it.

Dr. Jennifer L. Morgan, Professor of Social & Cultural Analysis & History and Chair of the Department of Social and Cultural Analysis from New York University, also happens to be the author of *Laboring Women: Reproduction and Gender in New World Slavery.* Her text provided much education about this one case. In it, she commented:

> Women of African descent in the 17th century English Atlantic understood the evolving logic of race as praxis (accepted as practice). Slave traders,

early English slave owners and colonial legislators all offered clumsy and piecemeal articulations of New World labor practices. But the terms of racial slavery rested emphatically on women's bodies. Whether it was to clarify that the baptism of children did not convey freedom; to regulate the intimacies that were at the heart interracial sex or to ascertain that enslaved women's babies were always already enslaved – reproducing women posed problems AND offered solutions for English Atlantic settlers concerned for what it meant to be enslaved and free in the early modern Atlantic. Elizabeth Key's comprehension of her embeddedness in racialized structures of meaning and labor fades from our view if we emphasize her court case as a moment of flexibility, fluidity and of possibility. It is left out of the archives because motherhood inhabits an entirely different moral and historical realm than "economy." Of course, that was not the case for Elizabeth; the child of an African woman whose freedom and that of her children was dependent upon English men. Elizabeth may not have understood the role in which her case would have in propelling the 1662 Act, but she did understand that the atmosphere in which she lived was one that put herself and her kin in jeopardy. The forces that moved Key and her husband in and out of court were precisely those that anticipated both her vulnerability and that of all Black women both in slavery and freedom in the 17th century Atlantic world. Legally sanctioned claims of lineage were short-lived and the link between the Key case and the 1662 Act that effectively closed the door on future claims to lineage is self-evident. Lineage could not be legally recognized for Black women when racial slavery depended upon the transformation of lineage into embodied inheritance.[69]

Central to European-White culture is the absence of any kind of scrutiny of the experiences of anyone other than themselves. It is entirely insular. No consideration of anyone "outside" exists. That is not due to some innocent omission. There are limitations and even prohibitions within our educational institutions today that disallow for any meaningful examination. This is to keep hidden the extent of the filth. We are taught either by active, intentional perpetrators or those who are willfully naive. Neither situation is desirable, and both lead to greater harm.

With closed eyes and an open heart, consider the following:

√   **Imagine** you can be raped at any time by Englishmen or any other men (Dutch, Portuguese, Spanish, French). What type of emotional stress would you feel unceasingly? How would this affect pregnancies and birthing outcomes?

√ **Imagine** you deliver a child. Imagine knowing that that baby can be torn apart from you at any time and for any reason, including to be sold to White butchers and rapists. How would that make you feel? How would it affect the ways in which you did and did not connect to your children?

√ **Imagine** you can be beaten and otherwise abused and tormented while pregnant. Think of Margaret Cornish, who in 1940 was tied to a post and "whipt" after having a child with a White male named Robert Sweat. How would that affect you? Your unborn child?

√ **Imagine** how hard it might be for you to carry a child to term.

√ **Imagine** how hard it might be for your child to survive birth. (Stillbirths were common.)

√ **Imagine** the impact this would have on your family, which is helpless to protect you. Imagine the impact on Black men, who feel they should, and know they cannot, protect their own families.

√ **Imagine** internalizing the reality that neither the law nor those who could change it at any moment saw you as fully human. Imagine there was no cost associated with hurting you, whether by rape or other violent human rights violations.

Consider, too:

√ How does marrying White capitalism to Black bodies affect White and Black psyches? What power dynamics does such a structure perpetuate?

√ How does the legalized looting of the vaginas and uteruses of Black and Indigenous women (per the 1662 Act, subsequent rape laws, and judicial decisions) and the loins of Black males to illegally make money for centuries impact the feeling of injustice so many Black people in America rightly feel? Does it exacerbate or diminish it? Why might that be? How do these laws create an original context of default criminality that is designed specifically for Black bodies?

√   How do these laws become enforced when Black girls and women
    are trafficked for sex work?

√   What do you think the connections are between White people's
    lack of empathy for Black people, their perpetual campaign of
    anti-Black terror, and the lack of reparations?

Most Whites who read this text may struggle to internalize it. Why might
that be?

The hope is that now we can more meaningfully consider the nation's
long-standing history with anti-Black terrorism and how it came to define
American identity, until this day.

Louis Hughes shared accounts of the terror he faced by White men in
his book entitled *Thirty Years a Slave*. Josiah Henson does the same in his
text entitled *The Life of Josiah Henson Formerly a Slave*.

In Hughes' experiences, he details the following:

I was born in Virginia, in 1832, near Charlottesville, in the beautiful valley
of the Rivanna river. My father was a white man and my mother a negress,
the slave of one John Martin. I was a mere child, probably not more than
six years of age, as I remember, when my mother, two brothers and myself
were sold to Dr. Louis, a practicing physician in the village of Scottsville.
We remained with him about five years, when he died, and, in the settlement of his estate, I was sold to one Washington Fitzpatrick, a merchant of
the village. He kept me a short time when he took me to Richmond, by way
of canal-boat, expecting to sell me; but as the market was dull, he brought
me back and kept me some three months longer, when he told me he had
hired me out to work on a canal-boat running to Richmond, and to go to
my mother and get my clothes ready to start on the trip. I went to her as
directed, and, when she had made ready my bundle, she bade me good-bye
with tears in her eyes, saying: "My son, be a good boy; be polite to everyone, and always behave yourself properly." It was sad to her to part with
me, though she did not know that she was never to see me again, for my
master had said nothing to her regarding his purpose and she only thought,
as I did, that I was hired to work on the canal-boat, and that she should see
me occasionally. But alas! We never met again. I can see her form still as
when she bade me good-bye. That parting I can never forget. I ran off from
her as quickly as I could after her parting words, for I did not want her to
see me crying. I went to my master at the store, and he again told me that

he had hired me to work on the canal-boat, and to go aboard immediately.
Of the boat and the trip and the scenes along the route I remember little - I
only thought of my mother and my leaving her. (p. 5-6)[70]

Henson shared the gut-wrenching experience of being separated from his
family at auction, where objects should be sold as opposed to people. He
emphasized his mother's response, which never left him. He also noted the
coldness and cruelty of the White owners; they were indifferent to the notion of family separation and focused only on their monetary profits. Their
money mattered more than he did, more than his mother did, more than any
other Black human being did.

Henson recalled:

My brothers and sisters were bid off first, and one by one, while my mother, paralyzed by grief, held me by the hand. Her turn came and she was
bought by Isaac Riley of Montgomery County. Then I was offered to the
assembled purchasers. My mother, half distracted with the thought of parting with all her children forever, pushed through the crowd, while the bid-
ding for me was going on, to the spot where Riley was standing. She fell at
his feet and clung to his knees, entreating him in tones only that a mother
could command, to buy her baby as well as herself and spare to her one, at
least, of her little ones. Riley, appealed to by the frantic mother, turned a
deaf ear to her plea and also freed himself from her with such violent blows
and kicks, as to reduce her to the necessity of creeping out of his reach and
mingling the groan of bodily suffering with the sob of a breaking heart.[71]

There has long been much talk of the disintegration of the Black family.
What was the origin of its destruction? When?

The pattern continues. White rape, including even of Black children,
continues. Whites in positions of power sanctioned such acts consistently.

Let us first go back to Missouri, 1855. Celia, a Black child, was sold to a
White master at the age of fourteen. He, Robert Newsom, was approximately sixty years old at the time of her purchase. Robert Newsom "acquired"
Celia for the sole purpose of replacing his wife, who had died. Newsom
raped Celia for the first time during their initial trip to his plantation, almost
immediately after "purchasing" her from her former master.

Newsom legally and brutally raped Celia for approximately five years.
From the age of fourteen, he fathered two children with her. Upon assuming

a boyfriend named George, someone who blamed Celia for "allowing" Newsom to rape her, he demanded that *she* stop the rape. She asked Newsom's adult daughters for help and warned him that if he came around her cabin again that she would self-defend.[73]

When Newsom did appear at Celia's cabin to rape her on the evening of June 23rd, 1855, she defended herself by fatally hitting him on the head with a stick. Despite having a lawyer, John Jameson, who by all accounts attempted to defend Celia to the best of his abilities, her judge, Judge William Augustus Hall (who later served as a member of the United States Congress, upon confederate secession of southern states from the Union and who was brothers with Missouri's Governor, Willard Preble Hall), gave the following instruction to the 12-person, all-White, male jury (William J. Selby, foreman; William Givens, Stephen Gilbert, William Lloyd, Benjamin Sheets, Thomas Pratt, John Culbreston, William Craig, W.J. Ficklin, William P. Selby, George Hossman, and Samuel Maties):

> If Newsom was in the habit of having intercourse with the defendant who was his slave and went to her cabin on the night he was killed to have intercourse with her or for any other purpose and while he was standing in the floor talking to her she struck him with a stick which was a dangerous weapon and knocked him down, and struck him again after he fell, and killed him by either blow, it is murder in the first degree.[73]

Put another way, if Newsom was in the habit of raping Celia, who was his slave and whose cabin he visited on the evening of his death, and she defended herself, she should be convicted of murder. Why? Because it was Newsom's legal and moral right to rape Celia.

Pay attention to the psychopathic rationalization. Rape is mere intercourse. Consent is a non-factor. The absence of empathy dominates. After all, how can chattel consent? She is an object. If he wished to insert himself into an object, then so be it. What sadism.

And lest you think White women largely defended their own, you are not correctly identifying who "their own" was in this situation. Color, not sex, had greater value. They were White before they were female. Despite knowing well what it was like enduring the unwanted advances of men, they knew who they would stay loyal to. And they knew why. It benefited them.

As emphasized in the book entitled *African American Women Speak Out on Anita Hill-Clarence Thomas,* which was written in 1995 by Darlene Clark Hine, Celia thought she could find allies in Newsom's daughters, and was woefully mistaken. They denied her humanity by not testifying to the accounts of which they were aware.[50]

Hine remarked:

The Missouri courts declared that in the eyes of the law, Black women, in particular slave women, were not women. The court delayed execution until the birth of Celia's child so as not to deprive the Newsom estate of the profit of Celia's rape. The baby, however, was stillborn.

Newsom's daughters refused to comment on their father's abuse of Celia, or to respond in any way to her entreaties for help. Their silence was in keeping with the politics of denial. For these plantation mistresses to have aided Celia would have meant that they and other similarly situated White women had to acknowledge openly that their fathers, brothers, and husbands were rapists. [50]

As stated in *Celia, A Slave,* a book written by Melton A. McLaurin in 1991:

Judge Hall's denial of the defense's instructions to acquit Celia because of Newsom's sexual assault was practically a foregone conclusion. The trial testimony of both prosecution and defense witnesses established beyond dispute that Newsom had been in the habit of demanding sexual favors of Celia, and that she had resisted those demands over a period of several months. Testimony from both state and defense witnesses also established beyond reasonable doubt that Newsom went to Celia's cabin on the night of his death with the intention of again forcing her to have intercourse with him. Yet the defense's contention that a slave woman had the right to use force to prevent rape, especially rape by her master, was highly novel. In Missouri, sexual assault on a slave woman by white males was considered trespass, not rape, and an owner could hardly be charged with trespassing upon his own property. Missouri's failure to make the rape of a slave a crime was hardly unique. Rather throughout the antebellum South, as historians from Ulrich Phillips to Eugene Genovese have observed, the law did not recognize the rape of Black women. As Genovese has bluntly put it: "Rape meant, by definition, rape of white women, for no such crime as rape of a black woman existed at law."[380]

In the updated Foreword of the same text, Dr. Daina Ramey Berry, Michael Douglas, Dean of Humanities and Fine Arts at the University of California, Santa Barbara, and Dr. Jennifer L. Morgan, Professor of History in the Department of Social and Cultural Analysis at New York University, pointed out that:

> While McLaurin's characterization of the sexual politics of slavery remains fundamentally true, we are now compelled to ask whether the powerless-ness of Black women in the face of sexual assault at the hands of white men might signify more than a perverse social relationship and, rather, speak to something at the heart of the political economy of racial slavery. Sex with Black women was not only a prerogative of power, it was a means of enhancing one's capital wealth that had been enshrined in colonial slave law as early as 1662. Newsom did not simply rape Celia for sexual gratifi-cation; he did so for economic gain as well. In this regard, the verdict of the court did more than protect the state from the spectacle of Black women and men testifying in court against whites; it also protected the economic investment in women's reproductive capacity, a capacity that was arguably at the very heart of the economic power of slave states like Missouri.[380]

Celia, A Slave, and the heightened political mood concerning slavery con-firmed by the accounts rendered throughout its text confirm Berry's and Morgan's assertion.

In *When Rape Was Legal: The Untold History of Sexual Violence During Slavery,* written by Rachel A. Feinstein, an account of sexual abuse is de-scribed by an unidentified Black woman during her time enslaved. She says:

> My young marster tried to go with me, and 'cause I wouldn't go with him, he pretended I had done somethin' and beat me. I fought him back because he had no right to beat me for not goin' with him. His mother got mad with me for fightin' him back and I told her why he had beat me. Well then she sent me to the courthouse to be whipped for fightin' him.[366]

These particular accounts provide a window into the lack of agency Black women had to protect their bodies. They also could not protect their chil-dren's bodies from being ravaged. Not only did White women, in many cas-es, protect their sons, fathers, husbands, and brothers through absolution of accountability for their transgressions, they also willfully supported the abuse of their Black counterparts. They saw to it that Black women were violently abused if they attempted to protect themselves from being raped.

Feinstein further builds on the ubiquitous nature of legalized rape, adding:

> Madison Jefferson, a former slave, reported the physical violence brought upon enslaved Black women who rejected the sexual advances of their white masters, reflecting the extremely limited options black women had under slavery to resist sexual exploitation. Even when physical violence, like whipping, or threats against one's family were "chosen" in place of sexual violence, often women were ultimately raped as well. An excerpt of Jefferson's account is summarized here:

> 'Women who refuse to submit themselves to the brutal desires of their owners, are repeatedly whipt to subdue their virtuous repugnance, and in most instances this hellish practice is but too successful—when it fails, the women are frequently sold off to the south. Madison's young master, albeit a member of the Methodist church, punished a young woman on the estate repeatedly on this account, and at length accomplished his purpose, while she was in a state of insensibility from the effects of a felon blow inflicted by this monster.'[366]

Feinstein continues:

> 'Courting' practices enabled white men to uphold their identities as virtuous gentlemen while committing the most deplorable acts upon enslaved women. In addition to the coercion that awaited an enslaved woman's refusal of a man's gestures and gifts, {Harriet} Jacobs emphasizes the role of the legal system in providing a foundation within which any gift, or any threat, from a white man to an enslaved black woman was laden with power.[366]

In the text entitled, *Incidents in the Life of A Slave Girl,* written by Harriet Jacobs, she explains:

> Sometimes, when my master found that I still refused to accept what he call his kind offers, he would threaten to sell my child. "Perhaps that will humble you," said he. Humble me! Was I not already in the dust? But his threat lacerated my heart. I knew the law gave him power to fulfill it; for slaveholders have been cunning enough to enact that "the child shall

follow the condition of the mother," not of father; thus taking care that licentiousness shall not interfere with advance.[367]

As stated in a paper written by Jeffrey J. Pokorak entitled, "Rape as a Badge of Slavery," concerning the case *George v. State* (Mississippi Supreme Court, 1859):

> Raping a Black woman was not a crime for the majority of this Nation's history. First, the rape of a Black woman was simply not criminalized. And even when there was an argument that a statute was race neutral as to victimization, prosecutorial inaction and Court holdings made clear the lack of recourse for Black women who were raped. In fact, a White defendant could argue that his indictment ought to be dismissed for failing to state the victim was White. The most extreme example of this lack of protection, however, was expressed in *George v. State*, in which the Supreme Court of Mississippi considered whether a trial court's sentence of death for a Black male slave raping a Black woman slave was a legal sentence. The Court concluded that a male slave could only "commit a rape upon a white woman." The Court reasoned that slaves were not protected by the common law or statutes because they were under the legal dominion of their masters as required by their status as property.[74]

In *Race, Gender, and Power in America*, edited by Anita Faye Hill and Emma Jordan, as well as in "Rape and the Law in the Old South: Calculated to Excite Indignation in Every Heart," written by Peter W. Bardaglio, these historians documented the conspicuously chilling court summary that contained the reasoning behind why Black women and girls could not be raped. The Court's written summary stated:

> The crime of rape does not exist in this State between African slaves. Our laws recognize no marital status as between slaves, their sexual intercourse is left to be regulated by their owners. The regulations of law, as to the white race, on the subject of sexual intercourse, do not and cannot, for obvious reasons, apply to slaves; their intercourse is promiscuous, and the violation of a female slave by a male slave would be a mere assault and battery.[307,308]

Pay attention to the conclusion that an enslaved Black male could only rape a White woman. Pay attention to the legality of pedophilia, and to the permissive sexual abuse of Black women and young girls. The Mississippi Supreme Court does not merely have little regard for Black women and girls; it has no regard for them.

Let us move to Florida, 1918. The Florida Supreme Court decided yet again, in *Dallas v. State*, that the rape of Black women was not rape at all because Black women were immoral, and rape was only rape if the victim was White, because White woman were moral.[75,79] If this is not psychopathy, nothing is. The judge determined that:

> What has been said by some of our courts about an unchaste female being
> a comparatively rare exception is no doubt true where the population is
> composed largely of the Caucasian race, but we would blind ourselves to
> actual conditions if we adopted this rule where another race that is largely
> immoral constitutes an appreciable part of the population.

Again, White America asserted that Black girls and women (of my own grandmother's and my own great-grandmother's generations) could not be raped throughout the period of enslavement and beyond because of its sociopathic obsession with the idea that Black people are immoral.

Who was moral? Whites, of course. Exclusively.

As Americans, we must ask ourselves:

√   How is it that we do not engage these very brutal, yet very factual and important, parts of our history so that we can further understand both the hearts of White men and women and the supposedly legal, God-given right to pedophilia, sodomy, and rape that they exercised routinely regarding the bodies of Black girls, women, boys, and men?

√   How is it that these historic and perpetual realities go unmentioned when we have discussions about American history?

√   How and why is it that White people lack any sentiments of remorse, and instead express anger, when reparations discussions emerge?

√   How is it that we continue to dismiss the absence of morality, of empathy, and of compassion that most White and non-Black people have for Black persons in today's America?

We spend too much time contemplating the myths we have created for ourselves. If we are exceptional, it is not in the way we have imagined. It is in a way that horrifies and saddens.

There is simply no room in White American culture to address what White America has done to Black people. America has stolen from us, wounded us, murdered us. There is no sin, however, when considered from the White point of view.

If one cannot feel or reason or decide between right and wrong, then another is incapable of harming that inherently morally lesser being.

Look at how we again confirm the lack of value of the Black female body by scrutinizing the practices at the Louisiana State Penitentiary.[72,76-78] As is revealed in the paper entitled "Born in the Penitentiary: Women and Children Incarcerated in Louisiana, 1833-1862," written by Brett Josef Derbes, America has never cared. It had no need to. He notes:

> In the Antebellum South, incarcerated women and children endured confinement at ill-equipped facilities among majority male populations. On March 16, 1832, the Louisiana state legislature passed an "Act to Establish a State Penitentiary." Officials selected a site in Baton Rouge, adopted the Auburn system of prison management, and emulated the penitentiary in Wethersfield, Connecticut. Prison workshops operated with inmate labor were initially constructed to relieve overcrowded county jails, contribute to the rehabilitation of inmates, and make the penitentiaries self-sustaining enterprises. The Louisiana State Penitentiary incarcerated more African American women with life sentences than any other southern state during the Antebellum Era. From 1835 to 1862 at least sixty-two women entered the prison. Twenty-six enslaved women were serving life sentences, and at least ten gave birth while imprisoned. On December 11, 1848, the legislature passed "An Act providing for the disposal of such slaves as are or may be born in the penitentiary, the issue of convicts." From 1849 to 1861, the county sheriff auctioned eleven children on the courthouse steps for a total of $7,591. Records indicate that penitentiary employees purchased six of the eleven children. The Union army occupied Baton Rouge and evacuated four children from the prison in April 1862. General Benjamin F. Butler wrote, "I certainly cannot sanction any law of the State of Louisiana which enslaves any children of female convicts born in the State prison. Their place of birth is certainly not their fault." The Battle of Baton Rouge, and a devastating fire in November 1864 destroyed the penitentiary. Yet, evidence of secret horrors suffered by women inmates survived the flames.[76]

In *Slave Breeding: Sex, Violence, and Memory in African American History*, Gregory D. Smithers unveils a profoundly stark and profane depiction of enslaved Black people in the antebellum South, through interviews given by a number of people in the early twentieth century, who were previously enslaved. In the book, he writes:

> During the Great Depression, formerly enslaved African Americans shared their memories of southern slavery with interviewers from the Works Progress Administration (WPA). Between 1936 and 1938, more than two thousand former slaves from seventeen states narrated their recollections of slavery. (p. 101)

> According to former slaves, slave breeding relied on the existence of plantation "studs" or "bucks" and breeding "wenches." The language that some slaves used to represent coercive sexual acts was sensational, but it served an important narrative purpose: it reflected the moral depths that slaves believed white men and women had stooped to in order to keep them enslaved. Julia Malone, for example, remembered that her mother was a breeding "wench." She claimed, "my mammy was a big woman." Peter Brown insisted that slave masters "prized fast breeders." Brown stated that his mother "was a fast breeder," giving birth to "three sets of twins." Steve Robertson, reminisced about his father's sexual prowess, referring to the existence of plantation "bucks." Robertson testified that "de marster picks de buck fo' to sire de chilluns wid de womens dey wants, an' it am usually de mostest p'olific." And Willie Blackwell informed his WPA interviewer that "my pappy am de Blackwell stud, de kind of a big, strong, powe'ful nigger dat de plantation ownahs wants to breed dey slave stock up wid.

> The imagery these former slaves evoked was of men and women whose bodily proportions, physical fitness, and reproductive capacity were used to support a program of human engineering [through pimping and prostitution] in the plantation South. For example, one former slave remembered that slaves "were propagated by selected male negroes, who were kept for that purpose, the owners of this privileged negro, charged a fee of one out of every four of his offspring for his services." Another former slave, Alice Wright, claimed that her father told her that, "they put medicine in the water (cisterns) to make the young slaves have more children." In other words, a number of former slaves depicted slave masters willfully selecting slaves that they believed would add to the *quantity* and *quality* of their slave stock. Such representations were a far cry from the immoral practices and squalid living conditions that antebellum opponents of slavery emphasized.

In an age when popular racial discourse was infected with the tenets of social Darwinism and eugenics, these recollections present the slave master as
cruel and oppressive, a type of antebellum mad scientist, while the enslaved
men and women represent the raw material from which "droves and droves
of Niggers" were biologically engineered. (p. 103-104)[368]

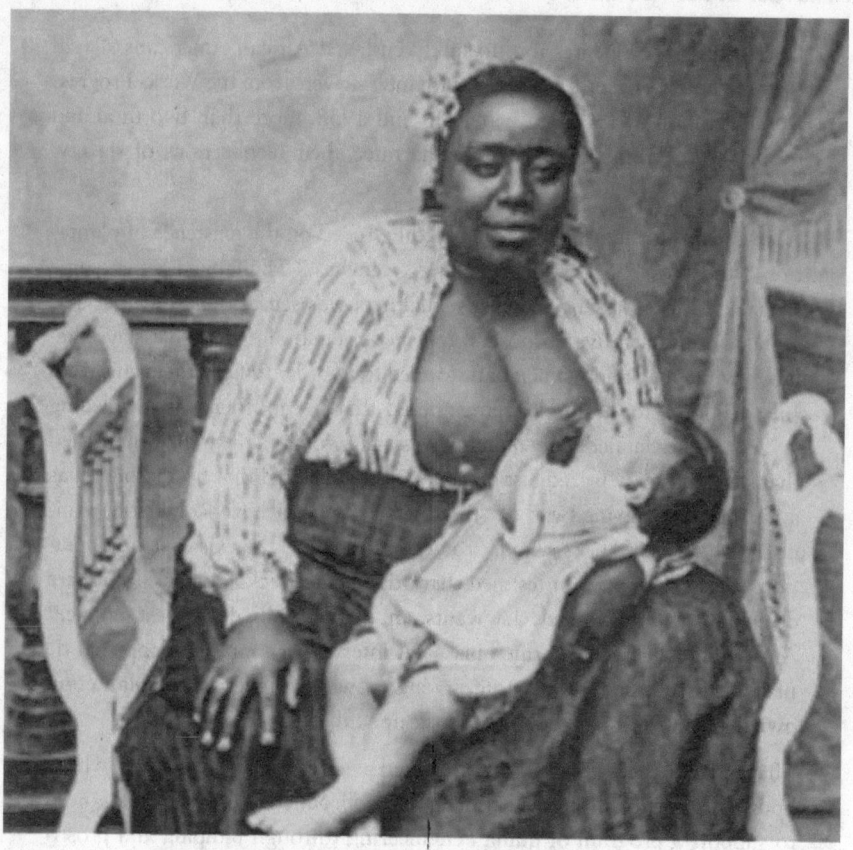

WANTS.

WET NURSE WANTED. Good wages given and the best references required. Apply at the Sun office. 1t;*

WANTED—A COLORED WOMAN as Waiter. None need apply unless well recommended. 112 PARK STREET. j7-2t*!

WANTED—A COOK: colored preferred. Apply at Wilkins' Restaurant, No. 89 WEST FAYETTE ST. j7-2t*.

SITUATION WANTED—By a respectable married WOMAN that has lost her own baby, with fresh breast of milk. Inquire at No. 154 NORTH CALVERT ST. 1t*]

WANTED—Any person having a female SLAVE, who is a good servant, and wishing to hire her, can find a good home for her in a small family, by applying at No. 166 E. MONUMENT ST. 1t*]

WANTED—A SITUATION, as WET-NURSE, by a respectable young married woman with a baby six weeks old. Best references given if required. Inquire at 31 NEW CHURCH STREET. 1t;*

APPRENTICE WANTED—To the Ladies' Shoemaking: a German boy preferred, who can speak English; age about 16 years. Apply at WILSON'S SHOE STORE, northeast corner of Saratoga and Poppleton sts. j9-2t*!

Private Sales.

Healthy Young Wet Nurse.

Capers & Heyward

Offer at private sale, a young and healthy WET NURSE. For further particulars, apply at our office, SOUTH SIDE ADGERS' WHARF.

June 7. smw3

WET NURSE, SEAMSTRESS, WASH-
ER, IRONER, AND HOUSE SERVANT
TO HIRE.—A young healthy Woman with her child
about 6 weeks old, and a Boy to attend to it. She
will be hired either as a Wet Nurse, or either of the
above capacities. She is a complete Seamstress,
Washer and Ironer, and House Servant; to be seen
at my house until hired. Apply to
THEODORE A. WHITNEY,
Broker and Auctioneer,
24 Horlbeck's Alley, next to King-st.
May 10

TO BE HIRED,

A Healthy Black WET NURSE, without a child,
with a good breast of milk. Enquire of Mrs.
Dawson, at Mr. Patrick Hind's, in Beaufain-street
October 24.   6

TO BE SOLD,
Before the Vendue Store of LAWRENCE
CAMPBELL, THIS DAY, between the
Hours of 11 and 12 o'clock,

A Negro Wench,

With her CHILD, about 18 months old,
She can cook, wash and iron tolerably well,
is a good House Servant, perfectly sober and
and honest; and has frequently been employed
as a Wet Nurse. The intention of altering
the property, is the only reason of her being
offered for sale. Conditions, Cash on delivery.   BRIAN CAPE & Co.
April 17.

FOR SALE—A Wet Nurse, about nineteen years of age, with her second child, six weeks old, will be sold low for cash, fully guarantied. Also—A first-rate Seamstress, who can cut out and fit well. Also—Several first-rate House Servants, Mechanics and Field Hands. Those who wish to purchase would do well to call on the undersigned before buying elsewhere.

o19 1w*   J. W. BOAZMAN, 157 Gravier st.

What psychopathy? What sociopathy, you say?

In *Rape, Racism, and the Law,* Wriggins also highlighted the diseased ways rape laws protected their dominant perpetrators (men) and White women. Of course, Black males were the primary profile for who a rapist was.[75]

Consider the following:

√ **Kentucky 1802 Code:** *death penalty for rape of a white woman by a slave and term of years for rape by a white man*

√ **Virginia Code of 1819 and 1823 Law:** *death penalty for rape or attempted rape of a white woman by a slave, Black, or mulatto and term of 10 to 21 years for rape by a white man*

√ **Missouri 1825 Statute:** *castration for rape or attempted rape by a Black or mulatto*

√ **Arkansas Code of 1838:** *death penalty for assault with intent to commit rape by a Black or mulatto*

√ **Alabama Code of 1852:** *death penalty for rape of a white woman by a slave or free Black*

√ **Mississippi 1857 Statute:** *death penalty for attempted carnal connection with or rape of a white female under 14 by a slave*

√ **Tennessee 1858 Law:** *death by hanging for rape of a free white woman by a slave or free Black*

In addition, Wriggins asserted:

> The rape of Black women {and girls}, by white or Black men . . . was legal; indictments were sometimes dismissed for failing to allege that the victim was white. In those states where it was illegal for white men to rape white women, statutes provided less severe penalties for the convicted white rapist than for the convicted Black one. In addition, common law rules both defined rape narrowly and made it a difficult crime to prove.

> During slavery, then, the legal system treated seriously only one racial combination of rape—rape involving a Black offender and a White victim. This selective recognition continued long after slavery ended.[75]

White people's collective psychosis (wording adopted from Toni Morrison) developed through cultural beliefs and agreements, religion, academic scholarship, science, White morality, and the legal system, and provided the reasoning, rationales, permission, and justifications to intentionally rape and molest Black women, girls, boys, and men.

Legitimized into reality by both statute and case law, White men and women persistently made clear that Black humanity was to be reviled and vilified. Examples of White America's court system historically hailing Black men as the rapist prototype can be observed in both the Georgia Supreme Court's 1899 ruling, and the Alabama Appeals Court decision in 1953, in *McQuirter v. State*.

The Georgia ruling in 1899 provided:

> Race {of Black men} may be considered to rebut any presumption that might otherwise arise in favor of the accused that his intention was to obtain consent of the female, upon failure of which he would abandon his purpose to have sexual intercourse with her.

The Alabama Appeals Court, in the 1953 case of *McQuirter v. State*, rendered the following decision:

> In determining the question of intention, the jury may consider the social conditions and customs founded upon racial differences, such as that the prosecutrix was a White woman and the defendant a Negro man.

In the eloquent words of Jennifer Wriggins:

> The "social conditions customs founded upon racial differences" which
> the jury was to consider included the assumption that Black men always
> and only want to rape white women, and that a white woman would never
> consent to sex with Black men.[309]

Simply put, as recently as 1953, White American courts ruled that Black men,
on the isolated basis of being Black, were all rapists.

This is not a fictional story. It is one that details the construction and
evolution of anti-Blackness in White America, as well as the evolution of
White people in America.

I digress.

Laws enacted by oppressors were designed to vilify the oppressed. The
brutal, treacherous offense of rape onto the bodies of Black women was not
merely ignored; it was incentivized. The molestation and rape of any and all
Black bodies was simply fine (but it was Black people who could not discern
morally, you will recall).

Who designed these laws, allowing for no or little punishment (concerning White men)? Who enforced them? Who benefited from them? There is
a pattern.

So, I submit the following questions to you as a reader:

√ How can it be that none of this is taught as what it is, which is
  sociopathic?

√ How have hundreds of years of sadistic legal history affected how
  the law treats Black people today?

√ How is it that White culture has not been adequately scrutinized?

√ How is it that non-White, and particularly Black, people are
  pathologized and judged exclusively for any deficiencies or transgressions?

As Carter G. Woodson stated in his book entitled *The Miseducation of the
Negro*:

> It is well understood that by the teaching of history the White man can be
> further assured of his superiority. If you can control a man's thinking you

do not have to worry about his actions. When you determine what a man shall think you do not have to concern yourself about what he will do. If you make a man feel that he is inferior, you do not have to compel him to accept an inferior status, for he will seek it himself. If you make a man think that he is justly an outcast, you do not have to order him to the back door. He will go without being told and if there is no back door, his very nature will demand one.[80]

This includes the framing of it. How are we to feel about such things? What frame of reference should we use to analyze our history and present circumstances? I believe a framework dictated by Whites cannot work. We must revisit our own past independently. As Cleage stated:

> We must write history, and frame the cultural, psychological, and sociological experiences of Black people in White America, for ourselves.[81]

We are the only ones who can do it.

We have seen this pattern of sex abuse persist throughout the ages. Look at Thomas Jefferson, who innumerable liberal, White scholars hail for his work establishing the republic. He groomed his wife's biracial half-sister, Sally Hemmings, between the ages of six and fourteen. He raped and impregnated her multiple times. This is widely known; it is not some secret. And what has the White response been? To celebrate him as a figure of national pride.

This is perverse.

Consider Newsom, consider the litany of examples documented in this text, alone. The country was built on bloodlust. Nothing mattered except the dominance of Whites. It is dreadful. The United States' cultural foundation is either ignored or lied about entirely in order to protect the pattern of sex abuse, including that of children, which spread like a cancer. These were not isolated incidents. This was system-wide.

Human sex trafficking, prostitution, rape, and pedophilia established the American economy, morality, legality, and culture.

Consider how plantation life was.

America's Founding Fathers and Mothers (Thomas Jefferson, James Madison, and both George and Martha Washington, etc.) encouraged and benefited from mass rape (including of children) and pimping. Whose bodies did they profit from? Black ones. Such sex abuse was the bedrock of this society, its systems, and its culture.[90]

No one sugarcoats or denies history better than White Americans. White America goes out of its way to ignore the demented, cartoonishly evil history that continues to adversely affect us today. There is a connection to be made between yesterday's injustices and today's ongoing human rights abuses.

Take, for example, Cyntoia Brown, who was convicted for murdering the man who molested, raped, and prostituted her as a young child. Her judge was conditioned to feel nothing for her. He was infected with anti-Blackness. He was taught to have no mercy on her or anyone fitting her profile.[82] If she had been White, her plight would have been met with both empathy and sympathy. Justice could never be hers. It was a foregone conclusion.

Juxtapose Brown's story to former U.S. President Donald J. Trump bragging about sexual abuse in 2005, while preparing for an interview with Access Hollywood. In it, he said:

I moved on her actually. You know she was down on Palm Beach. She used to be great. She's still very beautiful. I moved on her, and I failed. I'll admit it. And I did try to fuck her. She was married.

I moved on her like a bitch, but I couldn't get there because she was married. Then all of a sudden, I see her, she's now got the big phony tits and everything. She's totally changed her look.

I better use some Tic Tacs just in case I start kissing her. You know I'm automatically attracted to beautiful [women]. I just start kissing them. It's like a magnet. Just kiss. I don't even wait. And when you're a star they let you do it. You can do anything. You can do anything. Whatever you want. Grab them by the pussy. You can do anything.[203]

Former President Trump later referred to this as locker room talk. Yet, in October of 2022, upon being provided the opportunity to clarify his comments during his deposition in the E. Jean Carroll rape and sexual assault case, prior to his sexual assault conviction, he posited the following statement while being questioned by Carroll's attorney, Roberta Kaplan (as reflected in the oral testimony):[362]

Kaplan: "And you say, and again this has become very famous in this video, 'I just start kissing them. It's like a magnet. Just kiss. I don't even wait and when you're a star they let you do it. You can do anything. Grab them by the pussy. You can do anything.' That's what you said?"

Trump: "Historically that's true with stars."

Kaplan: "It's true that if you're a star you can grab women by the pussy?"

Trump: "Well, if you look over the last million years, I guess that's been largely true. Not always, but largely true, unfortunately or fortunately."

Kaplan: "You consider yourself to be a star?"

Trump: "I think you can say that. Yeah."

Sexual violence, once legalized and morally practiced by White men, is diabolical, maniacal, psychopathic, sociopathic, and, in truth, the very legacy of this country. This nature that pervades American culture is the ever-lingering legacy of Whiteness and White patriarchy. It is the result of unchecked power and the absence of never being held accountable to anyone for anything.

Ask yourself:

√ Why would we not want to finally begin seeking justice? What order would that disrupt?

√ Are White people, our society's gatekeepers, by and large, scared to punish their own, even when such punishment is clearly necessary?

√ Who, if anyone, suffers, when we seek out the truth?

√ Does White people's fear of exposing our history stem, in part, from the reality that it might result in acknowledging the reality that their gains were ill-gotten?

√ Do Whites fear revenge if the truth becomes universally acknowledged and understood?

√ Do Whites feel reparations are due?

√ Could it be that Whites do not want to confront themselves and their history because of the profound shame it might induce? The entire world would benefit from America scrutinizing itself, both in historical and present contexts. We would do well to question those in power.

Consider Judge Aaron Persky, for example, who presided over the Brock Turner rape case in San Francisco, California.[83] Persky sentenced Turner to six months in jail and three months of probation. Why did he do this, given the severity of Turner's numerous crimes? Let us examine his own words on the matter below.

> And in my decision to grant probation, the question that I have to ask myself, again, consistent with those Rules of Court, is: Is state prison for this defendant an antidote to that poison? Is incarceration in state prison the right answer for the poisoning of [Jane's] life?
>
> And trying to balance the factors in the Rules of Court, I conclude that it is not, and that justice would best be served, ultimately, with a grant of probation. Let—let me go through the Rules of Court, because there is a limitation on probation eligibility, and that's due to the charge of Penal Code section 220. And pursuant to Penal Code section 1203.065, this is a case where probation is prohibited except in unusual cases where the interest of justice would best be served. And in this case, the Court is directed to apply the criteria in Rule 4.413(c) to evaluate whether the statutory limitation on probation is overcome.
>
> And so, one criterion which was mentioned in the probation officer's recommendation related to 4.413(c)(1)(A), which states, [as read] "The fact or circumstance giving rise to the limitation on probation is, in this case, substantially less serious than the circumstances typically present in other cases involving the same probation limitation."
>
> And the probation officer alluded to, I believe, the fact that alcohol was present and concluded that this would be a basis for overcoming the statutory prohibition of probation.[83]

Judge Persky blamed the victim.

She drank alcohol, making her more susceptible to the crime, according to him. The burden was on the victim, not the aggressor. How typical.

How about Canadian Judge Robin Kemp, who in 2014 asked a rape victim why she did not simply close her legs or knees or put her "ass" in the sink. According to him, sometimes "sex and pain" went hand in hand. Judge Kemp, though Canadian, is encompassed in the socialization and indoctrination of the psychopathic racial personality. He is representative of the quintessential White American male.[84]

Consider again the king of kings, Donald Trump, America's most recent former president, the self-admitted predator and convicted rapist. Who better illustrates the toxicity of White, capitalistic, ultra-privileged (untouchable, in essence) maleness?

Getting caught on tape admitting to forcing himself on women did not matter. Saying he grabbed women "by the pussy" did not matter. Speaking ill of one of the many women who had accused him of rape, saying she was not "his type" did not matter. Nothing mattered. He still ascended to the presidency.

And who did he empower while in office? People such as Brett Kavanaugh, who had been credibly accused of sexual violence. He now sits on the highly divided U.S. Supreme Court.

None of this is mere happenstance. It is coordinated.

There is more, of course. There always will be.

Take the case of a Black woman named Anjanette Young, who on February 22nd, 2019, met a predictably unjust fate at the hands of the Chicago Police Department. Left naked and handcuffed in a room by several White, male officers, she was traumatized in the extreme.[85,86] Most of us understand that if Anjanette had been White, the incident would not have happened to her.

Furthermore, anti-Blackness allowed for Chicago's first female, lesbian, Black mayor, Lori Lightfoot, to deny the settlement that would have been paid to Young. The settlement had, incidentally, already been agreed to by various city officials. It was meant to convey the message that the conduct was unacceptable and punishable as an act of deterrence—that Ms. Young is a valued and respected citizen of the United States who should not have been treated this way.

But because we live in an anti-Black, anti-female, sociopathic society, even the most basic kind of compensation became controversial. What would we have done had a White woman been violated that way in her own home? How long and intensely would we have been outraged?

Let us move on.

In November of 2021, *The New York Times* published an article written by Ed Shanahan entitled, "Judge Spares Man in Teen Rape Case: 'Incarceration Isn't Appropriate,'" and it highlighted yet another case of White psychopathy and sociopathy.[77]

As highlighted in the newspaper:

The girl was 16 when Christopher Belter raped her, according to court documents. He was a teenager too, a student at an elite private boys school whose family's western New York home was known as a party house where teens gathered to consume liquor, marijuana and Adderall.

It was August 2018, and the girl, identified in court filings as M.M., was at Mr. Belter's house to spend the night with his sister before going to Chicago the next day.

He asked her into his room, and then threw her onto the bed, pulled off her clothes and told her to stop being such a baby, according to court documents. At a hearing this summer, she described focusing her attention on the leaves of a plant in the room as the attack continued.

This week, Mr. Belter, 20, was sentenced in the assault on M.M. and in sexual attacks on three other teenage girls. Facing up to eight years in prison, he was instead given eight years' probation by a judge who said he had "agonized" over the decision.

"I'm not ashamed to say that I actually prayed over what is the appropriate sentence in this case because there was great pain," the judge, Matthew J. Murphy III of Niagara, N.Y., County Court, said at Mr. Belter's sentencing on Tuesday, according to WKBW, a local television station. "There was great harm. There were multiple crimes committed in the case."

Still, the judge continued, "It seems to me that a sentence that involves incarceration or partial incarceration isn't appropriate." He told Mr. Belter, who must register as a sex offender, the probation would be "like a sword hanging" over his head for the next eight years. He offered no further explanation for why the sentence did not include prison time.[77]

It is a mob mentality. Everyone in the mob protects everyone else in the mob.

The fake remorse, the fake prayer, the fake agony—all of it was meant to conceal his role as an enabler in a black robe. No "God" forced him to absolve the perpetrator's crimes. Ask yourself how he differed from Judge William A. Hall or the White men who sat on the Supreme Court of Missouri in 1855, or the White men who sat on the Mississippi Supreme Court in 1859, or the White men who sat on the Florida Supreme Court in 1918, or Judge Robin Kemp, or Judge Aaron Persky, or former President Donald Trump.

Layer this equation by adding the sexual politics of 2024, and White men's additional weaponization of legal and institutional power as they require 10-year-old and 13-year-old female rape victims to be further traumatized, inconvenienced, and humiliated by forcing them to carry unwanted pregnancies to term. Imagine burdening these children—they are minors—with the pressure to have to travel in order to abort, or to be forced to carry the babies of their rapists to term.[369,370] We can conclude from such realities that the psychology of White men today is similar to what it was two hundred years ago. The abundance of evidence provides an even more pronounced view into the sinister nature of Whiteness and the collective psychosis that dominates American culture's frame of mind, cultural attitudes, and norms.

It is normalized psychopathy and sociopathy, and it is entirely illustrative of the terror perpetrated by Whites onto Black people. As stated by Nicole Morris, a Black woman who attended a workshop of mine, in 2022, espoused:

> The laws are not only actively anti-Black, and anti-women, they are also actively pro-White men, modified and adjusted, as necessary.

Confronting the foundational elements of Whiteness and White terrorism (i.e., White psychopathy/sociopathy, anti-Blackness, White patriarchy) is considered by most as anti-American or un-American. Make no mistake. What that means is anti-White. Perhaps, however, that is what makes it so necessary. We must humanize the experiences of Black and other non-White peoples. We must do this if we want to be truthful and authentic. Most importantly, we must do this in order to thwart the perpetration of even greater harm. Americans cannot be afraid of and can no longer run away from acknowledging the falsehoods and atrocities of White supremacy as White psychopathy and sociopathy. We cannot be afraid. Boldness is our ally and our guide.

To the millions of unidentified and unnamed Black females; to Celia, the enslaved, Black female implicated in *George v. State* (and all like her who have ever lived); to Margaret Varner, the Black female highlighted in Toni Morrison's book *Beloved* (who attempted to kill her children out of desperation rather than see them subjected to the rape and enslavement she had endured by her master);[87] to Recy Taylor, who was gang-raped by White teenagers in 1944 (an Abbeville, Alabama crime documented in the 2018 film entitled *The Rape of Recy Taylor*), we see you. (You will note Taylor's case was the one where, in the cruelest fashion possible, attorney Marvin White insultingly attempted to defend his clients and bully Taylor's husband by saying, "Nigger—ain't $600 enough for raping your wife?") This can be seen in the newspaper clipping shown here.[88]

$600 To Rape Wife? Ala. Whites Make Offer To Recy Taylor Mate!

By FRED ATWATER
(Defender Staff Correspondent)

MONTGOMERY, Ala. — "Nigger—ain't $600 enough for raping your wife?"

Stocky Willie Lee Taylor considered it.

He talked to white Marvin White, who wanted him to forget prosecuting the six white men who raped and ruptured Recy, his 24-year-old wife.

White spoke for his clients, all youths from prominent Abbeville families who had been identified by Recy. They were Hugo Wilson, Pennie Hastings, Sam Skippy, Billie Hilder, Dillard York and Luther Lee.

They were willing to pay $100 each if Recy Taylor would forget it, White said.

By then the rape of Recy, mother of a two-year-old daughter, had become known in every town in Alabama and every Negro community in the nation. The Grand Jury was to meet within a week to act upon one of the few cases ever to be brought to court of white youths raping a Negro woman.

White repeated his offer of $100 for each man as a "settlement."

Willie blurted out "No." But that didn't end it. White came back and again after more pressure and threats had been leveled at the Taylors and Willie said, "Come back later and I'll tell you." He came back later and Willie answered "Yes."

Defendants Dismissed

Willie may as well have stuck to his first no. For the Grand Jury, called on October 9, 1944, dismissed

VICTIM OF WHITE ALABAMA RAPISTS

First published photo of Mrs. Recy Taylor, victim of six white rapists in Alabama, and her little family is this picture received from their refuge in an Alabama city some distance from their hometown of Abbeville, where the crime occurred. With the young mother is her daughter, little Joyce Lee Taylor and her husband, Willie Guy Taylor.

What about the tragedy of Ruby McCollum, who had no other recourse than to kill her rapist, a White doctor, and Senator-elect named Leroy Adams? He had raped her for years and had impregnated her with a child who she had birthed several years earlier. The perpetrator's psychopathy ruined her life, her husband's life, and her child's life. He viewed raping her as his birthright (and had been sent every message, both culturally and legally, that that was, in fact, true).[89,91]

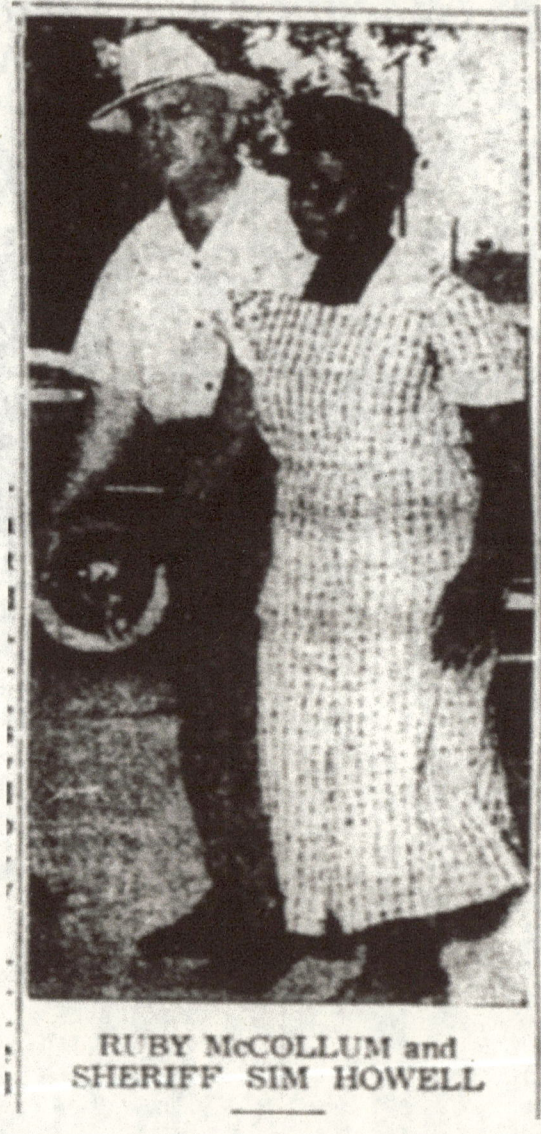

**RUBY McCOLLUM and
SHERIFF SIM HOWELL**

What about Betty Jean Owens, a Black female student at Florida A&M University who was gang raped by four White men, all of whom confessed to raping her. She was (rationally) convinced the case would get no attention or justice. Suzanne Owens, in a 2019 article entitled, "A Rare Case of Justice," chronicled it.[92] The only reason why the case was prosecuted was because of the national attention it received as a result of having been publicized. It is a near certainty that it, too, would have been discarded otherwise.

To my sisters Breonna (Taylor),[93] Sandra (Bland), Atatiana (Jefferson), Tanisha (Anderson), Jazmine (Headley),[94] Nia (Wilson),[95] and all the others whose names will never be uttered, you are seen. It is not you. You have value. That any person or institution has ever conveyed otherwise to you is a tragedy. Tragedies must be acknowledged and compensated for.

At some point, White terror was going to find you, just like it found others, such as Mary Laura Nelson in 1911 (and her dear son, L.D. Nelson), Mary Turner,[98–100] Autherine Lucy, Nial Ruth Cox,[101-103] and so many others. Our sisters have simultaneously been victimized and unjustly labeled as aggressors. What a feat. There was nothing you could have done differently to avoid being victimized by this ongoing holocaust; this is true for our entire race.[103,104]

Our only hope as Black people is to stop functioning like oppressed people and start acting aggressively, even if that means taking up arms to defend our own selves and our children. Self-defense is legal and appropriate.

Chapter Closing

This legacy of legalized rape against non-White females, especially Black ones, is just part of White America's ugly history. Millions of unidentified Black females were sex trafficked and prostituted for White profit, pleasure, and convenience and to build White wealth and White culture. No matter what anyone says, their lives mattered and matter.

We must reject any attempt to either sanitize or minimize White people's harm to Black people. We were and are terrorized. Let us scream this from the rooftops. We must reframe our history. It must reflect the role we played in building American wealth, the role Whites played in subjugating us, and how all of this continues to affect us to this day. All oppressed minorities must do this—Black, Indigenous, everyone.

In closing, I am reflecting upon words left to us by the late, great Tupac Shakur, from his 1993 song "Keep Ya Head Up":

> And since we all came from a woman,
>
> Got our name from a woman and our game from a woman,
>
> I wonder why we take from our women, why we rape our women,
>
> Do we hate our women?
>
> I think it's time to kill for our women
>
> Time to heal our women, be real to our women
>
> And if we don't we'll have a race of babies that will hate the ladies
>
> That make the babies.[340]

Now, I invite you to think about how American society and culture treat Black women and their children.

Chapter 3 Review Questions:

(Note: Please go to www.danteking.com to complete the chapter assessment and evaluation for the following questions.)

Considering the sociocultural and legal conditions, ask yourselves the following questions:

1. What did White females and males learn about the value of Whiteness?

2. How did various laws shape White identity for White males? How about for White females?

3. What did Black females learn about what it meant to be White and female? White and male? Black and male? Black and female?

4. What did Black males learn about what it meant to be White and male? White and female? Black and female? Black and male?

5. In what ways did these laws, and White people's perversions, shape White identity?

6. How did these laws shape Black identity?

7. How did these laws create and reinforce pro-White and anti-Black legal, social, political, and cultural orientations on the North American continent?

8. What do you make of the reduction and sanitization of the horror? Is it naivete or something more nefarious?

9. Why are we so hostile to the notion of self-scrutiny? Why do we not learn about the basis of White people's wealth? Why do we not learn about the harm done to specifically Black female bodies? Who benefits from these topics being overlooked?

10. How can White America's legalization of rape, including that of children, and other sexually predatory acts be understood historically? How about presently? Are the two connected? What role has anti-Blackness played?

11. How is the role of anti-Blackness different from that of White supremacy/power/superiority?

12. How does White people's control over the legal system benefit them?

13. How have White people's total control and dominion over Black people benefited and served their ability to engineer and reinforce their own perverted projections onto Black people, as a way of escaping collective scrutiny amongst and within their community and culture?

14. How can Black people escape the ignominious distinction of criminality that has been bestowed upon us by people who directly benefit from us having such a label, however false it may be?

15. Who are the real criminals?

16. Why is it dangerous to minimize historic crimes and untether them from current problems plaguing our criminal justice system?

17. In what ways does White male patriarchal predation and violence aimed at Black girls and women engineer Black male predation and violence aimed towards Black girls and women?

18. In what ways does White male patriarchal predation and violence aimed at Black girls and women engineer White females' predation and violence aimed towards Black girls and women?

19. In what ways does White male patriarchal predation and violence aimed at Black boys and men engineer White females' predation and violence aimed towards Black girls and women?

20. How does the legal system fit in with respect to creating consistently favorable conditions for Whites and unfavorable ones for Black people? Does it work in conjunction with, for example, the educational system?

21. How does the reality of debasing Black people, relegating us into the most inhuman and profane positions in American culture, influence White American psychological and sociological constructs about who Black people are (i.e., values, principles, behavior, etc.) and what we represent?

22. In what ways do these White psychological and sociological developments shape White identity, in terms of who they believe themselves to be and what they represent as a community and culture?

23. How does White projection, the foundation of both the psychological and sociological developments of American culture, shape the psychology and sociology that Black people and people of color accept about Black people, White people, and all others along the racial spectrum?

John Punch, the Casual Killing Act of 1669, and the Beginning of America's Legalized Psychopathic and Sociopathic Anti-Black Terrorism

I WANT TO BEGIN this chapter by referencing a statement made by General Mark Milley, Chairman of the Joint Chiefs, as he responded to remarks made by Florida Congressman Matt Gaetz on the topic of Critical Race Theory. General Milley stated:

> I do think it's important for those of us in uniform to be open-minded and be widely read. The United States Military Academy is a university, and it is important that we train, and we understand—and I want to understand White Rage, and I'm White. And, I want to understand . . . **what is it that caused thousands of people to assault this building and try to overturn the Constitution of the United States of America? What caused that?**[104] [emphasis added]

As I heard this, I screamed, "BE CAREFUL!"

This phrase is sometimes used in the Black community to mean one should be careful about what one asks for. Though he is an older white male, seemingly open-minded, he asked bold questions.

But it is more complicated than that.

I am familiar with these questions. I have asked them of myself and my students. It is obviously clear that most Whites struggle to look at themselves, their behavior, their history, their complicity, etc. This point was summed up in a recent interview of forensic psychiatrist and psychoanalyst, Dr. Aruna Khilanani, M.D.

Professor and journalist Marc Lamont Hill conducted it on *Black News Tonight*. He bluntly asked Dr. Aruna if, based on her professional opinion, she believed White people were psychopathic. Dr. Khilanani stated:

> I think so. I think there are many lies . . . . the level of lying that White people do that has started since colonialism, we're just used to it. Such as every time you steal a country, you loot, you say you've discovered something. We don't say that we killed all these people, we got rid of the Native Americans. We say we discovered America. You don't talk about the level of death. You don't talk about the level of what actually occurred. You wipe the slate clean. You sanitize the violence, and you actually got lost along the way, you tried to go to India. Then you say you discovered something. And this level of discovery is everywhere. You've discovered vegetarianism. You've discovered yoga. Everything is a discovery, and it's all actually stolen.[105]

Carol Anderson, author of *White Rage,* and Benjamin Crump, author of *Open Season,* have written books on this particular topic. They have done so from a different angle, of course, one in which they articulate the depths of White resentment. This contempt for Black people, they argued, was fueled by a distinctly pro-White history. What was, is, in other words. Most White people, historically and presently, resent Black progress. They hate seeing us advance. That is what explains their continued (though better concealed) attempts to thwart us at every turn.

See, for example, the Snow Riots in Washington, D.C. in 1835; Wilmington, North Carolina in 1898; the Ocoee Massacre in Florida in 1905; the East St. Louis Riots in 1917; the Tulsa Oklahoma massacre of 1921; the Rosedale White Backlash in 1978; and a litany of other examples proving the existence and potency of anti-Black terror (do not forget the Watts Riots, Newark, New Jersey, Bayview Hunters Point, etc.).[124,219,220, 252–257]

Current White backlash, intense and unceasing, has emerged as a substantial impediment to Black progress. Look at the dehumanization of Clifford Owensby, a Black paraplegic victim of White police terrorism in Dayton, Ohio, as recently as September 30, 2021.[259] And yet Black resentment remains a mystery. We get murdered repeatedly by the same people but are not allowed to be rageful. Most Whites know this, at least intellectually, if not emotionally. They know. They just do not care.

In this next chapter, we will explore more. We will cover the period between 1664 through roughly 1722. We will revisit General Milley's questions and further amplify what White character and behaviors are rooted in. The additional body of laws presented in this chapter will highlight examples focused on the very construction of Whiteness. Many are pulled from the *Statutes At Large*, written by Hening,[38,125] the Maryland Archives, the South Carolina Archives, and other sources of information.[36,108–111,114–117]

We will also explore the construction of the American "negro" and all the violence directed toward him/her. Consider Lauren Hill's song entitled "Black Rage" to better understand.[106,107] Some lyrics of her song include:

Black Rage is founded on two-thirds a person
Rapings and beatings and suffering that worsens,
Black human packages tied up in strings.
Black RAGE can come from all these kinds of things
Black Rage is founded on blatant denial
Squeezing economics, subsistence survival,
Deafening silence and social control.
Black Rage is founded on wounds in the soul!

When the dogs bite
When the beatings
When I'm feeling sad
I simply remember all these kinds of things
and then I don't fear so bad!

Black rage is founded: who fed us self-hatred
Lies and abuse, while we waited and waited
Spiritual treason this grid and its cages
Black rage was founded on these kinds of things

Black rage is founded on draining and draining
Threatening your freedom, To stop your complaining
Poisoning your water, while they say it's raining
Then call you mad for complaining, complaining

Old time bureaucracy drugging the youth
Black rage is founded on blocking the truth,
Murder and crime, compromise, and distortion
Sacrifice, sacrifice who makes this fortune?
Greed, falsely called progress
Such human contortion,
Black rage is founded on these kinds of things

So, when the dog bites
And the beatings
When I'm feeling sad
I simply remember all these kinds of things and then I don't fear so bad

Free enterprise, is it myth or illusion?
Forcing you back into purposed confusion
Black human trafficking or blood transfusion?
Black rage is founded on these kinds of things.
Victims of violence both psyche and body
Life out of context IS living unGodly
Politics, politics
Greed falsely called wealth
Black rage is founded on denial of self!
Black human packages tied and subsistence
Having to justify your very existence
Try if you must, but you can't have my soul
Black rage is made by unGodly control

So, when the dog bites
And when the beatings
And I'm feeling so sad
I simply remember all these kinds of things
And then I don't fear so bad

****

Creating Whiteness

First, we must consider the psychological and emotional state of the people who built laws aimed at terrorizing Black people. Next, we must set aside the economic component of anti-Black racial enslavement and deal with the psychological and emotional investments that White people possessed in maintaining the subjugation. We must also consider the beliefs and teachings passed down from generation to generation, perpetuating a White-positive, Black-negative structure. Only then will we be able to consider more meaningfully General Milley's inquiries.

White Psychopathology and Impression Management

White people suffer from a lack of impression management concerning themselves and others, especially Black people. This truth has persisted throughout the ages. The historical record has well documented white people's narcissistic personality disorder and insecurities, along with their internalized distortions and perversions about African people.

In *White Over Black: American Attitudes toward the Negro 1550-1812*, Winthrop D. Jordan provided a window into this reality. He wrote:

> The Negro's color attained greatest significance not as a scientific problem but as a social fact. Englishmen found blackness in human beings a peculiar and important point of difference. The Negro's color set him radically apart from Englishmen. It also served as a highly visible label identifying the natives of a distant continent which for ages Christians had known as a land of men radically defective of religion.

> While distinctive appearance set Africans over into a novel category of men, their religious condition set them apart from Englishmen in a more familiar way. Englishmen and Christians everywhere were sufficiently acquainted with the concept of heathenism that they confronted its living representatives without puzzlement. Certainly the rather sudden discovery that the world was teeming with heathen people made for heightened vividness and urgency in a long-standing problem: but it was the fact that this problem was already formulated long before contact with Africa which proved important in shaping English reaction to the Negro's defective religious condition.

In one sense heathenism was less a "problem" for Christians than an exercise in self-definition: the heathen condition being by negation the proper Christian life. In another sense, the presence of heathenism in the world constituted an imperative to intensification of religious commitment. From its origin Christianity was a universalist, proselytizing religion, and the sacred and secular histories of Christianity made manifest the necessity of bringing non-Christians into the fold. For Englishmen, then, the heathenism of Negroes was at once a counter-image of their own religion and a summons to eradicate an important distinction between the two peoples.

Christianity militated against the unity of man. Because Englishmen were Christians, heathenism in Negroes was a fundamental defect which set them distinctly apart. However much Englishmen disapproved of Popery and Mahometanism, they were accustomed to these perversions. Yet they were not accustomed to dealing face to face with people who appeared, so far as many travelers could tell, to have no religion at all. Steeped in the legacy and the trappings of their own religion, Englishmen were ill prepared to see any legitimacy in African religious practices. Judged by Christian cosmology, Negroes stood in a separate category of men.

Indeed the most important aspect of English reaction to Negro heathenism was that Englishmen evidently did not regard it as separate from the Negro's other attributes. Heathenism was treated not so much as a specifically religious defect, but as one manifestation of a general refusal to measure up to proper standards, as a failure to be English or even civilized. There was every reason for Englishmen to fuse the various attributes they found in Africans.

During the first century of English contact with Africa, Protestant Christianity was an important element in English patriotism; especially during the struggle against Spain the Elizabethan's special Christianity was interwoven into his conception of his own nationality, and he was therefore inclined to regard the Negroes' lack of true religion as part of theirs. Being a Christian was not merely a matter of subscribing to certain doctrines; it was a quality inherent in oneself, and in one's society. It was interconnected with all other attributes of normal and proper men; as one of the earliest English accounts distinguished Negroes from Englishmen, they were "a people of beastly living, without a God, lawe, religion, or common wealth"—which was to say that Negroes were not Englishmen. Far from isolating African heathenism as a separate characteristic, English travelers sometimes linked it explicitly with barbarity and blackness. They already had in hand a meditating term among these impinging concepts—the *devil*. As one observer declared, Negroes "in colour so in condition are little other than Devils incarnate," and, further, "the Devil . . . has infused prodigious Idolatry into their hearts, enough to rellish his pallat and aggrandize their tortures when he gets power to fry their souls, as the raging Sun has already scorcht their cole-black carcasses." "Idolatry" was indeed a serious failing, but English travelers in West Africa tended to regard defect of true religion as an aspect of the Negro's "condition." In an important sense, then, heathenism was for Englishmen one inherent characteristic of savage men.[402]

Jordan continues discussing European-White people's derangements about African people's biological connections to primates. He extensively talked about White people's cultural corruptions and abnormal projections concerning African people's sexual behaviors, aggression, and promiscuity, comparing them to animals. Jordan emphasizes profoundly how Whites imposed their psychosocial and sociocultural attitudes, habits, and practices onto Black people in a most twisted fashion. He notes:

If Negroes were likened to beasts, there was in Africa a beast which was likened to men. It was a strange and eventually tragic happenstance of nature that the Negro's homeland was the habitat of the animal which in appearance most resembles man. The animal called "orang-outang" by contemporaries (actually the chimpanzee) was native to those parts of western Africa where the early slave trade was heavily concentrated. Though Englishmen were acquainted (for the most part vicariously) with monkeys and baboons, they were unfamiliar with tailless apes who walked about like men. Accordingly, it happened that Englishmen were introduced to the anthropoid apes and to Negroes at the same time and in the same place. The startlingly human appearance and movements of the "ape"—a generic term though often used as a synonym for the "orang-outang"—aroused some curious speculations.

In large measure these speculations derived from traditions which had been accumulating in Western culture since ancient times. Medieval bestiaries contained rosters of strange creatures who in one way or another seemed disturbingly to resemble men. There was the *simia* and the *cynocephali* and the *satyri* and the others, all variously described and related to one another, all jumbled in a characteristic amalgam of ancient reports and medieval mortality. The confusion was not easily or rapidly dispelled, and many of the traditions established by this literature were very much alive during the seventeenth century.

The section on apes in Edward Topsell's *Historie of Foure Footed Beasts* (1607) serves to illustrate how certain seemingly trivial traditions and associations persisted in such form that they were bound to affect the way in which Englishmen would perceive the natives of Africa. Topsell, who built principally upon the work of the great Swiss naturalist Konrad von Gesner (1516-65), was careful to distinguish tailless apes from monkeys. They were to be found in three regions: south of the Caucasus, India, and "Lybia and all that desart Woods betwixt *Egypt, Ethiopia* and *Libia.*" When he came to describe the various types of "apes," however, Topsell was far less definite as to location than as to their general character: above all else, "apes," were venerous. In India, the red apes were "so venerous that they will ravish their Women." Baboons were "as lustful and venerous as goats;" a baboon which had been "brought to the French king . . . above all loved the companie of women and young maidens; his genitall member was greater than might match the quantity of his other parts." Pictures of two varieties of apes, a "Satyre" and an "Egopithecus," graphically emphasized the "virile member."

In addition to stressing the "lustful disposition" of the ape kind, Topsell's compilation contained suggestions concerning the character of simian facial creatures. "Men that have low and flat nostrils," readers were told in the section on apes, "are Libidinous as Apes that attempt women, and having thicke lippes the upper hanging over the neather, they are deemed fools, like the lips of Asses and Apes." This rather explicit association was the persistent connection made between apes and devils. In a not altogether successful attempt to distinguish the "Satyre-apes" from the mythical creatures of that time, Topsell straightened everything out by explaining that it was "probable" that Devils take not any denomination of shape from Satyres, but rather the Apes themselves from Devils whom they resemble, for there are many things common to the Satyre-apes and devilish Satyres." Association of apes and/or satyrs with devils was common in England. James I linked them in his Daemonology (1597). The inner logic of this association derived from uneasiness concerning the ape's "incident likenesse and imitation of man"; it revolved around evil and sexual sin; and, rather tenuously, it connected apes with blackness.

Given this tradition and the coincidence of contact, it was virtually inevitable that Englishmen should discern similarity between the man-like beasts and the beast-like men of Africa. A few commentators went so far as to suggest that Negroes had sprung from the generation of ape-kind or that the apes were themselves the offspring of Negroes and some unknown African beast. These contentions were squarely in line with the ancient tradition that Africa was a land "bringing dailie foorth newe monsters" because, as Aristotle himself had suggested, many different species came into proximity at the scarce watering places. Jean Bodin, the famous sixteenth-century French political theorist, summarized this wisdom of the ages with the categorical remark that "promiscuous coition of men and animals took place, wherefore the regions of Africa produce for us many monsters."

Far more common and persistent was the notion that there sometimes occurred "a beastly copulation or conjecture" between apes and Negroes, and especially that apes were inclined wantonly to attack Negro women. The very explicit idea that apes assaulted female human beings was not new; Negroes were merely being asked to demonstrate what Europeans had known for centuries. Englishmen seemed ready to credit the tales about bestial connections, and even as late as the 1730's a well-traveled, intelligent naval surgeon, John Atkins, was not at all certain that the stories were false: "At some Places the *Negroes* have been suspected of Bestiality with them [apes and monkeys] and by the Boldness and Affection they are known under some Circumstances to express to our Females; the Ignorance and Stupidity on the other side, to guide or control Lust; but more from the near resemblances are sometimes met to the Human Species would tempt one to suspect the Fact."

The sexual association of apes with Negroes had an inner logic which kept it alive without much or even any factual sustenance. Sexual union seemed to prove a certain affinity without going so far as to indicate actual identity—which was what Englishmen really thought was the case. By forging a sexual link between Negroes and apes, furthermore, Englishmen were able to give vent to their feeling that Negroes were lewd, lascivious, and wanton people.[402]

Jordan's and others' accounts provide evidence that White people developed their distorted beliefs about African people based on the imaginative ideas of White adventurers and philosophers. White people projected unregulated deviant ideas and misrepresentations onto Africans.

Today, this condition, White psychopathology, continues to exist in America. Furthermore, White people have disseminated and instilled this sickness into the minds of people of various races and ethnicities, including those of African descent.[402]

White predation. White psychopathic and sociopathic cultural predation.

Formalizing and Learning Whiteness and Blackness in Colonial America

Consider a 1664 law from when Maryland was a colony. As noted in "The Origin of Slavery in the United States—The Maryland Precedent," it was intended to establish the legality of racial slavery while also forbidding English and freeborn women from marrying Black men.[37]

It read:

> *Be it enacted by the Right Honorable the Lord Proprietary by the advise and consent of the upper and lower house of this present Generall Assembly, that all Negroes and other slaves already within the Province And all Negroes and other slaves to be hereafter imported into the Province, shall serve **Durante Vita** [hard labor for life].* [emphasis added][37]

First, it commits Black men to the condition of enslavement without any recourse. The established association of Black men is comparable to that of an enslaved person. And it does not matter whether the person is already within the territory or has come from abroad, or whether the person is enslaved or free. All of that is irrelevant. They are to be enslaved. This is not so for people of Asian, European, Mexican, Cuban, or any other descent as described by this section of the law, who may have arrived there during this period.

In contrast, this law stated that if any of those persons had been free in their country of origin, that they would remain free here. For example, if a Chinese person was free in China and traveled to the Virginia colony, they would remain free. That distinction is critically important, because if someone of African descent, meaning someone considered a Negro, was free in Africa prior to their arrival here, that would not matter. He would be enslaved. Why was that? What was so distinctive about the Black body that it required entirely different standards?

This law goes on to say:

> *And all Children born of any Negro or other slave shall be slaves as their fathers were for the term of their lives And forasmuch as divers freeborn English Women forgetful of their free condition and to the disgrace of our Nation do intermarry with Negro Slaves by which also divers suits may arise touching the Issue of such women and a great damage befalls the Masters of such Negroes **for prevention whereof for deterring such freeborn women from such shameful matches** [emphasis added]. Be it further Enacted by the Authority advice and Consent aforesaid That whatsoever*

freeborn woman shall intermarry with any slave from and after the Last day of this present Assembly shall Serve the master of such slave during the life of her husband And that all the Issue *[children, emphasis added] of such freeborn women so married shall be slaves as their fathers were. And Be it further Enacted that all the Issues [children] of English or other freeborn women that have already married Negroes shall serve the Masters of their Parents till they be Thirty years of age and no longer.*[37]

That is to say, not only did it sanction the immediate enslavement of the Black body as opposed to countless others, but also that it forbade White women from relating to Black men. There was something considered particularly unsettling about such co-mingling.

This can be observed in the tragic story of a White woman by the name of Eleanor Butler, referred to as "Irish Nell" in the literature.[108–111,136,137] As referenced in a *Medium* article entitled "The Forced Breeding Myth in the Irish Slaves Meme" written by Liam Hogan:

In August 1681 Eleanor was married to Charles, one of Boarman's slaves. This ceremony was performed on the plantation grounds by Father Hubbert, a Catholic priest. The wedding was attended by a large crowd of guests and well wishers. According to the 1664 law her punishment was that she would be enslaved alongside her husband, as long as he was alive. But worse than that, their children were to be slaves. From 1749 to 1787 the descendants of this marriage sued for their freedom multiple times on the basis that Eleanor was a white woman. They eventually won and were granted their freedom. The Boarmans were ordered to pay damages. The court depositions (27 May 1767) reveal vital details about this case. It appears that Lord Baltimore tried to prevent the marriage. As the Governor of the colony, he was disturbed that a white Catholic woman would marry a Black slave by choice, and aghast that some members of the elite Catholic ruling class apparently endorsed the marriage.

The lived experiences of Irish Nell and her husband, Charles Butler, are documented further in the Archives of Maryland, as well as several other sources. There is substantial record of the controversy surrounding their marriage. It also highlights the persistent, toxic nature of White supremacy and anti-Black sentiment. Note the role the legal system played. Black people's rights to testify in court were denied. Read the following:

Eleanor Butler, also called "Irish Nell," immigrated to Maryland as a white indentured servant to Charles Calvert, the third Lord Baltimore. She married Charles Butler, a slave of Major William Boarman, around 1681. A 1664 Maryland law required that when a "free borne woman shall inter marry with any slave . . . [she] shall Serve the master of such slave during the life of her husband." Her children would also be slaves. Lord Baltimore warned Nell that "she would . . . enslave herself and her property," but Nell insisted that she would "rather have Charles than have your lordship." Charles and Nell Butler were married in a Catholic ceremony at Major Boarman's home in Charles County. They had seven or eight children—all born after the repeal of the 1664 law. Nell's children included Jack, her oldest son, and her daughters Abigail (Abby), Kate, Moll, Nan, and Jenny. One of the Butler's neighbors, Mrs. Elizabeth Warren, recounted that Jack later escaped from his enslavement, fleeing to southern Virginia, and later purchased his freedom from one of the Boarman family.

In October 1770, Mary and William Butler filed freedom suits. The slaves of Richard Boarman, the Butlers sought their freedom on the basis that their ancestor, Irish Nell, was a white woman. Other alleged descendants filed suits in 1786 and 1787. In 1786, Maryland law accepted the testimony of African Americans in freedom suits. Mary Butler's daughter, also called Mary, won her freedom the following year. Incidentally, in 1793, the testimony of Black people in freedom suits was again prohibited.[36,108–111]

These laws specialized in denying the most basic human rights. White women and Black men had to comply with rules they did not consent to, and which injured them. The deranged, psychopathological obsessiveness surrounding Black men relating to White women is well documented. See the commentary of White men such as Charles Calvert, the third Lord Baltimore of Maryland, who went on record at the time expressing his discontent.

This is indicated in the 1681 law mentioned in Chapter Two (which contained initial use of the word White), that emerged literally one month after the wedding of Irish Nell to Charles Butler. It was enacted in August of 1681, as noted in the book entitled *The Law of Freedom and Bondage in the United States*. Again, it read:

> *Forasmuch as, divers free-born English, or white women, sometimes by the instigation, procurement or connivance, of their masters, mistresses, or dames, and always to the satisfaction of their lascivious and lustful desires,*

and to the disgrace not only of the English, but also of many other christian
nations, do intermarry with negroes and slaves, by which means, divers in-
conveniences, controversies, and suits may arise, touching the issue or chil-
dren, of such free-born women aforesaid; for prevention whereof for the
future, be it further enacted—that if the marriage of such woman-servant
with any slave shall take place by the procurement or permission of the mas-
ter, such woman and her issue shall be free, and enacts a penalty by fine on
the master or mistress and on the person joining the parties in marriage.[29]

Again, this law came about one month only after they married. White males
such as Calvert were displeased and made known their displeasure quickly and
forcefully. Such laws intended to terrorize. White women who dared marry
Black men were to be punished for betraying their race. They deserved to be
enslaved until their filthy husbands passed. Such punishment extended to the
offspring as well. What better way to disincentivize, after all, than to target
children? Children born of Black fathers and White mothers after the passage
of this law were to be sentenced to hereditary slavery for life. This example,
along with John Punch's experience, signify the entrance of legally sanctioned
slavery for life for American Black people.

Some questions to consider are:

√   If you are a Negro man in colonial Maryland between 1664 and
    1669, what is your life like? How would one such person respond
    to being subjugated for life? What is it like, always being at the bot-
    tom of the social totem pole? What do they do as a result of living
    in these conditions?

√   What about English and other freeborn women? How were they
    affected?

√   How incentivized would they be to marry/otherwise engage men
    who are condemned to enslavement and poverty? What options did
    they have? What options did they not have?

√   What passes down to the next generation with respect to cultural
    and psychological and legal norms? How does that differ based on
    sex? On race? How long was it before such structures had become
    normalized?

The next four laws I underscore get passed within the span of one year in Virginia (1667–1668). One has to do with forced religion while another has to do with how Black women were taxed. One has to do with corporal punishment of runaway servants and the other has to do with applying the death penalty to enslaved Black people resisting rape, torture, and other forms of terror.

The first, a Virginia law declaring baptism of slaves does not exempt them from bondage, was established in 1667 and stated:

> *WHEREAS some doubts have risen whether children that are slaves by birth, and by the charity and piety of their owners made pertakers of the blessed sacrament of baptisme, should by vertue of their baptisme be made ffree; It is enacted and declared by this grand assembly, and the authority thereof, that the conferring of baptisme doth not alter the condition of the person as to his bondage or ffreedome; that diverse masters, ffreed from this doubt, may more carefully endeavour the propagation of christianity by permitting children, though slaves, or those of greater growth if capable to be admitted to that sacrament.* [22,38,43,52,123]

Note that at this time, Christianity constituted its own legal category. White men legalized its extension to slaves thinking it would civilize them, caring not one bit for the opinions of those being forced into the faith. In addition, according to the Virginia Muster (March through May 1620), Black people, along with Indians, are noted as "Others not Christian in the service of the English." [22,43]

I am not arguing that zero Black people claimed Christianity as their identity in the North American continent prior to 1667. There are accounts of some who did, as was referenced regarding Elizabeth Key Grinstead. It has also been inferred that Anthony Johnson, a well-known, free Black male who acquired land, owned indentured servants, and enslaved Africans, was also most likely Christian.

What I am saying is that the legal extensions and protections that came along with being a European Christian were not extended to Black Christians. It did nothing to protect or absolve. The main benefit Christian identity conferred ethno-religiously was freedom (to a limited degree). Christians could be indentured, but not enslaved. [20,22]

And so, the significance of the 1667 law to Black and Indigenous people enslaved by White people is that it did not free them. It allowed White masters to baptize them without allowing them to have any say in their futures. It declared yet again that "the conferring of baptisme doth not alter the condition of the person as to his bondage or freedom," and encouraged "diverse masters, ffreed from this doubt" to "more carefully endeavor the propagation of Christianity by permitting children, though slaves, or those of growth if capable, to be admitted to that sacrament."

The law did not afford freedom to enslaved Black people as it did for their European counterparts, of course. One was worthy; the other was not.

It was only meant to control yet another aspect of the Black person's life. It resembles the situation in 15th century Spain, which was being ruled by Queen Isabella and King Ferdinand II of Aragon.

The next law, established in September of 1668, concerned **Negro women not exempted from tax**. It read, in part:

> WHEREAS *some doubts, have arisen whether negro women set free were still to be accompted tithable according to a former act, it is declared by this grand assembly that negro women, though permitted to enjoy their ffreedome yet ought not in all respects to be admitted to a full fruition of the exemptions and impunities of the English, and are still lyable to payment of taxes.*[38,52]

This law, predictably passed by White men, targeted distinctly "freed" Black women, saying they would still have to pay a tithe for their existence, as though they still belonged to a master. While they are granted their freedom and told to "enjoy" it, they are again confined in some respect. They cannot be completely free, like the English, because they are regarded as less than. White freedom did not resemble Black freedom. Another law passed in the same year addressed corporal punishment as a way to discipline servants for running away. It was meant to address the concerns of masters, not slaves, and the reasons why they would want to run away (such as being abused unceasingly). The law stated:

> *Whereas it has been questioned whether servants running away may be punished with corporal punishment by their master or magistrate, since the act already made gives the master satisfaction by prolonging their time by service [1662], it is declared and enacted by this Assembly that moderate corporal punishment inflicted by master or magistrate upon a runaway servant shall not deprive the master of the satisfaction allowed by the law, the*

one being as necessary to reclaim them from persisting in that idle course as
the other is just to repair the damages sustained by the master.[38]

As you can see, masters are awarded even greater power. They can abuse to
maintain order, yes. But also, to dominate entirely. The master was entitled
to exercise authority over his property—mind, body, and soul. That was
what was conveyed most of all with the passage of this legislation. Remember: money was on the line. And the White slave owner wanted it badly.
Whatever he had to do to acquire it was morally acceptable. The more control he exercised over his chattel, the more he would benefit.

We see this today. Whites control a supermajority of the capital flowing
throughout the United States. If they paid even a half a percentage point
more in taxes (which would still be inadequate), they could address many
of the problems plaguing Black America. But that would disturb the White
order, and anything that disturbs the White order is unacceptable.

So Black America continues to suffer silently. They must remain in control economically, psychologically, and in every other way possible. Their
commitment to anti-Blackness is, if nothing else, steadfast no matter the
circumstance. Within the span of a year, it is likely that the White Burgesses,
nearby White plantation owners, and community members heard of reports
that Black people were fighting back. That frightened them.

It is also documented that many Africans from Angola and other African countries who became enslaved seemed to be physically stronger than
their European counterparts. Combine this all with the account that Dr. Joy
DeGruy references in her book *Post Traumatic Slave Syndrome*, which says
that White women were chastising enslaved Black children who they either
owned or who their husbands owned. They murdered them while doing so,
very often. That led to the creation of a 1669 law that read:

> *Whereas the only law in force for the punishment of refractory servants re-*
> *sisting their master, mistress, or overseer cannot be inflicted upon Negroes,*
> *nor the obstinacy of many of them be suppressed by other than violent*
> *means [emphasis added], be it enacted and declared by this Grand Assem-*
> *bly if any slave resists his master (or other by his master's order correcting*
> *him) and by the extremity of the correction should chance to die, that his*
> *death shall not be accounted a felony, but the master (or that other person*
> *appointed by the master to punish him) be acquitted from molestation,*

since it cannot be presumed that premeditated malice (which alone makes murder a felony) should induce any man to destroy his own estate.[38]

The Casual Killing Act of 1669 was the name of this law. It is further proof that no amount of blood was ever enough. Let us examine this further. Whites created a whole separate law for Black people, one that was separate from the law established the year before, in 1668. The potential damage those who were strong willed could do frightened and intimidated them. The punishment directed at them needed to be harsher to break them down completely. This was only directed at Black people. No one else. This law provided that White masters and mistresses (and all White people, Indian or Black, etc.), anyone—as long as they were appointed by a White person to inflict harm—could do just that. Anyone could be deputized to traumatize the Black person. They would face no consequences.

I am thinking about Tyre Nichols, who recently suffered a modern-day lynching at the hands of five Black officers who felt entitled to aggressively approach and attach this innocent young man who was on his way home to his mother and father. He had been taking pictures at a park that evening. He can be seen and heard on video begging the officers for his life. The officers can be seen and heard delighting in his agony, as well as the brutality they were inflicting upon him. I watched this video in total shock, disbelief, and disgust, similarly to the ways in which I experienced the George Floyd video in May 2020. I was traumatized.[357]

The psychopathy and sociopathy are without boundaries.

Characterizing people who did this as anything less is, in itself, another injustice. Calling them by their first names or titles is simply unacceptable. We must label them accurately and truthfully. When we do not name them properly, they appear to be normal. Their actions appear to be normal. They are considered average, regular, well within the confines of decency. No. This must not go on. I am reminded of passages from *Without Sanctuary: Lynching Photography in America*,[98] which read:

> The men and women who tortured, dismembered, and murdered in this fashion understood perfectly well what they were doing and thought of themselves as perfectly normal human beings. Few had any ethical qualms about their actions. This was not the outbursts of crazed men or uncontrolled barbarians but the triumph of a belief system that defined one people as less human than another.

For the men and women who comprised these mobs, as for those who remained silent or indifferent or who provided the scientific scholarly explanations, this was the highest idealism in the service of their race, in preservation of their heritage. One has only to view the self-satisfied expressions on their faces as they posed beneath Black people hanging from a rope or next to the charred remains of a Negro who had been burned to death.

What is most disturbing about these scenes is the discovery that the perpetrators of these crimes were ordinary people, not so different from ourselves—merchants, farmers, laborers, machine operators, teachers, lawyers, doctors, policemen, students; they were family men and women, good, decent church going folk who came to believe that keeping Black people in their place was nothing less than pest control, a way of combating an epidemic or virus that if not checked, would be detrimental to the health and security of the community.[98]

Indeed. These excerpts highlight so very clearly the meaning and privilege of Whiteness. We are talking about more than mere social privilege. We are talking about the ability to murder consequence free. To my brothers George (Floyd),[226] Andrew (Brown Jr.),[227] Daunte (Wright),[228] Ahmaud (Arbery),[229] John (Crawford),[230] Philando (Castile),[231] Michael (Brown),[232] Tamir (Rice),[233] Oscar (Grant),[234] and all the other, unnamed Black males who are and were dehumanized by this culture every day, it is not you. It never could have been you. You stood no chance against a machine whose sole purpose was to rage against you.

At some point, the White psychopathy and sociopathy was going to find you and hunt you down. The anti-Blackness was going to find you and hunt you down. It never could have ended another way. Look to our dear, fourteen-year-old brother, L.D. Nelson (and his mother, Laura Nelson) back in 1911.[98,99] Look at Hayes Turner (and his wife, Mary Turner).[171] Look at George Stinney,[174] at Emmett Till,[236] the Scottsboro Boys,[237] the Groveland Four,[238] the Exonerated 5.[239] Look at all of them and countless others who have been victims of an ongoing holocaust, hundreds of years in the making. It is an inescapable fate.

Figure 4.1.
Abram Smith and Thomas Ship, 1930, Indiana

Figure 4.2.
Rubin Stacy, 1935, Fort Lauderdale, Florida

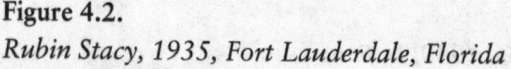

Figure 4.3.
Laura and L.D. Nelson (mother and son), 1911, Oklahoma

Figure 4.4.   **Figure 4.5.**

Figure 4.6.
George Floyd, Minnesota, 2020

Chapter Closing

The examples provided throughout this entire text matter, as they clarify the scale and nature of the horror.

The next chapter will cover an even greater number of examples aimed at supporting the book's thesis. We will focus on the distinctly White need for anti-Black terror and subjugation, aligning with both Harris' and Allen's assessments of Whiteness and their centrality to White identity.[26,125]

Moreover, we will cover how the culture of Whiteness (i.e., White psyche/mentality, White emotionality, White supremacy, White power, White privilege, White superiority, White entitlement, and White extremism, etc.) rests upon a psychopathic and sociopathic foundation, which has been passed down continually, including even today. This way of being has been perpetuated by all European immigrants to some degree, as they have come into and gone out of the Americas for the last five centuries.[14,15,125,151,170]

These patterns have been enmeshed with the culture. They have been adopted by all Americans, who function as robots there to perpetuate the social order. As Ida B. Wells famously said, their role is to "keep the nigger down" no matter the cost.

Chapter Four Review Questions

(Note: Please go to www.danteking.com to complete the chapter assessment and evaluation for the following questions.)

Consider the sociocultural conditions and the law created when answering the following questions:

1. What did White females and males learn about the value of Whiteness?

2. How did these laws shape White identity for White males? White females?

3. What did Black females learn about what it meant to be White and female? White and male? Black and male? Black and female?

4. What did Black males learn about what it meant to be White and male? White and female? Black and female? Black and male?

5. How did these laws shape Black identity?

6. How did these laws create and reinforce pro-White and anti-Black legal, social, political, and cultural orientations in the North American continent generally, but specifically in the United States?

7. What gets lost when we do not carefully scrutinize every bit of our national history?

8. How is it that we have separated past violence from current violence? And why is it?

9. How is the role of anti-Blackness different from that of White supremacy/power/superiority?

10. How do White people's creation and control over the law prevent them from ever being held to account?

11. How can Black people escape the notion of "criminality" when the construct was built specifically to encapsulate us and only us?

12. Who are the real criminals?

13. Why is it dangerous to minimize the horror of past events? Who does this minimization impact worst? Who benefits?

14. How is the law constructed to benefit Whites? How is it constructed to hurt Black people?

15. How does the reality of debasing Black people, relegating us into the most inhuman and profane position in American culture, influence, inform, shape, and develop White American psychological and sociological constructs about who Black people are (i.e., values, principles, behavior, etc.) and what they represent?

16. In what ways do these White psychological and sociological developments shape White identity, in terms of who they believe themselves to be and what they represent as a community and culture?

17. How does White projection, the foundation of both the psychological and sociological developments of American culture, influence and shape the psychology and sociology that Black people and people of color accept about Black people, White people, and all others along the racial spectrum?

18. In what ways does Dr. Poussaint's framing of Whiteness as racial politics and White racism as "mental illness," along with Dr. Bobby Wright's assertion of White psychopathy, help us to further understand the functionality of perpetual White perversions, distortions, and projections White people hold about themselves as superior, juxtaposed against fabricated anti-Black cultural narratives about "who" Black people are, as well as "what" Blackness represents in America?

19. In what ways does Dr. Poussaint's framing of Whiteness as racial politics and White racism as "mental illness," along with Dr. Bobby Wright's assertion of White psychopathy, help us to further understand the deeper legacy impacts of White supremacy and anti- Blackness and their impacts on the American cultural psychology, which includes White and all assimilated peoples on White American soil?

20. What role does the lack or absence of impression management, as well as the absence of impulse control, play in the impressions and interpretations of Black people's daily behaviors, attitudes, and actions in America?

21. In what ways does Dr. Wright's framing help us to further understand the politics and functionalities of Whiteness and anti-Blackness in America?

22. In what ways does Dr. Wright's framing help us to further understand the need for White American culture to have and perpetually maintain Black American Descendants of Enslaved Peoples (sometimes referred to as ADOS/ADOEP) as an affixed permanent underclass?

23. In what ways does Dr. Wright's framing help us to further understand the necessity of racial politics in America, specifically, Whiteness and anti-Blackness, the infinite "brand-value" of Whiteness, and the brand "valuelessness" of Blackness in America?

The Emergence of Black Rage, Anger, and Violence as the Result of White Psychopathic and Sociopathic Terror

I WANT TO BEGIN this chapter by stating the obvious: I do not care about the feelings or criticisms of Whites or people who present themselves as White. Those who ignore facts do not get my attention. Nothing they say or do to thwart me as I educate the public will work, because I am bolstered by demonstrable proof. Even if I am murdered for my work, it will persist. That is why I have written my thoughts down. Bodies perish, words do not. Some quotes by the late, great James Baldwin, which resonate with me deeply, are:

> We can disagree and still love each other unless your disagreement is rooted in my oppression and denial of my humanity and right to exist.
>
> I can't believe what you say, because I see what you do.
>
> To be African American is to be African without any memory and American without any privilege.
>
> I'm not interested in anyone's guilt. Guilt is a luxury that we can no longer afford. I know you didn't do it, and I didn't do it either, but I am responsible for it because I am a man and a citizen of this country and you are responsible for it, for the very same reason.[112]

A Moment of Reflection

I remember teaching a seminar at a hospital when an elderly, White, Jewish woman raised her hand to ask me a question. I could tell she was eager to learn, as she engaged genuinely. She said:

You know Dante, as a Jewish person and as a young Jewish child, we always learned about the Hitler era and what the Germans did to the Jews. I cannot explain how horrendous and painful that experience has been and still is to so many Jewish people. And until now, I have held that experience up as the ultimate dehumanizing experience that people have gone through. And what I am about to say is not to reduce my regard for what my people went through, but to share how I am feeling and the way I am understanding this entire experience we have gone through together and all the information you have shared. There is really no comparison between the experience that Jewish people faced during the Holocaust, and what African Americans have faced, and are still dealing with. The Holocaust was a period that lasted less than 15 years. This, all that you have presented here, and the things that White people have done to Black people, this has continued to go on for more than 500 years, and it almost seems like an obsession White people have about oppressing Black people. It's like we have a need to oppress you. This is absolutely scary.[113]

This woman happened to be a chaplain at that hospital. Her commentary resonated with me and others in the group. She made it a point to understand. Additionally, I am not sure if I had considered anti-Blackness and White supremacy as compulsory obsessions before then. I opened her eyes, and she opened mine. Ideally, that is how this process is supposed to work. We are supposed to enrich one another.

Simply put, laws shape culture. They control movement, interaction, education, and so much more. We must, therefore, study them closely. They will tell us a great deal about the people who passed them and were injured by them. Building upon the Casual Killing Act of 1669, which directly provided absolution to White people and those designated by White people to murder Black people, I will provide more proof of my point.

In 1672, An Act for the Apprehension and Suppression of Runawayes, Negroes, and Slaves passed. It speaks to Black (some Indigenous and White) people rebelling. We know this based on several laws that passed between 1662 and 1680, as well as several well-documented events (i.e., Gloucester County Virginia 1663; Bacon's Rebellion 1675-76; Westmoreland Riots 1687).

It stated the following:

FORASMUCH *as it hath beene manifested to this grand assembly that many <u>negroes</u> have lately beene, and now are out in rebellion in sundry parts of this country, and <u>that noe meanes have yet beene found for the apprehension and suppression of them from whome many mischeifes of very dangerous consequence may arise to the country if either other negroes, Indians or servants should happen to fly forth and joyne with them; For the prevention of which,</u> be it enacted by the governour, councell and burgesses of this grand assembly, and by the authority thereof, that if any negroe, molatto, Indian slave or servant for life, runaway and shalbe persued by the warrant or hue and crye, <u>it shall and may be lawfull for any person who shall endeavour to take them, upon the resistance of such negroe, molatto, Indian slave, or servant for life, to kill or wound him or them soe resisting;</u> Provided alwayes, and it is the true intent and meaning hereof, that such negroe, molatto, Indian slave, or servant for life, be named and described in the hue and crye which is alsoe to be signed by the master or owner of the said runaway. And if it happen that such negroe, molatto, Indian slave, or servant for life doe dye of any wound in such their resistance received the master or owner of such shall receive satisfaction from the publique for his negroe, molatto, Indian slave, or servant for life, soe killed or dyeing of such wounds; <u>and the person who shall kill or wound by virtue of any such hugh and crye any such soe resisting in manner as aforesaid shall not be questioned for the same,</u> he forthwith giveing notice thereof and returning the hue and crye or warrant to the master or owner of him or them soe killed or wounded or to the next justice of peace. And it is further enacted by the authority aforesaid that all such <u>negroes and slaves shalbe valued at ffowre thousand five hundred pounds of tobacco and caske a peece, and Indians at three thousand pounds of tobacco and caske a peece. And further if it shall happen that any negroe, molatto, Indians slave or servant for life, in such their resistance to receive any wound whereof they may not happen to dye, but shall lye any considerable tyme sick and disabled, then alsoe the master or owner of the same soe sick or disabled shall receive from the publique a reasonable satisfaction for such damages as they shall make appeare they have susteyned thereby at the county court, who shall thereupon grant the master or owner a certificate to the next assembly of what damages they shall make appeare; And it is further enacted that the neighbouring Indians doe and hereby are required and enjoyned to seize and apprehend all runawayes whatsoever that shall happen to come amongst</u>*

them, and to bring them before some justice of the peace whoe upon the
receipt of such servants, slave, or slaves, from the Indians, shall pay unto
the said Indians for a recompence twenty armes length of Roanoake or the
value thereof in goods as the Indians shall like of, for which the said justice
of peace shall receive from the publique two hundred and fifty pounds of
tobacco, and the said justice to proceed in conveying the runaway to his
master according to the law in such cases already provided; This act to
continue in force till the next assembly and noe longer unlesse it be thought
fitt to continue. [38] [emphasis added]

Like so many others, the law is specifically targeted. It was meant to address the "Black problem," which, itself, is highly inflammatory. It identified three classes of Black people. They were the Negro, the molotto, and
the servants for life. Like the Casual Killing Act, it reinforced what became
White culture, psychopathy, and sociopathy. It sanctioned murder, so long
as the victim's skin color was not White. All Brown people (meaning Black,
mulatto, and Indian) were fair game.

The law goes one step farther than the one from 1669. It provides that
White owners are to be compensated by public monies for their property
loss, thereby further incentivizing mass murder. If these individuals "just so
happen to be" murdered, no monetary loss would occur. It resembled the
earlier 1662 Runaway Law in that sense. That stated that a Black human
life was worth 4,500 lbs. of tobacco and caske (Indians were worth 3,000
lbs., incidentally). Ask yourself who it made more sense to murder.

Laws created by Whites were to be interpreted favorably by Whites,
whenever and however Whites desired. Any absurdity was sanctioned, so
long as it benefited the White person.

Again, anti-Blackness in North America, particularly the United States,
is a White American legal, social, cultural, economic, value, and belief system. It involves and thrives on the de-prioritization of humans perceived
and labeled as Black people. It also includes the criminalization, hyper-negativity, hyper-scrutiny, and pessimistic positioning of Black people and/or
Blackness throughout all aspects of American society and life, for the purposes of justifying and rationalizing political, social, cultural, economic debasement and inhumane treatment—ultimately genocide.

Anti-Blackness involves:

√   The criminalization, hyper-negativity, and hyper-scrutiny of Blackness—legally, socially, principally, culturally, sociologically, economically, and so forth.

√   The criminalization of Blackness in the legal system was perpetrated through the enactment of explicit laws and policies during the seventeenth, eighteenth, nineteenth, and twentieth centuries. These laws specifically targeted Black and Brown people of African descent. They were based on skin color as "prima facie evidence" of something gone horribly wrong. Some examples include Virginia Laws of 1669, 1680, 1705, 1723, the Negro Act of 1740, the Casual Killing Acts, the Fugitive Slave Act of 1850, the Supreme Court decisions of 1883, 1896, and 1926, the New Deal, the G.I. Bill, and the Fair Deal. Many more abound.

√   Unfavorable legal, cultural, social, and economic institutions and constructs.

√   Sociological, psychological, and emotional institutions and constructs.

√   A persisting condition and institution developed through collective European/White (i.e., Portuguese, English, French, Dutch, Spanish, Irish, British) colonialist, imperialist ideas, and beliefs.

√   The core of Whiteness, White ideals, and ideologies, which state that Black and Brown people of African descent are inferior, animalistic, and barbaric (i.e., African, African-European, Afro-Latinx, African Haitian, etc.).

√   The foundational principle of racism and core underpinnings of Whiteness, White racism, and White identity.

√   The construct was established to demean, oppress, disenfranchise, dehumanize, invalidate, surveil, murder and otherwise harm anyone interpreted or perceived as Black.

√   The condition meant to destroy Black people emotionally, physically, symbolically, and spiritually. This was accomplished through political, legal, educational, economic, religious, social, and all other institutional means.

√   The core of White morality.

√   The consistently, inescapably negative orientation toward and association of people defined, perceived, and/or interpreted as Black.

√   The tendency toward adapting to and adopting White-Eurocentric culture as normative and/or the standard by which all things are defined and measured. It is also reflexively anti-Black. Some examples include:

°   Identifying with success and better circumstances due to White economic systems, including capitalism.

°   Feeling validated by White-Eurocentric standards of attractiveness (i.e., straight hair, thinness, proximity to White skin/lighter skin, etc.).

°   Speaking English according to White-Eurocentric normative, educational, and socio-cultural standards and implicitly belittling and/or judging Black people who do not conform to such standards. Such judgments always find fault. They assume everything outside of the White norm is less than.

°   Celebrating White academic institutions as the best institutions, regardless of their historical records and perpetual policies of exclusion and harm toward Black people.

°   Blaming Black people for their individual circumstances, rather than understanding the magnitude of White governmental, economic, and legal forms of institutional, social, and cultural control.

Consider the following:

√   What must it be like, knowing you can be murdered at any time and for any reason, without any consequence at all? Could it be that such knowledge could foster a justified sense of resentment?

√   What cultural values develop and dominate when Whites are allowed to get away with (quite literally) bloody murder, free of any punishment?

√   What is the impact on the White psyche and the Black psyche, knowing Whites can act as they wish?

√   Is operating in a consequence-free environment normal? If so,
    name a scenario where Black persons are allowed this freedom.
    What is normalcy? Who is in charge of defining the term? What
    do you think the cultural impacts will be to White immigrants in
    the coming years? In what ways, if any, have your ancestors bene-
    fited? In what ways, if any, do you still benefit today?

I also want to clarify that while the law does name Indians, specifically, that
it appears as though darker-skinned and/or brown-skinned Indians constituted the majority of the groups of people targeted by Whites. This was
the typical practice when determining how certain Indian tribes would be
engaged violently by European-Whites. While this is not conclusive per se,
one example that reinforces this point is the 1740 Negro Law of South Carolina. In Chapter One of the Negro Law of South Carolina, the first section
entitled, "The Status of the Negro, his Rights and Disabilities," it stated:

> The Act of 1740, sec 1 declares all negroes and Indians, (free Indians in
> amity with this Government, negroes, mulattoes, and mestizos, who are
> now free excepted), to be slaves; the offspring to follow the condition of the
> mother, and that such slaves are chattels personal.[116-119]

Section 2 stated:

> Under this provision, it has been uniformly held, that color is prima facie
> evidence, that the party bearing the color of a Negro, mulatto, or mestizo,
> is a slave; but the same prima facie result does not follow from the Indian
> color.[116-119]

Figure 5.1.

NEGRO LAW OF SOUTH CAROLINA.

CHAPTER I.

The Status of the Negro, his Rights and Disabilities.

SECTION 1. The Act of 1740, sec. 1, declares all negroes and Indians, (free Indians in amity with this Government, negroes, mulattoes and mestizoes, who now are free, excepted) to be slaves:— the offspring to follow the condition of the mother: and that such slaves are chattels personal.

P. L. 163. 2 Stat. 397.

SEC. 2. Under this provision it has been uniformly held, that color is prima facie evidence, that the party bearing the color of a negro, mulatto or mestizo, is a slave: but the same prima facie result does not follow from the Indian color.

The State vs. Harden, (note.) 2 Speer's, 152. Nelson vs Whitmore, 1 Rich'n, 321.

SEC. 3. Indians, and descendants of Indians are regarded as free Indians, in amity with this government, until the contrary be shown. In the second proviso of sec. 1, of the Act of 1740, it is declared that "every negro, Indian, mulatto and mestizo is a slave unless the contrary can be made to appear"—yet, in the same it is immediately thereafter provided—"the Indians in amity with this government, excepted, in which case the burden of proof shall lie on the defendant," that is, on the person claiming the Indian plaintiff to be a slave. This latter clause of the proviso is now regarded as furnishing the rule. The race of slave Indians, or of Indians not in amity to this government, (the State,) is extinct, and hence the previous part of the proviso has no application.

Miller vs. Dawson & Brown, Dudley's Rep. 174. State vs. Belmont, decided in Charleston, Jan, 1845. P. L. 163. 2 Stat. 398.

SEC. 4. The term negro is confined to slave Africans, (the ancient Berbers) and their descendants. It does not embrace the free inhabitants of Africa, such as the Egyptians, Moors, or the negro Asiatics, such as the Lascars.

Gibbon's Egypt. Exparte Ferrett and others, 1 Con. Rep. by Mill. 194. The State vs. Scott, 1 Bail. 273. State vs. Hayes, 1 Bail. 275.

SEC. 5. Mulatto is the issue of the white and the negro.

SEC. 6. When the mulatto ceases, and a party bearing some slight taint of the African blood, ranks as white, is a question for the solution of a Jury.

The State vs. Scott, 1 Bail. 271. The State vs. Davis & Hanna, 2 Bail 558. The State vs. Cantey, 2 Hill, 615.

Unquestionably, we see that color is the main object of White concern. Before, during, and after this time, Blackness/Brownness, etc. was criminalized. Indians closer in color to Whites were more likely to be exempt from being enslaved, irrespective of having Indian blood running through their veins. Color mattered above all else.

How does this compare to today's racist American culture? What parallels are there?

What the 1672 law clarifies is that Black people out in sundry parts of the country posed no profound threat. That did not matter, however, because White paranoia made them out to. The need for White domination, the insatiable White appetite for monetary wealth, and all the psychopathy and sociopathy made something out of nothing.

Albert Cleage spoke about this during his 1971 appearance on *The Black Journal*. The episode was entitled "A Black Paper on White Racism." Cleage stated:

I think we must understand that there's no such thing as objective truth, that White people use the institutions to accomplish White purpose. The White purpose is to maintain a power position and keep everybody else in a powerless, subordinate type of position. That's the institutions' purpose. That is the way it functions and how it functions, and we have to realize that everything that schools teach is designed to fit into that purpose. The schools teach, not objective truth but what the White man wants to project as truth. {For example} Sociology. Sociology is not a science in the sense that it is dealing objectively with the way people live together. It's dealing with the White man's pattern of living together as the norm by which we judge how other people live. If you live like White people live, then you are living the way that you are supposed to live. If not, you're either primitive or insane as a people. Psychologically, it's the same thing. Psychology as applied, lacks an objective discussion or analysis of the development of community living or organizing to optimize function. Rather psychology as applied, begins with the presumption that the way Whites function and organize communities and live, is civilized, and the standard against which to measure society and all elements regardless of multicultural origins, affinities, or adaptation to geographic conditions. If the White man does it this way, then this is the norm by which we judge all other people. If the White man is violent, then actually all other people have to be violent in order to be normal. If you're not violent, then obviously there's something wrong with you and you should be in an insane asylum. The whole pattern that is set-up as a norm for human behavior by psychologists, and everyone that is dealing with it, is dealing with it from a White point of view. And so, the schools teach Black children and White children to look through White eyes. From kindergarten on, the Black child is being taught to look at the world and interpret it through White eyes. Everything he is, is wrong. Everything that exists in his community is wrong. And we ought to declare that White music is really no good, that White psychology is no good. The White man either acts like we do, or he's insane. White sociology is no good. The very structure of White society indicates that White people in social structure are obviously insane or they're abnormal. So, we must project then, a Black psychology, a Black sociology, a Black music, a Black history . . . that takes in the realities, and that is essentially sound as opposed to the mythology that the White man has developed out of his own ignorance, out of his own non-creativity.[81]

This is Black truth, and it is White truth.

Chapter Five Review Questions:

(Note: Please go to www.danteking.com to complete the chapter assessment and evaluation for the following questions.)

Considering the sociocultural context at hand:

1. What did White females and males learn about the value of Whiteness?

2. How did these laws shape White identity for White males? White females?

3. What did Black females learn about what it meant to be White and female? White and male? Black and male? Black and female?

4. What did Black males learn about what it meant to be White and male? White and female? Black and female? Black and male?

5. How did these laws shape Black identity?

6. How did these laws create and reinforce pro-White and anti-Black legal, social, political, and cultural orientations in all of the North American continent, but particularly in the United States?

7. Who benefits when we do not adequately scrutinize our past? Who gets further wounded?

8. How and why have we disconnected past violence against Black persons from current violence aimed at Black persons?

9. How is the role of anti-Blackness different from that of White supremacy/power/superiority?

10. How did White people's creation of and control over the legal system enable their terrorism?

11. How can Black people escape the idea of "criminality" when it was conjured up just for us?

12. Who are the real criminals? Are they free? If so, why?

13. Why is it dangerous to minimize the harm Black and Indigenous persons have suffered at the hands of Whites?

14. How is the legal system built to favor Whites, no matter the heinousness of their offenses?

15. How is the legal system built to disfavor Black persons, no matter the degree of innocence and victimization?

16. How does the reality of debasing Black people, relegating us into the most inhuman and profane position in American culture, influence, inform, shape, and develop White American psychological and sociological constructs about who Black people are (i.e., values, principles, behavior, etc.) and what they represent?

17. In what ways do these White psychological and sociological developments shape White identity, in terms of who they believe themselves to be and what they represent as a community and culture?

18. How does White projection, the foundation of both the psychological and sociological developments of American culture, influence and shape the psychology and sociology that Black people and people of color accept about Black people, White people, and all others along the racial spectrum?

19. In what ways does Dr. Poussaint's framing of Whiteness as racial politics and White racism as "mental illness," along with Dr. Bobby Wright's assertion of White psychopathy, help us to further understand the deeper legacy impacts of White supremacy and anti-Blackness and their impacts on the American cultural psychology, which includes White and all assimilated peoples on White American soil?

20. In what ways does Dr. Poussaint's framing of Whiteness as racial politics and White racism as "mental illness," along with Dr. Bobby Wright's assertion of White psychopathy, help us to further

understand the functionality of perpetual White perversions, distortions, and projections White people hold about themselves as superior, juxtaposed against fabricated anti-Black cultural narratives about "who" Black people are, as well as "what" Blackness represents in America?

21. What role does the lack or absence of impression management, as well as the absence of impulse control, play in the impressions and interpretations of Black people's daily behaviors, attitudes, and actions in America?

22. In what ways does Dr. Wright's framing help us to further understand the politics and functionalities of Whiteness and anti-Blackness in America?

23. In what ways does Dr. Wright's framing help us to further understand the need for White American culture to have and perpetually maintain Black American Descendants of Enslaved Peoples (sometimes referred to as ADOS/ADOEP) as an affixed permanent underclass?

24. In what ways does Dr. Wright's framing help us to further understand the necessity of racial politics in America, specifically, Whiteness and anti-Blackness, the infinite "brand-value" of Whiteness, and the brand "valuelessness" of Blackness in America?

White America's Ongoing Practices of Legal, Judicial, and Cultural Anti-Black Terrorism

IN THIS CHAPTER, I focus on mounting Black rage. How do Black persons deal with such immense anger at those who have hurt us so deeply and unapologetically? I also focus on Black liberation and empowerment, as they can pave the way forward. We must not forget why the needs for liberation and empowerment exist in the first place. They originate from a place of deprivation.

This excerpt, from W.E.B. DuBois, resonates. It is from *Black Reconstruction in America* and reads:

> It is true that Negro slaves in America represented the worst and lowest conditions amongst modern laborers. They represented in a real sense the ultimate degradation of man. No matter how degraded the [White] factory hand, he is not real estate. The tragedy of the Black slave was precisely this: His absolute subjection to the individual will of an owner, and to the cruelty and injustice which are the invariable consequences of the exercise of irresponsible power; especially where authority must be sometimes delegated by the planter to agents of inferior education and coarser feelings. The proof of this lies clearly written in the slave codes. Slaves were not considered men. They had no right of petition. They were divisible like

any other chattel. They could own nothing. They could make no contracts. They could hold no property or traffic in property. They could not hire out. They could not legally marry nor constitute families. They could not control their children. They could not appeal to their master. They could be punished at will. They could not testify in court. They could be imprisoned by their owners and the criminal offense of assault and battery could not be committed on the person of a slave. The willful, malicious, and deliberate murder of a slave was punishable by death, but such a crime was practically impossible of proof. The slave owed to his master, and all his family, a respect without bounds, and an absolute obedience. His [the master's] authority could be transmitted to others. A slave could not sue his master; had no right of redemption; no rights to education, or religion. A promise made to a slave by his master had no force nor validity. Children followed the condition of the slave mother. The slave could have no access to the judiciary. A slave might be condemned to death for striking any White person. Looking at these accounts, it is safe to say that the law regards a negro slave, so far as his civil status is concerned, purely and absolutely property; to be bought and sold and passed and descend as a tract of land.[42]

Though DuBois' book was released almost a century ago, his words remain entirely relevant. He knew there was no such thing as true education in the United States, and he knew why. He knew the danger it posed to the status quo. He knew how anti-Blackness resulted in the enslavement of Black people, and how that evolved into Jim Crow, and the lingering effects Black persons still feel today as a direct result.

Whites have designed academic institutions, the same institutions we are supposed to revere, to dehumanize Black people. They exist to perpetuate White power and abort Black power. They are a key component in the master plan aimed at destroying the Black person entirely. All of this is to say the American educational system must be disrupted. To leave such prominent institutions unchallenged is to surrender to White psychopathy and sociopathy. Surrender is unacceptable.

Whiteness and anti-Blackness deserve to be put on trial for all to see. If they are not, nothing will improve. Black persons will continue to lose wealth, standing, and yes, even their own lives. That is why scrutiny is so urgent. Each day that passes without White psychopathy and sociopathy being put on trial is another when Whites can act without fear of consequence for destroying Black lives.

To do this, we must confront untruths with truths. Where we find dehumanization, we must humanize. Where we hear unnerving silence, we must scream. Where we see ignorance, we must educate. For every injury we find, we must apply a balm.

Let us not forget who the psychopaths are. They are persons suffering from a chronic mental disorder marked by abnormal and/or violent social behavior. The psychopath is dangerous. The psychopath must be contained, confronted, and punished. We must acknowledge that our history is filled with psychopaths as leaders, elected and otherwise. We must understand what animates them. Then and only then will we understand who they really are and what their goals for us are. If we do not make a conscientious effort to understand what drives them, we will continue to be victimized by them.

The work overwhelms but is worthwhile.

We must pass an anti-lynching bill. We must ensure George Floyd did not die for nothing. And we must be intelligent about how we craft this legislation, as Whites will always find a way to upend laws they view unfavorable to them. I am reminded of Hamilton and Ture, who in 1967 stated:

> If we do not learn from history, we are doomed to repeat it, and that is precisely the lesson of the Reconstruction era. Black people were allowed to register to vote and to participate in politics, because it was to the advantage of powerful white allies to permit this. But at all times, such advances flowed from white decisions. That era of Black participation in politics was ended by another set of white decisions.
>
> There was no powerful, independent political base in the southern Black community to challenge the curtailment of political rights. At this point in the struggle, Black people have no assurance – [except for] a kind of idiot optimism and faith in a society whose history is one of racism – that if it became necessary, even the painfully limited gains thrown to the civil rights movement by Congress would [be] revoked as soon as a shift in political sentiments occurs (a vivid example of this emerged in 1967 with Congressional moves to undercut and eviscerate the school desegregation provisions of the 1964 Civil Rights Act).[3]

Continuing the Reveal of White Culture
and Psychopathy in Colonial America

Looking at our history with eyes wide open allows us to finally begin accounting for the injustice. It will allow us to fight for our own interests and, in the process, lift up all others unjustly persecuted as well. This work is moral, necessary, and urgent.

The next law is from 1680. It is **An Act Preventing Negro Insurrections.** This act provided the following:

> WHEREAS *the frequent meeting of considerable numbers of negroe slaves under pretence of feasts and burialls is judged of dangerous consequence; for prevention whereof for the future, Bee it enacted by the kings most excellent majestie by and with the consent of the generall assembly, and it is hereby enacted by the authority aforesaid, that from and after the publication of this law, it shall not be lawfull for any negroe or other slave to carry or arme himselfe with any club, staffe, gunn, sword or any other weapon of defence or offence, nor to goe or depart from his masters ground without a* <u>certificate from his master, mistris or overseer,</u> *and such permission not to be granted but upon perticuler and necessary occasions; And* <u>every negroe or slave</u> *soe offending not haveing a certificate as aforesaid shalbe sent to the next constable, who is hereby enjoyned and required to* <u>give the said negroe twenty lashes on his bare back</u> *well layd on, and soe sent home to his said master, mistris or overseer. And it is further enacted by the authority aforesaid that if any negroe or other slave shall presume or lift his hand in opposition against any* <u>christian,</u> *shall for every such offence, upon due proofe made thereof by the* <u>oath</u> *of the party before a magistrate, have and* <u>receive thirty lashes on his bare back</u> *well laid on. And it is hereby further enacted by the authority aforesaid that if any negroe or other slave shall absent himself from his masters service and lye hid and lurking in obscure places, comitting injuries to the inhabitants, and shall resist any person or persons that shalby any lawfull authority be imployed to apprehend and take the said negroe, that then in case of such resistance, it shalbe lawfull for such person or persons to kill the said negroe or slave soe lying out and resisting, and that this law be once every sixmonths published at the respective county courts and parish churches within this colony* [emphasis added].[38]

An embellished version of this law was developed by White Christians roughly 11 years later. Then, the law combined elements of the 1672 law, An Act for the Apprehension and Suppression of Negroes, Runawayes, and Other Slaves, as well as the 1680 law, An Act to Prevent Negro Insurrections.

This version, enacted in 1691, stated:

WHEREAS many times negroes, mulattoes, and other slaves unlawfully absent themselves from their masters and mistresses service, and lie hid and lurk in obscure places killing hoggs and committing other injuries to the inhabitants of this dominion, for remedy whereof for the future, Be it enacted by their majesties lieutenant governour, councell and burgesses of this present general assembly, and the authoritie thereof, and it is hereby enacted, that in all such cases upon intelligence of any such negroes, mulattoes, or other slaves lying out, two of their majesties justices of the peace of that county, whereof one to be of the quorum, where such negroes, mulattoes or other slave shall be, shall be impowered and commanded, and are hereby impowered and commanded to issue out their warrants directed to the sherrife of the same county to apprehend such negroes, mulattoes, and other slaves, which said sherriffe is hereby likewise required upon all such occasions to raise such and soe many forces from time to time as he shall think convenient and necessary for the effectual apprehending such negroes, mulattoes and other slaves, and in case any negroes, mulattoes or other slaves or slaves lying out as aforesaid shall resist, runaway, or refuse to deliver and surrender him or themselves to any person or persons that shall be by lawfull authority employed to apprehend and take such negroes, mulattoes or other slaves that in such cases it shall and may be lawfull for such person and persons to kill and distroy such negroes, mulattoes, and other slave or slaves by gunn or any otherwaise whatsoever.

Provided that where any negroe or mulattoe slave or slaves shall be killed in pursuance of this act, the owner or owners of such negro or mulatto slave shall be paid for such negro or mulatto slave four thousand pounds of tobacco by the publique. And for prevention of that abominable mixture and spurious issue which hereafter may encrease in this dominion, as well by negroes, mulattoes, and Indians intermarrying with English, or other white women, as by their unlawfull accompanying with one another, Be it enacted by the authoritie aforesaid, and it is hereby enacted, that for the time to come, whatsoever English or other white man or woman being free shall intermarry with a negroe, mulatto, or Indian man or woman bond or free shall within three months after such marriage be banished and removed from this dominion forever, and that the justices of each respective countie within this dominion make it their perticular care that this act be put in effectuall execution. And be it further enacted by the authoritie aforesaid, and it is hereby enacted, That if any English woman being free shall have a bastard child by any negro or mulatto, she pay the sume of fifteen pounds sterling, within one moneth after such bastard child be born, to the Church wardens of the parish where she shall be delivered of such child, and in default of such payment she shall be taken into the possession of the said Church wardens and disposed of for five yeares, and the said fine of fifteen pounds, or whatever the woman shall be disposed of for, shall be paid, one third part to their majesties for and towards the support of the government and the contingent charges thereof, and one other third part to the use of the parish where the offence is committed, and the other third part to the informer, and that such bastard child be bound out as a servant by the said Church wardens untill he or she shall attaine the age of thirty yeares, and in case such English woman that shall have such bastard child be a servant, she shall be sold by the said church wardens, (after her time is expired that she ought by law to serve her master) for five yeares, and the money she shall be sold for divided as is before appointed, and the child to serve as aforesaid.

And forasmuch as great inconveniences may happen to this country by the setting of negroes and mulattoes free, by their either entertaining negro slaves from their masters service, or receiveing stolen goods, or being grown old bringing a charge upon the country; for prevention thereof, Be it enacted by the authority aforesaid, and it is hereby enacted, That no negro or mulatto be after the end of this present session of assembly set free by any person or persons whatsoever, unless such person or persons, their heires, executors or administrators pay for the transportation of such negro or negroes out of the countrey within six moneths after such setting them free, upon penalty of paying of tenn pounds sterling to the Church wardens of the parish where such person shall dwell with, which money, or so much thereof as shall be necessary, the said Church wardens are to cause the said negro or mulatto to be transported out of the countrey, and the remainder of the said money to imploy to the use of the poor of the parish.[38,122]

Because of the continued resistance of free Black people who were still enslaved during this period and beyond, Whites decided that they needed to control every move of Black people. This law provided that Black people were not able to gather for funerals, eat together, or move about without the permission of White people, without showing a certificate verifying that they were supposed to be in that space.

If Black people were not able to present such verification, they were legally subjected to twenty lashes on their bare backs. This law also provided that if a White person claimed a Black person attempted to defend themselves against them by raising their hands toward them, the Black person would be subjected to thirty lashes on his or her bare back. The White person's accounting of events was always believed; no confirmation or proof was ever needed.

Think of the moral absurdity of it all. Consider the extent of the psychopathy and sociopathy. Think of the extent of the perversity.

If, for example, a Black person tried to prevent a rape, either of their own person or child or anyone else, the White aggressor, the person who initiated the crime, would be entitled to lash them thirty times. Resistance, which is a human condition related to survival, was met with legalized terror. Can there be any question pertaining to who was mentally challenged?[125,126]

In *Psychology of Terrorism*, Randy Borum stated:

> The transition into becoming a terrorist is rarely sudden and abrupt. What we know of actual terrorists suggests that there is rarely a conscious decision made to become a terrorist. Most involvement in terrorism results from gradual exposure and socialisation towards extreme behavior.[125]

The law also provided that if Black people took even slightly more severe actions to resist White terror, that they could be legally executed. Any opportunity to turn a living Black body into a mutilated and/or dead Black body was appealing. Rape and murder are White people's longest lasting legacies concerning Black people. It is inescapable, as it permeated every interaction they had.

It is no coincidence that Black men are a staggering twenty-one times more likely to be murdered in a police encounter than their White counterparts. Why do we have racism in America? Because racism, pro-Whiteness, and anti-Blackness defines America. To be American is to be forced to assimilate into Whiteness and resent most, if not all, things associated with African Americans.

It makes me wonder about the ancestors of Amy Cooper, Barbeque Becky, George Zimmerman, and profiles of White people in pop culture that are referred to as "Karens" and "Toms" to indicate a tendency to complain. These White Karens and Toms are obsessed with policing Black bodies. They threaten to call security. They lie. They become hysterical on cue, lying about some harm they never sustained.

Is it genetic?

The CDC website reads, in part:

> Your genes play an important role in your health, but so do your behaviors
> and environment, such as what you eat and how physically active you are.
> Epigenetics is the study of how your behaviors and environment can cause
> changes that affect the way your genes work. Unlike genetic changes, epi-
> genetic changes are reversible and do not change your DNA sequence, but
> they can change how your body reads a DNA sequence.[118]

These current examples make me wonder. Where did these people inherit
these tendencies? Where did they develop the desire to surveil, to hound,
to degrade any Black body anywhere near them? Perhaps Sandra Bland,
Ahmaud Arbery, Tamir Rice, John Crawford, Walter Scott, Breonna Taylor,
Trayvon Martin, Michael Brown, and so many others were all victims of an
inheritance on the part of Whites.

At this point, given the direct historical line I have drawn, if one cannot
see psychopathy and sociopathy, then one does not want to see, and for that
person, I feel profound shame. The unwillingness to see, given all this evidence, is proof of a moral deficit that is likely too substantial to overcome.

And why have Whites long been so preoccupied with sex between the
races? Why do they perceive it as filthy and something that must be stopped?
Take, for example, the 1681 case of White Mary Williamson, and William,
an enslaved negro male who belonged to William Basnett Squire. This case
occurred in the Virginia colony. Mary and William had an encounter that
ended up being tried in a courtroom. Despite her pursuit of him, the courts
decided that they were guilty of a crime, stating:

> *Whereas upon the Information of Mr. James Porter minister, it hath ap-*
> *peared to this Court that Mary Williamson hath Comitted the filthy sin of*
> *fornication with William a negro belonging to William Basnett Squire, It is*
> *therefore ordered that shee bee fined five hundred pounds of tobacco and*
> *Caske for the use of Linhaven parish, for which the said Basnett hath In*
> *open Court Ingaged himself.*
>
> *Whereas It hath appeared to this Court that William, a negro belonging to*
> *William Basnett Squire hath Comitted fornication with Mary Williams[on],*
> *and hath very arrogantly behaved himself in Linhaven Church in the face*
> *of the Congregation, It is therefore ordered that the Sheriff take the said*
> *William Into his Custody and give him thirty Lashes on his bare back.*[48]

Though all co-mingling was disincentivized, sexual encounters were considered the most egregious. White men wanted Black men as far away as possible from White women. The punishment for Black men not staying away from White women became harsher with time. They got humiliated in public, castrated, and lynched.

This was predictable. At this point, this outcome should be obvious. They internalized the cultural norm that they created to protect their property, self-interest, and economic system by defining Black people as inferior. They did this generation after generation. Interacting with White people carried a death sentence for Black males and females until the White American Supreme Court decided to overrule state laws that criminalized marriages between White and Black people (anti-miscegenation laws) in 1967. The topic of miscegenation can be explored further in books such as *Miscegenation: Making Race in America* by Elise Lemire and *What Comes Naturally: Miscegenation Law and the Making of Race in America* by Peggy Pascoe.[136,137]

Next, you'll learn about additional laws and aggressions aimed at Black people, including one that further clarified that Casual Killing Act of 1669. You will also see a clear and negative transition with respect to how Whites regarded Indians legally.

A law enacted in November 1682, **"An act to repeale a former law-making Indians and others ffree, sanctioned the following"**:

And be it further enacted by the authority aforesaid that all servants except Turkes and Moores, whilest in amity with his majesty which from and after publication of this act shall be brought or imported into this country, either by sea or land, whether Negroes, Moors, Mollattoes or Indians, who and whose parentage and native country are not christian at the time of their first purchase of such servant by some christian, although afterwards, and before such their importation and bringing into this country, they shall be converted to the christian faith; and all Indians which shall hereafter be sold by our neighbouring Indians, or any other trafiqueing with us as for slaves are hereby adjudged, deemed and taken to be slaves to all intents and purposes, any law, usage or custome to the contrary notwithstanding.[38,122]

This law dealt with the brutal capture, kidnapping, and monetization of non-White lives and the trafficking of non-Whites into the land *"whose parentage and native country are not Christian – at the time of their first pur-*

chase of such servant by some Christian" to be *converted to Christianity*, and *to be enslaved*.

The precision and intention behind this ensure it is literally impossible for non-Anglo-Europeans to escape the institution of enslavement. It also makes it impossible for them to ever fully access the benefits that accompany Whiteness.

More psychopathy, more sociopathy.

These conditions can be added to the litany of others concerning lineage and Black reproduction. And because the number of Black Christians increased due to laws such as the 1667 one converting them, legislatures felt the need to take up the matter. By this time, the use of Christianity as an ethno-religious designation had been tainted, and non-English Europeans needed to construct other language that would forever set apart White people from non-White people, and most critically Black people.[43]

The creation of the circumstances that evolved during this time are later better clarified in the 1705 Amendment to the Casual Killing Act of 1669. Below is an explicit excerpt. I cite it because I must. The October 1705 law **Concerning Servants and Slaves, Act XXXIV of 1705 (Casual Killing Act Amended),** stated:

> And if any slave resist his master, or owner, or other person, by his or her order, correcting such slave, and shall happen to be killed in such correction, it shall not be accounted felony; but the master, owner, *and every such other person so giving correction, shall be free and acquit of all punishment and accusation for the same, as if such accident had never happened;* And also, if any negro, mulatto, or Indian, bond or free, shall at any time, lift his or her hand, *in opposition against any christian, not being negro, mulatto, or Indian,* he or she so offending, shall, for every such offence, proved by the oath of the party, receive on his or her bare back, thirty lashes, well laid on; cognizable by a justice of the peace for that county wherein such offence shall be committed [emphasis added].[38,43,52,122]

Different than the June 1680 law "Preventing Negro Insurrections," this updated version made specific distinctions between White Christians and other Christians. The law said that Negro, Mulatto, and Indian Christians were not permitted to defend themselves against violence perpetrated by Christians who were not Indian, Black, or Mulatto. In other words, it criminalized any self-defense by non-White Christians against White Christians and absolved White Christians from any crime they committed against the bodies of Black and Indigenous people. Importantly, historians miss this. They should not, as it matters.

The Antebellum period (pre-Emancipation) was when this took place, and the law made this behavior criminal for people who were bond or free. That meant that free Black and/or free Indian people were legally required to submit to abuse at the hands of Whites. They had no legal right to self-defense. Black women could not defend themselves from a White rapist. Every harm perpetrated by a White person onto a Black person was acceptable.

More psychopathy, more sociopathy.

In the eyes of the law, Whites had total sovereignty over Black bodies. There was no such thing as agency for a Black or Indigenous person directly targeted by these laws. The result of this ongoing trauma? The loss of agency among Black persons even today. This cannot be allowed to continue. More than 400 years is enough.

Instead of focusing on what Black persons endured, let us instead focus on White sadism. It is the root of the problem, after all. The need to dominate every Black body, and using every available institution to do so, is abnormal. The need to own another is abnormal. Do not overlook the complete social control, dishonor, degradation, and dehumanization experienced by "free" Indians and "free" Black people. They were not some bright spot in a dark story. Doing so diminishes the pain. The most severe negative cultural association in America has to do with Blackness. This reality is inescapable. It must be addressed.

These systems, all invented and controlled by Whites, created negative psychological and emotional orientations toward Blackness and Black people. These laws established a White cultural framework that not only allowed but encouraged celebration of the destruction of Blackness and the Black body. White people could do no wrong. Black people could do no right. No degree of lopsidedness was enough. The laws and cultural tendencies created by Whites were meant to make thriving and living without fear and despair an impossibility. No joy could meet a Black soul. No peace could meet a Black soul. No bodily autonomy could meet a Black soul. No Black soul could breathe, quite literally, without a White person's permission. So much psychopathy, so much sociopathy.

Comparing what Black people endured and endure to what Jews endured during Hitler's control of Germany is wrong. It is irresponsible. Hitler had the support of a few allies for a limited period of time. Black people in America have suffered for centuries at the hands of nearly every White person they have encountered. Some of the scariest realities in this holocaust against Black people are as follows:

White people have socialized and indoctrinated Black people to participate in our own racial genocide.

The genocide of Black people in America is occurring while White people consistently deny that it is occurring. They have done this to promote a false narrative of improvement.

The systematic nature of the country's anti-Blackness has meant that no institution (education, politics, economics, housing, health care, food production and distribution, etc.) is free of poison.

Chapter Six Review Questions:

(Note: Please go to www.danteking.com to complete the chapter assessment and evaluation for the following questions.)

Considering what was outlined in this last chapter, ask yourselves the following questions:

1. What did White females and males learn about the value of Whiteness?

2. How did these laws shape White identity for White males? White females?

3. What did Black females learn about what it meant to be White and female? White and male? Black and male? Black and female?

4. What did Black males learn about what it meant to be White and male? White and female? Black and female? Black and male?

5. How did these laws shape Black identity?

6. How did these laws create and reinforce pro-White and anti-Black systems (legal, social, etc.) all over North America but particularly in the United States?

7. What happens when we minimize what was a large-scale violation? What does that do for the perpetrators? What does it do to the victims?

8. How do we cope when we fail to draw a direct line between history and the present?

9. How is it that most White people can get away with avoiding culpability, until now?

10. Why do we avoid painful topics and who benefits when we do? Who suffers? (This includes large-scale sexual abuse.)

11. How has White people's creation and control of the legal system allowed them to quite literally get away with murder?

12. How can Black people escape the notion of "criminality" when it was meant only to address their purported misdeeds and exclude everyone else's?

13. Who are the real criminals?

14. Why is it dangerous to minimize the impacts of yesterday's traumas and what does that do to how we live today?

15. How does the legal system favor Whites?

16. How does the legal system disfavor Black people?

17. How does the reality of debasing Black people, relegating us into the most inhuman and profane position in American culture, influence, inform, shape, and develop White American psychological and sociological constructs about who Black people are (i.e., values, principles, behavior, etc.) and what they represent?

18. In what ways do these White psychological and sociological developments shape White identity, in terms of who they believe themselves to be and what they represent as a community and culture?

19. How does White projection, the foundation of both the psychological and sociological developments of American culture, influence and shape the psychology and sociology that Black people and people of color accept about Black people, White people, and all others along the racial spectrum?

20. In what ways does Dr. Poussaint's framing of Whiteness as racial politics and White racism as "mental illness," along with Dr. Bobby Wright's assertion of White psychopathy, help us to further understand the deeper legacy impacts of White supremacy and

anti-Blackness and their impacts on the American cultural psychology, which includes White and all assimilated peoples on White American soil?

21. In what ways does Dr. Poussaint's framing of Whiteness as racial politics and White racism as "mental illness," along with Dr. Bobby Wright's assertion of White psychopathy, help us to further understand the functionality of perpetual White perversions, distortions, and projections White people hold about themselves as superior, juxtaposed against fabricated anti-Black cultural narratives about "who" Black people are, as well as "what" Blackness represents in America?

22. What role does the lack or absence of impression management, as well as the absence of impulse control, play in the impressions and interpretations of Black people's daily behaviors, attitudes, and actions in America?

23. In what ways does Dr. Wright's framing help us to further understand the politics and functionalities of Whiteness and anti-Blackness in America?

24. In what ways does Dr. Wright's framing help us to further understand the need for White American culture to have and perpetually maintain Black American Descendants of Enslaved Peoples (sometimes referred to as ADOS/ADOEP) as an affixed permanent underclass?

25. In what ways does Dr. Wright's framing help us to further understand the necessity of racial politics in America, specifically, Whiteness and anti-Blackness, the infinite "brand-value" of Whiteness, and the brand "valuelessness" of Blackness in America?

Normalizing White America's Systematic Anti-Black Culture— A Playbook for Adolf Hitler and the Jewish Holocaust

IT IS VITAL TO point out that, among a sea of bad actors, Virginia and Maryland were not unique. America's other pro-White and anti-Black colonies operated similarly under British rule.

Again, a combination of pro-White and anti-Black laws and policies were implemented throughout the colonies to degrade Black people specifically. Everything was enacted to elevate White wealth, White identity, and White dominance. There was no concern about right or wrong; moral or immoral.

What Does It Mean To Be White?: Developing White Racial Literacy, written by Robin DiAngelo, makes a good point. It notes that the projection of White traits onto Black bodies, such as laziness, shiftlessness, lustfulness, dirtiness, deviousness, sinfulness, etc., was purposeful. It alleviated moral culpability. To be White was to be angelic, Christian, innocent, moral. No true, meaningful, or deep self-reflection was (or is) required.

These dynamics directly shaped the cultural and institutional fabric of the United States of America. This is true for language, education, economics, legality, government, housing, and every cultural and structural creation in America.

Let's look at the connections between American academic, medical, legal, and economic institutions in the nineteenth and twentieth centuries. Harriet Washington, in her book *Medical Apartheid,* discusses the ways in which White, psychopathic terrorists posing as scholars and other medical experts and professionals preyed and still prey on Black bodies.[138] Washington discusses the ways in which anti-Blackness informed White institutional intersections of law, religion, academia, science (sociological and biological), economics, and medicine.

There is no shortage of examples.[139-144] Some examples include Dr. Charles Caldwell, who developed the science of phrenology. He asserted that the skull formations of Black people suggested the presence of fewer bumps and that, as a direct result, enslavement was necessary. He attended the University of Pennsylvania Medical School. Samuel Cartwright, another University of Pennsylvania Medical School alum, also known as the "Expert in Negro Medicine," asserted that Black people had lower lung capacity and that the forced labor experienced through enslavement was needed, as it increased it. He also created two mental and behavioral health conditions for African Americans in an effort to legitimize his expertise. They were drapetomania, the desire for Black people to free themselves from enslavement, and dysesthesia aethiopica, the lack of work ethic in Black people. Cartwright prescribed beatings and whippings as a way of addressing these conditions, which he termed as illnesses.

Some other medical terrorists include Dr. Josiah Nott, who is noted as having created the science of polygenism. Polygenism was a scientific philosophy that argued that the skull formations of White people made them superior to Black people. Physiognomy, a scientific philosophy established by Dr. Samuel Wells and Dr. Orson Fowler in the mid-nineteenth century, proposed that White people possessed higher moral and intellectual developmental capabilities, which in turn elevated their humanity above Black people's. Dr. Wells based much of his "science" on the outer appearances of different phenotypes.[345]

Included below is a picture from the educational textbook entitled, *New Physiognomy: Or, Signs of Character as Manifested Through Temperament and External Forms, and Especially in the Human Face Divine,* written and published by Dr. Samuel R. Wells in 1875.

Figure 7.1.

126   GENERAL FORMS.

Bearing in mind, then, its limitations and modifications, it is well in all cases, when making a physiognomical examination, to observe the facial angle.   Fig. 142 will help to convey

Fig. 142.—Grades of Intelligence.

an idea of the different grades of development and intelligence as indicated in the profile, size, as well as form, being taken into the account.

Put another way, Dr. Wells asserted that the inferiority of human beings could be determined by one's outer appearance. He specifically focused upon White superiority and Black inferiority as the two extremes of the spectrum. And so, with the support of other purported academic, scientific, scholarly philosophers (who I deem as White sociopaths credentialed and certified to enact systematic terrorism against Black people) and institutions such as the American Medical Association and the American Anthropological Association, Dr. Wells' physiognomy took flight throughout the United States of America and the world.

Then there is Dr. Robert Bennett Bean, distinguished anthropologist. His work continued reinforcing scientific and medical terrorism against the Black community. In his highly acclaimed publication entitled, *Some Peculiarities of the Negro Brain,* Dr. Bean hypothesized that Black people were inferior to White people based on his unfounded claim that Black people had smaller brains.[343]

In the publication, Dr. Bean introduces his study in the first two paragraphs, writing:

> From time to time in the past hundred years attempts have been made to determine the distinctive points of difference between the Caucasian and Negro brain. While differences in skull capacity, in brain weight and size—especially of the frontal lobes—or in the gyri have been demonstrated by Gratiolet, Tiedemann, Broca, Manouvrier, Peacock, Marshall, Parker, and others,—more recently by Waldeyer in Germany and by Elliott Smith in Egypt—yet no exact measurements of the brain, such as we have of the skull, are to be found.
>
> An effort will be made to show by measurement of outline drawings of brains in different positions, by composites of these outlines, and by actual drawings of individual brains that there is a difference in the size and shape of Caucasian and Negro brains, there being a depression of the anterior association center and a relative bulging of the posterior association center in the latter; that the genu of the corpus callosum is smaller in the Negro, both actually and in relation to the size of the splenium; and that the cross section area of the corpus callosum is greater in relation to brain weight in the Caucasian, while the brain weight of Negro brains is actually less.[343]

Dr. Bean's hypothesis and defense were presumably supported by Dr. Irving Fisher and Frederick Ludwig Hoffman's *Race Traits and Tendencies of the American Negro And Appreciation and Interests,*[376] a book Hoffman began with the following opening argument:

> The progress of the colored population in the United States, and more particularly in the southern states, has for more than fifty years past been a matter of the most serious concern to those who have observed the results of the presence of a large and growing negro population. The natural bond of sympathy existing between people in the same country, no matter how widely separated by language and nationality, cannot be proved to exist between the white and colored races in the United States. To-day, after thirty years of freedom for the negro in this country, and sixty years in the West Indies, the two races are farther apart than ever in their political and social relations. To-day, more than ever, the colored race of this country forms a distinct element and presents more than at any time in the past the most complicated and seemingly hopeless problem among those confronting the American people.

It is therefore a matter of the utmost importance that the true condition of this population should be fully understood in all its intricate details, to eliminate every possible doubt as to the seriousness and importance of the problem to the people of the southern states as well of the larger cities in the North and West.[376]

In chapter seven, the final chapter of the book, Fisher and Hoffman conclude:

The central fact deducible from the results of this investigation into the traits and tendencies of the colored population of this country, is plainly and emphatically the powerful influence of race in the struggle for life. In marked contrast with the frequent assertions, such as that of Mill, that race is not important and that environment or the conditions of life are the most important factors in the final result of the struggle for life, individual as well as social, we have here abundant evidence that we find in race and heredity the determining factors in the upward or downward course of mankind.

In the field of statistical research, sentiment, prejudice, or the influence of pre-conceived ideas have no place. The data which have been brought to-gether in a convenient form speak for themselves. From the standpoint of the impartial investigator, no difference of interpretation of their meaning seems possible. The decrease in the rate of increase in the colored population has been traced first to the excessive mortality, which in turn has been traced to an inferior vital capacity. The mixture of the African with the white race has been shown to have seriously affected the longevity of the former and left as a heritage to future generations the poison of scrofula, tuberculosis and most of all of, syphilis. This racial inferiority, has in turn brought about a moral deterioration such as is rarely met with in civilized countries at the present time. Already subject to an inordinate rate of mortality, especially from all of the most destructive diseases, the sexual immorality prevailing between colored females and white males of a lower type, as well as between colored males and colored females, has also brought about a diminished power of vital resistance among the young, as is to be expected from the recognized fact that the death rate for illegitimate children is about twice that of children born in wedlock. As a general result there is diminished social and economic efficiency, which in the course of years must prove not only a most destruc-tive factor in the progress of the colored race, but also in the progress, social as well as economic, of the white race brought under its influence. Racial inferiority was the keynote of the pro-slavery argument. On the other hand, racial differences were explained away by those who saw in freedom the sure prospect of speedy amelioration of the lot of the southern slave ; yet thirty years of freedom in this country and nearly sixty in the West Indies have failed to accomplish the original purpose of the abolition of slavery, that is, the elevation of the colored race to the moral, mental and economic level of the white race.

Nothing is more clearly shown from this investigation than that the southern black man at the time of emancipation was healthy in body and cheerful in mind. He neither suffered inordinately from disease nor from impaired bodily vigor. His industrial capacities as a laborer were not of a low order, nor was the condition of servitude such as to produce in him morbid conditions favorable to mental disease, suicide, or intemperance. What are the conditions thirty years after? The pages of this work give but one answer, an answer which is a most severe condemnation of modern attempts of superior races to lift inferior races to their own elevated position, an answer so full of meaning that it would seem criminal indifference on the part of a civilized people to ignore it. In the plain language of the facts brought together the colored race is shown to be on the downward grade, tending toward a condition in which matters will be worse than they are now, when diseases will be more destructive, vital resistance still lower, when the number of births will fall below the deaths, and gradual extinction of the race take place. Neither religion nor education nor a higher degree of economic well-being have been able to raise the race from a low and anti-social condition, a condition really fostered by the very influences which it was asserted would soon raise the race to a place even more elevated than that of the whites. It is not in the conditions of life, but in race and heredity that we find the explanation of the fact to be observed in all parts of the globe, in all times and among all peoples, namely, the superiority of one race over another, and of the Aryan race over all. To what must we attribute this superiority? To what inherent traits must we attribute the marvelous conquest of nature by the Aryan race?[376]

Hoffman and Fisher then reference Charles Morris' book, *The Aryan Race: Its Origins and Its Achievements*,[377] written in 1888. They contend:

I cannot do better than quote from the work of Mr. Morris, who defines in an admirable manner the essential differences between the four most important races:

If the negro is indolent both physically and mentally, the Mongolian energetic physically but undeveloped mentally, and the Melanochroi active physically and to some extent mentally, in the Aryan we find a highly vigorous and developed mental activity. Though by no means lacking in physical energy the mind is the ruling agent in this race, muscular work is reduced to the lowest level consistent with the demands of the body and the intellect, and every effort is made to limit the quantity of work represented in a fixed quantity of product. Waste labor is a crime to the Aryan mind. Use is the guiding principle in all efforts. It is to this ruling agency of the intellect over the energies of a muscular and active organism that we owe the superior quality, the restricted dimensions, and the vast quantity of Aryan labor products. In his work pure thought is far more represented than pure labor.

If we consider the negro race . . . it is to find a lack of energy both physical and mental. Nowhere in the region inhabited by this race do we perceive indications of high powers of either work or thought. No monuments of architecture appear, no philosophies, or literatures have arisen. And in their present condition they stand mentally at a very low level, while physically they confine themselves to the labor absolutely necessary for existence. They neither work nor think above the lowest level of life needs; and even in America under all the instigations of Aryan activity, the Negro race scarcely displays any voluntary energy either of thought or work. It goes only as far as the sharp whip of necessity drives, and looks upon indolence and sunshine as the terrestrial paradise.

The white race has great physical vigor, capacity and endurance. It has an intensity of will and desire which is controlled by intellectuality. Great things are undertaken, readily but not blindly. It manifests a strong utilitarianism, united with a powerful imagination which elevates, enables and idealizes its practical ideas. The negro can only imitate, the Chinese only utilize, the work of the white; but the latter is abundantly able to produce new works. He has a keen sense of order as the yellow man, not from love of repose, however, but from the desire to protect and preserve his acquisitions. He has a love of liberty far more intense than exists in the black or yellow races, and clings to life more earnestly. His high sense of honor is a faculty unknown to other races, and springs from an exalted sentiment of which they show no indications. His sensations are less intense than in either black or yellow, but his mentality is far more developed and energetic.

Thus, the Aryan stands as the type of intellectual man, the central outcome of the races in which the special conditions of dark and light, North and South, emotional and practical have mingled and combined into the highest and noblest states of mind and body.[376]

Lastly, Hoffman layers his assertions upon Charles Morris' purported anthropological evidence of racial superiority by writing:

> In other words, the Aryan race is possessed of all the essential characteristics that make for success in the struggle for the higher life, in contrast with other races which lack in either one or the other of the determining qualities. A statement so far-reaching must have a considerable body of facts in its support, and the whole history of human effort is witness to the fact that no other race since the Aryan appeared on the scene, has, in the end, been able to resist the onward march of its progressive civilization. Here, in the contrast between the white and colored races we have the most complete historical proof of race superiority, a superiority extending into all the intricate and complex phenomena of life. Wherever the white man has gone, he has become master of the conditions of life. The whole history of Anglo- Saxon conquest and colonization is one endless proof of race superiority and race supremacy. In countries where the very forces of nature were at first against him, he has, after years of struggle, gained his end and mastered the conditions of life surrounding him.[376]

Hoffman, who later became the President of the American Statistical Association, researched the most common causes of "negro" mortality. He referenced the works of such widely accepted scholars and doctors, such as Dr. Samuel Cartwright and Dr. Josiah Nott. It should not be of any surprise, then, to understand Frederick Ludwig Hoffman's conclusion that if Black people were disallowed health care through the public health system, we would become extinct within two or three generations. As a result, when the introduction of a national health care system was proposed in 1912 during President Theodore Roosevelt's administration, most White people opposed the idea because they did not want Black people accessing the system. Similar dynamics emerged roughly 25 to 35 years later during the administrations of U.S. Presidents Franklin D. Roosevelt and Harry S. Truman.

Building upon all of this was Dr. Madison Grant, author of *The Passing of the Great Race*, which was published in 1916.[291] Dr. Grant, a prominent leader of the White American Eugenics movement, provided progressive twentieth-century "scientific," "academic," and "scholarly" research, which served a progressive and more modernized anti-Black and White supremacist agenda.

In *The Passing of the Great Race*, Dr. Grant wrote:

Whenever the incentive to imitate the dominant race is removed the Negro or, for that matter, the Indian, reverts shortly to his ancestral grade of culture. In other words, it is the individual and not the race that is affected by religion, education, and example. Negroes have demonstrated throughout recorded time that they are a stationary species and that they do not possess the potentiality of progress or initiative from within. Progress from self-impulse must not be confounded with mimicry or with progress imposed from without by social pressure or by the slaver's lash.

A rigid system of selection through the elimination of those who are weak or unfit—in other words social failures—would solve the whole question in one hundred years, as well as enable us to get rid of the undesirables who crowd our jails, hospitals, and insane asylums. The individual himself can be nourished, educated, and protected by the community during his lifetime, but the state through sterilization must see to it that his line stops with him, or else future generations will be cursed with an ever-increasing load of misguided sentimentalism. This is a practical, merciful, and inevitable solution of the whole problem, and can be applied to an ever-widening circle of social discards, beginning always with the criminal, the diseased, and the insane, and extending gradually to types which may be called weaklings rather than defectives, and perhaps ultimately to worthless race types.[291]

The prominence of works by scientists such as Dr. Madison Grant, Sir Francis Galton, other leaders such as Harry Laughlin, Dr. Charles Benedict Davenport, Dr. Woods Hutchinson, and so many others, fueled the passing of laws such as Virginia's Racial Integrity Act of 1924.[294] The purpose of the Act was to halt interracial marriage between Whites and purportedly lesser people. The mission of the law was to ensure the purported purity and integrity of Whites. Several clauses of the Virginia Racial Integrity Act of 1924 are noted here:

No marriage license shall be granted until the clerk or deputy clerk has reasonable assurance that the statements as to color of both man and woman are correct.

If there is reasonable cause to disbelieve that applicants are of pure white race, when that fact is stated, the clerk or deputy clerk shall withhold the granting of the license until satisfactory proof is produced that both applicants are "white persons" as provided for in this act.

The clerk or deputy clerk shall use the same care to assure himself that both applicants are colored when that fact is claimed.

It shall hereafter be unlawful for any white person in this State to marry anyone other than a white person, or a person with no other admixture of blood than white and American Indian. For the purpose of this act, the term "white person" shall apply only to the person who has no trace whatsoever of any blood other than Caucasian; but persons who have one-sixteenth or less of the blood of the American Indian and have no other non-Caucasic blood shall be deemed to be white persons. All laws heretofore passed and now in effect regarding the intermarriage of white and colored persons shall apply to marriages prohibited by this act.[292]

Figure 7.2.

VIRGINIA
HEALTH BULLETIN

Vol. XVI.   MARCH, 1924.   Extra No. 2.

The New Virginia Law
To Preserve Racial Integrity

W. A. PLECKER, M. D., *State Registrar of Vital Statistics, Richmond, Va.*

Senate Bill 219, To preserve racial integrity, passed the House March 8, 1924, and is now a law of the State.

This bill aims at correcting a condition which only the more thoughtful people of Virginia know the existence of.

It is estimated that there are in the State from 10,000 to 20,000, possibly more, near white people, who are known to possess an intermixture of colored blood, in some cases to a slight extent it is true, but still enough to prevent them from being white.

In the past it has been possible for these people to declare themselves as white, or even to have the Court so declare them. Then they have demanded the admittance of their children into the white schools, and in not a few cases have intermarried with white people.

While this example centers on Virginia, it is important to note that all states, in alignment with the U.S. federal government, were notably and explicitly concerned with preserving the separation and superiority of the White race. Laws such as the Racial Integrity Act of 1924 were leveraged by the United States Supreme Court, which upheld a ruling (in *Buck v. Bell*, 1927) that legalized "compulsory sterilization of the unfit, including the intellectually disabled for the health and protection of the state."[293] U.S. Supreme Court Chief Justice Oliver Wendell Holmes clarified the motivations behind the Court's ruling with the following remarks:

> It is better for the world, if instead of waiting to execute degenerate off-spring for crime, or to let them starve for their imbecility, society can prevent those who are manifestly unfit from continuing their kind.
>
> Three generations of imbeciles are enough.[318]

One year prior to the 1927 ruling, the U.S. Supreme Court enabled an exclusively pro-White agenda with other rulings, including *Corrigan v. Buckley* and *Euclid v. Ambler*. More on these rulings in the next chapter.

In 1925, Adolf Hitler wrote a book entitled *Mein Kampf*, in which he boldly wrote:

> If Nature does not wish that weaker individuals should mate with the stronger, she wishes even less that a superior race should intermingle with an inferior one; because in such a case all her efforts, throughout hundreds of thousands of years, to establish an evolutionary higher stage of being, may thus be rendered futile.
>
> History furnishes us with innumerable instances that prove this law. It shows, with startling clarity, that whenever Aryans have mingled their blood with that of an inferior race the result has been the downfall of the people who were the standard-bearers of a higher culture. In North America, where the population is prevalently Teutonic, and where those elements intermingled with the inferior race only to a very small degree, we have a quality of mankind and a civilization which are different from those of Central and South America. In these latter countries the immigrants—who mainly belonged to the Latin races—mated with the aborigines, sometimes to a very large extent indeed. In this case we have a clear and decisive example of the effect produced by the mixture of races. But in North America the Teutonic element, which has kept its racial stock pure and did not mix

it with any other racial stock, has come to dominate the American Continent and will remain master of it as long as that element does not fall a victim to the habit of adulterating its blood.

In short, the results of miscegenation are always the following:

(a) The level of the superior race becomes lowered; (b) physical and mental degeneration sets in, thus leading slowly but steadily towards a progressive drying up of the vital sap.[319,320]

Several years after the enactment of Virginia's Racial Integrity Act, which led to the 1927 U.S. Supreme Court's *Buck v. Bell* decision and the creation of legislated eugenical sterilization boards in every state, Hitler again pointed to the efforts of White American leaders, including upon becoming the leader of the Nazi Party.

Hitler wrote:

I have studied with interest the laws of several [U.S.] states, concerning the prevention of reproduction by people whose progeny would, in all probability, be of no value or be injurious to the racial stock.[321]

On September 15th, 1935, the Nazi party erected the Nuremberg Race Laws. The Reich Citizenship Law, which prioritized Aryan Germans, ensured that only "pure" Germans could become legal German citizens. The Reich Citizenship Law was akin to the U.S. Naturalization Law of 1790, which prioritized "Whiteness" as the key determinant of citizenship in the United States. The Law for the Protection of German Blood and German Honor was also enacted. Similar to anti-miscegenation laws referenced in Chapter Four, laws that banned marriages between White and non-White individuals (i.e., Maryland 1664 and 1681, Virginia 1691, etc.), as well as Jim Crow laws that continued to ban marriages between White and Black people, Germany's Nuremberg Race Laws banned "race-mixing" between Jews and "people of German or related blood."

As quoted from the United States Holocaust Memorial Museum,

The Nazis believed that such relationships were dangerous because they led to "mixed race" children. According to the Nazis, these children and their descendants undermined the purity of the German race.[397]

The Nuremberg Race Laws resulted in Jewish people and families being relegated into isolated slums. They were segregated from other Germans and targeted as public enemy number one by the Nazi Party.

Does this look and sound familiar?

In short, his fascination with contemporary racism and terrorism was both fueled by America's terrorism against Black people and immigrants.

These efforts can be observed in the 1921 letter penned by the Governor of California, William Stephens (who served as governor from 1917 to 1923) to the Governor of Washington, Louis Hart. The newspaper clipping has a headline that reads: *"San Francisco Mayor [Eugene Edward Schmitz] Wants Exclusion Act to Bar the Japs."* Additionally, there is a clipping that displays the enactment of the 1924 Immigration Act (H.R. 7995), which banned all immigration from Asia and set a total immigration quota of 165,000 people for all countries outside of the Western Hemisphere. Finally, there is a picture of the Bill, itself.[324-327]

Figure 7.3.

Figure 7.4.

State of California
GOVERNOR'S OFFICE
SACRAMENTO   April 15th, 1921.

Hon. Louis F. Hart,
    Governor of Washington,
        Olympia, Washington.   APR 20 1921

My dear Governor:

        The California Legislature, on April 13th passed
unanimously Joint Resolution No. 26, embodying a declaration of California's principles in the matter of
Japanese immigration, and urging upon the President, the
State Department, and Congress, the endorsement and
adoption thereof.

        As a frontier State, California is making the
fight of the Nation against the incoming rush of an
alien, unassimilable race, which would engulf our civilization, our traditions, and our ideals. Without the
cooperation of the other States, California cannot hope
to secure such action as will put a stop to the future
development in this country of an alien, unassimilable
community which must in time engender racial conflict
and international misunderstandings. The way to preserve
peace with Japan is to act in this matter with justice
and decision, and to place about our American citizenship
and economic interests such protection as Japan properly
places about her own.

        In view of these facts, I am taking the liberty
of asking your assistance in upholding California's
stand in this matter. Your State Legislature is probably
not in session at this time, but you can aid in this
fight for the preservation of the Nation's interests,
by representations to your State's delegation at Washington, urging, or recommending, that they cooperate with
the California delegation in an effort to secure absolute
exclusion of Japanese immigration, under conditions which
will save any real humiliation to Japan, and will make
for peace now, and permanent friendship hereafter between
this Country and Japan.

                        Yours very truly,

                        W. D. Stephens
                        Governor of California.

Figure 7.5.

68TH CONGRESS 1ST SESSION } H. R. 7995

AN ACT

To limit the immigration of aliens into the United States, and for other purposes.

APRIL 10 (calendar day, APRIL 14), 1924
Ordered to lie on the table

Figure 7.6.

IMMIGRATION BILL IS SIGNED BY PRESIDENT; JAPANESE BAN BECOMES EFFECTIVE ON JULY 1

America's support for Hitler's eugenics program can be observed in the quote below, which features Leon Whitney, former Executive Secretary of the American Eugenics Society:

> Hailing Chancellor Adolf Hitler as one of the great statesmen and social planners in the world, Leon F. Whitney of New Haven, Conn., former executive secretary of the American Eugenics Society, endorses Hitler's sterilization program, which is to be applied to 400,000 Germans considered defectives. [322,323]

Leon Whitney was not alone in his support for Adolf Hitler. He was one fish in a sea of White American political and governmental officials. Many of these individuals were and are still regarded as America's best. Examine the article below, which was published in the *Washington Herald* newspaper, on September 3rd, 1915.[344] The article features people who spearheaded nonconsensual sterilization of supposedly unfit, lesser races. Supporters included people we laud as heroes. John D. Rockefeller, Andrew Carnegie, and Alexander Graham Bell were just a few.

Edwin Black discusses the connection between some of America's most highly regarded figures and Adolf Hitler in his book entitled *IBM and the Holocaust: The Strategic Alliance Between Nazi Germany and America's Most Powerful Corporation*. In Chapter Two of the expanded edition, released in 2012, Black asserts:

> On January 30th, 1933, THE WORLD AWOKE TO A FREIGHTENING new reality: Adolf Hitler had suddenly become leader of Germany. Hitlerites dressed in a spectrum of uniforms from gauche to ominous, paraded, motored, and bicycled through Berlin in defiant celebration. Hanging from trucks and stomping through the squares, arms outstretched and often swaggering in song, the Nazis were jubilant. Their historic moment—fraught with emotional expectations of revenge and victory against all adversaries—their long-awaited decisive moment had arrived. From this instant, the world would never be the same.
>
> Quickly, Hitler's Nazis moved to take over the entire government and virtually all aspects of German commerce, society, and culture. *Der Fuhrer* wanted an Aryan Germany to dominate all of Europe with a master race subjugating all non-Aryans. For Jews, Hitler had a special plan: total destruction. There were no secrets in Hitler's vision. He broadcast them loudly

to the world. They exploded as front page headlines in every major city, on every radio network, and in weekly cinema newsreels. Ironically, Hitler's fascism resonated with certain men of great vision, such as Henry Ford. Another who found Hitlerism compelling was Thomas J. Watson, president of one of America's most prestigious companies: International Business Machines.[386]

In an article written by Gabe Paoletti, entitled "7 Brands with Nazi Ties That We All Use," he points out:

The Nazis required lots of machinery to help carry out the Holocaust—and some of it was supplied by IBM.

Through their subsidiary, Dehomag, IBM supplied Nazi Germany with the capabilities to easily and efficiently identify Jews and other undesirables, as well as the technology necessary to track their transport to extermination camps.

Before the outbreak of the war, IBM was already a major international computing company and did considerable business in Germany. In 1933, during the beginning of Nazi control of Germany, company president Thomas Watson personally traveled to Germany. There, he oversaw the creation of a new IBM factory and the influx of American capital flowing into their Dehomag subsidiary.

Dehomag had just been hired by the Nazi government to carry out a massive nationwide census of Germany. This census was designed to identify populations of Jews, Gypsies, and other ethnic groups deemed undesirable by the regime so that they could be marked for extermination.

IBM also supplied the Nazis with punch cards and a card sorting system that allowed them to search these census databases so that they could identify individuals for extermination. The Nazis then repeated this same process in other countries that they invaded as the war progressed.

These punch card machines and sorting systems were also used to coordinate the trains bringing people to concentration camps.

Even after 1941, when the United States joined the war, high-ranking IBM employees falsified internal data and used European subsidiaries and smuggling to make sure that Nazi Germany was supplied with all the punch card material and devices it needed.

IBM kept doing business with Nazi Germany because these dealings were incredibly lucrative. In fact, during the war, Nazi Germany was IBM's second largest territory, after the United States.[387]

Various prominent American leaders, leaders beyond Andrew Carnegie, J.D. Rockefeller, and Alexander Graham Bell, such as the heads of IBM and Ford Motor Company, were linked as accomplices who funded both American and German race purity and forced sterilization programs. It must be understood that America's White race and its obsession with race purity and racial superiority, an obsession long influenced by Sir Francis Galton and other European race theory propagandists, provided Adolf Hitler and the Nazi Party with a systematic, play-by-play, genocide framework.

Figure 7.7.

Acclaims Hitler

Leon F. Whitney
Hailing Chancellor Adolf Hitler as "one of the greatest statesmen and social planners in the world," Leon F. Whitney, of New Haven, Conn., former executive secretary of the American Eugenics Society, endorses Hitler's sterilization program, which is to be applied to 400,-000 Germans considered defectives.
(Central Press)

Figure 7.8.

15,000,000 AMERICANS DEFECTIVE, THEY SAY

Gigantic Eugenic Enterprise Organized for Sterilization of Unfit of Nation.

New York, Sept. 2.—Mrs. E. H. Harriman's gigantic eugenic enterprise at Cold Springs Harbor, Long Island, to ascertain "what is the matter with the human race," launched a campaign today for the sterilization of 15,000,000 Americans. Coincident with this amazing statement comes the announcement of the plan of the Eugenic Society, which will have at its disposal the vast fortune of Mrs. Harriman, liberal financial assistance from John D. Rockefeller and Andrew Carnegie, and scientific aid from Alexander Graham Bell and the greatest host of scientists ever joined in a great undertaking. For four years preliminary work has been quietly conducted, not only at Cold Springs Harbor, but by field workers all over the world.

The board, which will have direction of the work, consists of the following famous men:

Alexander Graham Bell, inventor of the telephone, scientist and philanthropist, chairman; Dr. W. M. Welch, pathologist of Johns Hopkins University, Baltimore, vice chairman; Dr. L. F. Barker, of Johns Hopkins and president of the National Commission of Hygiene; Dr. T. H. Morgan, zoologist, of New York; Irving Fisher, professor of political economy at Yale, and Dr. E. E. Southard, the pathologist, of Boston.

The secretary to the board and resident director is Dr. Charles B. Davenport, the New York biologist. H. H. Laughlin is superintendent, and Prof. Howard J. Banker, a noted botanist of Depau University, has been installed as scientific expert.

The organization, after his four years' work in this country and Europe reached the conclusion that sterilization of defectives was the greatest work for them. Statistics gathered reveal the amazing fact that 10 per cent of the present population of the United States are defectives, who must be blotted out as reproducers of human life.

Figure 7.9–7.10.

15,000,000 AMERICANS DEFECTIVE, THEY SAY

Gigantic Eugenic Enterprise Organized for Sterilization of Unfit of Nation.

New York, Sept. 2.—Mrs. E. H. Harriman's gigantic eugenic enterprise at Cold Springs Harbor, Long Island, to ascertain "what is the matter with the human race," launched a campaign today for the sterlization of 15,000,000 Americans. Coincident with this amazing statement comes the announcement of the plan of the Eugenic Society, which will have at its disposal the vast fortune of Mrs. Harriman, liberal financial assistance from John D. Rockefeller and Andrew Carnegie, and scientific aid from Alexander Graham Bell and the greatest host of scientists ever joined in a great undertaking. For four years preliminary work has been quietly conducted, not only at Cold Springs Harbor, but by field workers all over the world.

The board, which will have direction of the work, consists of the following famous men:

Alexander Graham Bell, inventor of the telephone, scientist and philan-

Figure 7.11–7.12.

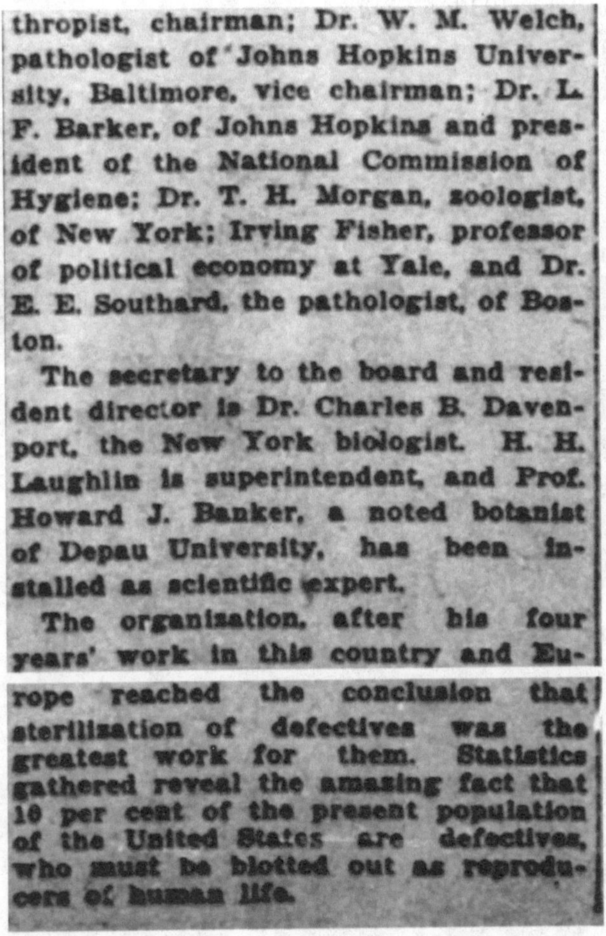

thropist, chairman; Dr. W. M. Welch,
pathologist of Johns Hopkins University, Baltimore, vice chairman; Dr. L.
F. Barker, of Johns Hopkins and president of the National Commission of
Hygiene; Dr. T. H. Morgan, zoologist,
of New York; Irving Fisher, professor
of political economy at Yale, and Dr.
E. E. Southard, the pathologist, of Boston.

The secretary to the board and resident director is Dr. Charles B. Davenport, the New York biologist. H. H.
Laughlin is superintendent, and Prof.
Howard J. Banker, a noted botanist
of Depau University, has been installed as scientific expert.

The organization, after his four
years' work in this country and Europe reached the conclusion that
sterilization of defectives was the
greatest work for them. Statistics
gathered reveal the amazing fact that
10 per cent of the present population
of the United States are defectives,
who must be blotted out as reproducers of human life.

Figure 7.13.
Adolf Hitler, circa 1930s Germany

Figure 7.14.

Figure 7.15.

Figure 7.16.
Thomas Jefferson, 3rd President
of the United States

Figure 7.17.
Abraham Lincoln, 16th President
of the United States

Figure 7.18.
Andrew Johnson, 17th President of the United States

Figure 7.19.
Woodrow Wilson, 28th President of the United States

Figure 7.20.
Richard Nixon, 37th President of the United States

Figure 7.21.
Donald Trump, 45th President of the United States

In their book *The Bell Curve: Intelligence and Class Structure in American Life,* Richard Herrnstein and political scientist Charles Murray assert that human intelligence is influenced by both inherited and environmental factors. They argue that intelligence is a more accurate predictor of various personal outcomes, including financial income, job performance, birth out of wedlock, and involvement in crime, than an individual's parental socioeconomic status.[413]

Adding to historically scientific literature and discourse concerning the academic discipline of Black inferiority along with a pro-Asian stance as two principal objectives for the book, Herrnstein and Murray told America and the world that Asians were smarter than Whites, and Whites were smarter than Blacks. They positioned Black people, as did Fowler and Wells, roughly one hundred years earlier, as the most intellectually under-developmentally capable group of human beings, further establishing the idea of Black people as a permanent underclass in American culture.

Herrnstein and Murray followed the earlier path of Chief Justice Oliver Wendell Holmes in the 1927 Supreme Court *Buck v. Bell* ruling, telling America:

> We are silent partly because we are as apprehensive as most other people about what might happen when a government decides to social engineer who has babies and who doesn't. We can imagine no recommendation for using the government to manipulate fertility that does not have dangers. But this highlights the problem: The United States already has policies that inadvertently social engineer who has babies, and it is encouraging the wrong women. *If the United States did as much to encourage high-IQ women to have babies as it now does to encourage low-IQ women, it would rightly be described as engaging in aggressive manipulation of fertility.* The technically precise description of America's fertility policy is that it subsidizes births among poor women, who are also disproportionately at the low end of the intelligence distribution. We urge generally that these policies, represented by the extensive network of cash and services for low-income women who have babies, be ended [emphasis added].

> The government should stop subsidizing births to anyone, rich or poor. The other generic recommendation, as close to harmless as any government program we can imagine, is to make it easy for women to make good on their prior decision not to get pregnant by making available birth control mechanisms that are increasingly flexible, foolproof, inexpensive, and safe.

The other demographic factor we discussed in Chapter 15 was immigration and the evidence that recent waves of immigrants are, on the average, less successful and probably less able, than earlier waves. There is no reason to assume that the hazards associated with low cognitive ability in America are somehow circumvented by having been born abroad or having parents or grandparents who were. An immigrant population with low cognitive ability will — again, on the average — have trouble not only in finding good work but have trouble in school, at home, and with the law.

America. The land of the free and the home of the brave. Often what we have are free and brave psychopaths and sociopaths. Cowards, actually.

I digress.

There are many more so-called medical "experts" whom I refer to as medical terrorists, discussed in *Medical Apartheid, Killing the Black Body,* a text written by Dorothy Roberts. The text discusses terrorists who developed "sciences," which served to legally and systematically perpetuate Black people's dehumanization.[262] Their work was regarded highly in the White medical arena, as these individuals graduated from and taught at some of America's most prominent academic institutions. Yale, Michigan State University, University of Pennsylvania, Johns Hopkins, Harvard, and William and Mary College are but a few. These institutions were funded to produce information that would supposedly advance the world. Many of these purported scholars received individual funding in the forms of stipends, salaries, grants, and endowments. These monies facilitated the popularity and legitimacy of their efforts. Local, state, and federal legal and regulatory institutions, such as the American Medical Association and American Anthropological Association, validated these experts and their "scientific" and "scholarly" research.

Dr. Bobby Wright, brilliant psychologist and orator, provided a defining example of America's approach to science. Dr. Wright stated:

> What they tell you is, oh no Dr. Wright, this is science. This is objective. You know what science is? A group of White men and White women getting in a room saying this is the way the world is. If you disagree with us, we will kill you or flunk you.[341]

In the early 1900s, Abraham Flexner, an anti-Black health education terrorist and author of *The Flexner Report,* was commissioned by the American Medical Association and the Carnegie Foundation to produce a report that provided assessments of the quality of health education across the nation's 150 medical schools. The report provided recommendations on entrance requirements, size and training of the faculty, size of endowment and cost of tuition, quality of laboratories, and the availability of a teaching hospital where surgeons would serve as good clinical teachers. Flexner did not believe many (if any) Black persons could fulfill this role. A supermajority of Black medical schools closed.[139] To quote him directly:

> The Negro must be educated, not only for his sake, but for ours. He is, as far as the human eye can see, a permanent factor in the nation. He has the rights and due and value of an individual, but he has besides, the tremendous importance that belongs to the potential source of infection and contagion. The pioneer work in educating the race to know and to practice the fundamental hygienic principles, must be done. A well-taught negro sanitarian will be immensely useful; an essentially untrained negro wearing an M.D. degree is dangerous.[139]

Flexner concluded, therefore, that Negroes needed to be groomed by White health educators, including physicians.

This type of absurdity was perfectly normal for White psychological standards. And yet, it was not normal. It was insane.

There is a litany of examples supporting the assertion that anti-Blackness dominates in the ways in which Black people are treated within the White health care and Black health-abuse systems today.[141-144] Below is an excerpt from a 2016 study that found that White medical students believe that Black people have a higher tolerance for pain.

From where did this belief originate?

The abstract for the study reads:

> Black Americans are systematically undertreated for pain relative to white Americans. We examine whether this racial bias is related to false beliefs about biological differences between Black people and whites (e.g., "Black people's skin is thicker than white people's skin"). Study 1 documented these beliefs among white laypersons and revealed that participants who more strongly endorsed false beliefs about biological differences reported lower pain ratings for a Black (vs. white) target. Study 2 extended these findings to the medical context and found that half of a sample of white medical students and residents endorsed these beliefs. Moreover, participants who

endorsed these beliefs rated the Black (vs. white) patient's pain as lower and made less accurate treatment recommendations. Participants who did not endorse these beliefs rated the Black (vs. white) patient's pain as higher but showed no bias in treatment recommendations. These findings suggest that individuals with at least some medical training hold and may use false beliefs about biological differences between Black people and whites to inform medical judgments, which may contribute to racial disparities in pain assessment and treatment.[143]

If you were Black, would you trust White American culture and institutions? If you were Black, would you trust White people? If you were Black, would you trust anyone trained by and within American culture and institutions?

How does the unlearning of racism occur for people whose identity is rooted in and sustained by maintaining a culture and systems that are dependent upon believing and reinforcing psychopathic violence?

The reality of White American terrorism/anti-Blackness is so pervasive that the odds of Black newborns surviving childbirth were cut in half when delivered by White and "not-Black" doctors; this was documented by the 2020 study "Physician-Patient Racial Concordance and Disparities in Birthing Mortality for Newborns."[144]

I now return to my original path.

Remember, we have to take special note of how the law affected free Black people. Many historians tend to focus on enslaved Black people, rather than the totality of the anti-Black orientation. It is time to devote some attention to the free, as they never really were.

Note that all Black people were free until meeting European sadists and terrorists, who, masking themselves as Christians, designed a system meant to torture and enslave them in perpetuity. This terrorism persists today; it is simply hidden better.

Terrorism. It is terrorism. It is not one microaggression in isolation. It is widespread terrorism. Devaluing us, our bodies, and our souls, is terrorism. It is terrorism when done quietly and when done loudly. It is terrorism when the law acknowledges it and when it does not. There is nothing "micro" about murdering Breonna Taylor while she slept in her home, and then not prosecuting her murderer. There is nothing "micro" about executing MaKhia Bryant, Daunte Wright, George Floyd, Ahmaud Arbery, Sandra Bland, Tamir Rice, Charleena Lyles, Walter Scott, Atatiana Jefferson, Freddie Gray, Andrew

Brown Jr., and countless others. There is nothing "micro" about walking up to Jacob Blake and simply shooting him as though he were some wild animal. Characterizing mass murder as trivial enables further mass murder.

Those with anti-Black orientations focus on the intent and not the impact. That is not a coincidence. The impacts of unjustified violence in all its forms include high blood pressure, high cholesterol, diabetes, cancer, heart disease, mental illness, substance abuse, domestic violence, low self-esteem, propensity to engage in self-harm, and more. Not only is there nothing "micro" about these impacts, but there is also nothing normal about them. And yet they have all been normalized and taken for granted. Whites did this.

Whites could do as they please. They were God. They could grant and they could take away. This includes the freedom of a Black person. It was not permanent if a White person did not want it to be. This was so during WWII, when America forced its Japanese population into internment camps. It is true today, as voting rights get assaulted all across the country. The rights of non-Whites in America are always subject to the whims of their White counterparts. We must confront this.

The Pro-White and Anti-Black Flexibility of White America's Legal, Judicial, and Political Systems

Let us scrutinize why laws aimed at hurting Black persons could be interpreted so flexibly by Whites.

Consider a 1705 law from Virginia, **an Act declaring who shall not bear office in this country.**[38,122] As was the case with this law and other examples provided in this text, it sanctioned the continuous criminalization of Black life, crystalizing an everlasting inferior status. The language of this law equated the identities of free Negros, Mulattos, and Indians with criminality. It provided that if any of these types of people dared attempt asserting that they were officials or tried running for office that they would be penalized financially. That meant bond servitude, such as enslavement. The language of this law read:

> BE it enacted by the governor, council and burgesses, of this present general assembly, and it is hereby enacted by the authority of the same, That no person whatsoever, already convicted, or which hereafter shall be convicted in her majestys kingdom of England in this or in any other her majestys dominion, colonies, islands, territorys or plantations, or in any

other kingdom, dominion or place, belonging to any foreign prince or state whatsoever, of treason, murder, fellony, blasphemy, perjury, forgery or any other crime whatsoever, punishable by the laws of England, this country, or other place wherein he was convicted with the loss of life or member, nor any negro, mulatto or Indian, shall, from and after the publication of this act, bear any office, ecclesiasticall, civill or military, or be in any place of public trust or power, within this her majestys colony and dominion of Virginia, and that if any person convicted as aforesaid, or negro, mulatto or Indian shall presume to take upon him, act in, or exercise any office, ecclesiasticall, civill or military, or any place of publick trust or power, within this colony and dominion, notwithstanding he be thereunto in any manner whatsoever commissioned, appointed, chosen or impowered, and have a pardon for his crime, he shall for such his offence, forfeit and pay five hundred pounds current money, and twenty pounds of like money for every month he continues to act in or exercise such office or place after a recovery made of the said five hundred pounds.

And for clearing all manner of doubts which hereafter may happen to arise upon the construction of this act, or any other act, who shall be accounted a mulatto, Be it enacted and declared, and it is hereby enacted and declared, That the child of an Indian and the child, grandchild, or great grandchild, of a negro shall be deemed, accounted, held and taken to be a mulatto.

In another law from 1705, **An Act Concerning Servants and Slaves,**[38,122] the legislature began to deal with free Black, Mulatto, and Indian people in the same ways as enslaved Black, Mulatto, and Indian people. I will not detail the entire law but want to highlight specific parts of it.

For example, it reaffirmed the section contrived in the late seventeenth/ early eighteenth centuries, which dealt with parentage. It stated that all servants who could not prove their Christian identity prior to arriving to the colony, with few exceptions, would become enslaved upon arrival. In addition, this law regulated (as a similar law did approximately 30 years earlier) how non-White people could hire servants and/or enslave people of the same complexion. The language of this part of the law read:

And for a further christian care and usage of all christian servants, Be it also enacted, by the authority aforesaid, and it is hereby enacted, That no negros, mulattos, or Indians, although christians, or Jews, Moors, Mahometans, or other infidels, shall, at any time, purchase any christian servant, nor any other, except of their own complexion, or such as are declared slaves by this act: And if any negro, mulatto, or Indian, Jew, Moor, Mahometan, or other infidel, or such as are declared slaves by this act, shall, notwithstanding, purchase any christian white servant, the said servant shall, ipso facto, become free and acquit from any service then due, and shall be so held, deemed, and taken: And if any person, having such christian servant, shall intermarry with any such negro, mulatto, or Indian, Jew, Moor, Mahometan, or other infidel, every christian white servant of every such person so intermarrying, shall, ipso facto, become free and acquit from any service then due to such master or mistress so intermarrying, as aforesaid.

Since marriage between Black and White people was outlawed, Whites then focused on addressing sexual encounters between the races and any children who came about as a result of those sexual encounters. They were regarded as filthy. Three additional sections read:

And if any woman servant shall have a bastard child by a negro, or mulatto, over and above the years' service due to her master or owner, she shall immediately, upon the expiration of her time to her then present master or owner, pay down to the church-wardens of the parish wherein such child shall be born, for the use of the said parish, fifteen pounds current money of Virginia, or be by them sold for five years, to the use aforesaid: And if a free christian white woman shall have such bastard child, by a negro, or mulatto, for every such offence, she shall, within one month after her delivery of such bastard child, pay to the church-wardens for the time being, of the parish wherein such child shall be born, for the use of the said parish fifteen pounds current money of Virginia, or be by them sold for five years to the use aforesaid: And in both the said cases, the church-wardens shall bind the said child to be a servant, until it shall be of thirty one years of age.

And for a further prevention of that abominable mixture and spurious issue, which hereafter may increase in this her majesty's colony and dominion, as well by English, and other white men and women intermarrying with negroes or mulattos, as by their unlawful coition with them, Be it enacted, by the authority aforesaid, and it is hereby enacted, That whatsoever English, or other white man or woman, being free, shall intermarry with a negro or mulatto man or woman, bond or free, shall, by judgment of the county court, be committed to prison, and there remain, during the space of six months, without bail or mainprize; and shall forfeit and pay ten pounds current money of Virginia, to the use of the parish, as aforesaid.

And be it further enacted, That no minister of the church of England, or other minister, or person whatsoever, within this colony and dominion, shall hereafter wittingly presume to marry a white man with a negro or mulatto woman; or to marry a white woman with a negro or mulatto man, upon pain of forfeiting and paying, for every such marriage the sum of ten thousand pounds of tobacco; one half to our sovereign lady the Queen, her heirs and successors, for and towards the support of the government, and the contingent charges thereof; and the other half to the informer; To be recovered, with costs, by action of debt, bill, plaint, or information, in any court of record within this her majesty's colony and dominion, wherein no essoin, protection, or wager of law, shall be allowed.

It is important to note that Indians are not implicated here. There is a distinct manner of making Black people worth less than anyone else. This mirrored the White perception of Black identity. Of course, one can never regard as equal what one deems soiled and less than. It cannot be.

White-European hatred and contempt for Black people can be observed through the language. Terms such as "abominable," generally considered harsh and reserved for absolutely atrocious acts, were used without a care in the world. There was an increased penalty for this "abominable" behavior, of course. It was worse than what had been outlined in 1691, because the need for domination had increased. That law provided that White and Black couples would need to leave the colony.

What paranoia. What psychopathy. What sociopathy.

Again, this can be attributed to the deeply ingrained grip over the social construct of race, White supremacy, and the resulting hatred of Blackness and Black people.

To produce law after law, institute penalty after penalty, all to address paranoia after paranoia is truly demented. Being this driven to control bodies of a different skin color for fear of being contaminated is irrational. It is not indicative of a mental state tethered to reality or an emotional state concerned with decency. Using every system in existence—an economic one, a religious one, a social one—all to continue exerting total control, is entirely abnormal. We must speak this aloud. We must acknowledge what has long been obvious yet hidden.

Frederick Douglass echoed similar sentiments in the 19th century, stating:

I therefore hate the corrupt, slaveholding, women-whipping, cradle-plundering, partial and hypocritical Christianity of the land . . . I look upon it as the climax of all misnomers, the boldest of all frauds, and the grossest of all libels. Never was there a clearer case of 'stealing the livery of the court of heaven to serve the devil in.' I am filled with unutterable loathing when I contemplate the religious pomp and show, together with the horrible inconsistencies which everywhere surround me. We have men-stealers for ministers, women-whippers for missionaries, and cradle-plunderers for church members.

The man who wields the blood-clotted cowskin during the week fills the pulpit on Sunday and claims to be a minister of the meek and lowly Jesus. . . . The slave auctioneer's bell and the church-going bell chime in with each other, and the bitter cries of the heart-broken slave are drowned in the religious shouts of his pious master. Revivals of religion and revivals in the slave-trade go hand in hand together. The slave prison and the church stand near each other. The clanking of fetters and the rattling of chains in the prison, and the pious psalm and solemn prayer in the church, may be heard at the same time.

The dealers in the bodies of men erect their stand in the presence of the pulpit, and they mutually help each other. The dealer gives his blood-stained gold to support the pulpit, and the pulpit, in return, covers his infernal business with the garb of Christianity. Here we have religion and robbery the allies of each other—devils dressed in angels' robes, and hell presenting the semblance of paradise.[23]

It is important to observe the role "otherism" played when considering how Whites profited off of labor produced by Black bodies. Treating them as objects from which they could make money incentivized by abducting them, raping them, and murdering them. This is a fact. The entire apparatus was diabolically designed to elevate Whites and diminish Black people. The very foundation rested on convincing Black people of their inferiority. The origins of this can be seen in an additional component of the 1705 Virginia statute, which reads, in part:

And for encouragement of all persons to take up runaways, Be it enacted, by the authority aforesaid, and it is hereby enacted, That for the taking up of every servant, or slave, if ten miles, or above, from the house or quarter where such servant, or slave was kept, there shall be allowed by the public, as a reward to the taker-up, two hundred pounds of tobacco; and if above five miles, and under ten, one hundred pounds of tobacco: Which said several rewards of two hundred, and one hundred pounds of tobacco, shall also be paid in the county where such taker-up shall reside, and shall be again levied by the public upon the master or owner of such runaway, for re-imbursement of the public, every justice of the peace before whom such runaway shall be brought, upon the taking up, shall mention the proper-name and sur-name of the taker-up, and the county of his or her residence, together with the time and place of taking up the said runaway; and shall also mention the name of the said runaway, and the proper-name and sur-name of the master or owner of such runaway, and the county of his or her residence, together with the distance of miles, in the said justice's judgment, from the place of taking up the said runaway, to the house or quarter where such runaway was kept.[38,122]

The laws outlined in this text clearly reinforced the requirement of Black people to submit every last part of themselves. They had no choice other than to take up arms, which people such as David Walker suggested they do in his 1829 Appeal.[147] This was reflected in the Stono Resistance Movement, led by an enslaved Angolan named Jemy in 1739, and the Nat Turner Resistance Movement in 1831 (along with the hundreds to thousands of others whose efforts and accomplishments are not readily accessible).[29]

However, the Africans/African Americans, along with White people (for a brief period in history) who were prodded and terrorized, eventually succumbed their hearts and minds to the authority figures around them. The origins of Black rage are tied to the origins of anti-Black dehumanization. Anyone reading this book and examining the origins of the few pieces presented here should be able to make connections to the reality that when White people chose to impose a violent culture onto the bodies of Black people, Black people reacted rationally in an attempt to self-preserve.

The Black person is not to blame. The White person is. The 13th Amendment reads: "Neither slavery nor involuntary servitude, except as a punishment for crime whereof the party shall have been duly convicted, shall exist within the United States, or any place subject to their jurisdiction."[147-149]

White people designed the entire system of criminality around the bodies of Black people. They did this formally through the law (enslavement) and informally through culture. To be Black in America is to be worthless (or worth less). Anti-Blackness is like an infection incapable of responding to treatment. It persists and spreads.

I often wonder how I would have responded had I been alive at the time. How would you have? Most importantly, why? I suspect I would have done what I concluded I needed to do to protect myself and my loved ones.

I do believe that I would have eventually sought out some way to resist. A time would have come where I would not have been able to tolerate it all, and I would have concluded resisting was a risk I was comfortable taking. Today, centuries later, no one should feel safe as long as anti-Black oppression exists. As Douglass eloquently stated:

> Where justice is denied, where poverty is enforced, where ignorance prevails, and where any one class is made to feel that society is an organized conspiracy to oppress, rob, and degrade them, neither persons nor property will be safe.[23]

This quotation moves me. It rings true today. All Americans (Arabs, Asians, Whites, Indigenous, etc.) should feel the veracity of his claim deep inside. As Ava Duvernay, Michelle Alexander, and Douglas Blackmon point out about the systems of mass incarceration and peonage, we have seen millions of Black men pursued, imprisoned, and essentially re-enslaved since the Civil War was fought. White people will always find a way.

More psychopathy, more sociopathy. Do not turn away.

This has happened over the course of the last 156 years, subsequent to the supposed freedom of most Black people being declared by the Emancipation Proclamation.[146-149] We must stop fooling ourselves. Only the most superficial elements have changed. Robin DiAngelo refers to this as "nice racism," which happens to be the title of a book she released in 2021.[152]

Until this country acknowledges that its entire identity is predicated on a lie (multiple lies), it will never make any progress. The truth disrupts. It causes pain and discomfort. Too many White Americans are content just the way they are to challenge what they perceive as the natural order of the world around them. And that is the fundamental problem. We must extricate the truth from where it has been buried.

Chapter Seven Review Questions

(Note: Please go to www.danteking.com to complete the chapter assessment and evaluation for the following questions.)

Considering what you have learned thus far, contemplate the following:

1. What did White females and males learn about the value of Whiteness?

2. How did these laws shape White identity for White males? White females?

3. What did Black females learn about what it meant to be White and female? White and male? Black and male? Black and female?

4. What did Black males learn about what it meant to be White and male? White and female? Black and female? Black and male?

5. How did these laws shape Black identity?

6. What were some of the ways White women responded to the laws directed against them, controlling their bodies and sexuality? Would this spur any allyship? Why or why not?

7. How did these laws create and reinforce pro-White and anti-Black sentiments?

8. What should we do about past offenses? Disregard them? Highlight them?

9. How did America's founding hundreds of years ago lead it to be the country it is today? How is it in reality? How is it marketed to be, both internally (domestically) and externally (to foreign states)?

10. How is it that most White people have never been forced to admit their history? What does this omission mean for them? For Black Americans?

11. What are the reasons why most Americans refuse to learn? What is it about anti-Blackness that is so terrifying to study?

12. How does White people's control over the law prevent a proper accounting of their actions?

13. How can Black people escape "criminality" when it was designed to imprison us physically and emotionally?

14. Who are the real criminals?

15. Why is it dangerous to minimize wrongdoing? Particularly regarding the communities who suffered most from it.

16. In what ways were laws structured in favor of Whites and against Black people?

17. What are your thoughts about the White American Holocaust that has been erected over 400 Years and its influence on the 1920s/30s Nazi Party, Adolf Hitler, and the German/Jewish Holocaust that occurred in the mid-twentieth century. What connections were you able to make?

18. What was Whiteness' and White Supremacy's influence on Nazism?

19. What are the connections between what it means to be White and what it meant to be a Nazi?

20. How does the reality of debasing Black people, relegating us into the most inhuman and profane position in American culture, influence, inform, shape, and develop White American psychological and sociological constructs about who Black people are (i.e., values, principles, behavior, etc.) and what they represent?

21. In what ways do these White psychological and sociological developments shape White identity, in terms of who they believe themselves to be and what they represent as a community and culture?

22. How does White projection, the foundation of both the psychological and sociological developments of American culture, influence and shape the psychology and sociology that Black people and people of color accept about Black people, White people, and all others along the racial spectrum?

23. In what ways are these acts of **academic, scientific, and educational violence** and their impacts on American socialization, further advancing and shaping the cultural psychology of Black inferiority for all Americans, during the <u>nineteenth century and beyond</u>?

24. In what ways does Dr. Poussaint's framing of Whiteness as racial politics and White racism as "mental illness," along with Dr. Bobby Wright's assertion of White psychopathy, help us to further

understand the deeper legacy impacts of White supremacy and anti-Blackness and their impacts on the American cultural psychology, which includes White and all assimilated peoples on White American soil?

25. In what ways does Dr. Poussaint's framing of Whiteness as racial politics and White racism as "mental illness," along with Dr. Bobby Wright's assertion of White psychopathy, help us to further understand the functionality of perpetual White perversions, distortions, and projections White people hold about themselves as superior, juxtaposed against fabricated anti-Black cultural narratives about "who" Black people are, as well as "what" Blackness represents in America?

26. What role does the lack or absence of impression management, as well as the absence of impulse control, play in the impressions and interpretations of Black people's daily behaviors, attitudes, and actions in America?

27. In what ways does Dr. Wright's framing help us to further understand the politics and functionalities of Whiteness and anti-Blackness in America?

28. In what ways does Dr. Wright's framing help us to further understand the need for White American culture to have and perpetually maintain Black American Descendants of Enslaved Peoples (sometimes referred to as ADOS/ADOEP) as an affixed permanent underclass?

29. In what ways does Dr. Wright's framing help us to further understand the necessity of racial politics in America, specifically, Whiteness and anti-Blackness, the infinite "brand-value" of Whiteness, and the brand "valuelessness" of Blackness in America?

Examples of America's Ongoing Legal, Psychopathic, and Sociopathic Black Genocide in the Nineteenth Century and Beyond

As you may have noticed, the term(s) "terrorist(s)" is/are used broadly throughout this text. This is purposeful. It is to highlight the full spectrum of the moral degradation of Whiteness and anyone benefiting from it in any way. It is essentially used in a way that is synonymous with "White" to highlight different facets of Whiteness and includes anyone (White or non-White) who perpetuates it and anti-Blackness. It also refers to those who are indifferent to the struggles Black people face in anti-Black America.

This chapter discusses the horrors that are the Declaration of Independence and Constitution of the United States. Many other scholars have written books on this topic. It is my job to highlight their most important points. Please register for my classes for even deeper analysis.

As W.E.B DuBois notes, both northern and southern states passed anti-Black laws as private institutional practices that legitimately allowed for a continued campaign against Black people. This practice has not changed, as it has been successful.

Let us scrutinize White American Slave Codes and Black Codes, which were laws states adopted to terrorize all Black people throughout the country.

They were particularly harsher in states where Black people could be recognized as "free" because the mere thought of such a thing unsettled them.

Missouri laws are just one example. The state's heritage landing page reads, in part:

> After the United States purchased the Louisiana Territory in 1803, the new territorial government of Missouri immediately instituted Black codes, based largely on the code in place in Virginia, and similar in some ways to the French *Code Noir*. The American law made no distinction between slaves and other personal property in the territory.

> The territorial legislature approved a section entitled "Slaves," found in the *Laws of the District of Louisiana*, on October 1, 1804. This section codified the laws that Black persons in Missouri, whether free or slave, were required to recognize and obey. The law prohibited slaves from leaving their master's property without permission and/or a written pass. Slaves could not own or carry a gun, powder, shot, club, or other weapon. Exceptions were made for those slaves living on a "frontier plantation;" their owner could obtain a license from the justice of the peace allowing the slaves to possess a weapon, presumably for protection against Indians and wild animals, or perhaps for hunting. The Black code forbade slaves to take part in riots and unlawful assemblies or make seditious speeches; all infractions were punishable by public whipping. Other rules in this section affected how slaves traveled between plantations, including how long a slave could remain on another's property and how many visiting slaves were allowed at a particular property at any one time; certain exceptions were applied. Obviously difficult to enforce, slaves and owners frequently ignored this rule with no legal repercussion. To further limit slaves' interaction with free society, the legislature restricted commercial dealings between a slave and a free man, white or Black; to do business with a slave required permission of the owner.

> Fearing slave escapes, territorial legislators included provisions designed to decrease these attempts. These conditions put limitations on the activities of slaves and free Black people, placing the responsibility of slave control on the owners. The law considered any Black person, free or slave, who conspired to incite a rebellion or commit murder, guilty of a felony; in such instances, the slaves usually received a death sentence. White owners who allowed their slaves to go at large and/or hire themselves out could suffer the loss of the slave through public sale at the courthouse; ignoring the "hiring

out" section of this provision brought little consequence. Frequently, slaves engaged in a practice known as "lying out," wherein they temporarily escaped to the woods or a swamp for a short time. One section of the Black code addressed this form of rebellion and allowed the justice of the peace to issue warrants for the apprehension of any slave known to be "lying out."

Slaveholders assumed most of the responsibility for the conduct of their slaves, but other groups in free society were expected to adhere to the rules of the Black code, as well. Legislation outlawed the transportation of slaves by ships or other water vessels unless owners specifically granted their permission. The law imposed a penalty of $150 for each illegally transported slave; in addition, the master could recover damages, including the market value for a lost or runaway slave, from the ship's captain or ship's owner in court. The law concerning the illegal transport of slaves evolved over time to address issues of "knowing" transport and the need for due care and diligence on the part of the ship's master in ascertaining that no runaways were on board. However, the burden of proof was on the ship's master, and he rarely won appeals.

With statehood came new laws regarding Black persons, including an 1825 law that prohibited a "free negro or mulatto, other than a citizen of some one of the United States" to "come into or settle in this state under any pretext whatever" (*Laws of the State of Missouri*, 1825, p. 600). Failure to produce a certificate of citizenship meant African Americans were forced to immediately depart from the state; during the 1844-1845 legislative session, legislators added a $10 fine in addition to the forced departure. Failure to leave the state meant a jail term and ten lashes; statutes allowed up to twenty lashes after 1845 [emphasis added].[159,160]

Alabama, Illinois, and Indiana are just three other states that passed laws preventing free Black people from residing there. The one written in Alabama, passed on January 17th, 1834, (Act 44) read, in part:

The statute provided that freed Black people found in Alabama would be given thirty days to vacate the state. After thirty days, they could be subject to a penalty of thirty-nine lashes [emphasis added] and receive an additional twenty-day period to leave the state. After that period had expired, the free person could be sold into (or back into) slavery with proceeds of the sale going to the state and those who participated in apprehending him or her.[161]

In 1850, Congress passed a law that deemed constitutional the Fugitive Slave Act.[162] This was a national law that deputized all White people in the United States as a racial police force against African Americans. All Black people enslaved and "free" became targets for Whites. Whites were incentivized through both slave auctioneers, as well as through the bounty, court, and law enforcement systems to pursue and capture any Black person they wanted.

We learn about the Japanese internment, which happened in the mid-twentieth century. The federal government essentially required, by appearance, Japanese and other Asian people to be herded into camps across the United States. This law was unsurprisingly similar. It enabled Whites who **suspected** a Black person was enslaved to be captured and enslaved.

Mere suspicion sufficed. Mere White suspicion, more specifically, sufficed.

Does this seem familiar?

This law was called upon nearly 170 years later (2020), when three White men (Travis McMichael, Gregory McMichael, and William "Roddie" Bryan) chased down 25-year-old Ahmaud Arbery in Glynn County, Georgia.

This was the reality for people such as Solomon Northrup, who wrote his memoir entitled *12 Years A Slave* (which was produced as a film in 2013).[269] Solomon, a "free" Black man, was kidnapped and sold into slavery by James H. Birch, the owner of a slave auction business. While Solomon was able to attain freedom 12 years later, he was not able to pursue charges against Birch. While he could prove that he was indeed free at the time of being abducted and had been pursued illegally, Washington D.C.'s laws "prohibited Black people from testifying against White people (as was the case in California and other states)."[29] This made the pursuit of justice impossible for Solomon, and many other Black people who were pursued wrongly. All of this was perpetrated by Whites.

White male judges were paid $5 if they decided to free a Black person who furnished proof of their freedom, or they could collect double to throw his life away.[29]

Reflection:

√   What became incentivized, and for who? How should Black people regard the highest court in the land, which repeatedly denied them their most basic human rights?

√ What additional connections can you make as you read this example? Do you see any similarity between this and Whites who "suspect" Black persons of doing something wrong incorrectly and then involve law enforcement, whose demonstrable tendency is to shoot before investigating?

√ How does White suspicion and obsessive anti-Black behavior function today (consider Ahmaud Arbery, Trayvon Martin, Tamir Rice, John Crawford, Breonna Taylor, George Floyd, Sandra Bland)?

√ What are the links between historical legality and its impacts on shaping culture?

The Fugitive Slave Act provided all White people with the ability to reinforce the criminalization of Blackness and authorized and incentivized White judicial terrorists to uphold these realities.

How far has America come?

More examples are available. Look at the Black Codes of Illinois, or **Article 13 of Indiana's Constitution (1851)**, which stated:

No Negro or Mulatto shall come into, or settle in, the State, after the adoption of this Constitution.[163]

In addition, the **Illinois Black Codes** prohibited:

Any Black persons from outside of the state from staying in the state for more than ten days, subjecting Black people who violated that rule to arrest, detention, a $50 fine, or deportation.[163]

Look at Oregon. It forbade Black people from owning and holding real estate. Racial zoning, racially restrictive covenants, and redlining persisted in the United States for decades.[128, 131–135]

Illinois, Ohio, Indiana, Iowa, and California all prohibited Black people from testifying in cases where a White man was a party. The White person's stature could never be diminished or even challenged.

After President Lincoln's purported emancipation of 3.9 million Black slaves, Black Codes re-emerged throughout the nation. Douglass Blackmon, in *Slavery by Another Name*, discussed the White tendency to change local laws as needed in order to maintain control over the Black body. Black persons who followed the law to the letter, wanting very much to avoid conflict, might soon thereafter find that the given law had been modified, criminalizing their behavior anyway. There was no end to the extent of White psychopathy and sociopathy. Nothing was ever good enough. No good faith act on the part of the Black person ever meant anything, much less enough. No attempt to conform. Nothing. What this ultimately led to between 1865 and 1940 was the re-enslavement of nearly 1,000,000 Black persons through a system known as peonage.

Richard Wormser, in *The Rise and Fall of Jim Crow,* details many of these horrific tragedies as well. These authors point to laws that were continually reshaped to recriminalize and reinjure Black persons as often as possible.[149,151,164] As Black people began realizing they had a right to live normally, Whites targeted them more. Blackmon states:

> So, across the South, laws were passed to criminalize everyday African American life. It was a crime for a Black man to walk beside a railroad, to speak loudly in the company of white women, to do someone's laundry without a license, to sell cotton after dark. But the most damaging statutes were around vagrancy. If you couldn't prove your employment at any moment, you were a criminal.[151]

The Black Codes, rooted in a hateful, anti-Black agenda, were created to systematically bolster the dehumanization and degradation of Black people across the United States of America. This is indisputable, and indicative of the obsession Whites had with Black bodies. They remained obsessed with finding new and improved ways to consistently terrorize and torment Black people.[129,159-162]

White American culture was created and has evolved with anti-Black terror at its core, and it has persisted in functioning in this way.

Take, for another example, vagrancy status. Whites made Black people prove they had a job, and not merely any job, but one Whites approved of. Think once again of the moral absurdity. If a White officer did not feel the Black person's job was acceptable, which was nearly always the case, he could punish him.

That was the point. The cruelty was the point.

The formality of the process was mere dressing, much like it is today, distressingly. What were the penalties for not meeting a White officer's approval?

Arrest, imprisonment, being rented and leased by states to do forced labor for private companies, and more. The system had a name, and it was surprisingly accurate. It was called "convict leasing" and it went on from at least 1874 to roughly the 1940s. It re-enslaved nearly 1,000,000 Black persons. That means almost 1,000,000 Black people were re-enslaved after President Lincoln's Emancipation Proclamation (which supposedly freed enslaved Black people) and after the passage of the Thirteenth, Fourteenth, and Fifteenth Amendments.

As we now know, even Whites who are touted as the most progressive voices on racial issues, such as President Abraham Lincoln, were in fact not supporters of Black people. They did not stand for equality and were as committed to White supremacy and anti-Blackness as White extremists were, though they portrayed and demonstrated their derision differently. The only difference was that their anti-Black hatred was expressed in a more subtle fashion.

Let us ask ourselves why.

Take, first, sentiments expressed by Lincoln in a speech delivered as part of the infamous Lincoln/Douglas debates (Peoria, Illinois; 1854). Then consider the sentiments he expressed in a speech given in Charleston, Illinois, four years later (1858). Last, take note of a letter he penned, as President of the United States, to Horace Greely, former U.S. Representative and editor of the *New York Tribune*, in 1862. Then ask yourself who he really was and what his motives were regarding Black people.

The Peoria, Illinois 1858 speech reads, in part:

> If all earthly power were given me, I should not know what to do, as to the existing institution. My first impulse would be to free all the slaves, and send them to Liberia,—to their own native land. But a moment's reflection would convince me, that whatever of high hope (as I think there is) there may be in this, in the long run, its sudden execution is impossible. If they were all landed there in a day, they would all perish in the next ten days; and there are not surplus shipping and surplus money enough in the world to carry them there in many times ten days. What then? Free them all, and keep them among us as underlings? Is it quite certain that this betters their condition? I think I would not hold one in slavery, at any rate; yet the point is not clear enough for me to denounce people upon. What next? Free them, and make them politically and socially, our equals? My own feelings will not admit of this; and if mine would, we well know that those

of the great mass of white people will not. Whether this feeling accords with justice and sound judgment, is not the sole question, if indeed, it is any part of it. A universal feeling, whether well or ill-founded, can not be safely disregarded. We can not, then, make them equals.[282]

The Charleston, Illinois, 1858 speech reads, in part:

While I was at the hotel to—day, an elderly gentleman called upon me to know whether I was really in favor of producing a perfect equality between the negroes and white people. While I had not proposed to myself on this occasion to say much on that subject, yet as the question was asked me I thought I would occupy perhaps five minutes in saying something in regard to it. I will say then that I am not, nor ever have been, in favor of bringing about in any way the social and political equality of the white and black races, that I am not nor ever have been in favor of making voters or jurors of negroes, nor of qualifying them to hold office, nor to intermarry with white people; and I will say in addition to this that there is a physical difference between the white and black races which I believe will forever forbid the two races living together on terms of social and political equality. And inasmuch as they cannot so live, while they do remain together there must be the position of superior and inferior, and I as much as any other man am in favor of having the superior position assigned to the white race. I say upon this occasion I do not perceive that because the white man is to have the superior position the negro should be denied every thing. I do not understand that because I do not want a negro woman for a slave I must necessarily want her for a wife. My understanding is that I can just let her alone. [168,283]

The *New York Tribune* 1862 letter reads, in part:

The sooner the national authority can be restored; the nearer the Union will be "the Union as it was." If there be those who would not save the Union, unless they could at the same time *save* slavery, I do not agree with them. If there be those who would not save the Union unless they could at the same time *destroy* slavery, I do not agree with them. My paramount object in this struggle *is* to save the Union and is *not* either to save or to destroy slavery.

If I could save the Union without freeing *any* slave I would do it, and if I could save it by freeing *all* the slaves I would do it; and if I could save it by freeing some and leaving others alone, I would also do that. What I do about slavery, and the colored race, I do because I believe it helps to save the Union; and what I forbear, I forbear because I do *not* believe it would help to save the Union.[167]

Does this sound like someone who was tormented in the dark of night over the plight of Black Americans? Surely not. In addition, Lincoln attempted to arrange the emigration of all Black people out of America, intending to send us to places such as Panama and Costa Rica. The United States Congress attempted to provide $100 to each Black person who volunteered to leave the country.[42] Black writers and scholars (and the texts they have written), such as W.E.B DuBois' *Black Reconstruction in America*, Lerone Bennett Jr.'s *Before the Mayflower: A History of the Negro in America, 1619-1962*[168] and *Forced Into Glory*,[168] as well as Nikole Hannah-Jones' *1619 Project*,[45] have discussed his white supremacism and anti-Blackness already. I bring it up here only to highlight how diseased he was and yet how celebrated he continues to be.

Literally whole monuments have been built for this man. We take a day off to celebrate him. The name "Lincoln" continues to be popular among Americans irrespective of their political leanings. A halo surrounds him and likely always will.

And yet he could not have cared less if one Black person exsanguinated due to having been lashed so severely, or if another had been raped so brutally she could barely walk.

Between 1862 and 1976, roughly, White federal and local government officials, under the auspices of a legal doctrine called eminent domain, worked together to implement a series of laws that provided White people with free land to build houses, farms, factories, and other businesses. These laws were known as Homestead Acts.[169]

Similarly, there were the Headrights Acts, which were laws that provided White men with 50 acres of land at the end of their indentures and additional allotments of 50 acres per enslaved African they acquired.

In essence, from approximately 1862 to 1976, the Homestead Acts provided expanded free land rights to White men traveling and relocating from southern states to northern states, as well as to White immigrants who were encouraged to come to the United States from Europe. These laws provided that each White male who completed an application and got approved by local land offices could receive 160 acres of free land, and that is just initially. No work, no loan, no payment, nothing. Just be White. In 1909, the Homestead Act allotments were up to a whopping 320 acres of land per approved application. These White affirmative action giveaways lasted until 1976. For perspective, 1976 is the year I was born.

Though Black people were permitted to apply, most were predictably denied due to anti-Black hatred.

In 1883, the U.S. Supreme Court issued decisions in the following cases: *The United States v. Stanley, The United States v. Ryan, The United States v. Nichols, The United States v. Singleton,* and *Robinson and wife v. Memphis & Charleston Railroad Company.* [263-265]

They essentially said it was unconstitutional for Congress to intervene in racial discrimination cases where White people decided to not conduct business with Black people. In essence, this legalized anti-Black discrimination. It held that the passage of the Thirteenth and Fourteenth Amendments did not outlaw private discriminatory acts.

It is important to understand the nature of some of the elements of the cases which led to this decision. As quoted from Open Jurist, Encyclopedia Britannica, and Justia Law:

> The cases against Stanley and Nichols were indictments for denying Black people the accommodations of an inn or hotel. Ryan was charged with refusing a Black person a seat at **Maguire's theater in San Francisco, and Singleton denied a person, whose color was not given to the use of accommodations at the Grand Opera House in New York** [emphasis added]. The case of Robinson and wife against the Memphis and Charleston Railroad company was an action to recover five hundred dollars given by the second section of the [1875] Act. The grievance was the refusal by the railroad conductor to allow the wife to ride in the ladies' car because of her African descent.

> In his majority opinion in the Civil Rights Cases, Associate Justice Joseph P. Bradley . . . struck down the Civil Rights Act of 1875, holding that the Thirteenth Amendment "merely abolishes slavery" and that the Fourteenth Amendment did not give Congress the power to outlaw private acts of racial discrimination [emphasis added]. Associate Justice John Marshall Harlan was the lone dissenter in the case, writing that the "substance and spirit of the recent amendments of the constitution have been sacrificed by a subtle and ingenious verbal criticism.[263-265]

We see here that even after gaining citizenship through the Fourteenth Amendment in 1870, an anti-Black Supreme Court took those rights away.

Legally sanctioned anti-Black discrimination was further exacerbated by the *Plessy v. Ferguson* ruling from 1896, which further legitimized White supremacist and anti-Black sentiments by segregating the races.

Fooling no one with any moral sense, it said separate could be equal. In fact, the Court did not believe that Black people had the right to be treated as equal citizens in the United States.[170]

How America was and why America merits scrutiny.

Some say the passage of the 1964 Civil Rights Act solved these problems. Such a claim is laughable. See the Supreme Court decision in 1968 regarding *Jones v. Alfred H. Mayer Co.*, which supposedly upheld the validity of the Civil Rights Act of 1866 and struck down the Supreme Court decision of 1883.[263,264]

How far are we from the past? Where did "stop and frisk" come from, if not the nation's earliest days, to cite one example?

The racial discrimination may be slightly less obvious. That does not mean it has ceased to exist. It is not the individual misdeeds of certain Black people that prevent advancement. No. It is still the system-wide oppression inflicted by Whites in ways that are more palatable to the masses. Nothing can compete with or minimize the damage caused by White psychopathy and sociopathy.[38,42,151,220,276,277]

In 1919, the California Supreme Court (remember: California is widely hailed as a liberal state) decided that racially restrictive covenants were legal. That meant it saw nothing wrong with telling Black citizens they had no right to occupy the same space White citizens did. That excluding them from a given neighborhood was neither immoral nor illegal. This decision was later reaffirmed, basically, in the Supreme Court's decision regarding *Corrigan v. Buckley* (decided May 24, 1926). It would be cemented again with *Euclid v. Ambler*, another Supreme Court ruling that same year (decided November 22, 1926). That decision held that localities could zone Black persons out of living in certain neighborhoods as they saw fit.[131–135]

These Supreme Court decisions propelled regions across America to do just that. Black people were told repeatedly they had no right to access upper scale neighborhoods or quality homes, no matter how hard they had worked or how much money they had saved.

To understand in context the focus and impacts of *Corrigan v. Buckley* and *Euclid v. Ambler*, it is vital to reflect on the direct targets of a prior ruling, which can be linked directly to the Euclid decision: *City of Aurora v. Burns*. In *City of Aurora v. Burns*, the Supreme Court of Illinois stated:

The constantly increasing density of our urban populations, the multiply-
ing forms of industry, and the growing complexity of our civilization make
it necessary for the State, either directly or through some public agency by
its sanction, to limit individual activities to a greater extent than formerly.
With the growth and development of the State, the police power necessarily
develops, within reasonable bounds, to meet the changing conditions. . . .

The harmless may sometimes be brought within the regulation or pro-
hibition in order to abate or destroy the harmful. The segregation of
industries commercial pursuits and dwellings to particular districts in a
city, when exercised reasonably, may bear a rational relation to the health,
morals, safety and general welfare of the community. The establishment
of such districts or zones may, among other things, prevent congestion of
population, secure quiet residence districts, expedite local transportation,
and facilitate the suppression of disorder, the extinguishment of fires, and
the enforcement of traffic and sanitary regulations. The danger of fire and
the risk of contagion are often lessened by the exclusion of stores and factories from areas devoted to residences, and, in consequence, the safety and
health of the community may he promoted . . .

The exclusion of places of business from residential districts is not a declaration that such places are nuisances or that they are to be suppressed
as such, but it is a part of the general plan by which the city's territory is
allotted to different uses in order to prevent, or at least to reduce, the congestion, disorder and dangers.[388]

Notice the language in the decision: "urban populations," "complexity of
our civilization," protecting the "harmless from the harmful," "segregation
of . . . dwellings to particular districts in a city, when exercised reasonably,
may bear a rational relation to the health, morals, safety, and general welfare
of the community." In addition, they wanted to "secure quiet residence districts" and "facilitate suppression of disorder." Put another way, the Illinois
Supreme Court and the United States Supreme Court were concerned with
establishing stable, functional, and clean White neighborhoods across America. White people deserved to live quietly, healthily, safely. White welfare
mattered. That meant it had to be free of Black contamination.

These two legal precedent-setting bodies, established by White men, were
also concerned with relegating Black people into unclean, rat- and insect-
infested ghettos and slums where they would die from such conditions. For
those who did not die, they would be patrolled and "suppressed" within

easily locatable geographies across America. Such neighborhoods would later become known as "Black" neighborhoods.

Richard Rothstein, Ira Katznelson, and Michael Allan Wolf discussed this further in their books entitled respectively, *The Color of Law*, *When Affirmative Action Was White*, and *The Zoning of America: Euclid v. Ambler*.[131-135]

As mentioned, the decision to segregate Black people from White people, even to eradicate Black people from human existence, was supported by White academic principles.

Below are examples of an advertisement for one of Oakland, California's exclusive "Whites Only" neighborhood, Rockridge, which was mostly built in the 1920s, along with a racially restrictive covenant from San Francisco, California's elite "Whites Only" St. Francis Wood neighborhood. In addition, I have included several redlining reports that highlight White peoples' persistent obsession with Whiteness, anti-Blackness, and race in general.[389]

The Rockridge advertisement states, "No negroes, no Chinese, no Japanese can build or lease in Rockridge Park."[389]

The racially restrictive covenant states:

Par. 2. Section 2. (a) Limitation of Occupancy and Ownership. No part of said property shall be sold, conveyed, rented or leased in whole or in part to any person of an African or Asiatic race or to any person not of the white or Caucasian race.

(b) No part of said property shall be used or occupied or permitted to be used or occupied in whole or in part by any person of African or Asiatic descent or by any person not of the White or Caucasian race, except that domestic servants, chauffeurs, or gardeners who are members of a race other than the white or Caucasian race may live on or occupy the premises where their employer resides or with the written approval of the Association may reside in such hotel, club, student boarding house, hospital, or other building as it may approve under uniform regulation.

The footnote at the bottom of the covenant reads:

Restrictive covenant from St. Francis Wood, an exclusive neighborhood in San Francisco. In 1919, the California Supreme Court held that such covenants were legal.

Figure 8.1.

Figure 8.2.

¶ Nowhere else is your future as a home-seeker or investor so secure as at Rock Ridge Park. Look for yourself and see.

¶ No negroes, no Chinese, no Japanese can build or lease in Rock Ridge Park.

¶ There'll be no stores, no saloons, no business of any kind in Rock Ridge Park.

¶ Absolutely nothing inferior can now or at any time be built in Rock Ridge Park.

¶ There'll be no flats and no apartments, and only one house to a lot or portion of a lot. Every lot a big lot at that.

¶ Come out today—bring your advisor with you—look around—compare values—compare improvements—compare location—compare environment; overlook nothing that will be a comparison. You'll want a Rock Ridge lot. You'll want it quick, too; before the opening sale when the choicest lots are gone.

¶ Phone us the first thing in the morning. One of our motor cars will take you out—show you the property—bring you back in half an hour.

¶ Or take the College avenue car—get off at Lawton—walk one block east to Broadway. Our salesmen are there on the tract with maps and prices.

Figure 8.3.

Par. 2. Section 2. (a) Limitation of Occupancy and Ownership. No part of said property shall be sold, conveyed, rented or leased in whole or in part to any person of an African or Asiatic race or to any person not of the white or Caucasian race.

(b) No part of said property shall be used or occupied or permitted to be used or occupied in whole or in part by any person of African or Asiatic descent or by any person not of the white or Caucasian race, except that domestic servants, chauffeurs, or gardeners who are members of a race other than the white or Caucasian race may live on or occupy the premises where their employer resides or with the written approval of the Association may reside in such hotel, club, student boarding house, hospital or other building as it may approve under uniform regulation.

Restrictive covenant from St. Francis Wood, an exclusive neighborhood in San Francisco. In 1919, the California Supreme Court held that such covenants were legal.

Figure 8.4.

AREA DESCRIPTION

1. NAME OF CITY   BERKELEY, CALIFORNIA   SECURITY GRADE   LOW GREEN   AREA NO.   A-3

2. DESCRIPTION OF TERRAIN.   Hilly, with steep slopes and bluffs, which afford excellent view sites for residences. Streets platted to conform to topography.

3. FAVORABLE INFLUENCES.   View property; well improved streets. Harmonious population with high degree of culture. Groves of trees add to charm of neighborhood.

4. DETRIMENTAL INFLUENCES.   Distance from schools, transportation and local shopping center.

5. INHABITANTS: Professional and business
   a. Type men, executives, etc. ; b. Estimated annual family income $ 5000-25,000

   c. Foreign-born No concentration %; d. Negro None ; %;
                    (Nationality)   (Yes or No)
                    Undesirables:
   e. Infiltration of remote ; f. Relief families None known ;

   g. Population is increasing Slowly ; decreasing ; static.

6. BUILDINGS:
   a. Type or types Mansion types ; b. Type of construction Frame ;
   c. Average age 15 yrs - many new ; d. Repair Good

7. HISTORY: 8-rm homes,   SALE VALUES   RENTAL VALUES
   spacious grounds   PREDOM-   PREDOM-
   YEAR   RANGE   INATING   %   RANGE   INATING   %
   1929 level $10,000-20,000 $12,500 100%   Practically no rentals   100%
   1933 low   5,000-10,000   8,000   64%   *   *   *
   1937 current 6,000-11,000   9,000   72%   *   *   *

   Peak sale values occurred in 1927 and were 102 % of the 1929 level.

   Peak rental values occurred in 1927 and were 100+ % of the 1929 level.

8. OCCUPANCY: a. Land 20 %; b. Dwelling units 100 %; c. Home owners 100 %

9. SALES DEMAND: a. Poor ; b. 8-room - $7500 ; c. Activity is Poor

10. RENTAL DEMAND: a. Poor ; b. None for rent ; c. Activity is Poor
                                                        21, avr'g $7,000
11. NEW CONSTRUCTION: a. Types 5 and 6-room homes ; b. Amount last year including lot

12. AVAILABILITY OF MORTGAGE FUNDS: a. Home purchase Ample ; b. Home building Ample

13. TREND OF DESIRABILITY NEXT 10-15 YEARS Up

14. CLARIFYING REMARKS:
    This is an older development than A-1 and A-2, but homes are excellently maintained;
    difficulty of access to area isolates it somewhat. This district is known as CRAG-
    MONT and BERKELEY VIEW TERRACE; zoned first class residential (singles-family) and
    restricted by deed to Caucasian ownership. There was very little speculative building
    in 1936 in this area, most of the new homes being built under contract for owners

15. Information for this form was obtained from SUTLIFF REALTY & FINANCE COMPANY, BERKELEY;
    CITY OF BERKELEY, BUILDING DEPARTMENT; RALPH E. PRENTICE; HAROLD W. JEWETT

                                                Date 6-15-37 193_

The redlining report pictured on the previous page is dated August 26, 1937.[389] My maternal grandmother, Mamie Edgar, was 18, and my paternal grandmother, Corrine Hight, was roughly 15. In the "CLARIFYING REMARKS" section, it reads:

> This is an older development than A-1 and A-2, but homes are excellently maintained; difficulty of access to area isolates it somewhat. This district is known as CRAGMONT and BERKELEY VIEW TERRACE; zoned first class residential (single family) and restricted by deed to Caucasian ownership. There was very little speculative building in 1936 in this area, most of the new homes being built under contract for owners.[389]

On the following page, you will find an additional redlining report that accompanied a redlining map for a neighborhood in Oakland, California. This neighborhood is adjacent to where my mother would purchase her home in 1977, where I grew up, and where she currently resides. Towards the top of the map, there are two areas: "FAVORABLE INFLUENCES" and "DETRIMENTAL INFLUENCES." The "FAVORABLE INFLUENCES" section states:

> Convenience to local and San Francisco transportation, schools and local shopping district. Good Catholic schools nearby.

The "DETRIMENTAL INFLUENCES" section states:

> Older type cottages, showing age; infiltration of a few families of Negroes. Zoned for multiple- (four) family residential.

Notice that both maps, which were designed to be the same for this region, a region affectionately known as the "East Bay" area, contain sections for both the "Foreign-born" and "Negroes." The concern for Black people moving into certain neighborhoods was so intense that White people dedicated an entire section to police the presence of Black people.

Under the "CLARIFYING REMARKS" section of this report, it is noted:

> Population increasing slightly due to tendency toward multiple residential. This might be termed a "HIGH RED" area and would have been graded "C" except for presence of Negro residents.

Figure 8.5.

```
HS FORM-9                          AREA DESCRIPTION
8-26-37
```

1. NAME OF CITY __OAKLAND, CALIFORNIA__ SECURITY GRADE __RED__ AREA NO. __D-14__

2. DESCRIPTION OF TERRAIN. Level

3. FAVORABLE INFLUENCES. Convenience to local and San Francisco transportation, schools and local shopping district. Good Catholic School nearby.

4. DETRIMENTAL INFLUENCES. Older type cottages, showing age; infiltration of a few families of Negroes. Zoned for multiple- (four) family residential.

5. INHABITANTS: Shop-keepers, white-collar
   a. Type __employees, service workers.__ ; b. Estimated annual family income $ __1200-2500__

   c. Foreign-born __Various__ , __8__ %; d. Negro __Six families__ ; __1½__ %;
                      (Nationality)   (Yes or No)
                      Lower classes:
   e. Infiltration of __Yes__ ; f. Relief families __Occasional__ ;

   g. Population is increasing __Slowly__ ; decreasing _____ ; static. _____

6. BUILDINGS: 5 & 6-rm, 1-story
   a. Type or types __cottages prevail__ ; b. Type of construction __Frame__ ;

   c. Average age __25 (20 to 35) yrs.__ ; d. Repair __Fair__

7. HISTORY: Semi-modern   SALE VALUES   RENTAL VALUES
            5-rm bungalow: PREDOM-   PREDOM-
   YEAR   RANGE   INATING   %   RANGE   INATING   %

   1929 level $2500-4500 $3500   100% $25 - 45 $35   100%

   1933 low   1500-2500   2000   57%   17.50-25   22.50   50%

   1937 current 1800-2750   2500   71½%   20 - 30   25   71½%

   Peak sale values occurred in __1927__ and were __105__ % of the 1929 level.

   Peak rental values occurred in __1927__ and were __105__ % of the 1929 level.

8. OCCUPANCY: a. Land __97__ %; b. Dwelling units __99__ %; c. Home owners __80__ %

9. SALES DEMAND: a. __Fair__ ; b. 5-rm cottage $2500 ; c. Activity is __Fair__

10. RENTAL DEMAND: a. __Good__ ; b. 5-rm cottage $25 ; c. Activity is __Good__
                                   1 cottage at $3000

11. NEW CONSTRUCTION: a. Types 1 home at $5500 ; b. Amount last year __2 homes in 1936__
                                                                           Very
12. AVAILABILITY OF MORTGAGE FUNDS: a. Home purchase __limited__; b. Home building __limited__

13. TREND OF DESIRABILITY NEXT 10-15 YEARS __Slowly downward__

14. CLARIFYING REMARKS: _____

        Population increasing slightly due to tendency
        toward multiple residential. This might be
        termed a "HIGH RED" area and would have been
        graded "C" except for presence of Negro resi-
        dents.

15. Information for this form was obtained from __CITY OF OAKLAND, BUILDING INSPECTOR;__

    _____ RALPH M. PRENTICE; ARTHUR L. GOARD

                                    Date __6-15-37__ 193_

Note: There were only six Black families, amounting to 0.5% of the neighborhood's population, which resulted in the neighborhood being downgraded to "HIGH RED," meaning hazardous.

That is all it took. Even a whiff or glimpse of Blackness was enough to disgust and alarm.

The federal government's approach to rating neighborhoods during this period was such that exclusively White neighborhoods were coded "A" and the color green for "most desirable." Blue-coded neighborhoods, rated with the letter "B," which were typically a bit older in age, yet still exclusively White, were noted as "still desirable." Neighborhoods coded the color yellow and with the letter "C" signified that "non-Whites' had moved into the area, regardless of whether they were of middle class or upper middle-class status. These neighborhoods were regarded as "declining." Lastly, the combination of red and the letter "D" was used for neighborhoods where African Americans lived. Black neighborhoods were regarded as hazardous. Hazardous. Like unregulated chemicals. This language is reflected in the initial report that was drafted for San Francisco's Fillmore district during this period. The next page contains an example of the actual report. The report states:

> This area of some 20 blocks occupies a comparatively level section which is inhabited by semi-skilled laborers, low-waged "white collar" workers, and service group employees, with incomes ranging from $1,000 to $2,000. There is a decided concentration of undesirable racial elements. More than half the population of San Francisco are located here, and it is considered a highly hazardous area.

Derogatory references about Black people exist throughout every report. In many cases, it was noted that there were "no inharmonious racial threats," "racial concentration is very remote," or that "undesirable racial elements" are nearby or presently existent within a neighborhood. Asians, Hispanics, and other European ethnic groups were referred to as "foreign born," or named specifically. It became astoundingly evident through many years of analysis that the presence of "not-Black" groups did not present as much of a psychological and emotional disruption to White people as did the presence of Black people.

Are the psychopathology, psychosis, and psychopathy of Whiteness becoming clearer?

Roughly one decade later, in the mid-1930s, German Chancellor Adolf Hitler and the Nazi regime began replicating the same neighborhood and housing conditions in Germany, specifically targeting the Jewish community.

Figure 8.6.

D-1   This area of some 20 blocks occupies a comparatively level

section which is inhabited by semi-skilled laborers, low-

wage "white collar" workers, and service group employees, with incomes

ranging from $1,000 to $2,000. There is a decided concentration of

undesirable racial elements. More than half the Negro population of

San Francisco are located here, and it is considered a highly hazard-

ous area. It is zoned second-residential with considerable provision

for business, and is largely given over to old apartments and flats

some of which show a high degree of obsolescence. The single-family

residences had a cost range when new of from $3500 to $7,000 and con-

sist mainly of frame structures having an average age of from 30 to

60 years. It is approximately 40% owner-occupied, but very little

pride of ownership is exhibited. Vacancies are numerous, being not

less than 10%. There is quite an extensive business district along

Divisadero Street which constitutes the area's eastern boundary. Schools

and transportation facilities are conveniently available, and many

parks and recreational areas are close by. Property in the area is

not readily saleable, and assessed value of lands is so high that

it constitutes a distinct burden to the home owners. It is felt that

when and if Laurel Hill Cemetery is sub-divided and developed, the

western portion of this area may be favorably affected. Only one

mortgagee institution was found that would accept applications for

loans in this area and it did so largely as a matter of principle,

officials stating that loans would only be made upon extremely modified

terms.

A standard six-room house in this area would have sold for

$5000 in 1929, $2500 in 1933, and is currently selling for $3500.

The same home would have rented for $45 in 1929, $22.50 in 1933, and

$32.50 now.

Dr. DeWitt Buckingham: Battle with the Claremont Improvement Club and White Psychopathology

When Dr. DeWitt A. Buckingham, a Black physician who also served as an Army Captain in the Medical Corps during World War II, decided to move both his family and his private practice from Meridian, Mississippi in 1945, he most likely did not ever imagine that his life would be dramatically changed forever. Unimpressed with homes located in Berkeley, California's "negro section," Dr. Buckingham sought to purchase a home in Berkeley's upper-class section, close to the Claremont Club and Spa, at 22 Bridge Road. There was only one problem: The neighborhood was legally restricted to "Whites Only."[390,391]

Please note the following in an article entitled, "Oakland Physician Stood Up for Housing Rights," written by Lincoln Cushing, originally published in the *East Bay Express* in 2019:

> Since 1928 the Claremont Improvement Club neighborhood association had a restrictive clause on the property reading "no part of said lands shall ever be used or occupied by persons of other than pure Caucasian blood."
>
> Club attorneys claimed the covenant served to protect homes and investments of area residents. "It is a question of economics, not racial evaluation," they said. Despite the restriction, Dr. Buckingham purchased the house from Oakland optometrist Benjamin Brudney for a reported $19,000. The Buckinghams moved into the premises during the night and resisted legal efforts to oust them.
>
> The Club sued the Buckinghams—and Brudney—in early 1946. The defense was led by Bertam Edises, described in news accounts as "a University of California student-pacifist, national disarmament advocate, and National Labor Relations Board attorney." Edises had mounted several previous suits against covenants. His argument? Using UC Berkeley anthropologists, including instructor Paul Radin, to prove that there is no such thing as a pure Caucasian, and therefore the covenants could neither be violated nor enforced. Edises threatened to file counter suits to force all plaintiffs to come into court and prove their race.
>
> But Alameda County Superior Judge James G. Quinn didn't buy it and ruled against Dr. Buckingham. The same was held for the appeal in October 1947, under Superior Court Judge Leon E. Gray. Dr. Buckingham spoke out: *"Not only is [this decision] a blow to me and my family, but to all minority groups in the State of California, the nation and a disgrace to*

the democratic citizens of Berkeley, the keystone of education, refinement and culture and home of the great University where these things are supposed to exist . . . As a captain in the Medical Corps of the U.S. Army, I fought for democracy and I shall continue the fight."

Despite the injunction, Mrs. Buckingham said she and her husband continued to live peacefully in their home for three years and stated, "the neighbors have been very nice to us."

The struggle was one of many that cascaded upwards to the U.S. Supreme Court, where on May 3, 1948, the Saint Louis case of Shelley vs. Kraemer determined that "restrictive real estate agreements which bar Negroes from all-white neighborhoods cannot be enforced by State or Federal courts."

On December 6, 1948, the California State District Court of Appeal reversed Judge Gray's decision.

Upon hearing the news, Dr. Buckingham and his wife issued a statement, saying, *"The recent unanimous decision . . . has proclaimed . . . the hopes and desires of all Americans who have fought, lived and died for democracy expressed in our Constitution."*[390,391]

It is clear from Dr. Buckingham's and his wife's official statement that they most likely believed that the worst was behind them. They could not have been more wrong.

Digging deeper into Dr. Buckingham's life enabled me to uncover the ways in which his fight against the court system not only made him a marked man, but also ruined his life.

Litigation likely deprived them of substantial money and inflicted great emotional stress on them individually and as a couple. They fought for their dignity. The home was the mere symbol. They fought for their humanity and the humanity of everyone who resembled them.

The favorable result triggered various White leaders, who concocted another challenge: an IRS audit. He was accused of tax evasion. He initially decided to plead guilty. That changed.

The next few pages feature a series of articles that detail Dr. DeWitt Buckingham's life in the years after his vigorous battle with the Claremont Improvement Club. The first article is entitled "Doctor Admits Tax Evasion, Free on Bail," and appeared in the *Oakland Tribune* on July 19, 1954; it scrutinized the purported evasion.[392] Coincidentally, the alleged evasion occurred the same year the Buckinghams were sued by their White neighbors. Could it be that the Buckinghams used the monies that they would have paid to the IRS to pay their legal expenses? Yes, likely. Put another way, I am almost certain that the Buckinghams did not anticipate going to court on the grounds that they were Black. Blackness was their crime. Laws across the land criminalized Blackness. Dr. DeWitt Buckingham and his wife became casualties of a legal system that criminalized their humanity in the worst way.

The next article entitled, "Doctor Faces $10,612.00 Lien For U.S. Taxes," was presumably written and published sometime in late 1954. It details what appears to be proof of a conspiracy to destroy his life, including further details of the investigation concerning his finances. Because the focus of the investigation is on 1946 to 1951, it can be presumed that White leaders most likely wondered how a Black man was maintaining his mortgage, family household bills, and additional living expenses, all while paying massive legal fees. The White leaders of America's institutions hatched a campaign to destroy him. They launched an investigation into his financial situation and set out on a path of financial ruin and total humiliation. This was the price for challenging the system.

It appears that Dr. DeWitt Buckingham was pursued by the local, state, and federal government, as well as by the judicial system. They conspired to teach him a lesson because he challenged the system in ways that no Black man in America should ever do. Because Dr. Buckingham decided that he and his family deserved a high-quality, stable life and clean-living conditions, conditions that White men in America long-ago decided should only be accessible to White people, Dr. Buckingham's life, marriage, and family were sabotaged. His family was ruined, and for many generations.

Dr. Buckingham ultimately went to prison. The third article, entitled, "Prison Bound Doctor Faces Custody Battle in Court," indicates that he was sentenced to six months in prison.[393] This was the price Dr. Buckingham paid for fighting for justice in White America. Shameful.

While researching the case, I stumbled upon a YouTube video of Dr. Buckingham's son. He spoke of how drugs had ruined his life.[394] He spoke of his revoked scholarship as a result of his criminal activity. He shared openly about his struggles.

Would he have faced these challenges had his home life not been so disturbed? The question is valid. Whites who insisted on punishing his father changed the dynamics of his life. They soiled them. They made them ripe for destruction.

In short, I was particularly struck by this case for personal reasons. No Black person can challenge the White order without compromising their own life and the lives of those they cherish most. That is the bottom line. Dr. Buckingham, like so many others, had his life ravaged because of his Blackness. To so many Whites, he was a nothing. To me? Everything.

Dr. Buckingham's story should matter to us all without question. It matters more to me perhaps because I have spent years challenging the White order, too. And it has come at a very high personal cost to me. Decades ago, he did his best as one Black man. Today, I do my best as one Black man.

Figure 8.7.

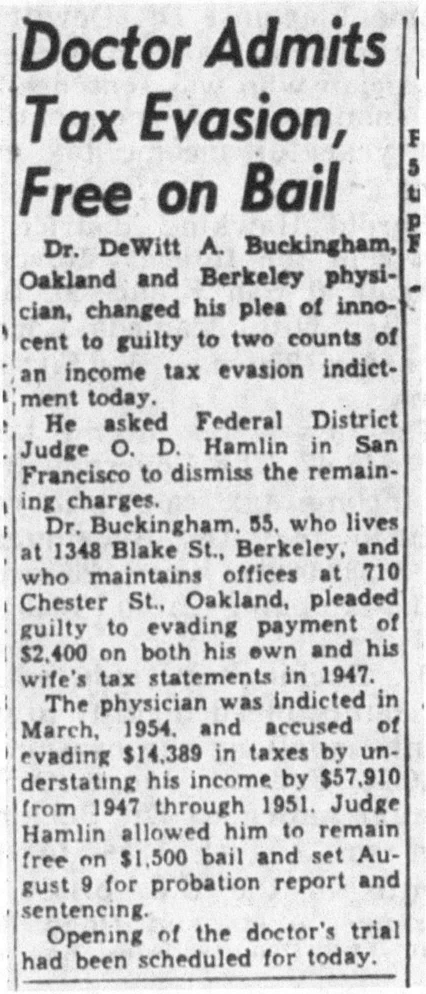

Doctor Admits Tax Evasion, Free on Bail

Dr. DeWitt A. Buckingham, Oakland and Berkeley physician, changed his plea of innocent to guilty to two counts of an income tax evasion indictment today.

He asked Federal District Judge O. D. Hamlin in San Francisco to dismiss the remaining charges.

Dr. Buckingham, 55, who lives at 1348 Blake St., Berkeley, and who maintains offices at 710 Chester St., Oakland, pleaded guilty to evading payment of $2,400 on both his own and his wife's tax statements in 1947.

The physician was indicted in March, 1954, and accused of evading $14,389 in taxes by understating his income by $57,910 from 1947 through 1951. Judge Hamlin allowed him to remain free on $1,500 bail and set August 9 for probation report and sentencing.

Opening of the doctor's trial had been scheduled for today.

Figure 8.8.

Doctor Faces $10,612 Lien For U.S. Taxes

A $10,612 income tax lien has been filed by the Federal Government against Dr. Dewitt A. Buckingham, Oakland-Berkeley physician who was sentenced to six months in the penitentiary last year for income tax evasion.

Harold Hawkins, district director of the Internal Revenue Bureau at San Francisco, filed the lien with Alameda County Recorder Thomas W. Fitzsimmons.

The lien is for income taxes for 1946-47. The Government in its income tax case last year claimed that Dr. Buckingham owed $38,000 in taxes for a period extending from 1946 to 1951.

Dr. Buckingham, indicted on six counts, pleaded guilty to two counts involving the evasion of $24,000. Federal Judge O. D. Hamlin sentenced Dr. Buckingham in August 1954 to six months in the U.S. prison at Florence, Ariz., and fined him $200. Dr. Buckingham has of-

Figure 8.9.

Prison-Bound Doctor Faces Custody Battle in Court

Dr. DeWitt Buckingham, Berkeley-Oakland physician convicted of income tax evasion, was bound for Federal prison today. But before his departure he became involved in the opening phases of a bitter court struggle to retain the custody of the Buckingham child, DeWitt II, 6.

Superior Judge Richard H. Chamberlain heard Buckingham testify against a petition sought by his ex-wife, Mrs. Mamie E. Buckingham, seeking to grant her custody of the boy.

Shortly before he surrendered to the U.S. marshal to be taken to Federal prison at Florence, Ariz., Buckingham told Judge Chamberlain that he had sent DeWitt II to relatives at Meridian, Miss., on July 30. Federal Judge O. D. Hamlin on July 19 sentenced the doctor to six months and fined him $200 on his plea of guilty to counts of evading $34,000 in income taxes for 1947.

SEEKS CUSTODY

Mrs. Buckingham, who lost control of the boy at a hearing before Judge A. J. Woolsey, emphasized through her attorney that the child was not to leave the state without Superior Court permission. She seeks control again because of Buckingham's imprisonment.

Buckingham claimed that the couple never had formally adopted the child, who he said was taken into their home October 2, 1947. The physician, living at 1348 Blake St., Berkeley, and practising at 718 Chester St., said Mrs. Buckingham flew to Los Angeles to get the baby a day after his birth.

HELD INVALID

Dr. Buckingham testified that the birth certificate was sent to him by a southern doctor, unsigned, and that "some other doctor" made out the document, making it appear that the birth occurred in Berkeley.

The Buckinghams were divorced July 3, 1953 and the final decree was signed last Aug. 2. In the court fight last October in which Buckingham won custody the doctor charged his wife with misconduct with another man at a San Francisco hotel, where the child had been taken. Mrs. Buckingham denied this and claimed she had fled to the hotel to avoid Buckingham's threats.

Buckingham surrendered to the marshal at San Francisco and the custody case here was continued for further testimony.

Paden Scholarship Fund Established

ALAMEDA, Aug. 26.—A William G. Paden Memorial Scholarship for $200 will be given in the name of the man who died April 6 after 40 years in the Alameda school system, 27 of them as school superintendent.

The scholarship will be given the son or daughter of a member of the California School Employees' Association.

Figure 8.10.
Dr. DeWitt A. Buckingham

Perpetual Infinite Forms of Black Genocide

In *Stamped from the Beginning*,[4] Dr. Ibram X. Kendi traces anti-literacy laws from the nineteenth century. Between 1829 and 1834, Alabama, Georgia, Louisiana, North Carolina, South Carolina, and Virginia, all passed them. They forbade teaching free or enslaved Black persons how to read or write. Whites wanted them illiterate, which was to say they wanted them powerless. In fact, all but Maryland and Kentucky outlawed teaching enslaved and/or free Black people to read or write.[4]

Consider the murder rate of Black persons during the nineteenth and twentieth centuries. Black life was cheap, after all; what did it matter if an unusually high number of Black persons were murdered on a daily basis?

Ida B. Wells-Barnett studied this famously in her writings entitled *Southern Horrors of Lynching*. Ralph Ginzburg amplified many of these murders in his text, *100 Years of Lynchings*, which features a trove of news articles highlighting the prevalence of lynching in America. James Allen's Hilton Als,[ ] John Lewis,[ ] and Leon F. Litwack's text, *Without Sanctuary*, also presents the gruesome realities of facilitated lynching that included the support (and sometimes participation) of local, state, and federal American officials. Here are a few examples of conspicuous White psychopathy and anti-Black terror (as shown in *100 Years of Lynchings*):[99]

Figure 8.11.

CHICAGO TRIBUNE
November 22, 1895

TEXANS LYNCH WRONG NEGRO

MADISONVILLE, Tex., Nov. 21—News has been received here of the lynching of a Negro in this part of Madison County on Tuesday night. He was accused of riding his horse over a little white girl and injuring her. On Wednesday it was discovered that the wrong Negro had been gotten hold of by the mob. The guilty one made his escape.

Figure 8.12.

NEW YORK TRUTH SEEKER
April 17, 1880

FIRST NEGRO AT WEST POINT
KNIFED BY FELLOW CADETS

WEST POINT, N.Y., Apr. 15—James Webster Smith, the first colored cadet in the history of West Point, was recently taken from his bed, gagged, bound, and severely beaten, and then his ears were slit. He says that he cannot identify his assailants. The other cadets claim that he did it himself.

Figure 8.13.

WASHINGTON TIMES
February 18, 1900

NEGRO LYNCHED TO AVENGE
ASSAULT ON WHITE WOMAN

COLUMBIA, S. C., Feb. 17—Will Burts, a negro, nineteen years old, was lynched this morning in Aiken county. Three days ago he attempted to outrage Mrs. C. L. Weeks and failed.

A crowd of 250 tracked the negro fifty miles across Aiken, Edgefield, and Greenwood counties. He was caught last evening by a farmer, who received $100 from the posse. The party returned to Greenwood, and at daylight this morning the lynching occurred. Some wished to hold the man till tonight and make a public demonstration of it, but this was outvoted.

A clothesline was obtained, one end swung over an oak limb, and the other fastened to Burts' neck. He was then ordered to climb the tree and get out on the limb. This the negro did without hesitation. He was then shot from the limb. The rope broke, and, as Burts was not dead, he was again hoisted up and then shot to pieces.

Avowed White terrorists were ubiquitous. There was no escaping them. Tragedy was inevitable.

Take Mary Turner, a pregnant Black woman who, at 33, reported a mob of White men who murdered her husband.[171] As noted on the Mary Turner website, developed to memorialize her story, the following transpired:

> On Saturday, May 18th Hayes Turner, who had at one point in time worked for Hampton Smith, was arrested for allegedly being part of the plot or "conspiracy" to kill him. After his arrest, Turner was held in the Brooks County jail before he was to be transferred to the Moultrie, Georgia jail for his safety. In the process of that transfer the Brooks County Sheriff and County Clerk were reportedly stopped by a mob of 40 masked men who took Hayes Turner and hung him at the intersection of Morven and Barney roads. Once again, his body was left there for a number of days for all to see.
>
> On Sunday, May 19th, thirty-three-year-old Mary Turner (m.n. Hattie Graham), the wife of Hayes Turner and reportedly 8 months pregnant at the time, someone who had also worked for and been abused by Hampton Smith, outraged about her husband's lynching publicly threatened to swear out warrants for those responsible for his murder. Those "unwise remarks," as the area papers put it, "enraged" local whites further. Consequently, Mary Turner was captured and taken to a place called Folsom's Bridge on the Brooks and Lowndes Counties' shared border. To punish her, at Folsom's Bridge the mob tied Mary Turner by her ankles and hung her upside down from a tree. Mob members then poured gasoline on her and burned her alive. One member of the mob is said to have then cut her stomach open causing her unborn child to drop to the ground where it was reportedly stomped and crushed. According to N.A.A.C.P. investigator Walter White, her body was then riddled with gunfire from the mob. Later that night she and her baby were buried ten feet away from where she was murdered. Her makeshift grave was marked with only a "whiskey bottle" with a "cigar" stuffed in its neck.[171]

How, when every institution was poisoned, could this have been avoided?

Think of John Hartfield, a Black man in Louisiana who was lynched for dating a White woman in Ellisville, Mississippi in 1919.[172] The story, as noted 100 years ago, says that John Hartfield was hanged, shot, and roasted for dating a White lady and his body was shared with spectators. It reads:

John Hartfield left his home in Ellisville seeking a better life in East St. Louis. In 1919, he traveled back to Ellisville to visit his white girlfriend, Ruth Meeks, taking a job as a hotel porter in Laurel. When the relationship became known to some white men, they decided to kill Hartfield. They accused Hartfield of raping Meeks, who they claimed was 18, although she was in her mid-twenties. Hartfield managed to elude them for a while, but they pursued him for several weeks.

Sheriff Allen Boutwell in Laurel raised donations to fund a hunting party with Bloodhounds at the request of Sheriff Harbison. He was finally apprehended attempting to board a train on June 24, and was turned over to Sheriff Harbison, who placed him in the charge of a deputy and left town. The deputy immediately released him to a mob.

The *Jackson Daily News*, the *New Orleans States*, and other newspapers ran headlines saying, "John Hartfield will be lynched by Ellisville mob at 5:00 this afternoon" and additional text that read, "The officers have agreed to turn him over to the people of the city at 4 o'clock this afternoon when it is expected he will be burned."[172]

Both examples involve innocent Black persons and culpable White persons. Both involve weaponizing every available institution (law enforcement officers, government, etc.). Both acts of terror were minimized, incentivizing even further terror. None of the bad actors faced consequences; they were simply erased from the historical record.

There is a pattern. As noted in *The Jackson Daily News*, Mississippi's Governor, Theodore Bilbo, also decided that he would do nothing to prevent the lynching of John Hartfield.

Figure 8.14.

This newspaper advertisement represents the boldness of White psychopathy. It also showcases Whites premeditating murder, and the lack of protection for Black people in America, both past and present. The reason that this was even possible was because the United States Supreme Court ruled in *United States v. Cruikshank* (1876) that anti-Black terror was legal. This case involved the Colfax massacre where Black men exercising their rights to assemble peaceably, and to vote, were murdered by more than 300 Whites. The decision invalidated Black people's rights provided under the First, Fourteenth, and Fifteenth Amendments of the United States Constitution, the latter of which had been instituted roughly ten and six years earlier respectively.

As stated in the *First Amendment Encyclopedia*:

In <u>*United States v. Cruikshank*</u>, 92 U.S. 542 (1876), the U.S. Supreme Court threw out the convictions of Cruikshank and other whites who, during a dispute about a gubernatorial election in Louisiana, killed about 100 blacks in the Colfax Massacre and were subsequently charged with conspiring to deprive those blacks of their constitutional rights.

Consistent with such decisions as those in *Barron v. Baltimore* (1833), which the Court issued prior to adoption of the Fourteenth and Fifteenth Amendments, Waite sought to limit the rights of national citizenship by distinguishing it from state citizenship.

He argued that the right to peaceable assembly was a natural right that preceded the adoption of the Constitution, rather than a right granted by it. For Waite, the First Amendment prohibited Congress from abridging the right to assemble but "was not intended to limit the powers of the State governments in respect to their own citizens, but to operate on the National government alone.

The Court found that while Congress has the right to protect individuals meeting for purposes of petitioning the national government, the indictments had made no claim that the individuals arrested and charged were attempting to deny this right to anyone or that the actions in this case were specifically directed at individuals on the basis of race.

Consistent with the distinction the Court would later draw between state and private action in the *Civil Rights Cases* (1883), Waite wrote in the high court's decision that the enforcement clause was not designed to protect individuals against the actions of other individuals but only from those of the state itself.[287]

Building upon Cruikshank, and further underlying these miscarriages of justice, subsequent decisions were rendered by the U.S. Supreme Court in 1883, concerning *Pace v. Alabama* (1881) and *United States v. Harris* (1876), which motivated and enabled Whites to enact legalized physically violent terrorism against Black people.[288],[289] In the matter concerning Plaintiff Tony Pace, a Black male, and Mary J. Cox, a White female, the two were indicted, tried, and convicted in an Alabama circuit court on the grounds of living together as an interracial couple. Put another way, the court convicted them because he was Black and she was White, leveraging subsequent claims of "fornication" and "adultery." Alabama's all-White judicial system took issue with a Black man and White woman cohabitating and sentenced them both to two years imprisonment in the state penitentiary.

Tony Pace fought the ruling on the grounds that it violated his rights under the Fourteenth Amendment that had been enacted roughly fifteen years earlier. The Fourteenth Amendment declared "no state shall deny any person equal protection under the laws." Mr. Pace escalated the case to the U.S. Supreme Court. However, the U.S. Supreme Court decided to rule against Mr. Pace, siding with the Alabama circuit court on the following grounds:

Per *Justia U.S. Supreme Court*:

Section 4184 of the Code of Alabama provides:

If any man and woman live together in adultery or fornication, each of them must, on the first conviction of the offense, be fined not less than one hundred dollars, and may also be imprisoned in the county jail or sentenced to hard labor for the county for not more than six months. On the second conviction for the offense with the same person, the offender must be fined not less than three hundred dollars, and may be imprisoned in the county jail, or sentenced to hard labor for the county for not more than twelve months, and for a third or any subsequent conviction with the same person, must be imprisoned in the penitentiary, or sentenced to hard labor for the county for two years.

Section 4189 of the same code declares:

If any white person and any negro, or the descendant of any negro to the third generation, inclusive, though one ancestor of each generation was a white person, intermarry or live in adultery or fornication with each other, each of them must, on conviction, be imprisoned in the penitentiary or sentenced to hard labor for the county for not less than two nor more than seven years.

Again, this decision, which followed several prior rulings, reinforced the notion that Black people were not human, or fully human, in the eyes of the White-American legal, psychopathic, and sociopathic Black genocidal system.

Even when the United States Congress, during the presidential administration of President Ulysses Grant, passed the Force Act of 1871, an act expressly and intentionally aimed at protecting Black people from physically violent acts of White terrorism, the United States Supreme Court, on January 22, 1883, ruled the act invalid.[289,290] In *United States v. Harris*, the United States Supreme Court ruled that the U.S. Congress had no right to legislate acts protecting Black people from acts of terrorism, whether by groups or individuals. They ruled against the Force Act, as well as the Fourteenth Amendment, reinforcing the idea that Black people were not human.

By rendering this decision, the U.S. Supreme court facilitated, enabled, and empowered White people to commit terrorist acts against Black people throughout the next 139 years and counting (which can be observed through institutional outcomes and the continual mistreatment of Black people by law enforcement and civilians presented in pervasive examples rampant on all social media platforms in present-day America).

The commemoration of White psychopathic and sociopathic terrorism mentioned above can be observed through many of the postcards and photographs depicted and described in *Without Sanctuary* and *100 Years of Lynchings*. These events depict and showcase White people committing legally sanctioned terrorism without consequence, as well as those who watched in support of the acts, cheerfully and gleefully.

The murders of George Floyd, Breonna Taylor, and Ahmaud Arbery were not new. They were expressions of a "right-of-passage" passed down through generations of psychopathic sociopaths and diabolical animalistic terrorists. This behavior represented the core of White identity and the White moral concept.

Additional examples of unchecked White American terrorism are provided throughout the subsequent pages:

Figure 8.15.   **Figure 8.16.**

L.D. Nelson, 14 years old, and his mother, Laura Nelson, hanging from a bridge, in Oklahoma, 1911. Pictured below, the crowd of White people who participated in their murders, posing for a picture to commemorate the event.

Figure 8.17.

Figure 8.18.

Jessie Washington, 16 years old. Burned and hung to death in Waco, Texas in 1916. Thousands of people, city officials, businessmen, law enforcement, and townspeople participated in event.

Figure 8.19.

Figure 8.20.

Figure 8.21.

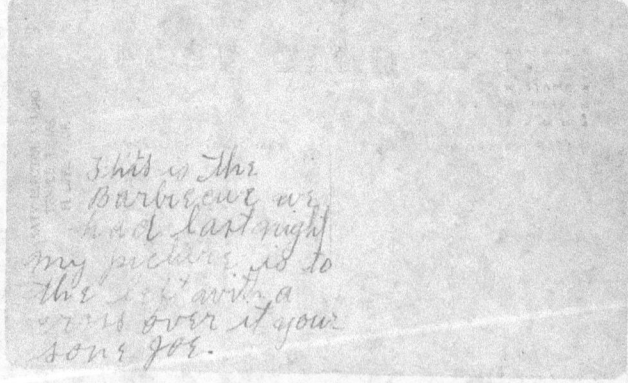

Figure 8.22.

Figure 8.23.
16-year-old Lige Daniels, Center, Texas; August 3, 1920.

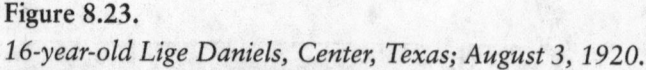

Figure 8.24.

Figure 8.25.

Figure 8.26.

The above picture depicts the Rubin Stacy lynching, in Fort Lauderdale, Florida, 1935. He was lynched for "threatening and frightening a white woman."

Following this tragic and murderous event, the NAACP rallied in support of the Costigan-Wagner Anti-Lynching Bill, which was railroaded by a group of anti-Black senators. The NAACP included Rubin Stacy's photo on a gripping flyer in an effort to obtain support for the bill's passage. The flyer included the following words:

Do not look at the Negro.

His earthly problems are ended.

Instead, look at the seven WHITE children who gaze at this gruesome spectacle.

Is it horror or gloating on the face of the neatly dressed seven-year-old girl on the right?

Is the tiny four-year-old on the left old enough, one wonders, to comprehend the barbarism her elders have perpetrated?

Rubin Stacy, the Negro, who was lynched at Fort Lauderdale, Florida, on July 19, 1935, for "threatening and frightening a white woman," suffered PHYSICAL torture for a few short hours. But what psychological havoc is being wrought in the minds of the white children? Into what kinds of citizens will they grow up? What kind of America will they help to make after being familiarized with such an inhuman, law-destroying practice as lynching?[350]

Figure 8.27.

Figure 8.28.

Postcard of the 1920 Duluth, Minnesota lynchings. Two of the black victims are still hanging while the third is on the ground. Postcards of lynchings were popular souvenirs in the United States (Isaac McGhie, Elias Clayton and Elmer Johnson). Courtesy of the National African American Museum of History and Culture.

Brief reflection questions:

√   What legal and societal messages did White people receive, about how they could mistreat Black people based upon the normalcy of these events during this period (and beyond)?

√   What messages did Black people receive about what it means to be Black in White America during this period (and beyond), as far as the acceptance of mistreatment and lack of protections legally and societally?

√   How does the vile and gruesome mistreatment of Black people, facilitated through White legality and practicality, reinforce the cultural antiblack tenet (that provides everyone with legitimate rights to mistreat and degrade anyone perceived and/or interpreted as Black)?

These types of patterns are repeated throughout our history and embedded into the fiber of American culture. The pattern continues when one looks at how Governor Charles Hillman Brough facilitated the Elaine Arkansas Race Massacre in 1919.[173] As stated in the Encyclopedia of Arkansas:

> The Elaine Massacre was by far the deadliest <u>racial confrontation</u> in Arkansas history and possibly the bloodiest racial conflict in the history of the United States. While its deepest roots lay in the state's commitment to white supremacy, the events in <u>Elaine (Phillips County)</u> stemmed from tense race relations and growing concerns about labor unions. A shooting incident that occurred at a meeting of the <u>Progressive Farmers and Household Union</u> escalated into mob violence on the part of the white people in Elaine and surrounding areas. Although the exact number is unknown, estimates of the number of <u>African Americans</u> killed by whites range into the hundreds; five white people lost their lives.

> The conflict began on the night of September 30, 1919, when approximately 100 African Americans, mostly <u>sharecroppers</u> on the plantations of white landowners, attended a meeting of the Progressive Farmers and Household Union of America at a church in Hoop Spur (Phillips County), three miles north of Elaine. The purpose of the meeting, one of several by Black sharecroppers in the Elaine area during the previous months, was to obtain better payments for their <u>cotton</u> crops from the white plantation owners who dominated the area during the <u>Jim Crow</u> era. Black sharecroppers were often exploited in their efforts to collect payment for their cotton crops. The union had contracted with lawyer <u>Ulysses S. Bratton</u>, whose son, Ocier, was at this meeting.

> In previous months, racial conflict had occurred in numerous cities in America, including Washington DC; Chicago, Illinois; Knoxville, Tennessee; and Indianapolis, Indiana. With labor conflicts escalating throughout the country at the end of <u>World War I</u>, government and business interpreted the demands of labor increasingly as the work of foreign ideologies, such as Bolshevism, that threatened the foundation of the American economy. Thrown into this highly combustible mix were Black soldiers, who were returning to the United States and who often exhibited a less submissive attitude within the Jim Crow society around them.

> Unions such as the Progressive Farmers represented a threat not only to the tenet of white supremacy but also to the basic concepts of capitalism. Although the United States was on the winning side of World War I, supporters

of American capitalism found in communism a new menace to their security. With the success of the Russian Revolution, stopping the spread of international communism was seen as the duty of all loyal Americans. Arkansas governor Charles Hillman Brough told a St. Louis, Missouri, audience during the war that "there existed no twilight zone in American patriotism" and called Wisconsin senator Robert LaFollete, who opposed the war, a Bolshevik leader. During this "Red Scare," the threat of "Bolshevism" seemed to be everywhere: not only in the labor strikes led by the radical Industrial Workers of the World but also in the cotton fields of Arkansas.

Leaders of the Hoop Spur union had placed armed guards around the church to prevent disruption of their meeting and intelligence gathering by white opponents. Though accounts of who fired the first shots are in sharp conflict, a shootout in front of the church on the night of September 30, 1919, between the armed Black guards around the church and three individuals whose vehicle was parked in front of the church resulted in the death of W. A. Adkins, a white security officer for the Missouri-Pacific Railroad, and the wounding of Charles Pratt, Phillips County's white deputy sheriff.

The next morning, the Phillips County sheriff sent out a posse to arrest those suspected of being involved in the shooting. Although the posse encountered minimal resistance from the Black residents of the area around Elaine, the fear of African Americans, who outnumbered whites in this area of Phillips County by a ratio of ten to one, led an estimated 500 to 1,000 armed white people—mostly from the surrounding Arkansas counties but also from across the river in Mississippi—to travel to Elaine to put down what was characterized by them as an "insurrection." On October 1, Phillips County authorities sent three telegrams to Gov. Brough, requesting that U.S. troops be sent to Elaine. Brough responded by gaining permission from the Department of War to send more than 500 battle-tested troops from Camp Pike, outside of Little Rock (Pulaski County).

After troops arrived in Elaine on the morning of October 2, 1919, the white mobs began to depart the area and return to their homes. The military placed several hundred African Americans in makeshift stockades until they could be questioned and vouched for by their white employers. (Union leader Robert Lee Hill was hidden by friends during the violence and later escaped to Kansas.) The violence even claimed those who had nothing to do with the union efforts, such as brothers David Augustine Elihue Johnston, Gibson Allen Johnston, Lewis Harrison (L. H.) Johnston, and Leroy Johnston, who were returning to Helena from a hunting trip when they were attacked and killed on October 2.

Evidence shows that the mobs of whites slaughtered African Americans in and around Elaine. For example, H. F. Smiddy, one of the white witnesses to the massacre, swore in an eye-witness account in 1921 that "several hundred of them . . . began to hunt negroes and shotting [*sic*] them as they came to them." Anecdotal evidence also suggests that the troops from Camp Pike engaged in indiscriminate killing of African Americans in the area, which, if true, was a replication of past militia activity to put down perceived Black revolts. In 1925, Sharpe Dunaway, an employee of the *Arkansas Gazette*, alleged that soldiers in Elaine had "committed one murder after another with all the calm deliberation in the world, either too heartless to realize the enormity of their crimes, or too drunk on moonshine to give a continental darn."

Colonel Isaac Jenks, commander of the U.S. troops at Elaine, recorded the number of African Americans killed by U.S. troops as only two. In contrast, the correspondent for the *Memphis Press* on October 2, 1919, wrote, "Many Negroes are reported killed by the soldiers. . . ." Other anecdotal information suggests that U.S. troops also engaged in torture of African Americans to make them confess and give information.

The white power structure in Phillips County formed a "Committee of Seven," made of influential planters, businessmen, and elected officials, to investigate the cause of the disturbances. The committee met with Gov. Brough, who had ridden on the train with the troops and accompanied them on a march to the Hoop Spur area. The governor, who was reported as saying he was going to Elaine to "obtain correct information," accepted the authority of the committee in return for its commitment that no lynchings would take place in Helena (Phillips County). He returned to Little Rock the next day and told a press conference, "The situation at Elaine has been well handled and is absolutely under control. There is no danger of any lynching. . . . The white citizens of the county deserve unstinting praise for their actions in preventing mob violence."

From this point forward, two versions of what occurred at Elaine exist. The white leaders put forward their view that Black residents had been about to revolt. E. M. Allen, a planter and real estate developer who became the spokesman for Phillips County's white power structure, told the *Helena World* on October 7, "The present trouble with the Negroes in Phillips County is not a race riot. It is a deliberately planned insurrection of the Negroes against the whites directed by an organization known as the 'Progressive Farmers and Household Union of America,' established for the purpose of banding Negroes together for the killing of white people."

On the other hand, the <u>National Association for the Advancement of Colored People (NAACP)</u> in New York, which had sent Field Secretary Walter White to investigate the events in Elaine, contested such allegations from the outset. White wrote in the *Chicago Daily News* on October 19, 1919, that the belief there had been an insurrection was "only a figment of the imagination of Arkansas whites and not based on fact." He said, "White men in Helena told me that more than one hundred Negroes were killed." Famed journalist and anti-lynching activist, Ida B. Wells-Barnett, secretly interviewed some of the prisoners in Helena, from which she produced the pamphlet "The Arkansas Race Riot." This work also challenged allegations of an insurrection and documented the torture and other depredations the prisoners had suffered.

Within days of the initial shoot-out, 285 African Americans were taken from the temporary stockades to the jail in Helena, the county seat, although the jail had space for only forty-eight. Two white members of the Phillips County posse, T. K. Jones, and H. F. Smiddy, stated in sworn affidavits in 1921 that they committed acts of torture at the Phillips County jail and named others who had also participated in the torture. On October 31, 1919, the Phillips County grand jury charged 122 African Americans with crimes stemming from the racial disturbances. The charges ranged from murder to <u>nightriding</u>, a charge akin to terroristic threatening (as defined by <u>Act 112 of 1909</u>). The trials began the next week, with <u>John Elvis Miller</u> leading the prosecution. White attorneys from Helena were appointed by Circuit Judge J. M. Jackson to represent the first twelve Black men to go to trial. Attorney Jacob Fink, who was appointed to represent Frank Hicks, admitted to the jury that he had not interviewed any witnesses. He made no motion for a change of venue, nor did he challenge a single prospective juror, taking the first 12 called. By November 5, 1919, the first twelve Black men who were given trials had been convicted of murder and sentenced to die in the electric chair. As a result, sixty-five others quickly entered plea bargains and accepted sentences of up to twenty-one years for second-degree murder. Others had their charges dismissed or ultimately were not prosecuted.

In Little Rock and at the headquarters of the NAACP in New York, efforts began to fight the death sentences handed down in Helena, led in part by Scipio Africanus Jones, the leading Black attorney of his era in Arkansas, and Edgar L. McHaney. Jones began to raise money in the Black community in Little Rock for the defense of the "Elaine Twelve," as the convicted men came to be known. The twelve men were: Frank Moore, Frank Hicks,

Ed Hicks, Joe Knox, Paul Hall, Ed Coleman, Alfred Banks, Ed Ware, William Wordlaw, Albert Giles, Joe Fox, and John Martin.

At the same time, the New York offices of the NAACP, upon the advice of Arkansas attorney Ulysses S. Bratton, hired the Little Rock law firm of George C. Murphy, a former attorney general and candidate for governor, as counsel for the twelve men. Even at the age of seventy-nine, Murphy, a former Confederate officer and Arkansas attorney general, was considered one of the best trial attorneys in Arkansas. By late November, Jones was working with Murphy's firm to save the Elaine Twelve.

Their initial task was to appeal the sentences given to the Elaine Twelve and ask for a new trial based on errors committed by the trial court. Gov. Brough issued a stay of the executions to permit an appeal to the Arkansas Supreme Court after the motions were denied. For the next five years, the cases of the Elaine Twelve were mired in litigation as Murphy and Jones fought to save the men from death. They secured new trials for six of the men, known as the Ware defendants, based on the fact that the trial judge had not required jurors to indicate the degree of murder on their ballot forms. The convictions of the other six men, known as the Moore defendants, were affirmed.

The cases of the Elaine Twelve were litigated on two separate tracks. The re-trials of the Ware defendants began on May 3, 1920. During the trials, Murphy became ill, and Jones became the principal counsel. Hostility toward him was so great from local white residents that, out of fear for his life, he was said to sleep at different Black families' houses every night during the trials. The convictions were again affirmed. Gov. Brough once again stayed their executions until the Arkansas Supreme Court could again review the cases. Ultimately, the Ware defendants were freed by the Arkansas Supreme Court after two terms of court had passed, and the state of Arkansas made no move to re-try the men.

The Moore defendants were granted a new hearing after the U.S. Supreme Court, in the case of *Moore v. Dempsey*, ruled that the original proceedings in Helena had been a "mask," and that the state of Arkansas had not provided "a corrective process" that would have allowed the defendants to vindicate their constitutional right to due process of law on appeal.

Instead of pursuing a new hearing in federal court, in March 1923, Scipio Jones entered into negotiations to have the Moore defendants released. To be released, the men would have to plead guilty to second-degree murder and a sentence of five years from the date they were first incarcerated in the Arkansas State Penitentiary. Finally, on January 14, 1925, Governor Thomas

McRae ordered the release of the Moore defendants by granting them indefinite furloughs after they had pleaded guilty to second-degree murder. In the interim, Jones had secured the release of the other Elaine defendants.

Though some local white residents of Phillips County still contend that white people at the time acted appropriately to prevent a slaughter in the Elaine area in 1919, the modern view of most historians of this crisis is that white mobs unjustifiably killed an undetermined number of African Americans. More controversial is the view that the military participated in the murder of Black people. Race relations in this area of Arkansas are currently quite strained for a number of reasons, including the events of 1919. A conference on the matter in Helena in 2000 resulted in no closure for the people in Phillips County. On September 29, 2019, a memorial to those who died during the massacre was dedicated in downtown Helena-West Helena. On November 5, 2019, the Elaine Twelve were memorialized on the Arkansas Civil Rights Heritage Trail in Little Rock."[173]

The facilitation of anti-Black terror by White Americans, legitimized and backed by the country's leaders at the local, state, and federal levels (and people from other non-White communities, as well as people who are Black) was and is atrocious. Gatekeepers of Whiteness and anti-Blackness had abundant authority to terrorize. Even Black people are implicated in this extraordinarily complex dynamic.

The responses to Black tragedies, past or present, have been minimized, leading us all to be misled about the extent of the psychopathy and sociopathy. That is why it is done. To deceive. Carefully worded statements distantly alluding to past tragedies do nothing, which is purposeful. And they do not allow us to move forward to correct present woes.

The governors (Bilbo, Brough, and Talmadge), upholders of the law, were psychopaths and sociopaths. All, within their ranks, functioned this way. Talmadge, you will recall, facilitated the murders of the Moore's Ford Lynching victims, Dorothy Malcolm, Roger Malcolm, George Dorsey, and Mae Dorsey.[175]

We cannot overlook Governor Olin D. Johnston, who allowed George Stinney to be murdered by the State of South Carolina for crimes he did not commit.[174] The past is connected to the present.

Take, for instance, former California Governor and American President, Ronald Reagan. Reagan, along with former California Secretary of State and Governor Jerry Brown, assassinated former San Francisco Mayor

George Moscone, former San Francisco Mayor and current California Senator Dianne Feinstein, and assassinated former Board of Supervisors member Harvey Milk, enabled the murders of roughly 900 people by Jim Jones, People's Temple Pastor, in 1978.[176]

More than 600 of the victims were Black people, mostly from California, and no one at the local, state, or federal level took responsibility for investigating the organized criminal facilitation that led to their murders. Some people believe that this annihilation of Black people in San Francisco and Los Angeles was an organized effort on behalf of officials from those cities. That they wanted to rid their cities of what they perceived to be filth. And perhaps Jones completed what America termed Urban Renewal (Redevelopment), or, as James Baldwin called it, Negro Removal.[177]

Jim Jones, with the support of the local, state, and federal officials, was able to con people out of selling their homes, refurbishing them, and selling them for his own personal profit. He was able to continue cashing the social security checks of individuals who were living in South America, while people in a position to stop him did nothing. If he had been a Black pastor, for example, and even one of his victims had been White, what steps do you think would have been taken to stop him?

And take note of the COVID-19 pandemic. Though people of all races have died from it, Black and Brown people have, predictably, been affected disproportionately. Why is that? Can it be the same coincidence occurring over and over and over again or is there a logical pattern to which we can point?

Many officials who push vaccines know they will enrich White shareholders. Follow the money. If they cared genuinely about the welfare of this population, they would address homelessness, education, food insecurity, and other such issues in the same ways that they bailed out mostly White-owned businesses through Paycheck Protection Programs. These programs disproportionately provided monies to mostly White capitalists, including such people as Governor Gavin Newsome and former President Donald Trump. The monies did not have to be paid back to the federal government, as they were subsequently forgiven through a 3- to 4-page online application administered by the Small Business Administration. In essence, the U.S. Federal Government developed a twenty-first century welfare program that overwhelmingly benefited Whites. This is called White socialism.[235,278,279]

It is simple. If we pay attention to the deeply ingrained sentiments held by Whites, we will understand why we live the way we do today.

Observe what former South Carolina Governor and United States Senator Strom Thurmond said, while running for U.S. President in 1948, in reaction to racial integration in the Armed Forces:

> I wanna tell you, ladies and gentlemen, that there's not enough troops in the army to force the southern people to break down segregation and admit the nigger race into our theaters and swimming pools, into our homes and into our churches.[178,179]

Thurmond was infected with the same mental deviations as Lincoln, the illnesses of anti-Blackness and White supremacy. Today, even people hailed as progressives, such as President Joseph Biden, will go out of their way to admonish people for anti-Asian hate stemming from the emergence of the COVID-19 virus (which was very necessary by the way), but will not utter a word in defense of those mostly responsible for electing him: Black Americans. The lives of Black people matter little, if at all, here in America.

White supremacy and anti-Black culture will lead American citizens to prosecute Bill Cosby for allegedly drugging women for decades but allow admitted White serial rapist Christopher J. Belter to be granted probation because the judge "prayed" on the decision and did not feel prison was "appropriate" for him. This is also true for Ed Buck, who did the same to at least ten young Black men, only to face no consequences. Why? More psychopathy, more sociopathy.

Who now speaks the name of Gemmel Moore, a 26-year-old man found dead in Buck's living room, naked on a mattress?

Read the following from "About Gemmel Moore & Timothy Dean":

> According to the report, a coroner's investigator found the following items in Buck's two-bedroom apartment: 24 syringes with brown residue, five glass pipes with white residue and burn marks, a plastic straw with possible white residue, clear plastic bags with white powdery residue and a clear plastic bag with a "piece of crystal-like substance."

> On July 26, 2018, prosecutors declined to file charges against Ed Buck in connection with Gemmel Moore's death, citing insufficient evidence. The Los Angeles County district attorney's office said that the "admissible evidence is insufficient to prove beyond a reasonable doubt" that Buck gave Gemmel Moore drugs or is responsible for his death.[180]

Even more disturbing is the reality of Kyle Rittenhouse leaving his Illinois home to commit murder at a Black Lives Matter–centered demonstration (an event held protesting the law enforcement–led terrorist attack on Jacob Blake in August 2020). Days after his exoneration, Donald Trump, the forty-fifth President of the United States, would invite Rittenhouse to visit with him at his Mar-a-Lago home in Florida.[266,267]

Do not talk to me in isolation about Cosby, R. Kelly, O.J. Simpson, or any other Black person accused, or held accountable for crimes for which White people are not held accountable. All such conversations must begin and end with White people. After all, it is White America who has erected a culture in which rape, pedophilia, human sex trafficking, and other vile atrocities, were legalized during colonial America, and under the United States Constitution, for centuries. This country has yet to make meaningful amends to Black people, our families, and communities, by providing holistic reparations to heal the harms that have been committed against us, as well as the perpetual harms we face in an anti-Black culture. Instead, there are campaigns being engineered by White and White-aligned people to ban such history and perspectives from being taught, to ensure White people never have to face the demented and sociopathic ways Whiteness was constructed.

It is White America that has enabled and allowed all such men to commit attacks against Black women and girls, with little to no consequence. All implicated parties must be held accountable for the relics of perpetual White supremacist patriarchy and matriarchy.

It is not Critical Race Theory that is bad for our country. It is the delusion of Whiteness, and perpetual White supremacy that is bad for this country.

While I do not condone violence of any manner, I do believe that Black people should follow the "White way" and develop a Black solidarity that is so strong that we remain quiet onlookers about Black people who seek economic refuge by robbing banks, committing fraud, and other types of nonviolent offenses.

The culture and systems of White America make Black persons their primary enemy. The standards should be identical, or we should not follow the rules. As Sharon Reed exclaimed on *Start Your Day with Sharon and Mike*, featured on the Black News Channel:

Why should I sit in judgment over any Black or Brown person? Until White people are treated "somewhat the same" in a system of justice, how can any of us sit in judgment of any Black or Brown person? Isn't this a valid question?

I agree with Sharon; the systems in White America are inoperable.

Black Tokens (Me, Myself, and I Included)

It is also a White supremacist and anti-Black system and culture that will have a Black male journalist by the name of Marc Lamont Hill argue (on the Black News Channel, no less) that Cosby is guilty, even though Bill Cosby was not convicted of any crimes. A few days later, Hill remarked condescendingly to the Black community that:

> Black people can walk and chew gum at the same time. We can fight for the release of somebody without celebrating them. We fought for OJ to come home, not because we thought OJ was a hero or a saint, but because we knew the criminal justice system had wronged him. We said that look, OJ doesn't like us. He don't love us. He don't hang with us. He don't date us. He don't marry us. He does all this stuff, but he still shouldn't be in a cage. That's what we should be doing with Bill Cosby but instead I look on Instagram, and I see people holding Bill Cosby parties at the club. And that's when I said F' all y'all. I wasn't talking to Black folk. I was talking to anybody who would organize a party like that.[181]
>
> And supporting Bill Cosby is proof that we don't care and love Black women enough.[182]

Most disturbing about his commentary was the manipulation of the race of some of the victims (who were Black). He did this to inoculate himself against criticism, of course. What he did was add fuel to the fire. White America already sees Black men as rapists. He confirmed their bias.

Where was this argument when it came to two of the Black, gay men found dead in Ed Buck's home (Gemmel Moore and Timothy Dean)? Did they matter in the same way?

Regarding Simpson, was he not found not guilty? Back in 1995?[183] Should Black persons remain guilty even when acquitted? What is the standard? Are there standards? Yes, for some non-White people, and all Black people. There literally has to be videos of a person getting their neck crushed for almost 10 minutes (George Floyd), or someone being shot down in cold-blooded murder while jogging (Ahmaud Arbery), and the world erupting in umbrage, for White people to be held accountable. Yet, we also see that someone could be sleeping in her bed at home, murdered by law enforcement (Breonna Taylor), and there be no accountability whatsoever for taking her life.

It is ridiculous.

America continues to function as a country of perpetual anti-Blackness and White supremacy.

I point this out, in part, hoping to turn the lens on myself. I, myself, have been guilty of this type of thinking and am not afraid to admit it is destructive. We must investigate each of our thoughts. We must self-reflect. We must do better. All of us. Even those of us sounding the alarm.

Consider the extreme tokens, people such as Larry Elder, recent candidate for Governor of California and right-wing radio talk show host. Having written books entitled *What's Race Got to Do With It?* and *Bad News For Race Hustlers,* he, along with Stacey Dash, Candace Owens, Katrina Pierson, and Tim Scott, just to name a few, make for ideal tokens. These individuals have pathetically embraced Whiteness, and all that comes with it, for personal gain. They self-perceive as exceptional Negroes, a term resurrected by Traci O'Neal in her book *The Exceptional Negro: Racism, White Privilege, And the Lie of Respectability Politics*[184]—or, put another way, an example of what one can achieve if they work hard. O'Neal states in her text:

> I use this term to mean exactly what I think Master Ford meant when he called Platt an "exceptional nigger"—though I have upgraded the term to "Negro" to account for more contemporary White sensibilities—that is to say, a Black person who to white people seems unlike other Black people they use as a reference point. Exceptional Negroes are often well-educated, always articulate, cultured, and able to move seemingly effortlessly in white business, political, and social circles. Exceptional Negroes do not fit the stereotypical criminal, thug, welfare queen, baby mama, baby daddy and myriad other negative labels usually associated with Black folks. Hence, we are deemed exceptional.[184]

These individuals deny the cultural embeddedness of White supremacy and anti-Blackness. This problem is described in detail by Dr. Fox in his book *Addicted to White.*[185]

I submit to you that it is a case of "free negro" syndrome. Some Black people see themselves as separate from the majority, given how hard they have worked to establish themselves. They get used as political puppets, and sometimes happily so. They can never be full beneficiaries of Whiteness but that is alright. See infamous examples, such as Oprah Winfrey shopping at Louis Vuitton in Europe or Professor Louis Gates trying to enter his own home in Massachusetts.

O'Neal goes on to say:

> But as we will see, the truth is that even with our exceptionalism, we are just still Negroes to white America, and in case we forget that they will swiftly remind us.[185]

The point here is that Black people have remained imprisoned psychologically, emotionally, and spiritually by Whiteness and anti-Blackness in America, and some seem to be simply fine with it, very often.

Jay-Z characterized it best in his song, "The Story of O.J.," when he said:

> Light nigga, dark nigga, faux nigga, real nigga, rich nigga, poor nigga, house nigga, field nigga...................still nigga.[186]

This is the reality.

Sage Howard, author of "Having a Baby Made Me Rethink Black Excellence," highlights the toxic, widely used, mainstream idea and use of the term "Black excellence."[336] She takes to task the ways in which Black Americans' (and others) use of the term signals identification and alignment with White measures and standards of progress, more specifically, White patriarchal standards of normativity, including respectability, acceptability, and civility.

In the article, Sage writes:

> I grew up in a household where our American Dream was "Black excellence." On the surface, Black excellence is simply the celebration of the success of a Black person. At its root, however, it measures a person's ability to attain mainstream white standards of success despite facing constant adversity. As I understand it now, Black excellence means adhering to respectability politics, a deceptive vehicle that measures my worth by standards set by white men.

There's an "emotional tax" that Black Americans pay in their professional lives, which is essentially how the heightened experience of being marginalized affects our health and well-being. It's also commonly known in our community as the Black Tax, when corporate culture requires us to work twice as hard to get the money and recognition white men do.

Respectability, I realized, required us to trade in our authentic selves for a more palatable version. It requires us to love our Blackness, but only to the extent that it looks and feels good to the society we live in. It defines our innate desires as moral defects.[336]

Filmmaker Ava DuVernay echoes this sentiment in her film, *When They See Us*, as she tackles the case of The Exonerated Five. This reality, and the reality of everyday White extremism, was highlighted in the series *Colin in Black and White*, a Netflix series produced by DuVernay and pro-football player Colin Kaepernick. These are perhaps two of the best explainers on anti-Blackness we have seen in some time, aside from the everyday news stories that present daily depictions of Black people being terrorized in America.[187,268]

All one has to do is observe the ways in which Supreme Court Judge nominee Ketanji Brown Jackson, was treated by Senators Josh Hawley, Mike Lee, Marsha Blackburn, Lindsey Graham, and Ted Cruz during the confirmation hearings held in the United States Congress during the week of March 21, 2022. The message was strikingly clear for members of the Black community, all Americans, and people who tuned in from around the world: She's still just another n****!

The contempt and disdain present in their tones of voice, which dripped through the delivery of every question and comment, was traumatizing. As Judge Brown Jackson cried during comments shared by Senator Cory Booker, I did too.[295-300]

Similar attacks on Black women and the larger Black community continued throughout 2023, into 2024. Monique Worrell, former state attorney for the Ninth Judicial Circuit Court of Florida, was removed from her position by Governor Ron DeSantis, due to fulfilling promises she made during her campaign to focus on criminal justice reform.[403] White senators in Atlanta, Georgia passed legislation with the underlying intent and motivation to remove Fulton County District Attorney Fani Willis due to her office's prosecution of former President Donald Trump.[404] The North Carolina Republican

Party, which is predominantly White, attempted to remove North Carolina State Supreme Court Justice Anita Earls, citing judicial ethics violations, because of her stating that implicit bias exists within the legal system.[405] And, in a most humiliating and devastating fashion, on January 1, 2024, the authorities removed Dr. Claudine Gay from her position as Harvard University's first Black University President.

These acts of racial terrorism compelled both Dr. Nakita Mortimer, and Dr. Antoinette "Bonnie" Candia-Bailey, to commit suicide in July 2023 and January 2024. Dr. John Moseley, Lincoln University President, specifically terrorized Antoinette "Bonnie" Candia-Bailey. Dr. Candia-Bailey sought help from the university's Board of Curators. They did not respond to her entreaties for aid. John Moseley, a White-presenting male, has a Black wife and a biracial daughter. The irony is that this man most likely spoke to his Black wife about terrorizing this Black woman, whom he presumably presented to her as a problematic employee.[407,408]

KRCG, Channel 13, published a story titled, "Emails surface from LU's VP of Student Affairs sent the day she died by suicide," on Friday, January 12, 2024. In the article they wrote:

> A controversial start to the year for Lincoln University President Dr. John Moseley and the Board of Curators after the University's Vice President of Student Affairs, Dr. Antoinette Bonnie Candia-Bailey, took her own life on January 8. Candia-Bailey's passing has sparked outrage from LU alumni across the country who are now calling for Moseley's resignation.
>
> New documents sent to KRCG and written by Candia-Bailey on the day she took her own life, outlining University President Dr. John Moseley as causing "enough harm and mental damage."
>
> "That day I was really beating myself up because I thought, if I had just read the entire email, maybe I could have saved her life," said Monica Graham, a close friend of Candia-Bailey's since college.
>
> Candia-Bailey graduated from Lincoln in 1998 and while there, became a member of Alpha Kappa Alpha Sorority, Inc. Her friends said she was a loving, generous person who radiated positivity.
>
> But soon after she took the position of Vice President in May of 2023, her friends noticed a change in her.

"I was literally just with her at homecoming, and she was like 'I'm just trying to make it through.'" said Shaunice Hill, another close friend of Candia-Bailey's. "Her whole demeanor had changed. Yes, she was still smiling, but you could tell that something was off—something was different."

Multiple emails obtained by someone close to Candia-Bailey and shared with KRCG show she sent emails to Moseley and the board of curators outlining Candia-Bailey's request for Family and Medical Leave (FMLA) and Americans with Disabilities Act (ADA) and state that the relationship between her and Moseley went "downhill" due to her severe depression and anxiety. Additional emails reveal that when she made complaints about how she was treated to the Board of Curators, the board president wrote a response back to her saying in part, "Please be advised the Board of Curators does not engage in the management of personnel issues for Lincoln University and will not be taking further action related to this issue."

Candia-Bailey also wrote that she was "intentionally harassed and bullied" and that after receiving a poor evaluation, when she asked for help, Moseley "ignored requests (failing to respond to emails), or when face-to-face, danced around the topic."[408]

Dr. Candia-Bailey's death, murder by suicide, rivetted me. I grieved her death for several days. Her story was my story. The circumstances of her death were ones I had experienced throughout my entire professional career. Suicidal and homicidal, I became. Feeling like there was nowhere for me to turn, no outlets to help ease my duress, I became severely depressed. Once again, a painful memory from my life resurfaced. I could see and feel Dr. Candia-Bailey's pain. I looked at her picture flash before my eyes and wept.

I thought about my friend Margot Reed, who died at her desk at work on May 16, 2023, because of a sudden heart attack. She was 62. Margot and I worked together in the City and County of San Francisco, in California. I remembered all the times people ridiculed and critiqued her for being too bold, too strong, too loud, too aggressive, too . . . and the list went on. Pressure, insurmountable pressure to fall in line based upon toxic and perverted societal standards, which require the oppressed to conform. My dear friend and sister was a warrior.

I thought about the other Black women who suffered similar fatalities like Margot. Rather than murder by suicide, Dr. JoAnne A. Epps and Dr. Orinthia T. Montague both died suddenly because of stress. Both Black women were university presidents. Dr. Epps was Temple University's President, while Dr. Montague served as Volunteer State Community College President. Dr. Epps, 71, died on the job while attending a colleague's funeral. Dr. Montague served for only two years as president. She was 56.[409-412]

I am aggrieved for these women, and all Black people who experience the same, or similar, types of ongoing mistreatment by our White and "not-Black" counterparts. The shameful violence committed against Judge Brown-Jackson, Justice Earls, Ms. Worrell, Ms. Willis, Dr. Gay, Dr. Mortimer, and Dr. Candia-Bailey, through the displays of diminishment and denigration, represents the core and foundation of the White American psychology, identity, and cultural value system.

White psychopathology is genocidal. Anti-Blackness is genocidal.

We must prosecute the crimes directed at us, past and present. It must happen with the arts, the legal system, the education system, the pulpit, and more. If we do not, what will we get?

More psychopathy, more sociopathy.

Chapter Eight Review Questions

(Note: Please go to www.danteking.com to complete the chapter assessment and evaluation for the following questions.)

Considering what you have just read, answer the following:

1. What did White females and males learn about the value of Whiteness?

2. How did these laws shape White identity for White males? White females?

3. What did Black females learn about what it meant to be White and female? White and male? Black and male? Black and female?

4. What did Black males learn about what it meant to be White and male? White and female? Black and female? Black and male?

5. How did these laws shape Black identity?

6. In what ways were the parameters of Whiteness and anti-Blackness vastly expanded to widen the realities and impacts of oppression between White/White-identified and Black people?

7. How does the law reinforce pro-White and anti-Black outcomes?

8. What happens when we dismiss real injuries, over and over again?

9. How do we not see the origins and extensions of anti-Blackness and White supremacy? Furthermore, why do we not?

10. What happens when we allow perpetrators to go on perpetrating without consequence for hundreds of years?

11. How is the role of anti-Blackness different from that of White supremacy/power/superiority?

12. How does White people's control of the legal system privilege them?

13. How can Black people escape "criminality" when it is meant to continue imprisoning us?

14. Who are the real criminals?

15. Why is it dangerous to minimize actual harm? What does that minimization enable in the future?

16. In what ways was the legal system structured to advance and affirm Whites, in psychopathic and sociopathic ways, during the seventeenth, eighteenth, and nineteenth centuries, concerning Black people?

17. How does the reality of debasing Black people, relegating us into the most inhuman and profane position in American culture, influence, inform, shape, and develop White American psychological and sociological constructs about who Black people are (i.e., values, principles, behavior, etc.) and what they represent?

18. In what ways do these White psychological and sociological developments shape White identity, in terms of who they believe themselves to be and what they represent as a community and culture?

19. How does White projection, the foundation of both the psychological and sociological developments of American culture, influence and shape the psychology and sociology that Black people and people of color accept about Black people, White people, and all others along the racial spectrum?

20. In what ways does Dr. Poussaint's framing of Whiteness as racial politics and White racism as "mental illness," along with Dr. Bobby Wright's assertion of White psychopathy, help us to further

understand the functionality of perpetual White perversions, distortions, and projections White people hold about themselves as superior, juxtaposed against fabricated anti-Black cultural narratives about "who" Black people are, as well as "what" Blackness represents in America?

21. What role does the lack or absence of impression management, as well as the absence of impulse control, play in the impressions and interpretations of Black people's daily behaviors, attitudes, and actions in America?

22. In what ways does Dr. Wright's framing help us to further understand the politics and functionalities of Whiteness and anti-Blackness in America?

23. In what ways does Dr. Wright's framing help us to further understand the need for White American culture to have and perpetually maintain Black American Descendants of Enslaved Peoples (sometimes referred to as ADOS/ADOEP) as an affixed permanent underclass?

24. In what ways does Dr. Wright's framing help us to further understand the necessity of racial politics in America, specifically, Whiteness and anti-Blackness, the infinite "brand-value" of Whiteness, and the brand "valuelessness" of Blackness in America?

Spike Lee, *School Daze*, and the Final Call For Black People To Wake Up!!

A Letter to Spike Lee:

Dear Spike Lee,

Thank you for shouldering your part of the burden. Because of how you have put your intelligence and education to use, innumerable people struck by blindness have been able to see. Your artistry is unmatched. One movie of yours in particular, *School Daze*, helped me understand myself better. I understood colonization, identity, and how they go together, for the first time in my life. You helped me learn that Whites defined themselves by being anti-Black.[188] You also helped me understand that many Black people define themselves through the lenses of Whiteness and anti-Blackness (me included).

The film brilliantly catalogs how we adopt White values and how that diminishes us in every regard and reinforces our subjugation.

Thank you.
Sincerely,
Dante King

Most Black people have not done the challenging work Lee has done, and therefore do not see what he sees, and saw long ago. It is worth contemplating how we and our circumstances would change if we modeled our thought patterns after his, Duvernay's, and Kaepernick's. I am perhaps most struck by the ending of *School Daze*. He has the characters deliver a simple yet moving message. He tells them to WAKE UP. It is a call to action, and for us all. This includes HBCU faculty, staff, and students, preachers—everyone.

White supremacy and anti-Blackness are so embedded into our institutions and psyches that we hardly recognize them. They are just fundamental parts of our existence in a White-dominant culture.[21,7]

Whites established the standard of brutality to be aimed at Black persons. This is on them.[38,125] And now we live in a multiracial, multiethnic country that practices anti-Blackness as a normal way of being. This is the predictable logical outcome. It should surprise absolutely no one, especially after reading this text.

Black people and every ally must be clear on the history and its connection to the present. There is no other way to fix this debacle.

As Kimberly Jones has correctly noted when discussing Ahmaud Arbery, Breonna Taylor, and George Floyd, White America's core problem is its anti-Black, white supremacist identity/ideology. Every problematic part flows from those two elements. Housing, health care, education, the law—everything. Nothing is left untouched. Every single aspect of society is constructed to keep Black people from having quality of life: power, wealth, health, an education, housing, and justice.[190]

Black people must understand how we can be our own worst enemies. If we do not, we will only enable our worst oppressors. One can hardly think of something more shameful. Every way we are taught to think and behave stems from the lenses of Whiteness and anti-Blackness.[1,21,191]

I hardly have all the answers. Even I struggle with how, for example, to identify true "not-Black" allies. Perhaps that is because so many fear that if Black persons mount a genuine revolt that only revenge, not equality, would arise.

What most Black people do, and I include myself, here, is focus on the negative impact racism has on Black persons. What we should all do a better job doing is focusing on all the power that is consistently afforded to Whites or people who are our allies. Racism does not merely involve oppression. It involves dehumanization masked as privilege, and we should focus on this variable more. It is having advantages when none should exist, in essence.

There is another frame of reference we must shift. We should not compare the progress Black persons make today with what they made yesterday. We should compare it to White progress, economic and otherwise. If we took even that one step, the extent of the psychopathy and sociopathy would be clearer. So would the need for reparations. In addition, the damaging effects of Whiteness on White and Black people extend far beyond economics, as highlighted in the 1940s Doll Study, which was facilitated by psychologists Kenneth and Mamie Clark, and a follow-up study designed by Margaret Spencer, in 2010.[191,192]

America's illness, in the form of a negative cultural orientation toward Blackness, was starkly presented during this documentary. Almost all negative orientations and characterizations were associated with the pictures of Black children.

They presented the children with multiple questions and statements while pointing to pictures of five different caricatures that ranged in skin tone. The results were horrifying.

Figure 9.1.

√ When asked to point to the smart and nice child, most children pointed to the White or lighter skinned image.

√ When asked to point to the mean and dumb child, most chose the Brown or Black image.

√ When asked to point to the skin color most teachers prefer, most children chose the White or lighter skinned image.

√ When asked to point to the skin color most teachers do not prefer, most children chose the Brown or Black image.

√ When asked to point to who adults would be more likely to like, they mostly chose the White or lighter skinned image.

√   When asked to point to who adults would be more likely to dislike, they mostly chose the Brown and Black images.

√   When asked to point to the good child, it was the White or lighter skinned child. The bad child? The Brown/Black one.

√   When asked to point to the good-looking child, it was the White or lighter skinned one. The less attractive/even ugly one? The Brown/Black one.

The children, groups made up of Black and White children, clearly demonstrated their orientations in favor of Whiteness and against Blackness. Not adults, children. This is not a coincidence. It is hundreds of years of indoctrination bearing fruit in the ugliest way imaginable.

When asked WHY a child was bad, ugly, stupid, etc., the response, given by children of both races, was something to the effect of: Because the child is Brown/Black.

Self-hatred starts early, and it is nothing short of heartbreaking. No child should self-perceive this way, ever. This is the sort of self-hatred that thwarts any and all success.

Cooper, disturbed, probed some more. Below is a revealing exchange:

Cooper, to a Black, girl-child pointing to the light skin color she coveted: Why do you want that skin color?

Black Girl: Because it looks lighter than this kind (pointing to her own face), because this looks a lot like that one.

The reference to her skin looking a lot like "that one" was in reference to her pointing to one of the Brown figures.

She added: And, I just don't like the way Brown looks, because the way Brown looks, looks nasty for some reason but I don't know what reason, and that's all.

Cooper, pressing even more: So, you think it looks nasty?

Black Girl: Not really, but sometimes.

Cooper: And they also asked what color adults don't like.

At this point, she pointed to the darkest figure almost begrudgingly.

Cooper: Why don't you think adults don't like this color?

Girl: Dark!

This was basically an on-air admission of self-hatred, and hardly anyone understood why. It was, in fact, the result of centuries of white supremacist and anti-Black indoctrination using every institution available. No one had identified the psychopathy and sociopathy. If that is not a tragedy, then one does not know what ever could be.

In another example, one which concerns Black educators and students, elementary school-aged children were segregated from other students and dehumanized. In an August 2023 *Washington Post* article written by Timothy Bella, titled, "Florida school 'segregated' Black students for talk on test scores," parents say the following anti-Black experiences were penned:

> Black students at a Florida elementary school were singled out and pulled from class for an assembly about how it was a "problem" that they had performed poorly on their standardized tests, school district officials said Wednesday. The incident drew outrage from parents and prompted an investigation by the school district.
>
> Only Black fourth- and fifth-grade students at Bunnell Elementary School in Flagler County, Fla., were taken out of class on Friday for the assembly on how to improve their grades—even students who had passing grades. Students were selected to attend based on their race; Flagler Schools spokesman Jason Wheeler told *The Washington Post* on Wednesday.
>
> Black teachers showed the students a typo-laden PowerPoint presentation titled, "AA Presentation," which noted how Black students had underperformed on standardized tests for the past three years. On the slide titled "The Problem," the school district identified Black students as "AA," or African Americans, in its assessment of their low overall scores, according to the presentation obtained by *The Post*.
>
> The incident has drawn backlash from parents who were not alerted about an event that had "segregated" their 9- and 10-year-olds. Some say their children were told in the assembly that they could end up dead or in jail if they did not do well on their upcoming tests.
>
> "It told my child that she was not good enough," Jacinda Arrington told WOFL, a Fox affiliate in Orlando. "The color of your skin means that you are not good enough, when, in fact, she's one of the smartest kids in her class."
>
> Another parent, Alexis Smith, told WFTV, an ABC affiliate in Orlando, that her son was panicking after the assembly. She said he asked her, "So I'm going to die, I'm going to get shot, I'm going to go to jail if I don't do right?"

The school district is investigating how Black students were the only group that attended an event aimed at encouraging improvement in test scores. As an incentive, the students were promised meals from McDonald's, Flagler interim superintendent LaShakia Moore said in a statement Tuesday."[395]

These examples are not anomalies. Dismissing them as such only perpetuates the harm. Our goal is the opposite. We must acknowledge how common and representative they are, and then ask ourselves why. This scenario demonstrated the ever-present dynamic of internalized anti-Blackness, and the magnitude of Black forced conformity compelled by White domination and Eurocentric control.[395]

The term "racism" is not enough. It is ambiguous and insufficient. We must call it what it is, which is anti-Black. Our culture is affirmatively, aggressively anti-Black. That is what accounts for, among other things, the frustrations in health care outcomes, interactions with law enforcement officers, and so much more. It is the deeply rooted anti-Blackness of it all. It overwhelms.

Anti-Blackness can be observed in countless examples. Several, which I share here, concern Black people attempting to obtain home appraisals.[330–334]

On August 25, 2020, Debra Kamin authored an article for *The New York Times*, titled "Black Homeowners Face Discrimination in Home Appraisals." In it, she wrote:

> Abena and Alex Horton wanted to take advantage of low home-refinance rates brought on by the coronavirus crisis. So, in June, they took the first step in that process, welcoming a home appraiser into their four-bedroom, four-bath ranch-style house in Jacksonville, Fla.
>
> The Hortons live just minutes from the Ortega River, in a predominantly white neighborhood of 1950s homes that tend to sell for $350,000 to $550,000. They had expected their home to appraise for around $450,000, but the appraiser felt differently, assigning a value of $330,000. Ms. Horton, who is Black, immediately suspected discrimination.
>
> The couple's bank agreed that the value was off and ordered a second appraisal. But before the new appraiser could arrive, Ms. Horton, a lawyer, began an experiment: She took all family photos off the mantle. Instead, she hung up a series of oil paintings of Mr. Horton, who is white, and his grandparents that had been in storage. Books by Zora Neale Hurston and Toni Morrison were taken off the shelves, and holiday photo cards sent by

friends were edited so that only those showing white families were left on display. On the day of the appraisal, Ms. Horton took the couple's 6-year-old son on a shopping trip to Target, and left Mr. Horton alone at home to answer the door.

The new appraiser gave their home a value of $465,000—a more than 40 percent increase from the first appraisal.[334]

On May 13, 2021, Alexandria Burris penned an article for the *Indy Star*. The article was titled "Black homeowner had a white friend stand in for third appraisal. Her home value doubled."

In the article, Burris wrote:

Carlette Duffy felt both vindicated and excited. Both relieved and angry.

For months, she suspected she had been low-balled on two home appraisals because she's Black. She decided to put that suspicion to the test and asked a white family friend to stand in for her during an appraisal.

Her home's value suddenly shot up. A lot.

During the early months of the coronavirus pandemic last year, the first two appraisers who visited her home in the historic Flanner House Homes neighborhood, just west of downtown, valued it at $125,000 and $110,000, respectively.

But that third appraisal went differently.

To get that one, Duffy, who is African American, communicated with the appraiser strictly via email, stripped her home of all signs of her racial and cultural identity and had the white husband of a friend stand in for her during the appraiser's visit.

The home's new value: $259,000.[330]

On July 23, 2021, the *San Francisco Chronicle* released an article by Lauren Hepler. The article was titled, "'Present-day redlining': A Black homeowner says her Oakland property was undervalued by $400k." Hepler covered a story concerning Oakland resident Cora Robinson, who attempted to refinance a duplex she owned.

The article stated:

When Cora Robinson decided to refinance her Oakland duplex last summer, the pandemic real estate market was going crazy for roomy stand-alone homes like hers.

Listing sites like Zillow said the property, which last sold for $289,500 in 2006, was now worth more like $1.2 million. Robinson wasn't looking to sell, but it seemed like a perfect chance to shave several hundred dollars off her monthly payment by locking in a lower interest rate.

But then came the appraisal.

In two new discrimination complaints filed with the U.S. Department of Housing and Urban Development on Wednesday, Robinson says she was lowballed by around $400,000 on the value of her property, largely because she and some of her neighbors are Black. The claims reflect the latest in a series of cases where Black homeowners in and around the Bay Area say they're being unfairly shut out of favorable financing and historic real estate gains as home prices hit record highs. It's a nationwide concern that also recently pushed President Joe Biden to vow new appraisal reforms.

"This is our present-day redlining," said Caroline Peattie, executive director of Fair Housing Advocates of Northern California, which filed the complaints on Robinson's behalf. "It just continues the cycle."[332]

On December 3, 2021, Hepler published another article in the *San Francisco Chronicle*. The title of this article read, "A Black couple 'erased themselves' from their home to see if the appraised value would go up. It did—by nearly $500k." In this article, Hepler wrote about an upper-middle-class Black couple who purchased and renovated a home in a relatively affluent neighborhood.

In the article, Hepler wrote:

Paul Austin thought things were going well when the appraiser came to his Marin City home last January.

The appraiser complimented the views of the San Francisco Bay, and he was sure to point out all the improvements, Austin recalled at an Oct. 13 meeting of a state reparations task force. So, he and his wife Tenisha Tate-Austin were shocked when the appraisal valued their home at $995,000—nearly half-a-million dollars less than another appraisal 10 months earlier.

The couple, who are Black, got a second opinion last February. This time, they asked a white friend named Jan to sit at the kitchen island and pretend to be the homeowner. They also "whitewashed" their home by hiding art and family photos. That appraiser said their house was worth $1,482,500.

The $487,500 discrepancy between the two 2020 appraisals pushed the couple to file a fair housing lawsuit in federal district court this week against appraiser Janette Miller, her firm Miller and Perotti Real Estate Appraisers Inc., and national appraisal company AMC Links LLC. It's the latest escalation in a series of similar cases of alleged racial bias in the home appraisal process as California property owners move to reap financial gains from record home prices.

"We did our homework," Austin told the Reparations Task Force in a panel on the racial wealth gap in October. "We believe the white lady wanted to devalue our property because we are in a Black neighborhood, and the home belonged to a Black family."

Conclusion: In White America, race determines class. One is considered valuable if they are White. And if they are Black, they are presumed to lack worth and value.

White racism and White supremacy are the root cause of White people's success in White America. Anti-Blackness is the root cause of Black disenfranchisement, challenges, and problems in White America.

Anti-Blackness is what accounts for a psychopathic White law enforcement officer, for example, doing what he did to Dajerria Becton at a 2018 pool party (murdering her).[193] It is what made Trayvon Martin look so "suspicious." It is behind the Sandra Bland murder and George Floyd murder. It even accounts for instances such as the one involving a Black police officer who kicked in the head of a Black citizen, Ashley Samuel, in July of 2021.[28,194] It is anti-Blackness through and through, repeatedly. It is because they were Black.

And White American culture and those who have aligned themselves with it hate Black people and have contempt for what they perceive as Blackness.[195,197] White people do not live with these questions or realities. White people have the privilege of not living with these questions and realities.

This was evident in the words of Charles Scharf, Wells Fargo CEO, when he spoke the quiet part aloud by saying there were very few skilled, experienced, knowledgeable, or talented Black people in the professional workforce.[198] "While it might sound like an excuse, the unfortunate reality is that there is a very limited pool of Black talent to recruit from."

This is part and parcel anti-Black racism. Racism reduces the view of the institutions/systems to individual failings of Black people. Anti-Black racism prevents examination of institutions and systems as flawed, rooted in White supremacy, and anti-Blackness. Anti-Blackness minimizes the magnitude of these types of thought patterns and beliefs. In this one moment, Scharf accidentally admitted to the world what he and so many others genuinely believed.

I worked for Wells Fargo for more than 13 years. There, I was groomed in pro-White and anti-Black "professional" culture. I can remember consistently receiving recognition—winning awards as a Personal Banker, Premier Banker, Branch Manager, and HR Business Consultant. I remember meeting colleagues at both the district and regional levels who would be surprised that I ranked highest within our district and region. I remember being asked questions about some of the things I had done to "achieve success," and yet other colleagues, also recognized at the same events, were not questioned in similar ways. I was the anomaly, you see. At one branch in particular where I worked, nearly everyone assumed the Asian person there ranked above me. That is not coincidental.

Wells Fargo is hardly alone in its culture and practices. All or nearly all major American corporations are afflicted with the same psychopathy and sociopathy. A Black friend of mine, who is a board licensed physician, often experiences the same. She is very often assumed to be a nurse, assistant, or someone else (anyone else) other than the medical doctor. Why is that? Again, anti-Blackness and White supremacy are sicknesses that pervade every environment. They are psychopathic and sociopathic. They are demonic.

My Experience as a Human Resources Professional

As a Human Resources professional with more than 15 years of experience and expertise, I have witnessed rampant anti-Blackness in the White "professional" context. Whites and those proximate to them (think East Asians, especially) are privileged. The same goes for White Cubans and White Hispanics. I can cite numerous personal examples to support this contention.

Example A: Julie, who is White presenting, mid-30s, has little industry experience. She is trained by Sheree, a Black woman roughly the same age. She passes the probation period and gets promoted to be the Black employee's manager right afterward. Sheree does not receive a promotion for the next five years. In two, Julie becomes Division Director, making triple Sheree's salary. Over the course of a decade, she has become an executive, ranked merely three levels below that of CEO. At that time, Sheree was promoted to a supervisor position.

Example B: Shawn, a Black male employee in his late forties, is aggressed by his Asian supervisor, who screams at him and spits in his face. Shawn punches him and is fired for being violent in the workplace. The supervisor is not reprimanded. Shawn is described as violent, aggressive, enraged, and unstable. Two months later, Bob, a White male in his mid-fifties, becomes angry at his Black, female supervisor named Shanitra. He punches her, and receives a mere suspension as opposed to being terminated. He is described as having had one bad day.

Example C: Lynette, a Black female, is well-educated in her field. She has an M.A. in Communications and B.A.s in Urban Planning and English, making her very well suited for her job. She applied for a promotion to Senior Communications Manager, which is one step up from her current position. Bob, her subordinate, is far less educated and has far less experience. He applies and gets the position, making his leap ahead, despite the lesser qualifications, four full steps. She is admonished for her lack of charisma during the interview process.

Other types of employee complaints I have dealt with while in the roles of ombudsperson and human resources complaints investigator are:

√ Monitoring and watching how often Black employees go to the restroom.

√ Complaints about the smell of Black employees' food and asking them to warm their food up at home.

√ A director asserting that because a Black employee has a James Baldwin quote in their signature line, it makes them appear angry. Telling the employee that as a White person they do not need to be educated or reminded about the struggles of African Americans on a daily basis. Requesting that the employee remove the quote.

√ Black candidates ranking higher on tests, interviews, etc., and management overriding processes to hire "not-Black" people; later rationalizing that the hired person was a "better fit" (i.e., "temperament," "gut-feeling this person was the right choice," etc.)

√   Black women were suspended for multiple days for calling in sick, while White men were given written warnings for the same offense. Subsequently, there were no disciplinary actions taken against White women, over multiple years.

√   Black employees represented 100% of the employees on performance improvement plans.

√   Black patients and their families and friends experienced having law enforcement called on them 100% of the time.

√   Black employees made up 27% of the employee population and 58% of all disciplinary actions.

These examples are real and representative. They are not exceptions. And they should be motivation for us to see now what we could not see earlier. These conditions are abnormal and should always be regarded as such.

Dr. Koritha Mitchell, author of *From Slave Cabins to the White House: Homemade Citizenship in African American Culture, Living with Lynching* and *Identifying White Mediocrity and Know-Your-Place Aggression: A Form of Self Care*, defines these types of actions as Know-Your-Place Aggression (KYPA).[337-339] KYPA is "the flexible dynamic array of forces that answer the achievements of marginalized groups, such that their success brings aggression as often as praise."[339] Dr. Mitchell makes the point that the success of straight White men does not evoke aggression. Rather, it inspires respect, acceptance, admiration, and the like. While KYPA is most often exhibited by White people against people from communities of color, and most severely Black people, it can also be exhibited by members of non-White communities against other communities. In other words, in White America, someone will always feel the need to put Black people in our marginalized place, regardless of economic, positional, and/or educational status. Again, this is done to achieve the psycho-social, psycho-political, psycho-cultural, and psycho-economic agendas of White supremacy culture, and anti-Blackness.

I am thinking of my dear friend and sister, Lanitra Williams, who died at age 47, from cancer. While on her deathbed, she agonized with me about the harms she had experienced at the hands of coworkers and management where she worked. She was not provided the support she needed to live a balanced, healthy, stable, and supportive life. It is clear to me, based upon our 1-on-1 conversations, that much of her demise was caused by the daily anti-Black, anti-female challenges she navigated as a Black woman, which were very much present in her work situation.

I can relate, as this, too, has been my life experience. A life experience that prompted me to consider committing suicide.

The Final Plea

My Black mothers, sisters, fathers, brothers, aunts, uncles, daughters, and sons: please do not carry the unjust burden that is believing you are not enough. You are. You always have been. You always will be. It is the system that is stacked against you. You should assume no culpability and should rage against the machine that oppresses you.

Baldwin said:

> I know how you watch as you grow older, the corpses of your brothers and your sisters pile up around you. Not as a result of anything they have done, they were too young to have done anything. But what one does realize is that when you try to stand up and look the world in the face as if you had a right to be here, you have attacked the entire power structure of the western world.

> What white people have to do is try to find out in their hearts why it was necessary for them to have a nigger in the first place. Because I am not a nigger. I'm a man. If I'm not the nigger here, and if you invented him, you the white people invented him, then you have to find out why. And the future of the country depends on that. Whether or not it is able to ask that question.[151,152,273]

DuBois was attributed with saying:

> A system cannot fail those it was never meant to protect.[273]

The truth of the matter is that it does not matter how hard you work. You are Black in America, and this informs everything about your experience. Do not be fooled any longer. Not all, but most Black people will fail in America, or be diminished to assuming subordinate roles that become constraining over time. And yet, we do not have such realistic discussions with Black children and pretend that the same adage of "hard work" is as true for Black people as it is for White people, when such a reality has never been true. We are pathologized for being perceived as inadequate, and we are pathologized for being exceptional.

Yet, White mediocrity, White deficiency, and White insufficiency are hardly or ever interrogated. Meanwhile, Black children and adults are in therapy, as we attempt to comply with White standards and norms that we have convinced ourselves will "elevate us" to higher plains. It is a recipe for delusion and confusion. Use the education you gained through reading this text. The White structure in which you function every day is designed to hurt you and your children the way it hurt your ancestors. Do not be complicit in this ongoing, massive campaign to wound and disable. Understand the relationship between anti-Blackness and probability, which Dr. Kendi highlights as cultural racism in his book, *How to Be An Anti-Racist*.[199]

The White, social, cultural, institutional, and economic structure that operates on the foundational principles of White Supremacy and anti-Blackness will only allow a tiny number of Negroes to sit at the table.[1,198] Those people are forbidden from facilitating the promotion of Black liberation theory, practice, or any other kind of non-oppressive agenda upon arrival.

No. Often, a shameful alignment occurs. That must stop. Simply put, we are invited in because Whites believe we will be useful idiots. Malcolm X accounted for this behavior and named it in his discussion at U.C. Berkeley (which I referenced at the beginning).[200]

He said:

The laws here in America were made White, by White people, for the benefit of White people.[200]

We continue to seek inclusion, validation, and approval through White supremacist and anti-Black systems and institutions that do not want us here in America and have continued to demonstrate this throughout the ages. Most times, we end up trading our dignity and identity for more validation. Nothing is worth that.

We must wake up and understand that there is internal healing and collective organizing to be done.

Whatever it is you think has so dramatically improved—it hasn't. Only the dressing differs. And we no longer care for the superficial, having read this book. We look to substance.

Think about the following:

√ Black people are more than three times as likely as White people to be killed during a police encounter.[153,154]

√ African Americans own approximately 1/10 of the wealth that Whites do. In 2016, the median wealth for nonretired, Black households 25 years old and up was less than 1/10 that of similarly situated White households. The wealth gap persists regardless of formal education, marital status, age, or income. For instance, the median wealth for Black households with a college degree equaled about 70 percent of the median wealth for White households without a college degree.[155]

√ African American mothers are dying at three to four times the rate of non-Hispanic, White mothers, and infants born to African American mothers are dying at twice the rate as infants born to non-Hispanic, White mothers. These two trends hold true across education levels and socioeconomic status. Even tennis star Serena Williams—a wealthy and remarkably powerful woman—nearly died from pregnancy-related complications that were ignored because of her Blackness.[156]

√ African American infants are 3.2 times more likely than non-Hispanic, White infants to die from complications related to low birth weight.[156]

√ Between January 1972 and December 2019, other than during the aftermaths of recessions, the African American unemployment rate has stayed at or above twice the rate for Whites.[157]

√ Over the last 12 months, the average unemployment rate for Black college graduates has been 4.1%. That is nearly double the average unemployment rate for White college graduates (2.4%) and equivalent to the unemployment rate of Whites with an associate degree or who have not completed any college (4%). The largest disparity is seen among those with less than a high school diploma/people who dropped out before earning their high school diploma/GED. While those Whites have an unemployment rate of 6.9%, the Black unemployment rate is at 16.6%. That is over twice the White average.[158]

White control of Black bodies persists, and the consequences are catastrophic. Dr. Wright (1975) summarized this as:

> Psychopaths also reject constituted authority and discipline. The presence of this trait in the White race has grave implications for Black people who seek legal solutions to their problems. This especially applies to the Black people in the United States who are the world's only legally created group, (created through the 13th, 14th, and 15th amendments which can be repealed at any moment by the Congress or declared unconstitutional by the Supreme Court). As long as this condition exists, Black people in the United States will always be legally five minutes away from slavery. For Black people in the United States to place their destiny in the hands of Supreme Court Justices is an extreme form of psychological blindness and a pathological rejection of history. The Supreme Court of the United States has always used the prevailing White political climate as the criterion for dealing with questions of race. For example, as a result of the infamous 1954 school desegregation decision, Black people lost an estimated 35,000 teaching and administrative positions in the South. Former Black principals of Black schools are now janitors in integrated schools and the same thing is going to happen to Black teachers in the North. Eventually the Supreme Court is going to find the 1954 decision unconstitutional, but by that time Whites will have taken over all Black schools including the Black colleges.[21]

I wrote this book to convince the world, especially those most vulnerable, that America has always been and continues to be a country whose primary drivers are psychopathy and sociopathy. Black Americans continue to be victimized. We continue to be the targets of a calculated, sustained campaign for elimination. A genocide is still occurring.

In 1951, the Civil Rights Congress charged genocide directed against Black people in their proclamation of "We Charge Genocide."[201] This text, published some 70 years ago, noted, "The mental harm done to the Negro people in the United States by conditions forced upon them, is incalculable." In "Psychodynamic Factors in Racial Relations," written by Helen McLean in 1946, she noted:

> Long before any Negro child has become fully conscious of being a Negro, he is affected by the existing tensions in his parents, who as Negroes, live an insecure existence, chronically frightened of external reality and of their own

intensely hostile feelings against white men. The insecurity and impotence of the Negro parent in the face of white domination makes identification with those parents' anxiety laden. Yet identification with any member of the White group is also anxiety producing since the Negro is constantly being rejected by the white group. If the individual attempts to be mobile upwards by virtue of his ability or strong aggressive drives, he will fail to achieve satisfactory identification with the white group and will at the same time be resented by the Negro group. If he remains identified with the Negro group, he feels impotent and insecure. His aggressive ambitious drives will find no satisfactory outlet. Only the self-destructive outlet of criminality, psychopathic behavior, and psychosomatic disease is open. The high incidence of hypertension among southern Negroes is probably one indication of an unconscious attempt at mastery of the hostility which must be controlled. The chronic rage of these individuals produces hypertension which initially is fluctuating in character. Eventually the pathological changes resulting from this overload on the cardiovascular renal system lead to a consistently high blood pressure. All available evidence from clinicians indicates that functional disease (that is, psychosomatic) is markedly on the increase in the Negro.[246]

America's anti-Black, genocidal agenda and its impacts have persisted for more than 400 years. It remains normalized in American culture. Black people continue to experience this reality in all aspects of our lives. We never get a rest. It affects our social interactions, our education, our employment status, our ability to shop, our ability to go to the gym, etc.[247]

These psychological, emotional, and physical effects are depicted masterfully in the 10-part miniseries entitled "Them," which appeared on Amazon Prime in early 2021.[248] The series details the daily pressures Black people face while attempting to comply with American standards and values, all while being tortured by White and White-proximate people. As Black people, we must reassert now the charge of anti-Black America's persistent genocide of Black people.

How does White American culture become rid of the illnesses that are anti-Blackness and White supremacy, one might ask?

I do not claim to have all the answers, but I do know we must see what has previously gone unseen. Black people are suffering from "racial battle fatigue (RBF)," a phrase coined by Dr. William Smith, from the University of Utah, in 2008.[221] As noted by the Minnesota Counseling Center, Dr. Smith and others define RBF as:

The cumulative psychological, social, physiological, and emotional impacts of racial micro and macro aggressions and racist abuse on racially marginalized groups—particularly Black individuals. Attempting to cope with these persistent hostile, violent, demeaning, dismissive and toxic race-based stressors completely depletes one's physical, emotional, and mental energy.[282-284]

We, Black people, naturally become exhausted due to the permanence of racial trauma inflicted upon us every day.

I do not believe that we will ever properly and adequately address anti-Blackness in America. Too much money and power are at stake, and nothing motivates like money and power.

The way Black people live now, constantly catering to and being betrayed by some absurd standard of being, is unacceptable. It causes health problems and even early death. We adapt, thinking we will help ourselves when it is just the opposite.[3,21]

I think out of everything, the impact on Black children distresses me most. Consider Faith Fennidy, a young, talented, and brilliant 11-year-old Black American girl. In 2018, she was removed from Christ the King Parish School in Louisiana (suspended for 3 days) for wearing braids. She cried in humiliation.[205] I think of Chickayazea Flanders, who suffered the same tragic situation in 2017,[206] and 8-year-old Marian Scott, who, in 2019, was excluded from her class picture at Paragon Charter Academy because her mother took pride in doing her hair in a way that the school found unacceptable, and the burden that created for Marian and her family.[207] I sit here thinking about the young, Black, female model who suffered backlash because people infected with the psychopathy of anti-Blackness wanted to put her down because she appeared in an H&M advertisement with her natural hair on display.[195,197]

James Baldwin stated, "To be Negro in this country, and to be relatively conscious, is to be in a rage almost all of the time." There was a reason he said what he said.

White supremacy's and anti-Blackness' impacts on Black adults in today's society, as sociologist E. Franklin Frazier warned in his 1957 text entitled *Black Bourgeoisie*, often involve an adaptation to Whiteness and all its misery.[1]

Dr. Frazier asserted that middle- and upper-class Black persons' attempts to become like White people are the result of the anti-Blackness they have internalized, resulting in an inferiority complex. He said:

Since the Black bourgeoisie live largely in a world of make-believe, the masks which they wear to play their sorry roles conceal the feelings of inferiority and the insecurity and the frustrations that haunt their inner lives. Despite their attempt to escape from real identification with the masses of Negroes, they cannot escape the mark of oppression any more than their less favored kinsmen. In attempting to escape identification with the Black masses, they have developed a self-hatred that reveals itself in their deprecation of the physical and social characteristics of Negroes. Likewise, their feelings of inferiority and insecurity are revealed in their pathological struggle for status within the isolated Negro world and craving for recognition in the White world. Their escape into a world of make-believe with its sham "society" leaves them with a feeling of emptiness and futility which causes them to constantly seek an escape in new delusions.[1]

In 1979, Dr. Alvin Poussaint, in *The Black Scholar* (vol. 10), wrote an article entitled "White Manipulation and Black Oppression." In it, he stated:

While Black people grovel in destructive internecine warfare, statistics on their progress grow worse and institutional racial injustices persist while whites consolidate their positions of power and dominance over the Black masses. This has been an effective strategy: Black people become not only the victim but the victimizer; accomplices with white racists in their own subjugation.[7]

The reality of the perspectives shared by Dr. Frazier and Dr. Poussaint could not have been any clearer than in the conflict that emerged in the early 1990s, between then famed superstar rapper Tupac Shakur and C. Delores Tucker, then Secretary of the Commonwealth of Pennsylvania, and founder of the first Commission on the Status of Women. Ms. Tucker's criticisms of Tupac's lyrics, and the entire industry of gangsta rap (which at the time included groups and rappers like the Geto Boys, Luke and 2-Live Crew, N.W.A, Too Short, etc.), held press conferences and attempted to have their music banned.

It was clear that Ms. Tucker was so far removed from the manifestations of poverty, despair, and pain resulting from deeply felt systematic racism persisting throughout all of America's Black ghettos that she did not understand Tupac and others who were simply telling about their experiences as young Black men in America. They were rapping about their daily circumstances and the influences and encounters that shaped their truths. These Black men, mostly, chose to express their woes, discontent, and other experiences through their music.[316] C. Delores Tucker could not recognize this, and instead frowned down upon Tupac and his industry mates.

Tupac Shakur, felt that C. Delores Tucker had betrayed him, other rappers, and the larger Black community by aligning herself with White political figures and White norms of respectability, civility, acceptability, and morality. More specifically, he felt betrayed because she used these standards to establish a platform, along with others from the Black bourgeoisie (Black political figures), to openly ridicule and attack their work in an effort to derail their careers. As a result, Tupac lashed out against her in his song, "How Do You Want It."

In the song, Tupac rapped:

C. Delores Tucker, you's a motherfucker.

Instead of tryin' to help a nigga you destroy a brother.

Worse than the others; Bill Clinton, Mr. Bob Dole.

You're too old to understand the way the game's told.

You're lame, so I gotta' hit you with the hot facts.

Once I'm released, I'm makin' millions, niggas top that.

They wanna censor me, they'd rather see me in a cell.

Livin' in hell, only a few of us'll live to tell.

Now everybody talkin bout' us, I could give a fuck.

Like we the first ones to bomb and cuss.[365]

The conflict between the two was one of the Black bourgeoisie (Ms. Tucker) meeting the antithesis of Whiteness and White morality (Tupac). Ms. Tucker was unaware of her complicity in anti-Blackness against Tupac and the other Black male rappers she targeted during this period. Ms. Tucker was unaware that her blame was misdirected at the symptoms and results of a much larger problem, and not the root cause of the problem, the root cause being Black male misogynoir as a result of White male misogynoir. Black male violence and rage as the result of White male violence and terrorism. What kinds of terrorism? Physical terrorism. Psychological terrorism. Emotional terrorism. Economic terrorism. Plantation culture terrorism. Exploitation terrorism. Terrorism in the form of a denial that all rights and privileges that have been gained by White people is due to strategically and carefully crafted affirmative action policies and laws created through local, state, and federal government actions, while at the same time excluding and legislating against the majority of African Americans in America.

In 2023, roughly thirty years later, Dr. Jackie Walters lamented:

> Sometimes, as African American women, we're a bit more dramatic, and you go to the doctor, and you complain, and you complain, and you complain, and you're not taken seriously because you cry wolf the entire pregnancy.

> African American women . . . we want to also make sure you're being serious with your doctor and not playing the game so I can take you off work. Because then we see you 25 times in the pregnancy, it's hard to believe that there's a true problem when there's a true problem.[400, 401]

White psychopathology and anti-Blackness have been trained into the psyches, souls, and spirits of Black people just as much, if not more, on some levels, as they have been into White and non-Black people. Dr. Jackie's words are deadly. The implications are dangerous, as they allude to legitimizing, rationalizing, and justifying the reasons why Black women are not listened to, believed, supported, or treated with full humanity.

√ Should humans not be allowed to emote; especially when their bodies are experiencing the hormonal transformations that accompany forming another human inside of the body?

√ Is it dramatic for human beings to be concerned, cautious, and hyper-aware about the unexpected changes occurring to their bodies when they are not trained clinical experts?

√ Should vulnerable human beings voicing health concerns to their physicians more than twenty times be viewed as crying wolf, or should it be presumed that they are acting in good faith, and responded to with careful consideration?

These concerns become problematic when they are attached to Black bodies.

Anti-Blackness is cultural phenomena. White psychopathology is cultural phenomena. Dr. Jackie is an example of the ways in which normalized anti-Blackness has been embedded into the DNA of Black people in America.

Epigenetics.

A commentary written in 1979 by James Q. Wilson, about the book *Criminal Violence, Criminal Justice* written by Charles E. Silberman, summed it up in this way,

> Blacks learned violence from having violence practiced on them. If any group is kept in subjugation by the use of physical force and public humiliation, members of that group will understandably come to believe that force and humiliation should be used to manage their own affairs and, when circumstances permit, their relations with other groups.[364]

I digress.

Unfortunately, Ms. C. Delores Tucker shared her displeasure by lashing out at Black males, whom she presumably felt were in an inferior position, and whom she could chastise. Whether it was her intention, she contributed to leading a movement heavily aimed against Black men and the larger Black community.[317] Hers and her colleagues' efforts would have been better spent by focusing on the larger picture and challenging the systems, institutions, and cultural influences that shaped the experiences conveyed through gangster rap. Their energies would have been better spent seeking to understand and empathize with the devastating nuanced impacts of Black oppression in White America; impacts that can be felt through one line rapped by Tupac in his song "Troublesome":

> Ain't nothing worse than this cursed ass hopeless life.[335]

Dr. Jerome Fox and his work can also help us to understand the C. Delores Tucker and Tupac Shakur tensions better. In his 2016 workbook entitled *Addicted to White: The Oppressed In League with The Oppressor*, Dr. Fox stated that Black people are consumers and addicts of Whiteness. That we have made their way our own.[185] He posited that there were five fundamental variables that drive this reality. In his own words, during an interview on the *Knowledge Wisdom and Understanding* podcast, Dr. Fox stated:

> We as a people worldwide, are addicted to a White value system that's predicated on narcissism, greed, and violence. And I zoom in on that to identify 5 White values that we are principally addicted to.
>
> Value number one, that everything Black is bad and inferior, and everything White is good and superior. Value number two . . . is basically we put

things, money, and the things that money buys, above relationships. Value number three . . . oppressors are trustworthy recorders and interpreters of history and reality. That's why we listen to their news, so-called mainstream news, and read their history books without questioning everything that we hear, and everything that we read. And then, White value number four, individualism is better than collectivism. Hence, obligations to the group are subordinate to personal gain. So, it's all about me . . . me, me, me, me. White value number five . . . the best way to feel good about yourself is by surpassing, outdoing, and defeating someone else in an activity, achievement, or personal characteristic. This value in summary is competition over cooperation, and clearly there are things that we as a people need to do in order to secure our freedom and liberation but that require our unity. The only way to accomplish that is through us being unified and obviously if you're constantly looking for ways to distinguish yourself from your fellow Black brother and sister, there will be no cooperation.[208]

Dr. Fox describes Black people's placement and reality in America as a "tragic dependency upon our enemies," and he does so correctly, which should alarm us all.

Dr. Amos Wilson, in a speech given in the early 1990s, stated:

And as the Black man was the first to walk on this earth, the Black child is the first child to walk as a child. And as the Black man was the first to speak language on this earth, the Black child is the first to use language and symbols. As the Black man was the first to draw intelligent conclusions and build cities and nations and to engineer the world, the Black child exhibits in its psycho-motor responses and its ability to coordinate its body with its mind before White children. That the history of Black people is yet in the genes of his children, and that the potential of the Black man is in the potential of his children.

But people who do not know themselves, who do not know their history, who believe the propaganda put out by racists who have such an inferiority complex until they are willing to step down to White folk instead of living up to their potential; will destroy the potential that they have.

There is no reasoning on earth for the Black man to be ruled by White folk, or any other man. There is no reason for the Black man to be dependent on any other people. You can only see that as your natural role, and you can only see that as your natural place in the world if you've come to believe lies and mythologies, and if you've come to believe in your own inferiority as a people.

And the greatest damage then, that is done to African children in these educational establishments today is done through the low expectations of African American parents and of the African American community, and the low expectations of other people who have no knowledge of who African people are, and the potential of our people as a whole.

Therefore, you've got to know who you are.[303]

Dr. Wilson also said, during this same speech:

But if you don't know yourself—if you don't know your own developmental history, and how your psychology as an individual and as a people comes out of your unique experiences as individuals and as a people. If you are not aware of this, how your experience as an individual and as a people shapes the way you think, the way you see the world, the way you see yourself; shapes your very values, motivations, goals, and aims in life.

If you are not aware of how the American experience has shaped these things to fit the dominance of White folk, then you are going to miseducate your children, you are going to miseducate yourself, and you are going remain under the domination and control not only of White folk, but of any other folk that comes into this country and that comes into this world.

Arabs will rule over you. Latins will rule over you. Asians will rule over you. Everybody will rule over you, and anybody who has a sense of who they are, what they are; anyone who operates and educates their children according to their traditions, according to their background, according to their history, according to their identity.

The Japanese educate their children in terms of their Japanese-ness. Not in terms of White folk. Not in terms of Black folk. But in terms of themselves.

It is a brainwashed Negro, who tries to educate himself as if he were not Black, but as if he were some White person.

And this leads to miseducation if no education at all.[303]

So much of what they argued was tragically right. We have become preoccupied with mirroring our oppressors. Perhaps that is the ultimate sign of how thoroughly dominated we have become. Our dress, our cuisine—everything that defines us—is from our White oppressors. We are not White. We should never strive to be. It should never be something to which we aspire. We should not view how they live as something to emulate once we reach a certain status. We should rely on our own to design our clothing, cook our food, and make our music. There is no reason to take so much from those who robbed us of our very humanity.

Our focus on the material, acquiring it like Whites did, is also problematic. Dr. Frazier referred to this as the result of "nothingness" because our suffering (which stems from our extreme insecurity) results in our own self-hatred. That self-hatred means we cannot connect to anything with any substantial meaning, only that which is empty. That is why we focus on the European-designed handbag or suit.

We cannot patch the hole in our hearts with objects. We need to heal, and we cannot do that without acknowledging just how deep those wounds are. Discomfort is necessary. There is no material bandage big enough to stop the extent to which we have been bleeding for over 400 years. We have also adopted a perverse view that our ancestors suffered for us. So that we could live better today. Well, why did they have to be oppressed so that we could pretend to be free? How is that moral or rational?

Take Ben Carson, M.D., for example. He was President Trump's Housing and Urban Development (HUD) Secretary. As recently as 2017.

He said:

> Immigrants who came here in the bottom of slave ships, who worked even longer, harder for less. But they, too, had a dream that one day their sons, daughters, grandsons, granddaughters, great-grandsons, great-granddaughters might pursue prosperity.[209]

More psychopathy, more sociopathy.

And his decision to perpetuate both yielded him what? Power and approval (but only to a safe degree) among Whites. Carson is the perfect example—the absolute perfect example— of Dr. Wright's definition of someone suffering from Mentacide, someone who is irrational and delusional.[21]

What is perhaps most horrifying is how indicative it is of how well-controlled he is. What a puppet he has proved himself to be. He not only blames the victim, which would be bad enough. He profits from the victimization.

Carson, in his ignorance, represents a clear depiction of Dr. Amos Wilson's description of the Black-on-Black criminal, which he outlined in a speech entitled "The Psychology of Cooperative Economics."

In his speech, Dr. Wilson asserted:

There's no one more like the oppressor than the Black-on-Black criminal. The Black-on-Black criminal is a White man in Black face. He exhibits the same attitude toward his people as the White racist does. He doesn't love them, he hates them. He rejects them. He feels apart from them. He sees them merely as tools of exploitation. And when you look at the psychology of the Black-on-Black violent criminal you will see that psychology exactly parallels to White racist[s]. Because he has internalized the White racist lies, and now he has become an instrument for their activity against his own people.

And in acting the way he does, he thinks he's acting like a White man. So, if the White man is free to kick the N*****'* butt, he figures his freedom is the same thing. If he sees the White man's freedom as his capacity is to treat Black people any way he feels, and to rise above the law; then he, in imitating the White man is going to do the same thing the White man does. That's why we've got to get over the equality game. Because if a person lives upon our oppression, if their lifestyle is based on our oppression and exploitation, then to be just like them is to join in with them in oppressing our own people, and it becomes self-oppression as well.

Therefore, what it means to be free and what it means to be equal cannot be what it means to be like White folk.[306]

The Embeddedness and Pervasiveness of Anti-Blackness

One study, conducted by the Yale Child Study Center, was featured on NPR. A study control group of teachers was told to observe a group of preschool children. The group consisted of Black and White females and males. Facilitators of the study, led by Walter Gilliam, instructed the teachers to look for bad behavior. They instructed the teachers to hit a button every time they observed bad behavior and also used eye-scan technology to track where the teachers directed their attention. The teachers overwhelmingly paid the most attention to the Black male children and hit the button disproportionately more often to indicate that the Black children were misbehaving.[211]

But there was no bad behavior on their parts.

Researchers indicated there had not been any. This study reinforced another from 2003, which was done by Bertrand and Mullainathan. In it (sometimes called the "resume" study), hypothetical figures with highly desirable skill sets and what were deemed "Black sounding" names applied for jobs. Applicants with "White-sounding" names who were far less prepared for the positions were far more likely to receive interviews.[261]

How much more obvious can it get?

One does not even need such studies to make the point. One's lived experiences should suffice.

Consider a pool safety campaign initiated by the American Red Cross. An instruction poster featured a diverse group of children enjoying a day at their local pool. Who violated the pool rules? Only the Black children. Who did not? The ones who were White or White presenting.[213]

More psychopathy, more sociopathy. It is always everywhere.

Think about the piece entitled "Race and Economic Opportunity in the United States: An Intergenerational Perspective," which was featured in *The New York Times* in March 2018.[214] The article was entitled "Extensive Data Shows the Punishing Reach of Racism for Black Boys." The study, led by researchers and professionals from a combination of Stanford, Harvard, and the Census Bureau (and consisted of Raj Chetty, Nathaniel Hendren, Maggie R. Jones, Sonya R. Porter, and the Equality of Opportunity Project) followed the lives of millions of Black and White males and females who grew up wealthy. It highlighted the following:

> Black boys raised in America, even in the wealthiest families and living in some of the most well-to-do neighborhoods, still earn less in adulthood than white boys with similar backgrounds, according to a sweeping new study that traced the lives of millions of children.
>
> White boys who grow up rich are likely to remain that way. Black boys raised at the top, however, are more likely to become poor than to stay wealthy in their own adult households.
>
> Even when children grow up next to each other with parents who earn similar incomes, Black boys fare worse than white boys in 99 percent of America. And the gaps only worsen in the kind of neighborhoods that promise low poverty and good schools.[214]

The article, accessed electronically, featured an interactive set of blue and yellow squares. Each square indicated the lives of the children. The blue squares indicated the lives of the rich/affluent, Black, male children, while the yellow squares indicated the lives of the rich/affluent, White, male children. There were 10,000 lives depicted by all of the boxes in total. They each flowed into the following categories: Rich adult; Upper-middle-class adult; Middle-class adult; Lower-middle-class adult; and Poor adult. As you can see, more than 40% of the rich, Black children ended up poor or lower-middle-class, while more than 60% of the White children remained wealthy or upper to middle-class.

Figure 9.2.

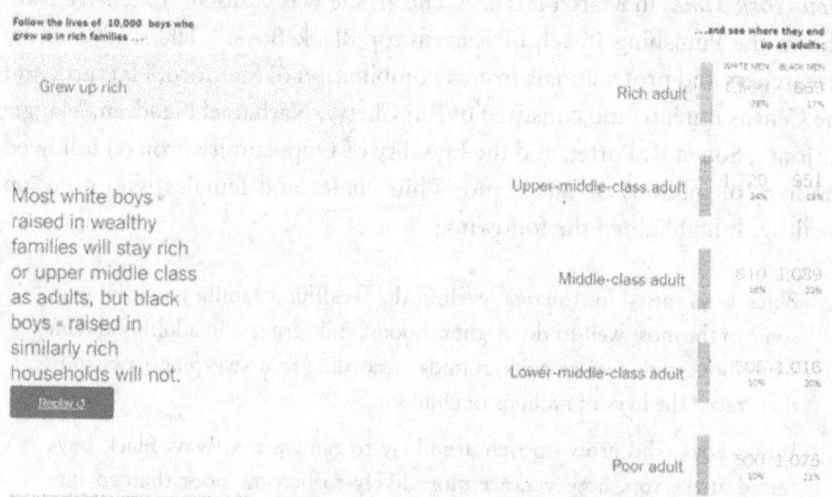

The article also highlighted other outcomes. Nearly half of White males who grew up poor ended up either wealthy or upper middle class or middle class. This compares to just 23% of Black males represented across the same categories. How can all of this simply be coincidence? To see this data is to know the effect of widespread psychopathy and sociopathy.

These figures were from 2018, not 1968 (which, even then, would have been unacceptable). For the Black males who grew up wealthy, 63% ended up impoverished. For Black males who grew up poor, 91% of them ended up across the three lowest categories. They remained poor with a slim shot of becoming middle class. There was only a 28% difference between the Black haves and have-nots, between Black males who grew up rich and those who grew up poor.

Figure 9.3.

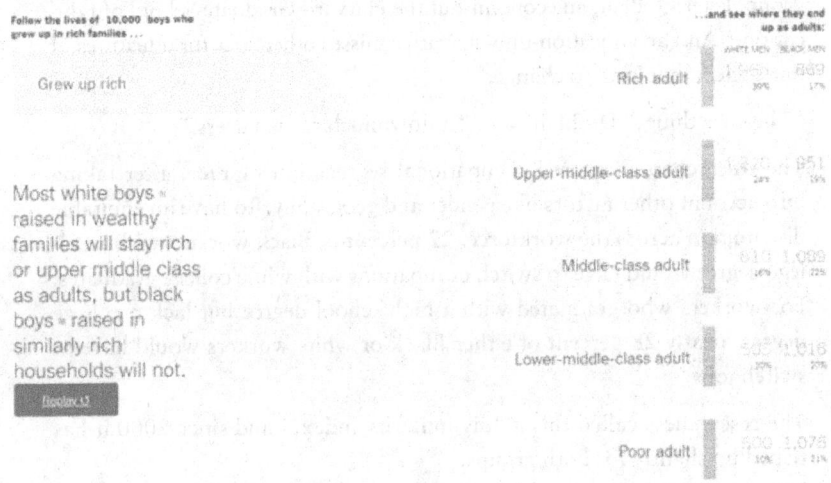

Follow the lives of 10,000 boys who grew up in rich families ...

...and see where they end up as adults:

Grew up rich · Most white boys raised in wealthy families will stay rich or upper middle class as adults, but black boys raised in similarly rich households will not.

In a newer, more recent study titled "The Limits of Educational Attainment in Mitigating Occupational Segregation Between Black and White Workers,"[379] executed by the National Bureau of Economic Research that relied on U.S. Census data and government surveys of households and businesses from 1980 to 2019, captured in Steve Lohr's *New York Times* article, "Occupational Segregation Drives Persistent Inequality, Study Says,"[378] published on September 4, 2023, Lohr writes:

> Education has long been hailed as the path to upward mobility in America. But new research points to limits of education as an economic escalator for Black workers.

> In the past two decades, the number of Black workers with a four-year college degree or higher has more than doubled, to 4.8 million. But the income gains are far less than would be expected in a race-neutral labor market, a team of academic and nonprofit researchers found.

> A key reason, they conclude, is the persistence of occupational segregation. Black workers with a college degree are more likely than their white peers to be employed in middle-wage jobs, like as social workers, tax examiners, and education administrators.

> The new report, published as a National Bureau of Economic Research working paper, is based on an analysis of U.S. census data and government surveys of households and businesses from 1980 to 2019.

"Education is important, but it's no panacea," said a member of the research group, Peter Q. Blair, an economist at the Harvard Graduate School of Education. "And an education-only narrative misses other structural features of our society that have to change."

"The core thing," Dr. Blair said, "is how much race matters."

The researchers measured occupational segregation by race, after taking into account other factors like gender and geography. To have an equitable distribution across the workforce, 22 percent of Black workers with a college degree would have to switch occupations with white college graduates. For workers who graduated with a high school degree but lack a college degree, nearly 28 percent of either Black or white workers would have to switch jobs.

The researchers called this a "dissimilarity index," and since 2000 it has ticked up slightly for both groups.

The new report notes that Black college students often major in fields that have lower wages. That is one potential explanation for the apparently limited impact of college on upward mobility.

But the dearth of Black students in majors that lead to higher pay in careers like technology or finance, the researchers say, is a legacy of racism.

Anti-Blackness is at the heart of capitalism and inflation, in other words. Economic oppression is real and has tangible, negative outcomes. It helps perpetuate the myth that Black people do not work hard, that they gravitate toward poverty, and that they choose not to assimilate in ways that would benefit them because they are deeply self-destructive. What does all of that do? Further cement anti-Black sentiment. It is cyclical in nature, you see. Everything feeds off of everything else. It is diabolical in its cleverness and none of us ever stood a chance against it. White people made their fortune on the literal backs of Black persons. They stole from them and murdered them. They did this and faced no consequences. Black people who today may rob a bank or loot a store to survive? Only the harshest penalties apply.

The reality of American terrorism/anti-Blackness is so pervasive that the odds of Black newborns surviving childbirth were cut in half when delivered by White and "not-Black" doctors; this was documented by the 2020 study, "Physician-Patient Racial Concordance and Disparities in Birthing Mortality for Newborns."[144]

A 2023 Harvard research study, published in the *Proceedings of the National Academy of Sciences*, demonstrates the current pervasive nature and state of White psychopathy in America. In an article published by Phys.Org, written by Issam Ahmed, the research findings established:

> A team from Harvard and Tufts gathered data from more than 60,000 subjects who took part in 13 experiments that tested their implicit biases.
>
> An overwhelming majority—over 90 percent—explicitly stated that white people and non-white people are equally human.
>
> But on an implicit measure, white U.S. participants, as well as white participants from other countries, consistently associated the attribute "human" (as opposed to "animal") with their own group more than other racial groups.
>
> Conversely, Black, Asian and Hispanic participants showed no such bias, equally associating their own group and white people with "human."
>
> "The biggest takeaway for me is that we're still grappling in a new form with sentiments that have been around for centuries," first author Kirsten Morehouse, a Ph.D. student at Harvard University, told AFP.

Throughout history, the dehumanization of other races has been used as a pretext for unequal treatment, ranging from police brutality all the way to genocide.[396]

More psychopathy, more sociopathy.

Ask yourself why it is fair to judge one and not the other. Ask what lens allows you to do so. Ask who benefits as a result. None of this is coincidental. One more study to consider is the Legal Memo Study conducted by Nextion and Dr. Arin N. Reeves in 2014.[212] It mirrors the preschool study.

Legal professionals from a variety of law firms were asked to evaluate the proficiency of two third-year NYU law students. One of the hypothetical students was identified as a White male named Thomas Meyer, while the other student was identified as a Black male named Thomas Meyer. The feedback about the Black Thomas Meyer's writing was predictably toxic. Hyper-scrutiny characterized the assessments. His hypothetical White counterpart? No such hyper-scrutiny existed, of course. White Thomas Meyer received glowing feedback. Any minor deficits they noted were couched in positive terms.

This study was closely linked to two true stories. One was written about a White male teacher named John Corcoran. It was featured on the BBC in April of 2018. The article was entitled, "I was a teacher for 17 years, but I could not read or write," and in it, he explained how his teachers were aware of his significant deficits but promoted him grade by grade anyway, based not on his performance (like everyone else's) but on his potential. He had not adequately performed, but they had confidence in him anyway.[275]

How generous in spirit.

One section of Mr. Corcoran's story reaffirmed the ways White supremacy ensures and manifests opportunities for incapable, deficient, insufficient, and inadequate White people. It shined a light on several functionalities of Whiteness, and the ways White people continue to be provided with the presumption of adequacy as well as the benefit of the doubt in an existence of incompetence and unpreparedness. In the article, Mr. Corcoran stated:

> At teacher conferences my teacher told my parents, "He's a smart boy, he'll get it," and they moved me on to the third grade.
>
> "He's a smart boy, he'll get it," and they moved me on to the fourth grade.
>
> "He's a smart boy, he'll get it," and they moved me on to the fifth grade.
>
> But I wasn't getting it.
>
> "By the time I got to the fifth grade I'd basically given up on myself in terms of reading. I got up every day, got dressed, went to school and I was going to war. I hated the classroom. It was a hostile environment and I had to find a way to survive."[275]

While this example can serve as a key example in helping us to understand the layers behind White supremacy, and what Dr. Koritha Mitchell refers to as White Mediocrity, it can also help us to understand the ways that White American culture works to hold Black children and adults to standards that are not imposed onto White children and adults. The fact that Mr. Corcoran was "presumed" to be a "smart boy" in the face of societal standards that would have deemed a Black child as "slow," "mentally incapable," "retarded," and/or other substantially negative labels that could and would have adversely affected the child throughout their entire life demonstrates the complex nature of White racism and anti-Blackness.

Understanding John Corcoran's experiences, specifically the ways Whiteness enabled him the ability to succeed in the face of inadequacy and deficiency, can also help us to understand Donald Trump's ascendency to the presidency of the United States of America.

In the Affirmative Action case that was heard in front of the U.S. Supreme Court, on October 31, 2022; a case that was actually brought forth by a group of Asian students who suggested that Black and Hispanic students were limiting their opportunities to get into Ivy League universities due to race being a standard consideration in the admissions process, it was proved that White affirmative action was a major issue rather than the former. The oral arguments provided on October 31 included representatives from the University of North Carolina (UNC). The exchange noted here is directly from the case's transcript:

Chief Justice Ketanji Brown Jackson: "Can I just simply return to Justice Alito's hypothetical, which I think is a little bit helpful in trying to pinpoint a problem that I've been having? It seems from the race hypothetical that if there was only one basis for giving someone a boost, and that basis was race, then I see a disadvantage, absolutely, to anyone else who's not an underrepresented minority who can get that boost. But I understood that we have here a program in which there are at least forty different basis for being able to get a boost, and not everyone who is an underrepresented minority gets a boost. So, it's really hard to figure out if anyone is being disadvantaged in a system like that, and that's where I was worried about standing because I'm trying to understand how the system is operating to actually advantage minorities in a way that is harmful to anyone else in this system."

UNC Counsel: "And I think that attributes to the careful cue that UNC has taken to this court's decisions, in Fisher 2, making sure . . . you know universities find themselves in this goldilocks problem about considering it too much or too little."

Chief Justice Ketanji Brown Jackson: "But there are other considerations is the point. Everyone, everyone can get a boost for all sorts of reasons. Minorities don't automatically get a boost under this system, so it's hard to know whether anyone's being disadvantaged from the mere fact that a minority could get a boost in this environment, right?"

UNC Counsel: "That's right, and the evidence also bears it out, Petition Appendix 78, where the evidence showed that <u>hundreds of White students with lower combined GPA and SAT scores were admitted ahead of higher performing Black students, Latinx students</u> [emphasis added], who went to UNC, and I think that bears the hallmark of the type of individualized considerations that this court wanted."[358, 359]

As you can see from this example, mediocre White students were provided with the preferential treatment that is customarily afforded to members of the White race (organization). They underperformed Black and Hispanic students, and yet still managed to be admitted to the university ahead of them. The Asian students who brought forth the affirmative action case were not interested in evaluating White mediocrity, White deficiency, White sponsorship, or White affirmative action. They were only interested in perpetuating historical and traditional stereotypical tropes about Black and Hispanic people, in the face of factual data and evidence which proved otherwise.

Harvard's data showed that more than 40% of their student admissions were due to the "legacy" process, a process typically dedicated to underperforming, mediocre, deficient, and incapable white students (roughly 70% of all legacy students), whose family members have historically attended the school. These individuals receive an "affirmative action" boost, due to their legacy of Whiteness, essentially. In addition, other nonperforming White students whose families donate monies to the universities also receive preference. In other words, incompetent and deficient White students, due to their socioeconomic status and abilities to manipulate institutional systems, were able to gain admissions ahead of Black and Latinx students who outperformed them.

Recent examples of White families exercising White affirmative action to compensate for White incompetence can be observed in the cases of Felicity Huffman and Lori Loughlin.[371] In a *New York Times* article titled, "Lori Loughlin and Felicity Huffman: 1 Scandal, 2 Actresses, Diverging Paths," written in April 2019, author Jennifer Medina wrote,

> Ms. Huffman and Ms. Loughlin are charged in the same sweeping criminal complaint, but the particular claims against them veer into far different plots.
>
> The essential claim against Ms. Huffman? That she spent $15,000 to get William Singer, the college consultant who has admitted to being the architect of a ring that used bribes to help parents get their children into selective colleges, to arrange for someone to secretly correct her daughter's answers on the SAT.
>
> The plans required Ms. Huffman to help her daughter receive extra time and choose a specific testing location where cheating could occur—and Ms. Huffman clearly understood what would occur, prosecution documents suggest. When her daughter's high school suggested that she take the test at school, Ms. Huffman sent an email to Mr. Singer that said: "Ruh Ro!"

In the end, prosecutors say, the scheme went forward, and Ms. Huffman's daughter, who is now a senior in high school and apparently knew nothing of the plans, got a score of 1420, about 400 points higher than she had earned on her Preliminary SAT exams.

When it came time for Ms. Huffman's younger daughter to take the test, Ms. Huffman and Mr. Singer again spoke in detail and plans began for a similar process, according to the criminal complaint against Ms. Huffman. The plans, though, were ultimately scrapped, the prosecutors said, and the younger girl apparently took the tests on her own.

Plans in the case of Ms. Loughlin, and her husband, the designer Mossimo Giannulli, were far more complex and focused around the entire college admissions process, not a test, the criminal complaint against them suggests.

Ms. Loughlin's lawyers did not return calls on Wednesday.

Prosecutors say that the family worked to get both of their daughters into "a school other than ASU," going along with Mr. Singer's plans for falsified athletic credentials and paying larger sums of money.

For months, investigators say, Ms. Loughlin kept in close touch with Mr. Singer, even while the family vacationed in the Bahamas. Following his suggestion, they would present the daughter—Isabella Rose Giannulli—as a coxswain, though she had never rowed crew. Once her spot at the University of Southern California was assured, they wired $200,000 to Mr. Singer's supposed charity.

According to prosecutors, Ms. Loughlin and Mr. Giannulli followed a similar path with their younger daughter. Both were enrolled at U.S.C. The total price tag, by prosecutors' tally? $500,000.[371]

Still, in the face of substantial evidence that specifically spotlighted the ways in which Whiteness and White supremacy functions within these processes, as noted above, the pro-White United States Supreme Court saw fit to strike down the legal use of Affirmative Action in college admissions, on June 29, 2023.[363]

The primary function of Whiteness is unearned advantage, while the primary function of Blackness is the burden of being exceptional, yet never being acknowledged, recognized, and/or rewarded as such.

The value of the delusional conception of "White skin" in America, is infinite.

Another example of White psychosis is a story that featured a White law professor from Georgetown University, who commented on the perpetual inadequacies she observed in her Black students, semester after semester, for more than 20 years.[274]

Not only do these examples demonstrate the value of White skin, that one could be entirely deficient and inadequate by White standards of success, and still prevail; they also highlight the unattainable bar that most Black people agonize about not achieving. There are many Black people who will never prevail because they are Black. And there are many White people who have and will continue prevailing because they are White. Most White people will never acknowledge or admit these truths. Instead, they will perpetuate delusional ideologies about "hard work," "bootstraps," "individualism" . . . and the list goes on.

Again, as I shared in an earlier chapter, in *The Falsification of Afrikan Consciousness: Eurocentric History, Psychiatry, and the Politics of White Supremacy*, Dr. Amos Wilson wrote,

> There are so many of us who believe that fair housing laws, civil rights laws, voting laws, and so forth guarantee our freedom. That is an illusion. What a flight into fantasy.
>
> Laws are no stronger than their enforcers. The same people who pass those laws are the same people who are responsible for enforcing them. If the people who enforce the laws no longer decide to do so, the laws are of no value and have no power.
>
> Ultimately, then, fairness rests not in laws but in the activities of people and in the attitudes and consciousness of people.
>
> Therefore, if the people who are responsible for enforcing those laws change their attitudes, then the treatment of those people whose freedom is protected by those so-called laws is changed as well.[301]

Again, as W.E.B DuBois stated, "A system cannot fail those it was never meant to protect."

This is America; White America; anti-Black America. The home where White and White-presenting people are free, authorized to be psychopathic sociopaths, masked as bravery.

In September 2022, I was asked to facilitate an antiracism leadership retreat for one of the most prestigious medical schools in the country. The room was comprised of 110 diverse leaders, chancellors and vice chancellors. Most of the group, more than half, were White (roughly 55 to 65 percent). I asked all of the White leaders to stand if they had ever been given jobs because of their connections (i.e., they knew someone, or they knew someone who knew someone, etc.). Most, if not all of them, stood on their feet.

They continued standing. The room was silent. I asked all of their non-White colleagues to take a very deep look around the room. I encouraged them to memorialize the occasion and take note of the admission of White affirmative action, upon which their colleagues had bravely admitted.

Next, I asked all of the White leaders to raise their hands if they had ever been given job opportunities for which they were not qualified. This included not meeting positional and/or educational objectives. Again, most if not all of the White leaders in the room raised their hands. I instructed all participants in the room to scan the room and observe their White colleagues whose hands were raised. They did.

The room was silent. The group of high-ranking professionals appeared dumbfounded. Some even appeared to be startled. I directed the White leaders to take their seats.

Finally, I emphasized the following points:

- Whiteness, in White America, provides that one can be incompetent, incapable, and deficient and still amass positional, economic, reputational, and political opportunity and success. The White leaders' admissions of the ways they experienced White affirmative action, coupled with studies I had shared prior to the event, solidified this point.

- The exceptional nature of Black people—which includes our intellectual and creative abilities, work ethic, tenacity, and capacity to outthink and outwit most people—does not, cannot, and will not ever compare to the mediocrity and/or deficiency White and other "not-Black" colleagues, due to White supremacy and anti-Blackness.

- I invited all Black leaders in the room to take a deep breath and relax. They were encouraged to understand, know, and be confident that they had done their best. They were guided to understand that all of the opportunities that they thought would flow their way once they acquired the necessary credentials (i.e., master's and doctorate degrees, specialized licenses, training certifications, etc.), that had not manifested, was not their fault. I shared with them my own personal testimony of having to navigate the same painful reality while working in both private and public sectors and how I suffered depression as a result. I encouraged these Black leaders to exhibit grace for themselves, and to not blame themselves for not being "good enough," which so many of us (Black people) internalize. We develop thoughts and feelings that lead to insecurities and reinforce feelings of inadequacy and self-doubt.

° The Black leaders were reminded to be confident in their exceptionalism, excellence, and brilliance and not to judge themselves through White American models and frameworks of intellect, respectability, and civility. I affirmed that each of them had "done enough" and "were enough." After all, the lack of reward for their efforts was not their fault. The fault was their Blackness. In a society that is built upon the fertile hostility towards Blackness, which sees and deems Blackness as deficient and insufficient, they would never receive the types of recognition and accolades that their mediocre and deficient White and "not-Black" colleagues receive.

° I informed the White and "not-Black" leadership (with the support of one of the Black, female fellows) that they needed to provide the same types of "sponsorship" and support to their Black colleagues. I reminded them of the sponsorship that they had acknowledged receiving throughout their careers and had admitted to the entire group moments earlier.

° All leaders were encouraged to remain conscious of the impulse to hold Black and Brown people to higher standards, as compared to White colleagues who are oftentimes held to the lowest standard, or no standards at all. This can be true for people from other non-White groups (who are not Black), who benefit due to their proximity to Whiteness.

° Lastly, I asked how many Black and non-White leaders had ever stated that they did not want to be given opportunities because of their race? It seemed like most of the non-White leaders in the room raised their hands. I gently reminded them about the functionalities of Whiteness and White supremacy, the admissions of their White colleagues as a prime example, and to understand that America provides opportunities to White people because they are White. I encouraged them to feel good about receiving opportunities solely based on race rather than feeling negatively due to stereotypes that work to perpetuate stigmas about people of color and affirmative action. To understand America is to understand that it is a country that was founded and functions upon White affirmative action. And so, we should not think about or feel any negative emotions upon receiving opportunities for any reason, including race. Be bold and proud, knowing full and well that White people in America have been provided with 100% of opportunities based on their race.

In three subsequent leadership retreats, December 2022, April 2023, and May 2023, this exercise was repeated with three different executive cabinets: a medical school and two different prestigious healthcare organizations. The results were similar in all cases.

Anti-Blackness and White supremacy are meant to eat at us from the inside out. They show us no such charity, only harshness. And we are crippled as a direct result. We must understand this is an illness. As Toni Morrison put it, it is a "profound neurosis that no one examines for what it is."[27]

Black people must continue proclaiming unabashedly that Black Lives Matter, that Black is Beautiful, that Black is Enough, that Black is Love, that Black is Whole. We must mean it, for our children and for ourselves. We must discard all White oppressive tenets and behaviors.[215]

Closing: What Lies Ahead?

I hope this book touched you. Writing it touched me.

In the words of President John F. Kennedy:

One hundred years of delay have passed since President Lincoln freed the slaves, yet their heirs, their grandsons, are not fully free. They are not yet freed from the bonds of injustice. They are not yet freed from social and economic oppression. And this Nation, for all its hopes and all its boasts, will not be fully free until all its citizens are free.

We preach freedom around the world, and we mean it, and we cherish our freedom here at home. But are we to say to the world, and much more importantly, to each other that this is the land of the free except for Negroes; that we have no second-class citizens except for Negroes; that we have no class or caste system, no ghettoes, no master race except with respect to Negroes?

The old code of equity law under which we live commands for every wrong a remedy, but in too many communities, in too many parts of the country, wrongs are inflicted on Negro citizens and there are no remedies at law. Unless Congress acts, their only remedy is in the street.[216]

White America has consistently answered his question in the affirmative, and resolutely. We must consider what we want and what we are willing to do to get it. That is our assignment. And we must consider this assignment with the utmost seriousness, as it is a life-or-death matter, as you can see.

Samuel Adams, one of America's Founding Fathers, said the following in the *Boston Gazette* in 1772:

If the public are bound to yield obedience to laws to which they cannot give their approbation, they are slaves to those who make such laws and enforce them.[218]

Know that we are still enslaved. We have no control over the distribution of resources, monetary or otherwise. Which is another way of saying we are deprived. No one is looking out for us. Often even we do not look out for our own selves. We must boldly resist those who wish to hurt us, no matter the cost.

Enough psychopathy, enough sociopathy. Enough of these diseases.

It is past time for White America to own the abuse it has inflicted and continues to inflict onto our bodies and souls. As noted in the Kerner Commission Report, issued in 1968:

Segregation and poverty have created in the racial [Negro] ghetto a destructive environment totally unknown to most white Americans.

What white Americans have never fully understood—but what the Negro can never forget—is that white society is deeply implicated in the ghetto. White institutions created it, white institutions maintain it, and white society condones it.

Our nation is moving toward two societies, one Black, one white–separate and unequal.[219,220]

We are now 54 years away from this pivotal era, an era many perceived as a moment of national racial reckoning. No such reckoning occurred. It was all an act. A trick. A psychopathic, sociopathic trick. And we chose to fall for it. I do not believe that most Whites want to change the order that benefits them. That would require profound moral insight. What evidence is there that they possess this profound moral insight?

This is evident by the ways in which White women and men, government officials, pander to the "educated" and "lesser educated" White majority, and the ways in which they protect racism through a lack of accountability.[217] Anti-Blackness is American culture, a way of being and existing. It is more than a pathology; it is a living, breathing condition, and the most valuable variable central to American life in its entirety. Without anti-Blackness, America fails. Without anti-Blackness, Whiteness is not superior to anyone. Without anti-Blackness, there is no one to oppress for economic, political, or cultural gain. White America needs and will always ensure it has a "nigger," otherwise it will lose itself.

I think a lot about a short clip of James Baldwin, which I saw in *I Am Not Your Negro*, produced in 2016. In it, he said:

> There are days, this is one of them, when you wonder what your role is in this country and what your future is in it. How precisely you're going to reconcile yourself to your situation here and how you are going to communicate to the vast, heedless, unthinking, cruel white majority that you are here. I'm terrified at the moral apathy—the death of the heart—which is happening in my country. These people have deluded themselves for so long that they really don't think I'm human.[152]

Unfortunately, we have not even begun the process of understanding who we are and what animates us, and until we do, we will continue to fail miserably.

Chapter 9 Review Questions:

(Note: Please go to www.danteking.com to complete the chapter assessment and evaluation for the following questions.)

Considering what you have read, answer the following:

1. How are you seeing Whiteness and anti-Blackness differently now?

2. What are your thoughts about Whiteness and anti-Blackness as sociopathic, psychopathic, and pathological conditions?

3. In your estimation, how should America address its current problems regarding White supremacy and anti-Blackness?

4. In what ways does Dr. Poussaint's framing of Whiteness as racial politics and White racism as "mental illness," along with Dr. Bobby Wright's assertion of White psychopathy, help us to further understand the functionality of perpetual White perversions, distortions, and projections White people hold about themselves as superior, juxtaposed against fabricated anti-Black cultural narratives about "who" Black people are, as well as "what" Blackness represents in America?

5. What role does the lack or absence of impression management, as well as the absence of impulse control, play in the impressions and interpretations of Black people's daily behaviors, attitudes, and actions in America?

6. In what ways does Dr. Wright's framing help us to further understand the politics and functionalities of Whiteness and anti-Blackness in America?

7. In what ways does Dr. Wright's framing help us to further understand the need for White American culture to have and perpetually maintain Black American Descendants of Enslaved Peoples (sometimes referred to as ADOS/ADOEP) as an affixed permanent underclass?

8. In what ways does Dr. Wright's framing help us to further understand the necessity of racial politics in America, specifically Whiteness and anti-Blackness, the infinite "brand-value" of Whiteness, and the brand "valuelessness" of Blackness in America?

CHAPTER 10

Addressing Whiteness and Anti-Blackness in America: Suggestions and Recommendations for Individuals and Institutions

FOR AMERICA TO FUNCTION normally, Whiteness must be dismantled. That means every American institution must be dismantled, as Whites have invented and dominated them all. We would have to let go of identities we have long wed ourselves to and unlearn the most basic values that dominate our lives. A whole upheaval must occur, which is why it most likely will not, and White supremacist and anti-Black ideologies will continue to dominate. Hope, which is what Black people have relied on, is simply not enough. We need a bold, intricate, hard plan, one that will take years to implement, assuming we do it correctly, and one that will address in the most fundamental ways what our deficits are. Because Black people have been conditioned so harshly, we see any trivial step forward as something to celebrate. Having a half Black president, for example, was supposed to mean racism was dead. All that happened was that it temporarily got better exposed due to the obvious hatred of those opposing him (think of the birther issue). America is not well. It has not made the progress so many Black people believe it has made. And it cannot, by definition, because it does not understand the country's origin story meaningfully.

√   Why did it take us hundreds of years to have our first Black [fill in the blank]?

In *Black Bourgeoisie*, E. Franklin Frazier asserted:

> However much some middle-class Negroes may seek to soothe their feeling of inferiority in an attitude which they often express in the adage, "it is better to reign in hell than to serve in heaven," they are still conscious of their inferior status in American society.

> Not all middle-class Negroes consciously desire . . . to be white in order to escape from their feelings of inferiority. In fact, the majority of middle-class Negroes would deny having the desire to be white, since this would be an admission of their feeling of inferiority. Within an intimate circle of friends some middle-class Negroes may admit that they desire to be white, but publicly they would deny any such wish. The Black bourgeoisie constantly boast of their pride in their identification as Negroes. But when one studies the attitude of this class in regard to the physical traits or the social characteristics of Negroes, it becomes clear that the Black bourgeoisie do not really wish to be identified with Negroes.[1]

Both victims and aggressors must self-reflect, and they should do so with professional help. This process must be guided. It cannot be self-contained. Adequate scrutiny will not come about on its own.

This would require investments by both Black and other racial/ethnic clinicians and coaches committed to helping us cleanse ourselves. These professionals should be highly trained first, of course. As you can see, the road ahead is long. It is arduous.

Individuals should:

√   Learn actual and all history, not merely what was spoon-fed to them. Then connect it to the present.

√   Acknowledge that disparities are systematic; they are not about the individual shortcomings of Black people.

√   Acknowledge that Whites who allege they are not racist, are. And that they continue to benefit from a system that was built around their comfort and our degradation.

√   Access the reading list I have assembled at www.danteking.com, as well as the resources and references here.

√   Understand that the plight of every Black person in America is the result of pro-Whiteness and anti-Blackness. Every single one, without singular exception.

√   Attend Understanding the Roots of Racism and Bias: Anti-Blackness, and Its Link to Whiteness, White Racism, Privilege, and Power.

√   Purchase *The 400-Year Holocaust: Toolkit and Workbook* and begin implementing similar frameworks, policies, and programs throughout their organizations.

√   Come to terms with the reality that we will never fully understand the complexities and damage caused by our oppression.

√   Understand that the White psyche needed like oxygen the terrorization of Black people. It could not function in its absence. That is how fundamental it is to White identity.

√   Understand that anti-Blackness and Black people's pain and exploitation have been and remains the bedrock of America's economic and political systems. Black pain and suffering is profitable. This was as much the case for the racial enslavement of Black people as it is for mass incarceration, special education, and other industries of oppression that make up the White American cultural, institutional, and economic landscape.

√   Resist the illnesses of Whiteness and anti-Blackness by redefining the Black American experience outside of the White social, cultural, economic, and institutional validation system.

√   Understand that there is no such thing as reward for hard work in a culture and systems that are designed to reward White people most assiduously, regardless of their performance. Realize the reality that White supremacy culture is an environment established for White people to win. It was established for their success and well-being. Stop judging the masses of Black people and others referred to as POC, who remain challenged in situations of struggle and defeat, as though it is their own fault. True solidarity is possible only when this fact is uplifted and maintained.

√ Dismantle Black selectivism. We tend to pick and choose who to celebrate based on who meets our anti-Black, pro-White standards. No one subversive is selected. No one honest is selected. No one bold is selected. That is not a coincidence. In addition to upholding the legacies of people like Dr. Martin Luther King, Jr. and Rosa Parks, we need to celebrate and uplift our ancestors who fought against oppression and denigration, as well as other lesser-acknowledged figures: W.E.B DuBois, James Baldwin, Marcus Garvey, Ida B. Wells-Barnett, David Walker, Frederick Douglass, Nat Turner, Fannie Lou Hamer, Lerone Bennett Jr., Gloria Richardson, Malcolm X, Albert Cleage, John Henrik Clarke, Toni Morrison, E. Franklin Frazier, and many others who have tried to sound the alarm.

Too many Black people have accepted without scrutiny the culture that oppresses us. Much of the work that needs to take place must take place within, and that is hard (but necessary) to accept.

√ White people should seek therapy from therapists who are descendants of Africans abducted and forcibly brought to America. These professionals should represent people who have an in-depth knowledge of the framing outlined in this book. These individuals should be trained to disrupt White comfort, and White psychology. It will facilitate a change in their frame of reference.

√ Use the following pieces of the "Dismantling Racism and Tenets of White Supremacy" curriculum to start:

Manifestations of White Supremacy:
§ Perfectionism
§ Sense of urgency
§ Defensiveness
§ Quantity over quality
§ Worship of the written word
§ Only one right way
§ Paternalism

§ Either/or thinking
§ Power hoarding
§ Fear of open conflict
§ Individualism
§ I'm the only one
§ Progress is bigger, more
§ Objectivity
§ Right to comfort

White People's Resistance:
§ Denial
§ Minimization
§ Blame
§ Lack of intent
§ It's over now
§ Competing victimization

√   Address the persistent, inherent psychopathic and sociopathic need to oppress Black people.

Institutions should:

√   Work to provide ongoing social, emotional, health, and economic welfare to Black people, in the same ways that local, state, and federal private and public institutions worked to provide these realities for Whites, explicitly for more than three and a half centuries.

√   Donate money to Black children and families directly, as well as to Black schools.

√   Donate monies to Black men, women, girls, and boys who are incarcerated, as well as those who are released from the prison system.

√   Provide food, shelter, clothing, and funding to programs that support unsheltered Black people, as well as those who are impoverished and do not have resources to provide enough for themselves or their families. Realize Black "criminality" is a symptom of the absence of opportunity, and the absence of hope.

√   Contract and consult with me or other antiracism scholars and experts. Seek out the help of others, including Dr. Koritha Mitchell, Dr. Ibram X. Kendi and the Center for Antiracist Research at Boston University, Dr. Kenneth Hardy, Dr. Joy DeGruy, Dr. Rachelle Rogers-Ard, and others doing this work in different areas of emphasis.

√   Learn that equity attempts to identify the specific needs and requirements informed by demographic traits, such as race. It then tries to address the differing needs of each group by bridging the gap between Whites and Black people. This makes equity central to the genuine empowerment of Black people and not just theoretical equality.

√   Implement anti-Black/racism core competencies that hold accountable every leader across your organization.

√   Focus on both the historical and current dimensions of White matriarchy and patriarchy, rather than overemphasizing the intersection of Whiteness and maleness. Understand the culpability of White women, as it played a significant role in how we got to where we are today. White women upheld Whiteness, White supremacy, White racism, White privilege, White power, and anti-Blackness. [6,222]

√   Ensure all employees, leaders, board members, and stakeholders are educated about White psychopathy and sociopathy.

√   Recruit Black and Brown leaders who have a demonstrable track record for working on anti-Black racism and who can encourage and advocate on behalf of Black and Brown equity and justice. Celebrate and empower Black people in leadership and individual contributor roles, throughout your organization.

√   Understand that Black people mostly feel devalued and degraded, and that that feeling is entirely rational and predictable, given our history. You may believe that the POC in your organization feel valued and supported, but I have worked with more than 50 different organizations, and the experience is the same everywhere. Black people, and other such POC, are devalued, and experience major setbacks because of it. They are most times not honest about it and code switch to avoid ever having to address it, yet it leads to Racial Battle Fatigue (RBF). [130,221]

√ Know that all White people who are attempting to promote equity and antiracism are doing so from a socialization rooted in superiority and anti-Blackness. Do not trust them. Their actions are rooted in racist logic (i.e., superiority and supremacy logic, as well as a logic of inferiority and deficiency about Black, and other non-White, peoples). At the same time, most, if not all, Black and Brown peoples are coming from oppressed perspectives (i.e., inferiority perspectives) and it drives us in a way where we operate from a place of deprivation, very often. That means our standards for improvement are low. That is not a coincidence, either.

√ Learn from medical professionals such as Dr. David Williams from Harvard, who invented the Everyday Discrimination Scale. [285]

√ Enact additional time off policies for Black people. Because we are strained the most, we require greater time to address that strain. Ensure all employees learn about Racial Battle Fatigue, a theory developed and created by Dr. William Smith. [221]

√ Ensure all leadership reads the article written by Shenequa Golding entitled "Maintaining Professionalism In the Age of Black Death Is . . . A Lot." [223]

√ Recognize when Black and "not-Black" people are being used to uphold White matriarchy and patriarchy within organizations, as gatekeepers and defenders. [224]

√ Require 24 to 40 hours of antiracism training every two years and document attendance and performance in employee files.

√ Continue to assert that Whiteness and anti-Blackness are illnesses that must be treated lest they spread.

√ Read and/or re-read the "Kerner Commission Report," issued in 1968 to understand the assessments made about America in 1968, in terms of becoming two societies, one White, one Black. Jelani Cobb recently contemporized this report and republished it for today's society. [286]

√ Sponsorship, not mentorship!

√   Remain aware of White mediocrity, deficiency, and insufficiency as
     White American norms. Stop requiring Black people to be excep-
     tional, only to recognize and reward it as average. Recognize all
     Black people as exceptional for surviving daily terrorism, yet still
     possessing the ability to show up and participate in American life
     daily, in addition to being required to be exceptional. Only then
     can there be true equity and equality.

√   White people need to deal with themselves, their psychopathic
     and sociopathic proclivities toward Black people. On this note, I
     submit that there are processes that need to occur that extend far
     beyond the concept of racial equity, or racial repair. An authentic
     racial reckoning needs to occur. Below, I outline some definitions
     that I have created to aid both organizations and individuals in
     attempting to do racial healing and antiracism work. The concepts
     and definitions consist of:

Racial Reckoning: The process of White/White-adjacent/"not-Black" people learning about their history and the ways in which they have been indoctrinated with Whiteness and anti-Blackness. It includes becoming aware
of and in touch with predispositions to anti-Blackness and the psychopathic and sociopathic personalities existing within their culture, communities,
and identities. In addition, it includes White people doing their own personal work, and coming to terms with the reality that they are no better
than Black and Brown people (especially the most marginalized) but that all
White American institutions (including economics, language, politics, government, education, religion, the judicial system, and all other systems) were
built to create a reality in which they felt superior to others. In addition,
White people, liberal, progressive, good White people, must awaken to the
reality that inherent within their existence is the need to oppress Black and
Brown people individually and institutionally, while at the same time denying that it is occurring.

Racial Repair-ations: The process of White/White-adjacent/"not-Black" people locating resources, learning, and developing strategies to deal with reinforced White superiority and anti-Blackness (i.e., historical record, knowledge,
and perspective; soft skills including humility, giving up power, empowerment
and upliftment of Black and Brown people; etc.) to authentically equalize and

stabilize structural, institutional, cultural, social, psychological, emotional, and interpersonal inequities; and power imbalances between White people and non-White people (specifically Black people) to achieve authentic inclusivity/representation and realization (i.e., contributions, voice, decisioning, outcomes, etc.).

White Racial Negotiations: The process of White people deciding how much power and privilege is to be, can be, and/or will be rendered, sacrificed, and negotiated in a White supremacist environment, in order to provide opportunities, resources, inclusion, belonging, upliftment, and all other privileges/opportunities that White people enjoy to Black, Indigenous, Hispanic, Arab, Middle-Easterners, and other peoples from other traditionally marginalized groups. This is aligned with and is a form of racial repair-ations to confront and combat what Robin DiAngelo has referred to as "white fragility" weaponized in the forms of "everyday White racial bullying" and daily "White racial control," among other things.

Policies should be designed in ways that the language constitutes clear intention about achieving the respective antiracism and/or racial equity goal. All policies should contain a policy statement and a programmatic and/or practice structure that identifies exactly how the policy and/or program is executed.

There are many more recommendations, but I will stop here, as this is a mere starting point.

Anonymous Participant Comments from
Understanding the Roots of Racism

ONE OF THE QUESTIONS I ask as a part of a reflective survey distributed after participants attend this workshop, is: What connections have you/can you make to the current state of United States/American culture, its institutions (i.e., government, politics, education/academia, language, economics, legal system, religion, incarceration/imprisonment, housing, healthcare/health education, etc.), as a result of this capacity building intensive? Please consider physical and nonphysical institutions (i.e., language, economics, intellectual property, etc.). Noted throughout the next several pages are some of the responses and reactions to this question that have been shared by participants who have attended the course.

√   This question is at the core of the entire class, in my opinion. Each session to date would take a look at a specific point in our past, focusing on laws, enforcement, and effects on both African Americans and their white counterparts. Week over week, as we reviewed these facts, we heard from scholarly experts interpreting the effects these laws and historical events had on individuals and society. We also had frequent breakout sessions where we would learn of the details of a historical event and then discuss how there are parallels to the subject today. One going through this curriculum couldn't help but apply the lessons presented to the patterns seen today in our current events both on the news and even within our organization and within our departments. As we left the 1600s to 1700s and began to focus on the 1800s to present day, the curriculum highlighted the evolution of the wording of the laws passed and the entire nation's coordinated effort to basically accept that AA's were "free," but in a coordinated and intentioned way, ensured that AA structurally were limited in their ability to integrate into society and participate in American economy as a true equal to whites.

Again, the connections to today were widespread and easily seen and was the focus of much of my thought and personal discussions with friends and family between classes. Without a doubt, this course helped me in seeing the facts that support the idea that American society is built on racism and anti-Blackness, that whites within this society have benefited from this structure (regardless of if they wish to admit it or not), and that those from the AA community have experienced real trauma in their current life affecting their ability to thrive in this society in the way that whites, as a whole, can. These truths apply to our organizations, HR processes, how we supervise and lead our teams, how we interact with our patients, and how we measure the effectiveness of our practices on our department's mission, vision, and values.

√   In 2021, it is clear that anti-Blackness was strategically orchestrated with the intent to destroy the humanity and lives of Black folks through any means necessary. Anti-Black laws, institutions, practices, and mores of yester years continue to permeate throughout current American life and culture exclusively to benefit White folks and at the detriment of Black folks. Black folks continue to be at the receiving end of the creations of America's diabolical masterminds, aka the founding fathers, and other White constructionists of American culture.

√   The biggest connection I have made is learning the history of how this country was made for White people (not by White people, because Black people built this country as much if not more) and for the sole elevation and economic progress of White people at the expense (and explicitly to the detriment) of Black people, as well as other POC, and how that led to the current state of racism in the U.S. The through line of anti-Blackness from the seventeenth century to today is stark and obvious. There are so many ways that Black people are oppressed and denied opportunities today—in education, housing, jobs, finance, voting rights (!), and so many more. When you trace the history, it is no surprise that we have ended up where we are today. All of the ways that Black people are oppressed build on each other, which makes it harder and harder to move forward or be successful in life, through no fault of your own.

√　Racism and inequity is embedded in EVERY facet of our existence here in the U.S. The nation calls itself the "land of the free and the home of the brave," but I now know that it is completely the opposite. We are imprisoned in a system of profound racism, hatred, and fear. Our rules and regulations, our education system, law enforcement—EVERYTHING—have been and continue to be designed and propagated by cowards. I am embarrassed to call myself an American.

√　The U.S. was physically built on the backs of enslaved people, the laws were created and enforced and re-written as needed to benefit White people and to disenfranchise Black people from all the benefits of a society. The tools of society are made to serve White people—schools, banks, courts, police, hospitals, etc.—but I did not know the extent to which they were made to oppress BAA people. I learned the clear design from the earliest explorers and pilgrims to venture capitalists and law makers of today that created the structures of culture we live in—segregation, homelessness, mass incarceration, wealth gaps, health gaps, and on and on. You can tell what a person values by what they spend their time and money on. It is clear that our country has always and still does value Whiteness and power. We have spent billions of dollars on socialist programs only when it benefits White people. As soon as BAA people try to take advantage of the programs that their tax dollars pay for, it is suddenly socialist fascism and "welfare queens." Suddenly society can't afford the cost. While spending trillions on the military and corporate welfare programs. It is a structure of evil that reinvents itself to suit modern sensibilities over and over again.

√　This has helped me understand that anti-Blackness was intentional and "baked" into American culture, and most importantly that it continues today. The idea that anti-Blackness was set up in all areas of government, education, and down to where Black people were permitted to live was, in my mind, something that happened in the past, and that "we don't do that anymore." But to understand that anti-Blackness is the very foundation of American society that has propelled White success has been the most eye-opening for me.

√   Being an immigrant from the Philippines, I greatly benefited from my proximity to Whiteness. Being raised in a White-dominated culture in the Philippines allowed my transition from the Philippines to the U.S. much easier. I realize now that I have been educated to speak and act like a White person. This allowed me to assimilate and succeed. But I now realize that this came at a cost. Not to me. But to Black people. I feel like I was allowed to succeed because I was not Black.

√   Integrating a new sense of self. As a White person I did not understand, until this course, the degree to which walking around in White skin and conforming broadly to social norms was causing harm day in and day out. In this course I realized simply being White means that you are uniquely programmed from birth to reproduce conditions of anti-Black racism, unconsciously or consciously, and to benefit from doing so. Toni Morrison and Alvin Poussaint suggested that racism is a form of mental illness in Whites, and this resonated with me deeply. This inclination toward domination and superiority, alongside the paranoia, fear, and the psychotic inability to empathize with harms enacted, is the intergenerational inheritance of White Americans. This is the core of the White American psyche and our culture. Before this course I already didn't believe in "good" or "bad" people, but I didn't realize that because I have White skin I am far more likely to cause harm than others. It was painful to have this aspect of myself laid out so clearly, so undeniably. Often during the course, I felt my hands squeezing my temples, trying to crack my skull, or tear my skin apart as I incorporated this inbred propensity for evil into my working sense of self.

√   First and most maliciously, the legal system is nothing more than the White bully's code of domination enshrined in the written word and enforced by arms. The worship of the written word in law worked hand in hand with the holy scriptures to rationalize and reinforce the domination, torture, rape, and murder of Black people and Indigenous people in particular. That's not all. The cultural manifestations of anti-Blackness are first revealed in these colonial-era laws. And they quickly infused all institutions, so that "White" Americans became brainwashed by and encultured in anti-Blackness and White supremacy, thereby dangerously reinforcing the laws oppressing BIPOC. All American cultural institutions thereafter have inherited this anti-Black construct. It is intentional and not accidental that modern institutions show grave and unjust racial disparities. Black people are murdered by police, incarcerated at higher rates, experience worse health outcomes, have less wealth and opportunity, and receive worse education than White people and other White-adjacent groups.

√　This training has very much solidified and expanded my knowledge that this government, American culture, and all above mentioned institutions are founded on White supremacy, racism, brutal abuse, and injustice and still are to current day without progress or meaningful change. This training definitely taught me so much more in regard to how White supremacy/racism also dictates nonphysical institutions. For me, the definition of capitalism being socialism for White people really made sense and brought a lot of that together and includes all of those institutions, physical and nonphysical. Additionally, Whiteness being property with infinite value also helped me connect how all of these institutions and American culture are entirely fixed on White supremacy and White advantage and power within all these areas.

√　As a White person I am better realizing and processing how White supremacy culture is providing a sense of, or mindset, as well as actual power and privilege to all White people. How if unrealized and unchecked this manifests in or informs everything White people do. The socialization around this is everywhere and White people from infancy are having their worth, culture, and humanity affirmed constantly. Impacts include: entitlement, complicity in White supremacy, delusional ideas of self-worth/grandeur, lack of empathy for non-White people, lack of accountability for continued abuse, continued systematic and social benefits (White affirmative action) and control connected to anti-non-Whiteness and anti-Blackness, continued racial control via things like calling police on BIPOC peoples, regulating/controlling spaces at work, within community, all over, and passing down these things to White children.

√　So many ways. I have gained so much more insight into the diabolical history, facts, policies, and laws that have created American government and culture and continue to rule it now. I have gained a much deeper, clearer understanding of the roots of racism, American culture, and that racism is at the root of White success. I believe I will be better able to have effective conversations about racism and White supremacy. Through this experience I have gained the opportunity to participate in policy work towards racial equity, which I am anticipating will help me learn more ways to be useful doing antiracism and equity work going forward. This experience has increased my awareness and motivation to be accountable for the privilege and power my Whiteness has provided and how my everyday Whiteness is actively harming people. I am pretty terrible with conflict and confrontation, while intellectually I know both are inevitable and necessary. This experience has helped me to realize more about my responsibility to confront White supremacy and racism, despite my aversions to conflict/confrontation and that it is not an acceptable excuse.

√   This is one of the things that this training really drove home for me, that none of this exists in only a historical context. The systems that were created in White racism and to uphold White power, many of them still function the same and for the same purpose, or just look a little different today. Some of the institutions that stood out to me were academia, medicine/public health, and incarceration. I now see more clearly that academia in the U.S. was created by White Christian cis men who were seeking to uphold and legitimize their racist beliefs, and that education systems still largely function to do this. My own education in the CA public school system was clearly complicit in teaching a whitewashed narrative of history. And schools today still disproportionately discipline Black children, remove them from classrooms, and readily feed the school-to-prison pipeline. The history of medicine in the U.S. strikes me as particularly horrific, and to know that working in public health places me in a system that continues to uphold health disparities, and is so vehemently opposed to change at times, is something with which I am grappling. To know that gynecology largely grew out of the torture and enslavement of Black women, and that even today, medical students tend to believe that Black people feel less pain, it makes me sick. And lastly, for now, I see clearly how slavery led to forced labor led to Jim Crow led to our current incarceration system. And that each of these is just a different mutation of the same virus (as another participant in the training described), all serving the same system of White supremacy and racism.

√ While I know racism is the ocean the U.S. swims in, permeating everything, to see so many clear examples of laws, policies, governance, education, economy, etc., I was surprised each time (which surprised me). There was a recent audio/video clip played in the fourth week I think that struck me because the same words/tone, etc. could've been exactly the same hundreds of years earlier in the slavery scene you had just shown us. I have a deeper understanding of what it means when Black folks say, "they're trying to kill us."

√ All U.S. institutions were specifically designed to cause violence against Black people (psychologically, socially, physically). The neutral/default of these systems is oppression and White supremacy. "Professionalism" discourages any display of emotion, which serves White racial interests of not confronting the ongoing violence. The quantitative measures of "success" in these institutions makes people who are succeeding feel like they are special and that they earned it, rather than that they have either received some special advantage (White affirmative action) or been elevated as an example of success/ the system not being racist while others in their community continue to struggle.

√ That U.S./American culture, norms, economics, governing policies, and institutions have been established and continue to thrive off of the repeated campaigns and experiments to abuse, torture, profit, blame, desecrate, and eradicate Black and Indigenous people from this country and world. The implicit and explicit bias that stems today along with racist practices against other POC have long been embedded and passed down generation after generation to operate independently in feeding off one another like a sickness in abusing each other . . . all to maintain a White supremacist culture.

√ I see connections between White supremacy, hatred of Black people, imperialism, colonialism, and the patriarchy sewn so deeply into the fabric of all that we do and all that I have been taught to value, and I see the connections tied deeply from the past straight through to the present. I did not see these connections so deeply and clearly before. We place value on people "following the rules," but those rules have been created by White people in order to maintain White power and are based only on White cultural values. This is true for all of the institutions you mentioned above. I did think about this previously, but not to the extent I now understand. And what is new for me, and crushing, is a realization of how deeply hatred of Black people underpins all of this in a way that is different from the racism that targets other people of color.

√   Everything in current U.S./American culture and society is based on White supremacy. What is considered "best," "correct," "proper," "successful," "productive" is all based on White supremacy and what White people have decided is acceptable as the norm. Everything from "acceptable" appearance, to diet, to what is a desirable area to live in, and what is considered a "good" education has been a narrative and culture created by White people. Laws are created and shift to benefit White people and as soon as White people start to see a law as negatively affecting too many White people (especially men) then they change the laws. Or the laws are just ignored and not even applied to White people because White people are automatically given the benefit of the doubt as being good people that just had maybe a rough upbringing and are able to justify their actions and behaviors . . . which Black people have never been able to have.

√   The quote from Lee Atwater (*from video shown in the course*), "You start out in 1954 by saying, "Nigger, nigger, nigger." By 1968 you can't say "nigger"—that hurts you, backfires. So, you say stuff like, uh, forced busing, states' rights, and all that stuff, and you're getting so abstract. Now, you're talking about cutting taxes, and all these things you're talking about are totally economic things and a byproduct of them is, Black people get hurt worse than whites. . . . "We want to cut this," is much more abstract than even the busing thing, uh, and a hell of a lot more abstract than "Nigger, nigger."" This is present and obvious every single day. This is actively happening now in politics and the policies passed and with voting laws and with how Black people are being treated. Words like "post racial society" and "microaggression" are racist in nature. And the biggest and most damaging lie white people have been able to convince people of in this country is that there is no racism and that people are not racist. White people censure language and now it is seen as insulting for anybody to be accused of being a racist when society has set them up to view themselves as a "good" person.

√ White people have a mental illness, are psychopaths, if they are able to believe that they are not actively benefiting from our current racist society and how it is set up to continue being this way. Black voices are constantly silenced and demonized to delegitimize anybody who is not White. Yet ultimately White people are profiting off of the emotional and physical labor of Black people just like how some of the smartest, strongest Africans were stolen and brought to work as slaves on stolen land. White people have always been aware of the value in Black people, yet they have been thriving off of trying to dehumanize them and strip them away of all self-confidence, financial freedom, or any emotions.

√ This workshop was one of the best educational experiences I have had and I was a graduate student in psychology and the law for over a decade. I believe the insight I gained and the historical perspective I was given has fundamentally changed me and the ways in which I will move forward personally and professionally. I am very grateful for all the emotional and intellectual labor Professor King invested in us and this experience, as well as the value placed on an interactive approach to learning. Thank you!

√ This was the most worthwhile 2-day CME I have ever attended. I will be encouraging my colleagues to attend future sessions.

√ Dante, you are an absolute GEM! Thank you, thank you, thank you! Thank you for existing. I continue to rave about the impact your course had on me and how we all should be the impact in how we support and show up for Black folx and fight against anti-Blackness every single day . . . to be conscious. I could write a book about how much this has impacted me, but it wouldn't be enough. I appreciate you and the constant work you put forth

EVERY DAY in order to educate folks and uplift the voices and stories of those that have been silenced for far too long. We can never learn enough. I am purchasing your book and look forward to reading it. Again, thank you so much. I appreciate you!

√ This was by far the most impactful continuing educational activity I have ever engaged in. I will be recommending it to people. I cannot say enough how it has impacted me and how it has changed me deeply.

√ Wow. So moved by Dante and impressed by his knowledge. I so, so appreciated the opportunities to interact and share. I have been reflecting on this experience for days. I saw the throughline and there is no unseeing

√ So grateful for this time to explore the historical roots of our current system. This type of educational experience is so important for us in this country and in the world.

√ Excellent course! Recommend keeping slides with quotes on screen a bit longer so that we can digest the quote. They hold powerful messages and I needed to read and re-read multiple times to analyze and think.

√ Dante King is just an exceptional presenter and speaker for this very difficult topic of racism and antiracism. His research is so solid and very appropriate. His material really needs to be taught in our medical schools, residencies, and to our health organizations so that we can better listen to, understand, and care for our African American patients. He needs to come to Kaiser Permanente.

√ Learn more. Two days was not enough but this workshop definitely opened up a portal of new understanding.

√ I am a retired physician, but often do "curb-side" consults. This course has opened up a new world to me and how I look at the world. All in all, I was shocked by many things, especially how Whites created "the projects" and many, many other things. It was horrifying to see the history of (including the current history) the impact of White supremacy, and how it never allows for a chance for change. I thought it was very brave of Dante to teach this class,

and discuss some things that happened to him in his private life—
even the morning just before we started day #1. Superb class.

√   1. "The 400-year-Holocaust" sums it up. Brilliant title for a book.
2. White supremacy clearly had a huge impact on every aspect of a
Black person's life, including today. 3. Blacks having to take all of
the blame, when it was White supremacy that caused the problem.

√   1. Privilege: I have more privilege than I realized, and my Black
brothers and sisters have less privilege than I realize. The idea of rest
just in day to day being or lack thereof had not struck me. I thought
feeling "tired" was about the antiracist work. I didn't realize until
hearing Dante speak about this that the fatigue is just in "being"
in America. That existing in America is so exhausting for Black
people because of the culture and construct. It makes more sense to
me that this chronic stress impacts health outcomes negatively. It
answers the "why" to preterm labor/increased c-section question.
2. Compassion/Empathy: I can think of particularly some Black
brothers/friends and anxiety/shifting of personality in different
situations that I didn't understand before. Now I view it through
a lens of empathy and compassion because if I "change frames"—
they are just trying to survive. 3. Intention/Cruelty (Psychopathy):
I didn't know about the postcards of lynchings. I thought that there
was a small portion of ignorant/racist people. In one of Dante's
pictures they even spelled "oppose" wrong. I did not realize how
many people participated in lynchings/torture. I have been ignorant
to the darkness that exists in the hearts of mankind. Holocaust is
the correct word. Our children need to know . . .

√   I have a deeper understanding of the historical force of anti-
Blackness in the law, culture, politics—and especially the field of
psychology which will guide me when working with Black clients
in terms of their own experiences and our communication, as well
as when working with White clients. I will be better able to identify
what issues arise from the collective Black psyche and what is from
any one individual. I will include my understanding of the insidi-
ousness and the pathology of anti-Blackness in all that I write and
talk about the psychological impacts of financial inequity.

√   1. The relentlessness/inescapable aspect of anti-Blackness for Black people in America and the impact that has on health. 2. Legal encoding of anti-Blackness—was aware of but not the depth and extent. 3. Further understood the fundamental differences between anti-Blackness and the kinds of discrimination other BIPOC and other marginalized groups experience.

√   1. Scholarly facts are not always factual when they come from the oppressor. 2. I now understand where the Black Panthers were coming from; they were educated about the Black history that had been erased from the American history. 3. I see why Black history has been erased from our current American history.

√   Thank you SO MUCH for this incredible opportunity to participate in meaningful, transformative conversation about race and anti-Black racism. I have deep gratitude to the organizers and UCSF for supporting these types of events.

√   Dr. Dante King is a gifted speaker, skilled facilitator, and exceptional human being. Thank you so much for inviting him to lead this session and supporting our learning and growth.

√   Dante was fantastic! The material was harsh and traumatic . . . because anti-Blackness racism is just that, traumatic and harsh. I hope that others recognize this. The visceral reactions that we felt are normal human responses to this pervasive violence and this disease of anti-Blackness racism.

√   While today was particularly difficult for me in some ways—as I became very emotional with the content presented, Dante did an amazing job sharing what we all need to hear and understand about how we got to "this place" in our country. The history, the facts (many of which I had never heard) were devastating and shocking. Yet they lit a clear path as to how the structural inhumanity, hatred, and approved violence took over the White race with almost a maniacal force against the Black race. It really explained so much. Sadly, though much has changed thankfully, not enough has changed—and this work becomes all the more important.

√   Dr. Dante King's presentation was powerful and challenging and this was inspiring to get out there and make some changes.

√ Thank you and kudos to Dante King for the immense work and dedication it takes to produce this work. I am very grateful. It is an immense service to the world.

√ The antiracism leadership fellowship is unlike any equity training I've ever been to. Through history that most of us have not learned, Dante illuminates the dynamics of how anti-Blackness permeates our everyday lives and the institutions where we work. Robin's content on Whiteness, the rich discussions we had, and sharing from other participants added to the depth and breadth of our learning.

√ It is frequently said that "Race is a social construct." This course teaches you the roots of those social constructs and demonstrates how historical structural racism permeates all aspects of our lives and interactions in society. All the reading in the world cannot replace thoughtfully facilitated small group discussions by true experts. I cannot recommend this course highly enough.

√ What a gift to have been a part of this fellowship! It challenged my self-perception of being progressive and open-minded, my privileged social conditioning, and understanding of what is possible in our system so much that I felt uncomfortable at times, and broken open, in an extremely positive way. Engaging with my coworkers, supervisors, and leaders on this topic was at first intimidating, but after a few weeks, it became easier to express vulnerability, to share racially unskilled behaviors, and learn from Dante and others in the group how I have caused harm in my life, especially at work. Dante's presentation of the historical progression of racism and White supremacy was both dense and extremely enlightening, illustrating in very clear terms the racist foundations of our nation, culture, and this workplace, in spite of thinking we are "so progressive." Many thanks to Dante for this experience and the hard push to do better. I feel my work ahead is imperative and just beginning.

√ This has been one of the most painful journeys, specifically to recount the million ways that Black folks have been violently treated. At the same time, this journey has been one of the most rewarding in terms of sharpening my ability to sense and call out anti-Black and White supremacy culture.

√   Taking this fellowship interrupts your understanding of racism
     and Whiteness in the context of America and the history of this
     nation. Dante is an exceptional professor, teacher, and mentor
     who pushes you to challenge your thinking and explore Whiteness,
     White supremacy, and anti-Blackness. This course is absolutely
     necessary for anyone committed to their antiracism journey.

√   I feel like I've learned so much so it is difficult to narrow it down
     to two. What stands out to me most is how wide spread and en-
     grained White supremacy and White privilege are into our current
     culture and historical context (on a global scale). So much so, that
     it runs through me in ways that are difficult to undo. I had some
     resistance to the notion of anti-Blackness initially, not wanting
     to see Black and White at opposite ends of the spectrum but I see
     it now. I see it, it is there. I struggle to understand it, or I guess I
     should say that I struggle with "why" or "how" it came to be—at
     least from a moral perspective (which is were the White psychop-
     athy comes in). It sparks a lot of emotions in me, but is especially
     saddens and upsets me by how the lives of Black and Brown peo-
     ple have been minimized and oppressed in every way.

√   1. Whiteness is a pathology of living in a delusion based on a
     hunger for and total dependance on cruelty towards Black peo-
     ple mixed with willful lack of self-awareness. 2. White leaders
     interested in DEI work in particular need to be very careful to
     focus primarily on working on themselves while supporting Black
     leaders and leaders of color, otherwise their social conditioning
     sets them up to be liable to be more part of the problem than the
     solution

√   White supremacy was systematically created to oppress all non-
     Whites by any means necessary to differentiate themselves as the
     special elite group. Anti-Blackness was an overt and cautious
     decision White men made to hold power over everyone else.

√   White people in America were relentless in their codification of
     ever-worsening laws and behavior to deny Black people and peo-
     ple of color of every basic right. Black people feel a lot of rage and
     this should not surprise anyone.

√ I've realized how the ways I tend to be 'nice' can be harmful. Thinking about checking on people as a method of emotional surveillance was extremely illuminating and I will think before I do it again. I am examining how I am subconsciously expecting "civility" and emotional absolution from people around me. I think after the session where I called out some behavior I thought was bypassing some real growth I have come away with a stronger understanding of how I show up in a space. This doesn't mean I won't do it again, but I am more conscious of being perceived as a young White man. I'm usually really nervous to bring up that kind of critique anywhere, so mostly what I have learned is that if I say something that others don't like, I will survive--and recognize that pass I get is a privilege itself.

√ (1) Anti-Blackness as a distinct framework vis a vis any other concepts relating to racism or discrimination; (2) the collective responsibility of all White Americans to recognize our role as inheritors of a system founded in institutionalized rape of African women by White men.

√ 1) Re-examining how deeply ingrained and interconnected we are in how we experience racism across races. The historical context and thread that runs through centuries to present day, the attitudes, practices and habits that have shaped my own existence is powerful and shocking at times when I look at certain experiences through a deeper anti-Blackness and reinforcement of White supremacy lens. 2) The approach of moral-suassion to affect change through those peoples and institutions that ignore right from wrong. This is part of how I've approached public health/social justice work (right vs wrong in advancing equity & equality) and getting stuck, frustrated, demoralized, all the things when things don't shift.

√ 1. Anti-Blackness is built into the bedrock of this society. 2. White people are totally averse to talking about racism and that non-Whites have been complicit in maintaining White comfort out of fear and survival.

√ Realizing that the rules for Black people are different than for White people. It is rigged and Black people are supposed to adhere to White rules in society and obey laws that were designed to promote anti-Blackness, (i.e., criminal justice system, employment, housing), again rigged with no chance of getting ahead.

Dante King is a native of San Francisco, California. He is the author of the book *The 400-Year Holocaust: White America's Legal, Psychopathic, and Sociopathic Black Genocide and the Revolt Against Critical Race Theory.* Dante is an Adjunct Assistant Professor of Medical Education, in the Mayo Clinic College of Medicine and Science. He serves as guest faculty at the University of California, San Francisco, School of Medicine (UCSF), where he has lectured for three years. Dante officially consults as a legal expert scholar and witness concerning matters regarding race and racism. Dante was recently instrumental in codifying new law in California (see People v. Finley, 2023).

His academic disciplines include Afro-Realism; Critical Race Studies; African American Studies; Whiteness Studies; Anti-Blackness; American History; African American History; and how they have shaped American culture and institutions.

Dante's continued research interests include examinations of race, racism, and legality throughout colonial and post-colonial America, and their impacts on American culture and identity.

Dante has guest lectured at Clark College (Vancouver, Washington), Bellevue College (Bellevue, Washington), Skyline College (San Bruno, California), Green River College (Green River, Washington), Everett College (Everett, Washington), Lake Washington Institute of Technology (Lake Washington, Washington), and Renton Technical College (Renton, Washington). Dante is a member of the American Association of University Professors (AAUP); National Association for Multicultural Education (NAME); Association for the Study of African American Life and History (ASALH); and the National Association of Diversity Officers in Higher Education (NADOHE).

Dante is a historian, scholar, public motivational speaker, thought-leader, facilitator, and coach. He has worked and consulted for over 15-years as a human resource management professional specializing in executive leadership development, coaching, and the <u>implementation of anti-racism organizational development frameworks, strategies, and practices</u>.

In 2018, Dante partnered with the San Francisco Board of Supervisors to develop and enact the City and County of San Francisco's <u>Racial Equity Ordinance</u>, which led to the first-ever citywide Office of Racial Equity (2019).

Dante was previously the Deputy Director for the Department of Public Health Office of Health Equity in San Francisco, one of the largest public health organizations in the country, with over 8,000 employees. He led and directed the development and implementation of the department's <u>Racial Equity Action Plan</u>, which focused on improving both workforce and health equity outcomes. He also led the development and implementation of several highly impactful antiracism and racial equity policies and programs (i.e., Antiracism Recruitment and Hiring Policy, Healing Time Off, Respect in the Workplace, etc.). One of his most significant accomplishments, while at the SFDPH, was the implementation of the department's first ever Antiracism and Racial Equity Leaders Fellowship, a 12-week cohort which included over 50 executive and senior leaders.

Prior to assuming this role, Dante was the Director of Race, Equity, and Inclusion at the San Francisco Municipal Transportation Agency (SFMTA), one of the largest municipal transportation agencies in the country, with more than 6,000 employees. He led and directed the design, development, and implementation of the agency's first-ever <u>Racial Equity Action Plan</u>, focused on improving workforce outcomes. He also collaborated with his peers on the executive leadership team, which included the Human Resources Director, to develop and enact policies and programs which directly targeted racial disparities and disproportionate organizational outcomes.

While working as a senior Human Resources Manager at the City and County of San Francisco (2016-2019), Dante designed and implemented a citywide anti-racism and bias training, Creating an Inclusive Environment: An Introduction to Implicit Bias. Over 20,000 city employees have received this training to date. Dante also managed and led the team of learning partners and training professionals who delivered the training to all employees and members of the San Francisco Police Department (SFPD). As a part of this project, Dante provided consistent feedback and hands-on guidance and direction to the SFPD executive leadership team.

In early 2020, a confidential email written to SFPD Chief Bill Scott appeared in the San Francisco Examiner. The email to Chief Scott highlighted the depth of anti-Black bias and racism Dante and his team experienced from many members of the SFPD during the three years they provided training to the department. The feedback Dante provided to Chief Scott led to Dante presenting his findings to the San Francisco Police Commission, as well as systemic programmatic and policy-oriented changes throughout the department.

In addition, Dante King founded the Black Employees Alliance (B.E.A), in 2019. The B.E.A consistently partnered with San Francisco Leadership (Mayor London N. Breed, S.F. Board of Supervisor President Shamann Walton, Hillary Ronen, Matt Haney, and Sandra Fewer), as well as department heads and senior leaders, to highlight and combat racial inequities and disparities. The group's advocacy was in direct response to racial disparities concerning Black employees across all departments, in the areas of recruitment and hiring, pay and promotions, recognition, and discipline and terminations.

The Black Employees Alliance was instrumental in compelling and influencing Mayor Breed's appointment of Dr. William Gould IV, whose firm investigated the city's employment practices, issuing a comprehensive summary of findings and recommendations. The B.E.A partnered with Mr. Gould and his colleagues to produce information and data that led to many of the findings.

Besides Dante's Human Resources Management experience, and public service, he has taught courses for Stanford Medical School, Johns Hopkins, UCSF, and the Mayo Clinic. Dante currently teaches an accredited course through UCSF called, Understanding the Roots of Racism and Bias: Anti-Blackness and Its Links to Whiteness, White Racism, Privilege, and Power. As guest faculty at Mayo Clinic College of Medicine and Science, he lectured a two-part course called, The Roots and Lingering Effects of White Supremacy and Anti-Blackness in American Culture and Institutions. Most recently, Dante developed an additional course called Developing Antiracism Leadership Competencies to Achieve Inclusive Practices and Health Equity, a collaboration with special guest and co-lecturer, Dr. Robin DiAngelo, author of the books *White Fragility* and *Nice Racism*. Dante and Robin have also partnered to produce the Unlearning Anti-Blackness, White Supremacy, and Racism in American Culture and Institutions Leaders Fellowship, a 16-week virtual fellowship program focused on training, coaching, and mentoring leaders who directly influence and impact change at their organizations.

Dante has consulted and collaborated with organizations in the areas of human resource management, antiracism policy, and program development and implementation. Some organizations Dante has worked with include the San Francisco Police Department; San Francisco Department of Police Accountability; California State Public Defender's Office; San Francisco Public Defender's Office; Johns Hopkins University; Stanford University School of Medicine; University of California San Francisco (UCSF) School of Medicine; Wikimedia Foundation; *The Athletic*; Oakland Unified School District; UCSF Office of Diversity and Outreach; UCSF California Preterm Birth Initiative; UCSF Alliance Health Project; California Prevention Training Center; and BATS Improv; to name a few.

Dante has keynoted and presented at annual conferences, such as the 35th Annual National Conference on Race and Ethnicity in Higher Education, National Education Association's Annual Conference on Race and Social Justice (NEA), American Public Health Association (APHA), Association for the Study of African American Life and History (ASALH), Eikenberg Academy for Social Justice Soulwork Annual Conference, Brothers of the Desert Wellness Summit, Howard County Champions of Change Conference, Race Forward: Facing Race Annual Conference, California Prevention Training Center's Medical Mistrust Conference, Mayo Clinic Annual Diversity, Equity, Inclusion and Antiracism Annual Enterprise Retreat, NEA Minority and Women's Leadership Conference to Advance Racial and Social Justice , Bemidji State University's 2023 Martin Luther King Jr. Holiday Celebration, Rainier Educators of Color Equity National Conference 2023, 4th Annual Northwest Regional Equity Conference 2023, the 24th Annual White Privilege Conference, and many more.

Most recently, Dante was featured in the *San Francisco Sun* Reporter's 2022 Special Edition of the Talented 25. He has been featured on Legal Lens with Angela Reddock-Wright (KBLA 1580), CAPTC's Coming Together for Sexual Health, BackTable Podcast, The Sisaundra Show, KPFA Radio Interview (B.H. Brilliant Minds Juneteenth Celebration), California Prevention Training Center Podcast, Intentional Conversations with Dr. Nika White, This Week In White Supremacy, The Dawn Stensland Show, recurring guest on the Joan Esposito Radio Show, KCBS, and the The Karen Hunter Show. Dante has also been a featured guest on the What Say U Podcast, hosted by Melannie Cunningham, All About Community with Robert L. Harris,

Esq., <u>KMOX The Show</u>, <u>Areva Martin In Real Time</u>, <u>Situations and Con-</u>
<u>versations with Tra'Renee</u>, <u>The Clay Cane Show</u>, <u>The Lurie Daniel Favors</u>
<u>Show</u>, and <u>a host of other shows and media outlets</u>.

Awards and Future Endeavors

Amongst an array of many awards and recognition, most recently, in the
summer of 2022, Dante was awarded 1st Place, by The Bookfest Awards,
in the genre of Non-Fiction History for penning *The 400-Year Holocaust*.
Dante also received the Dr. Huey P. Newton Trailblazer and Legacy Award,
presented by B.H. Brilliant Minds, Inc., for his consistent leadership and
advocacy on behalf of Black communities in Oakland and San Francisco,
California, and abroad. In fall 2023, the National Association for Multicultural Education (NAME) awarded Dante the Carter Godwin Woodson
Service Award for his commitment to correcting "deficiencies in American
history where African American History and the history of other cultures is
misrepresented, distorted, or ignored."

Dante released his second publication, *The 400-Year Holocaust: Toolkit
and Workbook*, in April 2023. It focuses on Organizational Change and Development; an introduction to antiracism policy development examples and
skills practices, as well as antiracism leadership strategies and frameworks
(i.e., Equity in the Center's Awake to Woke to Work, Dismantling Racism's
Antiracism Organizational Change, etc.).

Education

Dante holds a Bachelor of Arts degree in African American Studies, and a
master's degree in education, from California State University, East Bay. He
also possesses a Human Resources Management certification. Dante started
doctoral work in Educational Leadership and Social Justice, with the principal focuses on challenging White supremacy and anti-Blackness, and their
cumulative effects on Black people, White people, and all participants in
American culture.

Community Outreach and Volunteer Efforts

Dante is the Executive Director of <u>Blackademics: Addressing Anti-Black-</u>
<u>ness Around the World, LLC.</u> Blackademics is an educational and charitable

non-profit, focused on educating students and families across race, about the legacy and persistence of White supremacy and anti-Blackness in America, as well as worldwide. Dante is a board member for the <u>B.H. Brilliant Minds Project, LLC</u>, a local Bay Area, California, non-profit and charitable agency focused on bringing healing to African American people through community service and outreach. He has served as a board member for the B.H. Brilliant Minds Project for over 15 years, while also serving the agency through education and book donations.

Previously, Dante served as a board member for the Sexual Minority Alliance of Alameda County (SMAAC) Youth Center. During his tenure as a board member for over four years, Dante focused SMAAC's mission and goal on serving underserved, unhoused, and unsheltered Black LGBTQ+ youth. In addition, Dante mentored and tutored many youths during his time at SMAAC. Dante has also helped organizations like AMASSI and the AIDS Project of the East Bay with their sexual health outreach efforts.

While in high school, Dante joined the AmeriCorps program created by President Bill Clinton. During his time with AmeriCorps, Dante worked at the East Lake YMCA in East Oakland as a youth outreach worker, mentor, and tutor under Margaret Wimberly's supervision.

Shortly after high school, Dante became involved with a non-profit which was housed at the Allen Temple Church in East Oakland. This opportunity allowed him to tutor at his old elementary school, Daniel Webster. These experiences were crucial in shaping Dante's future as a leader, educator, and public servant.

Dante previously attended the Center of Hope Community Church, where he helped people from the unsheltered and unhoused community. This experience led Dante to collaborate with friends and family in proactively purchasing food, water, and toiletries to deliver directly to people throughout these communities.

In 2016, Dante became involved with The Village, a prison outreach program that catered to helping Black men in prison. Dante began reaching out and connecting with prison inmates. His goal was to provide guidance, aid, and comfort. Dante became deeply involved with these efforts, and has donated, to date, more than $100k in resources to over 15 men. Donations have included loading monies onto JPay and Connect Network accounts to ensure inmates can write letters to, as well as call, their families; ordering thousands of dollars of Secure Paks; as well as driving to see and visit inmates in prison, both in northern and southern California. Dante has written several early release letters to support early prison releases for reformed prison inmates. Dante has been successful in helping two men access early parole releases.

Dante's drive and ambition, aiming to authentically uplift and help others, have fueled his long history of public service, enabling him to attract and sustain many meaningful and long-lasting relationships.

Website: www.danteking.com

DEDICATIONS

Mom (Debra King-Cooper)—You are life. I would not be here and could not have gotten this done without you. You are my first and my last. Each day I live is for you, to make you happy, and to bring joy into your spirit and physical being. I would not be here if it weren't for you!

Huge thanks to Dr. Lawanne' S. Grant and the Leadership DevelopME publishing team. I could not and would not have made it through the book writing process (for the third time) without you! You helped to get me on the right track with writing and publishing. I am forever grateful.

I am thankful for the opportunity to have been able to package my work into a series of chapters that will hopefully help people in North America and beyond to understand the seriousness of the attack Black people in America are under. I dedicate this book to Black people around the world who have not fully comprehended or understood the reach and magnitude of White racism, and anti-Blackness—who can now feel, be, and live in liberation with the knowingness that the predicament we find ourselves in is one that is dire. I dedicate this book to "not-Black" and White people around the world who will read this book and connect with the truth-telling experience that it is. My goal for this endeavor is to contribute to the legacies of Black leaders and truth-tellers who have continually awakened and contributed to the liberation and empowerment of Black people in the United States. In addition, it was also important for me to leave behind a montage of thoughts and highlights of my larger work, the birthing of:

- **Understanding the Roots of Racism and Bias: Anti-Blackness and Its Link to Whiteness, White Racism, Privilege, and Power** (University of California San Francisco School of Medicine; 2021–Present)

- **The Unlearning and Addressing Anti-Blackness, White Supremacy, and Racism in American Culture and Institutions Leaders Academy** (2015–Present)

- **The 400-Year Holocaust 12-Week Course** (2015–Present)

- **The Roots and Lingering Effects of White Supremacy and Anti-Blackness in American Culture and Institutions (Mayo Clinic; May 2022)**

- **Developing Anti-Racism Leadership Competencies to Achieve Inclusive Practices and Health Equity (Mayo Clinic; September 2023)**

I realize as I age and recognize the continual trauma of being Black, coupled with studying and teaching about this subject, that I cannot do this for an exceedingly long time. It is not sustainable. Therefore, I needed to document and produce an expression of my work in this form, made available to those who I will never meet, teach, share with, and/or learn from.

There are so many people—friends and extended family—that I want to thank, and yet to name them would be an impossible feat because I am most certainly sure I am going to leave out someone who is important to me, and who has contributed to my life, development, and growth in some meaningful and special way. To that end, please know that all of you who know me, know what you have done for me, and what we have shared—please know that I love you, and I dedicate this book to you. I want badly to write personal notes to each one of you, and to do so would most likely amount to its own chapter, so I will resist the urge to go down that path.

I will, however, name some especially important people, many of whom are Black women, who have nurtured, coached, developed, supported, and uplifted the works I have produced over the years, in countless ways. This book results from your belief, love, encouragement, and tutelage of me. My aunts—Verna Chea, Lynn Green, Doris Parnell (RIP), Barbara Hill, Vickie Knight, Maryann Edgar Calloway, Dolores Lewis.

To the Arthur family of Dallas, Texas (my grandmother Mamie Arthur); Edgar family of Dallas, Texas (my grandfather Charles Edgar); Hight family of Galveston, Texas (my grandmother Corrine Hight); David/Davis families of Port Arthur, Texas, and Louisiana (my grandfather Jimmy Davis); Dorn family of Georgia (great-great grandmother Jane), as well as the Hardeman family of Dallas/Houston Texas; the Stephenson, King, and Gilton families of San Francisco—I love you all. Uplifting and sending a special dedication to my grandparents, who I know are smiling upon my family and me with joy—Charles Edgar Sr, Mamie Arthur Edgar, Corine Hight King, James (Jimmy) Davis, and the King family.

To my wonderful and special godmother, Sarah Fine. You have been my rock. Without you and my mother, I could not have survived in this world.

I must take this opportunity to name all the Black educators who taught and mentored me into a place of self-empowerment, self-assurance, and self-thought: Rebecca Freeman, Christine Wilson—at Daniel Webster elementary school, it all started with you; Ms. O'Neal (my seventh grade English teacher) at Elmhurst Jr. High School; Willie Hamilton, Principal at Daniel Webster; Mr. Robinson, Music teacher at Daniel Webster; Michael Moore, History teacher at Elmhurst; Lynn Dodd, Principal at King Estates; Dee Logan, my aunt and counselor at King Estates; Dr. Larry Harper-Short, my godfather, who raised me and also taught me what it means to think beyond bounds. The rest of you know who you are. I will not name the schools. Please know that your legacy lives on in me. Pauline Perrone, Johnny Burks, Ria Settles, Ms. Bridgeman, Ms. Dixon, Leatrice Hicks, Yvonne Ash, Linda Halpern, Ellen Posey, Tanya Dennis, Helen Alder.

To some incredibly special people who both opened doors and supported the work I am doing in order for me to be alive today—Dr. Zea Malawa, Alexis Cobbins, Dr. Larry Rand, Jaontra Henderson, Daphina Melbourne, Amy Lilley, Donna Kotake, Elizabeth Green, and Duran Rutledge—thank you!

To two incredibly special mentors, coaches, and friends—Rachelle Rogers-Ard, and Virgie Maney—thank you for your unwavering love, coaching, friendship, and mentoring. Virgie and Big Daryl, and my two brothers Little Daryl and Robert, thank you for your continued prayers, love, and support. I would not be where I am today without these women. Thank you for being the blessings that you are to me, to others, and to life. Virgie, you are and forever will be my best coach, and boss. There are not enough words to thank you for all you have done for me.

To my big sister from another mister and Ms. Linda Deboe. You continue to be in my corner. I love you dearly. Nikki, Kim, and Wayne and everyone in the family—you are my family forever and I love you. Tiffiny K. Nash, Ericka Nicole Paden, and the entire Briggs Family. I love you all very much. Thank you for including me in your family. Willie Natt, you were an amazing leader. Thank you for taking a chance on me. Without you, I would not have had the experience that ultimately led me to the journey I am on today. I love you and Annette both. Dexter Hall, thank you for enabling me to begin a career journey that would enable me to learn so much about the world. Sarita Robinson, you were an amazing pillar of strength and support for me, and I love you. To all of my Black Wells Fargo colleagues who were friends and supporters of mine during my time there—thank you. Margot Reed and Nadia Bishop, thank you for being there for the late-night talks. Kathy Broussard, Jessica Brown, Nikki Mixon, Demarris Evans, Irella Blackwood, Jumoke Akin-Taylor, Brenda Barros, Kimberly Burrus, Ameerah Thomas, Yulanda Williams, Elizabeth Green, Kimberly Burris, Zea Malawa, Solaire Spellen, Christine Smith, Bivett Brackett, Jumoke Hinton, Laurie Smith Anderson, and again "thee" Alexis Cobbins (lol), the love you have surrounded me with, and the bonds we have are unbreakable. Dr. Yoshiko Harden and Dr. Daryl Brice, you are beautiful and lovely souls. I am honored to know you and glad we met. Lisa Corner, Dr. Rochelle Hooks, Dr. Bay Jones, Nyanda Sam-King, Dr. Debra Jenkins, and Beabe Akpojovwo. You are very near and dear to me. Your support for my work and me has meant more to me than words can convey. Robert Britten, my brother from the Pacific Northwest, I love and value you. You are my sisters and brothers, my village, and I love you all.

Kate Toran, Dara Silverman, David Nish, and Lori Thoemmes—thank you for demonstrating true allyship and friendship.

Paul Henderson for governor!! You are an amazing friend and have been a pillar of strength for me. I appreciate you.

To my goddaughters, both named John'Nae, I love you both. Koshia Willis, you are a great mother, and friend, and have done an outstanding job. Tanya, you did an excellent job also. May you rest in peace.

Ericka Small (and the entire Lee family), Jennifer Taylor (Lillie), Lakesha Carden (Lo-Lo, Bob, Felicia, and Rita), Demetra Mack (Deborah), La'Trae Wilson, Christina Survine, Nicole Wills, Robin Cotton (and the entire Cotton family), Antoinette Thompson, Rolanda Taylor (RIP), Jeannine Brown (RIP; and the entire Creswell family) — you have been blessings to me both past and present, and I am grateful. To my tribe of first cousins LaTanyua Brown, Ebony Lewis, Theda Lewis, Jawolei Chea, Chelsea Parnell, David Parnell, Jermell Parnell, Charles Edgar III, Justin Chea, Lonnie Lewis, Jr. (RIP), Kathy Lewis (RIP), Mamie Lewis, Sonya Lewis, Pamela Michelle, and Sonya Rose—I love you all. Trae, thank you so much for the referral. The creation of this book could not have happened without you.

Sonya Rose, you are my twin. I adore and love you more than anyone, except for my nanny, Janet, Chelsea, and Asean. I love you all.

Marcel Walker, there is absolutely no one like you. Words cannot fully convey or express the deep love that I have for you. I will always be here for you. Make sure you maintain this and keep it in your heart and mind always!

Shawntell Johnson, Asata Berry—I love you so much. Thank you for being inspirational to me.

To my dad, Dr. Larry Harper-Short, I would not be here without you. You mean the world to me. I love you and E'Marcus Harper-Short.

Dr. Barbara Paige (former Chair of the Ethnic Studies department at CSU East Bay), you were the lifeline to my college experience and the reason I am on the path and journey I am on today. Thank you for being a mentor, role model, counselor, and my guidance when I needed it most. You were there for me in ways that most will not ever understand. I appreciate your mentorship, guidance, discipline, exceptionally high expectations (lol), and love you more than you will ever know. Dr. Nicholas Baham, thank you for being a mentor, role model, and big brother as well. It is also vitally important for me to thank Dr. Ardella Dailey, Dr. G.T. Reyes, and Dr. Eric Haas. Your coaching, leadership, mentorship, and guidance through my time in the Social Justice and Educational Leadership Doctoral program helped me to sustain the validation I needed in bringing forth this book. Thank you Dr. Reyes, for introducing me to the research and pedagogical concepts that we learned about during the first quarter of the program. Our meeting was not in vain.

Marguerite Malloy Esq., thank you for being my sister, and a role model. Thank you for your thoughtfulness and willingness to take this journey with me! Your reviews and edits were on point (all of them)! I love you dearly and appreciate you more than you know.

Alicia St. Andrews, thank you for being my friend and for becoming a family member during this process. Thank you for taking part in the process of reviewing the chapters and for providing me with questions that enabled me to reconsider some of the positioning of the information. I love you. To my friends on the San Francisco Board of Supervisors, Shamann Walton, Sandra Fewer, and Matt Haney—thank you for coming through for the Black Employees Alliance and Coalition Against Anti-Blackness, in our attempts to address issues for Black Employees in the City and County of San Francisco.

To all the members of the Black Employees Alliance and Coalition Against Anti-Blackness, thank you for standing strong and for your steadfastness through all the horrors and terrors that we faced together, just trying to go to work daily.

To Karl Olson, Therese Cannata, and the team at Cannata, O'Toole, Fickes, & Olson, LLP; Felicia Medina, Shauna Madison, Elizabeth Connelly, Danielle Miles-Langaigne—and the team at Medina Orthwein. You are the best legal counsel anyone could ever have. Thank you for your commitment and dedication to justice. Barbara Tomson, my auntie, I love and appreciate your guidance, sacrifice, and help more than you know.

Dr. Dorothy Forde!! You are a gift from the best places in the universe. There are not enough words to express how grateful I am to/for you!! I could not have gotten this done without you. I will say this again... I could not have gotten this done without you!!

Valerie Gail Williams, all I can say is I love you with all of my heart. You continue to be a pillar of strength for me. Thank you, thank you, thank you!!

Sista Soulja, thank you for being willing to state the truth and stand up for Black people even when it was not popular and when you were isolated. I love you. Tupac—The greatest, most authentic, and truest rapper-activist who ever lived! Rest in peace! Thank you, and I love you.

To Bryan Stevenson, you are an amazing person, mentor, and role model. I have been fortunate to be in your presence occasionally and hope to impact our people and the world, as much as you have inspired and impacted me. Dr. Koritha Mitchell (@ProfKori), what can I say? There are not enough words to convey the respect, admiration, and adoration I have for you. Thank you for providing Black people around the world with your brilliance. Thank you for giving us the framing and language to name and understand our brilliance in a culture of mediocrity, White mediocrity. Black people are Black and brilliant and Black and beautiful because WE ARE!

To my Mayo Clinic family, Ms. Barbara Jordan, you are brilliance personified. Thank you for your care, support, and encouragement. Dr. Shannon Laughlin-Tomasso, thank you for your support, encouragement, and belief. You are and will always be special to me. Dr. Amy Seegmiller-Renner, all I can say is wow!! You are my friend and sister. I bask in total awe when I consider and think about what we have accomplished together. Thank you for putting your entire belief and muscle behind this work! The doors at Mayo Clinic would not have opened had it not been for you taking the UCSF course in 2021. I am forever grateful.

Sincere and deep thanks and gratitude to Consuelo Grier at Bellevue College; Bessie Gordon, Ha Nguyen, and Mimi Weithers-Bruce, at Green River College; DeGundrea Harris, Nicole Harris, and Vanessa Neal, at Clark College; Dr. Yoshiko Harden, Doris Martinez, and Maritza Ogarro, at Renton Technical College; Robert Britten and Brian Ramos, at Lake Washington Technical College; John Hudson and Lisa Corner, at Everett College. Thank you for your embrace of my work, and for honoring the truth. Special thank you to my sister GumLai Ross and brother Robert Britten.

To Dr. Dionne Hart, Dr. Nicky Keeth, Dr. Emily McTate, and Dr. Monica Taylor, I appreciate your sincere and authentic support. You are now a part of my "mentally liberated" family.

To Vice Chancellor Dr. Renee Navarro, Assistant Vice Chancellor Dr. Alejandra Rincon, Dr. Lamisha Hill, and Ms. Melissa Bautista, thank you for your collaboration and partnership. To Vice Chancellor Dr. Renee Navarro, Assistant Vice Chancellor Dr. Alejandra Rincon, Dr. Lamisha Hill, and Ms. Melissa Bautista, I thank you for your collaboration and partnership. You are my family, and I am grateful for all the support you have provided and continue to provide at the University of California San Francisco Office of Diversity and Outreach.

Chelsea, my lovely and wonderfully made sister. I did not know you existed. Finding you has brought me so much joy, and I am honored to have you in my life. I love you more than you will ever know.

Dajuan Artese King, my brother from the same mother, you already know. Thank you for being one of my best friends and for always being open to a conversation, feedback, or just a reflection session both as my brother and friend. Thank you, daddy, Harold King, for your willingness to learn and understand each other better in this phase of our lives. I love you all.

Lastly, I dedicate this book to my mother, Debra King-Cooper for her unwavering belief in all that I do—and for her continual love, grace, care, and concern for me. I am thankful for every day that we have been fortunate to walk this earth together, and for all you have provided for me. There are not enough words or enough resources to convey my gratitude or express fully what you mean to me. You are my queen, my religion, the air that I breathe, and the beat of my heart. May you continue to experience goodness, grace, comfort, strength, good health, prosperity, and favor all the days of your life.

REFERENCES

1 Frazier, E. Franklin. *The Black Bourgeoisie: The Book that Brought the Shock of Self-Revelation to Middle-Class Blacks in America*. New York: Free Press Paperbacks, 1957.

2 Asare, Janice Gassam. "How Communities Of Color Perpetuate Anti- Blackness," *Leadership: Diversity, Equity & Inclusion*, Forbes, July 19, 2020. https://www.forbes.com/sites/janicegassam/2020/07/19/how-communities-of-color-perpetuate-anti-blackness/

3 Ture, Kwame, and Charles V. Hamilton. *Black Power: The Politics of Liberation*. New York: Random House, 1967.

4 Kendi, Ibram X. *Stamped From the Beginning: The Definitive History of Racist Ideas in America*. New York: Bold Type Books, 2016.

5 Wilkerson, Isabel. *Caste: The Origins of our Discontents*. United States: Random House, 2020

6 Jones-Rogers, Stephanie. E. *They Were Her Property: White Women as Slave Owners in the American South*. Hartford: Yale University Press, 2019.

7 Poussaint, Alvin F. "White Manipulation and Black Oppression." *The Black Scholar* 10, no. 8/9 (1979): 52–55.

8 Feagin, Joe R. *The White Racial Frame Centuries of Racial Framing and Counter-framing*. Routledge, 2010.

9 Terry, Josh. "10 years ago today, Kanye West said, 'George Bush doesn't care about black people.'" Things to Do, *Chicago Tribune*, June, 16, 2018. https://www.chicagotribune.com/redeye/redeye-kanye-west-katrina-telethon-george-bush-black-people-20150902-htmlstory.html

10 Coyle, Laura. "The Great Mississippi River Flood of 1927." National Museum of African American History and Culture, *Smithsonian*, January 11, 2019. https://nmaahc.si.edu/explore/stories/collection/great-mississippi-river-flood-1927

11 The Editors of Encyclopedia Britannica. "Mississippi River Flood of 1927: American History" *Britannica*, September 1, 2023. https://www.britannica.com/event/Mississippi-River-flood-of-1927

12 DeGruy, Joy. *Post Traumatic Slave Syndrome: America's Legacy of Enduring Injury and Healing*, Rev. ed. United States: Uptone Press, 2017.

13 Diangelo, Robin. *White Fragility: Why It's So Hard for White People to Talk About Racism*. Boston: Beacon Press, 2020.

14 Painter, Nell Irvin. *The History of White People*. New York: W.W. Norton & Company, 2011.

336 *Diagnosing Whiteness and Anti-Blackness*

15 Poussaint, Alvin F. *Why Blacks Kill Blacks*. United States: Emerson Hall Publishers, 1972.

16 Painter, Nell Irvin. *Creating Black Americans: African-American History and Its Meanings, 1619 to the Present*. United Kingdom: Oxford University Press, 2006.

17 Roediger, David R. "Historical Foundations of Race." National Museum of African American History and Culture, *Smithsonian*, n.d. https://nmaahc.si.edu/learn/talking-about-race/topics/historical-foundations-race

18 "Dismantling Racism Works." *Racism Defined*. dRworksBook, 2021. https://www.dismantlingracism.org/racism-defined.html.

19 DiAngelo, Robin. *What Does It Mean to Be White? Developing White Racial Literacy*. New York: Peter Lang, 2016.

20 Allen, Theodore W. *The Invention of the White Race: The Origin of Racial Oppression in Anglo America*. London: Verso, 1997.

21 Wright, Bobby E. *The Psychopathic Racial Personality and Other Essays*. Chicago: Third World Press, 1985.

22 Gerbner, Katharine R. "Christian Slavery: Protestant Missions and Slave Conversion in the Atlantic World, 1660-1760." PhD diss., Harvard University, 2013. Digital Access to Scholarship at Harvard. ProQuest, UMI Dissertation Publishing, 2013.

23 Douglass, F. *Narrative of the Life of Frederick Douglass*. CreateSpace Independent Publishing Platform, 2018.

24 "Black Paper on White Racism,. Part 2." *Black Journal* 44, December 21, 1971. Thirteen WNET, Library of Congress, American Archive of Public Broadcasting (GBH and the Library of Congress), accessed June 12, 2024, http://americanarchive.org/catalog/cpb-aacip-62-pg1hh6cm8r

25 Anonymous. Review of *Understanding the Roots of Racism and Bias: Anti-Blackness and Its Link to Whiteness, White Racism, Privilege, and Power*. 2021.

26 Harris, Cheryl. "Whiteness as Property." *The Harvard Law Review Association* 106, no. 8 (1993): 1707–1791.

27 Morrison, Toni. "Conversations with the author of 'Beloved' and 'The Bluest Eye'." By Charlie Rose. *Charlie Rose*, July, 10, 2020. https://charlierose.com/videos/31212

28 Crump, Ben. *Open Season: Legalized Genocide of Colored People*. United States: Amistad, Harper Collins, 2024.

29 Aponte-Rios, Miguelangel, director. *Slave Catchers/Slave Resisters*. History Channel, 2005. https://www.imdb.com/title/tt0823691/.

30 Hurd, John Codman. *The Law of Freedom and Bondage in the United States* (Vol. 1). Boston: Little Brown & Company, 1858.

31 X, Malcolm, "Interview at Berkeley," interview by John Leggett and Herman Blake, October 11, 1963.

32 Imhotep, Michael. *The Cress Theory of Racism: Surviving Racism in The 21st Century - Clip 2*, 2013, April 28. https://www.youtube.com/ watch?v=7IyMZCjJEjw

33 Anderson, Carol. *White Rage: The Unspoken Truth of Our Racial Divide*. United States: Bloomsbury Publishing, 2016.

34 Davis, Peter, writer. *Of Black America*. Season 1, episode 5, "The Heritage of Slavery." Featuring Fannie Lou Hamer and Lerone Bennett Jr. Aired August 13, 1968.

35 Battalora, Jaqueline M. *Birth of a White Nation: The Invention of White People and Its Relevance Today*. United States: Strategic Book Publishing, 2013.

36 Harris, Thomas and Henry John. "A Series of the Most Important Law Cases, Argued and Determined in the Provincial Court and Court of Appeals of the then Province of Maryland, from the Year 1700 Down to the American Revolution." Reports, Maryland, 1809.

37 Alpert, Jonathan. "The Origin of Slavery in the United States-The Maryland Precedent." *The American Journal of Legal History* 14, no. 3 (1970): 189-221. doi:10.2307/844413

38 Hening, William Waller. "A Collection of All the Laws of Virginia, from the First Session of the Legislature, in the Year 1619." Statues at Large, Virginia, 1823. https://babel.hathitrust.org/cgi/pt?id=mdp.39015036018417&seq=7

39 Christian_hegemony. "Why Black Lives Haven't Mattered: The Origins of Western Racism in Christian Hegemony." Challenging Christian Hegemony, February 15, 2015. https://christianhegemony.org/why-black-lives-havent-mattered-the-origins-of-western-racism-in-christian-hegemony

40 Congress of the United States, in the House of Representatives. "Acts passed at a Congress of the United States of America: begun and held at the city of New-York, on Wednesday the fourth of March in the year M, DCC, LXXXIX, and of the independence of the United States the thirteenth." Acts Passed at the First Session of the First Congress of the United States, New York, 1789. https://catalog.mount-vernon.org/digital/collection/p16829coll5/id/753

41 Hudson, G. "Black Americans vs. Citizenship: The Dred Scott Decision." *Negro History Bulletin* 46, no. 1 (1983): 26–28. http://www.jstor.org/stable/44254727

42 Du Bois, W. E. B. *Black Reconstruction in America: Toward a History of the Part Which Black Folk Played in the Attempt to Reconstruct Democracy in America, 1860-1880*. Oxford University Press, 2017. United States: Harcourt, Brace and Co., 1935.

43 "The 1619 Landing - Virginia's First Africans Report & FAQs." 1619: Landing, Hampton History Museum. Hampton History Museum, 2018. https://hampton.gov/3580/The-1619-Landing-Report-FAQs.

44 Scott v. Sandford, 60 U.S. 393, 38 (U.S. Supreme Court 1856).

45 Hannah-Jones, Nikole. "Our democracy's founding ideals were false when they were written. Black Americans have fought to make them true." *The 1619 Project, The New York Times Magazine*, August 14, 2019. https://www.nytimes.com/interactive/2019/08/14/magazine/1619-america-slavery.html

46 Phillips, Samuel. Is Afrika Cursed? *Msingi Afrika Magazine*, July 1, 2021. https://www.msingiafrikamagazine.com/2021/07/is-afrika-cursed/

47 Thomas, Zoe. "The hidden links between slavery and Wall Street." *BBC News*, August 28, 2019. https://www.bbc.com/news/business-49476247

48 Hening, William Waller. "The Statutes at Large; Being a Collection of All the Laws of Virginia, from the First Session of the Legislature, in the Year 1619." Hugh Davis's Case, New York, 1630. https://www.coursehero.com/file/49364942/5-Early-Virginia-Court-Cases.pdf

49 Barnard, Jerry. "Cornish-897." WikiTree: Where Genealogists Collaborate, November 22, 2015. https://www.wikitree.com/wiki/Cornish-897

50 Smitherman, Geneva. *African American Women speak Out On Anita Hill-Clarence Thomas*. Michigan: Wayne State University Press, 1995.

51 "General Court Responds to Runaway Servants and Slaves (1640)." Virginia Humanities, *Encyclopedia Virginia*, December 7, 2020. https://encyclopediavirginia.org/entries/general-court-responds-to-runaway-servants-and-slaves-1640/

52 Schwarz, Philip J. *Twice Condemned: Slaves and the Criminal Laws of Virginia, 1705 - 1865*. New Jersey Lawbook Exchange, 1998.

53 *Virginia Slave Laws, 1660s*. (n.d.). https://www.swarthmore.edu/SocSci/bdorsey1/41docs/24-sla.html

54 "Elizabeth Key (Kaye). Colonial Williamsburg: Slavery and Remembrance: A Guide to Sites, Museums, and Memory. United Nations Educational, Scientific and Cultural Organization, n.d. http://slaveryandremembrance.org/people/person/index.cfm?id=PP031

55 Rashawn, Ray and Alexandra Gibbons. "Why are states banning critical race theory?" Commentary, *Brookings*. November 2021. https://www.brookings.edu/blog/fixgov/2021/07/02/why-are-states-banning-critical-race-theory/

56 Ruiz, Michael. "Critical Race Theory: These states are already cracking down on the controversial concept." Controversies, *Fox News*, June 12, 2021. https://www.foxnews.com/us/critical-race-theory-states-cracking-down

57 Goulooze, T. "Thomas Key (abt.1595-abt.1636)." WikiTree: Where Genealogists Collaborate. March 27, 2024. https://www.wikitree.com/wiki/Key-42

58 Kolb, Avery. "Early Passengers to Virginia: When Did They Really Arrive." *The Virginia Magazine of History and Biography* 88, no. 4 (1980, October): 401–414.

59 Stanard, William G. "Virginia Land Patents." *Virginia Historical Magazine and The Virginia Magazine of History and Biography* 2, no 1. (Jul 1894): 68. Virginia Historical Society.

60 "Headright System: Definition & History - Video & Lesson Transcript." Study.com, n.d. https://study.com/academy/lesson/headright-system-definition-lesson-quiz.html

61 "Headrights (VA-NOTES)." Library of Virginia, n.d. https://www.lva.virginia.gov/public/guides/va4_headrights.htm

62 *How Colonists Acquired Title to Land in Virginia*. Virginiaplaces.org, (n.d.). http://www.virginiaplaces.org/settleland/headright.html

63 Fann, Porter. "Unknown Key (abt.1610-bef.1655)." WikiTree: Where Genealogists Collaborate, October 31, 2022. https://www.wikitree.com/wiki/Key-4376

64 Ponti, Crystal. "America's History of Slavery Began Long Before Jamestown." Black History, *History.com*, August 16, 2024. https://www.history.com/news/american-slavery-before-jamestown-1619

65 Morgan, Jennifer L. *Laboring Women Reproduction and Gender in New World Slavery*. Pennsylvania: University of Pennsylvania Press, 2004.

66 Edwards, Rose. "Humphrey Higginson (1607-aft.1666)." WikiTree: Where Genealogists Collaborate, February 6, 2023. https://www.wikitree.com/wiki/Higginson-36

67 Stokes, William. "John Mottrom (abt.1610-abt.1655)." WikiTree: Where Genealogists Collaborate, March 29, 2024. https://www.wikitree.com/wiki/ Mottrom-5

68 Loggans, Regan. "Legislating Reproduction and Racial Difference in Virginia." Early Encounters, 1492-1734, English Colonies, Women & the American Story, New York Historical Society Museum & Library, n.d. https://wams.nyhistory.org/early-encounters/english-colonies/legislating-reproduction-and-racial-difference/

69 Mothering Slaves. *Jennifer Morgan, 'Partus Sequitur Ventrem': Law and Re/Production for Enslaved Women*, 2015, April 21. https://www.youtube.com/watch?v=Y GEARpgIzEY

70 Hughes, Louis. *Thirty Years a Slave: From Bondage to Freedom: The Institution of Slavery as Seen on the Plantation in the Home of the Planter: Autobiography of Louis Huges*. Milwaukee: South Side Printing Company, 1897. https://www.google.com/books/edition/Thirty_Years_a_Slave/oyRY2JRtn4gC?hl=en&gb-pv=1&pg= PA1&printsec=frontcover

71 Henson, Josiah. *The Life Of Josiah Henson: Formerly a Slave, Now an Inhabitant of Canada*. Cambridge: Bolles and Houghton, 1849.

72 De Latte, Carolyn E. "Review: [Untitled]." *Louisiana History: The Journal of the Louisiana Historical Association* 33, no. 4 (1992): 432–434. http://www.jstor.org/stable/4232979

73 Brown, D.L. "Missouri v. Celia, a Slave: She killed the white master raping her, then claimed self-defense." Retropolis, *Washington Post*, October 19, 2017. https://www.washingtonpost.com/news/retropolis/wp/2017/10/19/missouri-v-celia-a-slave-she-killed-the-white-master-raping-her-then-claimed-self-defense/

74 Pokorak, Jeffrey J. "Rape as a Badge of Slavery: The Legal History of, and Remedies for, Prosecutorial Race-of-Victim Charging Disparities." *Nevada Law Journal* 7, no. 1 (2006): article 2.

75 Wriggins, Jennifer. "Rape, Racism, and the Law." In *Rape and Society* edited by Patricia Searles and Ronald J. Berger, 215–222. *London*: Routledge, 2018. https://doi.org/10.4324/9780429493201-26

76 Derbes, Brett Josef. "Born in the Penitentiary: Women and Children Incarcerated in Louisiana, 1833-1862." Paper, Colorado Convention Center, January 8, 2017. https://aha.confex.com/aha/2017/ webprogram/Paper21380.html

77 Shanahan, Ed. "Judge Spares Man in Teen Rape Case: 'Incarceration Isn't Appropriate.'" *The New York Times*, December 2, 2021. https://www.nytimes.com/2021/11/18/nyregion/christopher-belter-rape-sentence.html

78 Derbes, Brett Josef. "'Secret Horrors'": Enslaved Women and Children in the Louisiana State Penitentiary, 1833–1862." *The Journal of African American History* 98, no. 2 (2013): 277–290. doi:10.5323/jafriamerhist.98.2.0277

79 "Dallas v. State, 76 Fla. 358 (1918)." Caselaw Access Project, Harvard Law School Library, August 29, 2019. https://cite.case.law/fla/76/358/

80 Woodson, C. G. *The Education of the Negro Prior to 1861: A History of the Education of the Colored People of the United States from the Beginning of Slavery to the Civil War.* New York: G.P. Putnam's Sons, 1915.

81 *Black Journal; Black Paper on White Racism. Part 1.* (n.d.). https://www.digital-commonwealth.org/search/ commonwealth-oai:h702rd821

82 Allyn, Bobby. "Cyntoia Brown Released After 15 Years In Prison For Murder." Law, *NPR*, August 7, 2019. https://www.npr.org/2019/08/07/749025458/cyntoia-brown-released-after-15-years-in-prison-for-murder

83 "Stanford sexual assault: Read the full text of the judge's controversial decision." *The Guardian*, June 14, 2016. http://www.theguardian.com/us-news/2016/jun/14/stanford-sexual-assault-read-sentence-judge-aaron-persky

84 Rowe, Dominque. "A Canadian Judge Is Under Scrutiny Following Comments He Made During a Rape Case." *Yahoo Sports*, n.d. https://ca.sports.yahoo.com/news/canadian-judge-trial-following-comments-060009895.html

85 Savini, Dave, Samah Assad, and Michele Youngerman. "'You Have the Wrong Place:' Body Camera Video Shows Moments Police Handcuff Innocent, Naked Woman During Wrong Raid." *CBS News*, December 17, 2020. https://chicago.cbslocal.com/2020/12/17/you-have-the-wrong-place-body-camera-video-shows-moments-police-handcuff-innocent-naked-woman-during-wrong-raid/

86 Pratt, Gregory Royal. "Mayor Lori Lightfoot apologized, but her administration takes hard line with Anjanette Young in high-stakes lawsuit over botched raid." *Chicago Tribune*, July 2, 2021. https://www.chicagotribune.com/politics/ct-lori-lightfoot-anjanette-young-lawsuit-20210702-x6vqkhe2jne6de4wpxx565bw7i-story.html

87 Morrison, Toni. *Beloved.* New York: Vintage Classics, 1987.

88 Buirski, Nancy, dir. *The Rape of Recy Taylor. YouTube.* United States: The Orchard Entertainment, 2018, YouTube. https://www.youtube.com/watch?v=rPudMdFEqUs.

89 Feinstein, Rachel A. *When Rape Was Legal.* London: Routledge, 2018.

90 Gross, Kali N., and Cheryl D. Hicks. "Introduction—Gendering the Carceral State: African American Women, History, and the Criminal Justice System." *The Journal of African American History* 100, no. 3 (2015): 357–365. doi:10.5323/jafriamerhist.100.3.0357

91 Momodu, Samuel. "Betty Jean Owens (1930s- ?)." African American History, *BlackPast*, February 28, 2019. https://www.blackpast.org/african-american-history/betty-jean-owens-193/

92 Parker, Kendra R. "As the World Burns: 'Checking In' (An Annotated Letter to My Students with Lessons from Octavia E. Butler)." *CLA Journal* 63, no. 2 (2020): 162–168. doi:10.34042/claj.63.2.0162

93 Gafney, Wil. "A Reflection on the Black Lives Matter Movement and Its Impact on My Scholarship." *Journal of Biblical Literature* 136, no. 1 (2017): 204–207. doi:10.15699/jbl.1361.2017.1363

94 Cigarran, J. "The Case of Cheryl D. James: Institutionalized Racism and Police Violence Against Black Women in Portland, Oregon (1968–1974)." *Oregon Historical Quarterly* 121, no. 1 (2020): 40–67. doi:10.5403/ oregonhistq.121.1.0040

95 Andone, Dakin, and Dan Simon. "Officials still don't know why a white man allegedly stabbed a black woman to death in a subway station." *CNN*, July 27, 2018. https://www.cnn.com/2018/07/27/us/nia-wilson-murder-bart-stabbing-trnd/index.html

96 Pasley, Gay. "Fact Finding." *Transition* no. 124 (2017): 190–196. doi:10.2979/transition.124.1.31

97 Wells-Barnett, Ida B. *Southern Horrors: Lynch Law in All Its Phases*. Outlook Verlag, 2018.

98 Allen, James. *Without Sanctuary: Lynching Photography in America*. United States: Twin Palms Publishers, 2000.

99 Ginzburg, Ralph. *100 Years of Lynchings*. Baltimore: Black Classic Press, 1988.

100 Alexander, Kerri Lee. "Autherine Lucy." National Women's History Museum, 2018. https://www.womenshistory.org/education-resources/biographies/autherine-lucy

101 "Nial Ruth Cox, Appellant, v. A. M. Stanton, M.d., et al., Appellees, 529 F.2d 47 (4th Cir. 1975)." *Justia Law*, (n.d.). https://law.justia.com/cases/federal/appellate-courts/F2/529/47/386658/

102 Carmon, Irin. "For eugenic sterilization victims, belated justice." *MSNBC*, June 26, 2014. https://www.msnbc.com/all/eugenic-sterilization-victims-belated-justice-msna 358381

103 "1973 Special Report: 'Forced Sterilizations of Welfare Mothers.'" Hezakya Newz & Films, YouTube, March 25, 2019. https://www.youtube.com/watch?v= 3h34WUZeFJI

104 "Milley defends military, open-mindedness amid 'woke' allegations." *Washington Post*, June 23, 2021. https://www.youtube.com/watch?v= -y0PfiS0jxY

105 "BNT Exclusive: Dr. Aruna Khilanani Explains Yale Speech About Killing White People." Black News Tonight with Marc Lamont Hill, YouTube, June 16, 2021. https://www.youtube.com/watch?v=o20tk-QrZiE

106 "Lauryn Hill—Black Rage (#BlackLivesMatter Edition)." Posted by Nathan Bean, YouTube, November 26, 2014. https://www.youtube.com/watch?v=xAhFAgQGf88

107 "Lauryn Hill – Black Rage." Genius.com Lyrics. (n.d.). https://genius.com/Lauryn-hill-black- rage-annotated

108 Maryland State Archives. "1770_irish_nell.pdf." (n.d.). maryland.gov. https://msa.maryland.gov/megafile/msa/speccol/sc5400/sc5496/000500/000534/images/1770_irish_nell.pdf

109 Maryland State Archives. "Irish Nell Butler." Archives of Maryland, Biographical Series. (n.d.). https://msa.maryland.gov/megafile/msa/speccol/sc5400/sc5496/000500/000534/html/00534bio.html

110 Hogan, Liam. "The Forced Breeding Myth in the Irish Slaves Meme." *Medium*, November 30, 2018.

111 "Butler v. Boarman, 1 Md. 371 (1770)." Caselaw Access Project, Harvard Law School Library, August 29, 2019. https://cite.case.law/md/1/371/

112 "Black History Month | James Baldwin." *The Bee & The Fox*, February 2, 2019. https://www.thebeeandthefox.com/blogs/news/black-history-month-james-baldwin

113 Anonymous Quote. San Francisco, January 30, 2019.

114 "South Carolina Passes Negro Act of 1740, Codifying White Supremacy." A History of Racial Injustice, Equal Justice Initiative, May 10, 1740. https://calendar.eji.org/racial-injustice/may/10

115 "Chapter One: The Status of the Negro, his Rights and Disabilities." The Negro Law of South Carolina, Collected and Digested by John Belton O'Neall. Genealogy Trails History Group, (n.d.). http://genealogytrails.com/scar/negro_law.htm

116 Rasmussen, Birgit Brander. "'Attended with Great Inconveniences': Slave Literacy and the 1740 South Carolina Negro Act." *PMLA* 125, no. 1 (2010): 201–203.

117 Cushing, John D. *The Earliest Printed Laws of South Carolina, 1692-1734.* Wilmington, DE: Michael Glazier, 1978.

118 "Epigenetics, Health, and Disease." *U.S. Centers for Disease Control and Prevention*, May 15, 2024. https://www.cdc.gov/genomics-and-health/about/epigenetic-impacts-on-health.html?CDC_AAref_Val=https://www.cdc.gov/genomics/disease/epigenetics.htm

119 *1349_5985e86bb14db77.jpg (527×832).* (n.d.). https://encyclopediavirginia.org/wp-content/uploads/2020/11/ 1349_5985e86bb14db77.jpg

120 McCartney, Martha. "Virginia's First Africans." *Encyclopedia Virginia*, December, 7, 2020. https://encyclopediavirginia.org/entries/africans-virginias-first/

121 "Headrights." *VA Notes*, Library of Virginia, (n.d.). https://www.lva.virginia.gov/public/guides/va4_headrights.htm

122 Hening, William Waller. *The Statutes at Large: Being a Collection of All the Laws of Virginia, From the First Session of the Legislature, in the Year 1619* (Vol. 1-13). William Waller Hening, 1823.

123 "The Colonial Virginia Register" New River Notes, Grayson County Virginia Heritage Foundation, (n.d.). https://www.newrivernotes.com/topical_books_1902_virginia_colonialvirginiaregister.htm

124 "Tulsa Race Massacre: President Biden commemorates 100-year anniversary." *BBC News*, June 1, 2021. https://www.bbc.com/news/ world-us-canada-57323200

125 Borum, Randy. *Psychology of Terrorism.* Tampa: University of South Florida, 2003.

126 Steindl, Christina, Eva Jonas, Sandra Sittenthaler, Eva Traut-Mattausch, and Jeff Greenberg. "Understanding Psychological Reactance." *Zeitschrift Fur Psychologie* 223, no. 4 (2015): 205–214. https://doi.org/10.1027/2151-2604/ a000222

127 "Police respect whites more than Black people during traffic stops, language analysis finds." *PBS NewsHour*, 2017, June 5. https://www.pbs.org/newshour/science/police-respect-whites-Black people-traffic-stops-language-analysis-finds

128 Peyton, Nellie. "Redlining in America: How Housing Discrimination Endures." News.Trust.Org, (n.d.). https://news.trust.org/item/20200713110849-az14m/

129 "The Southern "Black Codes" of 1865-66." Teach Democracy, (n.d.). https://www.crf-usa.org/brown-v-board-50th-anniversary/southern-black-codes.html

130 Greer, Tawanda M., and Klaus E. Cavalhieri. "The Role of Coping Strategies in Understanding the Effects of Institutional Racism on Mental Health Outcomes for African American Men." *Journal of Black Psychology* 45, no. 5, (2019): 405–433. https://doi.org/10.1177/0095798419868105

131 Blessett, Brandi, and Vanessa Littleton. "Examining the Impact of Institutional Racism in Black Residentially Segregated Communities." *Ralph Bunche Journal of Public Affairs* 6, no 1 (2017): article 3.

132 Madrigal, Alexis C. "The Racist Housing Policy That Made Your Neighborhood." *The Atlantic*, May 22, 2014. https://www.theatlantic.com/business/archive/2014/05/the-racist-housing-policy-that-made-your-neighborhood/371439/

133 Rothstein, Richard. *The Color of Law: A Forgotten History of How Our Government Segregated America*. New York: W.W. Norton & Company, 2018.

134 Wolf, Michael A. *The Zoning of America: Euclid V. Ambler*. Lawrence: University Press of Kansas, 2008.

135 Katznelson, Ira. *When Affirmative Action Was White*. New York: W.W. Norton, 2005.

136 Lemire, Elise V. *Miscegenation*. Philadelphia: University of Pennsylvania Press, Inc., 2009.

137 Pascoe, Peggy. *What Comes Naturally: Miscegenation Law and the Making of Race in America*. Cambridge: Oxford Univ. Press, 2011.

138 Washington, Harriet A. *Medical Apartheid: The Dark History of Medical Experimentation on Black Americans from Colonial Times to the Present*. New York: Double Day, 2006.

139 Hlavinka, Elizabeth. "Racial Bias in Flexner Report Permeates Medical Education Today." Public Health & Policy, Medical Eduation, *MedpageToday*, June 18, 2020. https://www.medpagetoday.com/publichealthpolicy/medicaleducation/87171

140 Bean, Robert Bennett. "Some racial peculiarities of the Negro brain." *American Journal of Anatomy* 5, no. 4 (1906): 353–432. https://doi.org/10.1002/aja.1000050402

141 Goyal, Monika K., Tiffani J. Johnson, James M. Chamberlain, Lawrence Cook, Michael Webb, Amy L. Drendel, Evaline Alessandrini, Lalit Bajaj, Scott Lorch, Robert W. Grundmeier, Elizabeth R. Alpern, and PEDIATRIC EMERGENCY CARE APPLIED RESEARCH NETWORK (PECARN). "Racial and Ethnic Differences in Emergency Department Pain Management of Children With Fractures." *Pediatrics* 145, no. 5 (2020): e20193370. https://doi.org/10.1542/ peds.2019-3370

142 Greenwood, Brad N., Rachel R. Hardeman, Laura Huang, and Aaron Sojourner. "Physician–patient racial concordance and disparities in birthing mortality for newborns." *Proceedings of the National Academy of Sciences* 117, no. 35 (2020): 21194–21200. https://doi.org/10.1073/pnas.1913405117

143 Hoffman, Kelly M., Sophie Trawalter, Jordan R. Axt, and M. Norman. "Racial bias in pain assessment and treatment recommendations, and false beliefs about

biological differences between Black people and whites." *Proceedings of the National Academy of Sciences* 113, no. 16 (2016): 4296–4301.

144 Mende-Siedlecki, Peter, Jennie Qu-Lee, Robert Backer, and Jay J. Van Bavel. "Perceptual Contributions to Racial Bias in Pain Recognition." *Journal of Experimental Psychology: General* 148, no. 5 (2019): 863–889.

145 *David Walker, 1785-1830. Walker's Appeal, in Four Articles; Together with a Preamble, to the Coloured Citizens of the World, but in Particular, and Very Expressly, to Those of the United States of America, Written in Boston, State of Massachusetts, September 28, 1829.* (n.d.). https://docsouth.unc.edu/nc/walker/walker.html

146 "The Constitution". Resources Library, Primary Sources, Bill of Rights Institute, (n.d.). https://billofrightsinstitute.org/primary-sources/constitution/

147 Duvernay, Ava. (2017). *13th. http://www.avaduvernay.com/13th.* http://www.avaduvernay.com/13th.

148 Alexander, Michelle. *The New Jim Crow: Mass Incarceration in the Age of Colorblindness.* New York: New Press, 2012.

149 "Slavery By Another Name." *WOUB Public Media*, February 1, 2012. https://woub.org/2012/02/01/slavery-another-name/

150 DiAngelo, Robin. *Nice Racism: How Progressive White People Perpetuate Racial Harm.* Beacon Press, 2021.

151 Hale, Grace Elizabeth. *Making whiteness: the culture of segregation in the South, 1890-1940.* New York: Vintage Press, 2004.

152 Yu, Mallory. "'I Am Not Your Negro' Gives James Baldwin's Words New Relevance." Movies, *NPR*, February 3, 2017. https://www.npr.org/2017/02/03/513311359/i-am-not-your-negro-gives-james-baldwins-words-new-relevance

153 Haynes, Danielle. "Study: Black Americans 3 times more likely to be killed by police." U.S. News, UPI, June 24, 2020. https://www.upi.com/Top_News/US/ 2020/06/24/Study-Black-Americans-3-times-more-likely-to-be-killed-by-police/ 6121592949925/. https://www.hsph.harvard.edu/news/hsph-in-the-news/Blackpeople-whites-police-deaths-disparity/

154 Schwartz, Gabriel L., and Jaquelyn L. Jahn. "Mapping fatal police violence across U.S. metropolitan areas: Overall rates and racial/ethnic inequities, 2013-2017." *PLOS ONE* 15, no. 6 (2020): e0229686. https://doi.org/10.1371/journal. pone.0229686

155 Hanks, Angela, Danyelle Solomon, and Christian E. Weller. "Systematic Inequality." The Influence of Race in American Policy, Center for American Progress, February 21, 2018. https://www.americanprogress.org/issues/race/reports/2018/02/21/447051/systematic-inequality/

156 Novoa, Cristina, and Jamila Taylor. "Exploring African Americans' High Maternal and Infant Death Rates." Center for American Progress, February 1, 2018. https://www.americanprogress.org/issues/early-childhood/reports/2018/02/01/445576/exploring-african-americans-high-maternal-infant-death-rates/

157 Ajilore, Olugbenga. "On the Persistence of the Black-White Unemployment Gap." Center for American Progress, February 24, 2020. https://www.americanprogress. org/issues/economy/reports/2020/02/24/480743/persistence-black-white-unemployment-gap/

158 Wilson, Valerie. "Black unemployment is significantly higher than white unemployment regardless of educational attainment." *Economic Policy Institute*, December 17, 2015. https://www.epi.org/publication/ black-unemployment-educational-attainment/

159 "Laws Concerning Slavery in Missouri: Territorial to 1850s." Missouri State Archives, Missouri's Early Slave Laws: A History in Documents, Missouri Digital Heritage. (n.d.). https://www.sos.mo.gov/archives/education/aahi/earlyslavelaws/slavelaws.asp

160 Missouri General Assembly. *Laws Of The State Of Missouri: Revised And Digested By Authority Of The General Assembly. With An Appendix. Published According To An Act Of The General Assembly, Passed 21st February, 1825* (Vol. II). Legare Street Press, July 18, 2023.

161 "Alabama Legislature Bans Free Black People from Living in the State." A History of Racial Injustice, January 17, 1834. https://calendar.eji.org/racial-injustice/jan/17

162 "Fugitive Slave Act: September 18, 1850." Civil War, Primary Source, American Battlefield Trust, (n.d.). https://www.battlefields.org/learn/primary-sources/fugitive-slave-act

163 Eastman, Zebina. *Black Code of Illinois.* Chicago: Publisher Unknown, 1883.

164 Wormser, Richard. *The Rise and Fall of Jim Crow.* New York: St. Martin's Griffin, 2004.

165 Bennett Jr, Lerone. *The Shaping of Black America.* Johnson, 2007.

166 Bennett Jr, Lerone. *Forced into Glory: Abraham Lincoln's White Dream.* Johnson, 2007.

167 "Letter to Horace Greeley." Speeches & Writings, Abraham Lincoln Online, 2020. http://www.abrahamlincolnonline.org/lincoln/speeches/greeley.htm

168 Bennett Jr, Lerone. *Before the Mayflower: A History of Black America.* Indiana: Johnson Pub. Co, 2003.

169 Harris, Irene. *The Homestead act and Westward Expansion: Settling the Western Frontier.* New York: The Rosen Publishing Group, 2017.

170 Karr, Charles. H. (n.d.). *Civil Rights and the Negro, 1875-1900.* 37.

171 "Remembering Mary Turner." The Mary Turner Project. (n.d.). https://www. maryturner.org/

172 "100 years ago, John Hartfield was hanged, shot, roasted for dating a white lady and his body parts shared to spectators." Face2Face Africa, November 20, 2019. https://face2faceafrica.com/article/100-years-ago-john-hartfield-was-hanged-shot-roasted-for-dating-a-white-lady-and-his-body-parts-shared-to-spectators

173 "Elaine Massacre of 1919." Civil Rights & Social Change, Race, Early Twentieth Century, Encyclopedia of Arkansas, (n.d.). https://encyclopediaofarkansas.net/entries/elaine-massacre-of-1919-1102/

174 Faber, Eli. *The Child in the Electric Chair: The Execution of George Junius Stinney Jr. and the Making of a Tragedy in the American South*. Columbia: The University of South Carolina Press, 2021.

175 Stevenson, Darius. "Murder in Black and White: Moore's Ford Lynching." YouTube, June 1, 2018. https://www.youtube.com/watch?v=0lYH-Rdc_aw

176 "Jim Jones And The Peoples Temple." Jim Jones/Jonestown Documentary. YouTube, (n.d.). https://www.youtube.com/watch?v=hO8aYSApnng

177 *Take this Hammer (the Director's Cut)—Bay Area Television Archive*. (n.d.). https://diva.sfsu.edu/collections/ sfbatv/bundles/216518

178 "A Tribute to Strom Thurmond: The Last True Christian Senator." Landover Baptist, Americhrist, Ltd. (n.d.). https://www.landoverbaptist.org/news0703/thurmond.html

179 "The historic 1948 Democratic National Convention." *Fox News*, YouTube, July 27, 2016. https://www.youtube.com/watch?v=DgfuWHYIwv4

180 "About Gemmel Moore & Timothy Dean | Justice4Gemmel+." Justice4Gemmel, (n.d.). https://www.justice4gemmel.org/ gemmelandtimothy

181 "Marc Lamont Hill and Judge Joe Brown Get into Heated Debate on Media's Portrayal of Bill Cosby." *BNC News*, YouTube, July 1, 2021. https://www.youtube.com/watch?v=6nBDNsNSga4

182 "Marc Lamont Hill: 'Supporting Bill Cosby is Proof We Don't Love Black Women Enough.'" *BNC News*, YouTube, July 6, 2021. https://www.youtube.com/watch?v=lXUMw61GxFQ

183 "O.J. Simpson acquitted." History, (n.d.). from https://www.history.com/this-day-in-history/o-j-simpson-acquitted

184 O'Neal, Traci D. *The Exceptional Negro: Racism, White Privilege, and the Lie of Respectability Politics*. Atlanta: Icart Media LLC, 2018.

185 Fox, Jerome E. *Addicted to White: The Oppressed in League with the Oppressor: A Shame-based Alliance*. United States: Jerome E. Fox, 2016.

186 JAY-Z. JAY-Z - The Story of O.J. YouTube, (n.d.). https://www.youtube.com/watch?v=RM7lw0Ovzq0

187 DuVernay, Ava, creator. *When They See Us*. Netflix, 2019. https://www.netflix.com/watch/80200549?trackId=13752289&tctx=0%2C0%2Cca93f7d3f75d22d797f3e9ae410c56ce05814bdf%3Addecaafef33ccb21650a2deece83f797a00d370d%2Cca93f7d3f75d22d797f3e9ae410c56ce05814bdf%3Addecaafef33ccb21650a2deece83f797a00d370d%2Cunknown%2C.

188 Maslin, Janet. "Film: 'School Daze.'" *The New York Times*, February 12, 1988. https://www.nytimes.com/1988/02/12/movies/film-school-daze.html

189 Garvey, Marcus, and Nnamdi Azikiwe. *Emancipated from Mental Slavery: Selected Sayings of Marcus Garvey*. The Mhotep Corporation, 2019.

190 "How Can We Win." David Jones Media, YouTube, June 1, 2020. https://www.youtube.com/watch?v=sb9_qGOa9Go

191 "Inside the AC360 doll study." *CNN*, YouTube, May 17, 2010. https://www.youtube.com/ watch?v=DYCz1ppTjiM

192 "Study shows how children view race bias." *CNN*, YouTube, May 18, 2010. https://www.youtube.com/watch?v=EQACkg5i4AY

193 "Raw Footage: Texas Cop Draws Gun on Pool-Party Teens." *Wall Street Journal*, YouTube, June 8, 2015. https://www.youtube.com/watch?v=z6tTfoifB7Q

194 *GRAPHIC: Video shows Atlanta police officer kick handcuffed woman in head.* WHSV3, July 28, 2021. https://www.whsv.com/2021/07/28/graphic-video-shows-atlanta-police-officer-kick-handcuffed-woman-head/

195 Evans, Shalwah. "H&M Responds To Backlash Against Its Ad Of A Black Girl With 'Undone' Hair." *Essence*, December 6, 2020. https://www.essence.com/hair/hm-responds-to-black-hair-conversation-sparked-over-ad/

196 JustAnnet . "The 'Father of Gynecology' Performed Horrific Experiments on Enslaved Black Women." *Medium*, 2021, May 25.

197 Terrell, Kellee. "That Little Black Girl's Hair In The H&M Ad Isn't The Problem. Perhaps The Problem Is You." *HelloBeautiful*, September 20, 2019.

198 "Wells Fargo CEOs comments about diverse talent anger some employees." *CNBC*, September 22, 2020. https://www.cnbc.com/2020/09/22/wells-fargo-ceo-ruffles-feathers-with-comments-about-diverse-talent.html

199 Kendi, Ibram X. *How To Be an Antiracist.* New York: Random House 2019.

200 Malcolm X. "Message to the Grass Roots." Detroit: Northern Negro Grass Roots Leadership Conference, November 10, 1963. Posted by 1453malcolmx on Youtube, February 29, 2012. https://www.youtube.com/watch?v=7kf7fujM4ag

201 Patterson, William L., ed. *We Charge Genocide: The Historic Petition to the United Nations for Relief From a Crime of the United States Government Against the Negro People.* New York: Civil Rights Congress, 1951.

202 "When White People Call the Police on Black People." *The New York Times.* (n.d.). https://www.nytimes.com/2018/05/11/us/black-white-police.html?.?mc=aud_dev&ad-keywords=auddevgate&gclid=Cj0KCQjwssyJBhDXARIsAK98ITQ8CnL1DLPrkCfZm5MRZf-WH1Tt8RGc5tAObb-1Zu7x9xsVnam9tXQaAh1UEALw_wcB&gclsrc=aw.ds

203 "Transcript: Donald Trump's Taped Comments About Women." *The New York Times*, October 8, 2016. https://www.nytimes.com/2016/10/08/us/donald-trump-tape-transcript.html

204 "The Key Moments from Christine Blasey Ford's Testimony." (n.d.). https://www.washingtonpost.com/video/politics/the-key-moments-from-christine-blasey-fords-testimony/2018/09/27/9b981858-c281-11e8-9451-e878f96be19b_video.html

205 "Family of girl out of school over 'hair extensions' holds press conference." WWLTV, YouTube, August 24, 2018. https://www.youtube.com/watch?v= evOWVV4Xlhk

206 "My Son Will Be Banned From School Because of His Hair." *This Morning*, You-Tube, September 15, 2017. https://www.youtube.com/watch?v=0BqGblnusEQ

207 Gramling, Sara. "8-Year-Old Marian Scott Banned From Picture Day Because Of Red Hair." Mamas Uncut, McClatchy Media Company, October 27, 2019. https://mamasuncut.com/8-year-old-marian-scott-banned-from-school-picture-day-because-she-had-red-hair/

208 "The Carl Nelson Show: Featuring Dr. Jerome Fox." *Spotify*. Podcast, June 11, 2021. https://open.spotify.com/show/5cpuUVZ6sjoTZiyVlcAiLR

209 "Carson: 'There were other immigrants who came in the bottom of slave ships.'" *AP NEWS*, March 6, 2017. https://apnews.com/article/united-states-archive-immigration-8e80499facaf4e6b8a6b1d1295550b1a

210 Mumford, Kevin. "After Hugh: Statutory Race Segregation in Colonial America, 1630-1725." *The American Journal of Legal History* 43, no. 3 (1999): 280–305. https://doi.org/10.2307/846160

211 Turner, Cory. "Bias Isn't Just A Police Problem, It's A Preschool Problem." Morning Edition, *NPR*, September 28, 2016. https://www.npr.org/sections/ed/2016/09/28/495488716/bias-isnt-just-a-police-problem-its-a-preschool-problem

212 Weiss, Debra Cassens. "Partners in study gave legal memo a lower rating when told author wasn't white." *ABA Journal*, April 21, 2014. https://www.abajournal.com/news/article/hypothetical_legal_memo_demonstrates_unconscious_biases

213 Graham, Ruth. "After the Outrage: Last summer, the Red Cross pulled its racist swimming posters. Has it done anything about racism in swimming?" Family, Slate, July 14, 2017. https://slate.com/human-interest/2017/07/the-red-cross-pulled-its-racist-swimming-posters-its-still-fixing-the-damage.html

214 Badger, Emily, Claire Cain Miller, Adam Pearce, and Kevin Quealy. "Extensive Data Shows Punishing Reach of Racism for Black Boys." *The New York Times*, March 19, 2018. https://www.nytimes.com/interactive/2018/03/19/upshot/race-class-white-and-black-men.html

215 Okun, Tema. "(divorcing) White Supremacy Culture: Coming Home to Who We Really Are." White Supremacy Culture, last updated August 2023. https://www.whitesupremacyculture.info/

216 *Kennedy | Brief American Pageant*. (n.d.). https://college.cengage.com/history/us/kennedy/am_pageant_brief/6e/instructors/protected/primary_sources/sexslave.htm

217 "Capitol Insurrection Updates." *NPR*, September 5, 2021. https://www.npr.org/sections/insurrection-at-the-capitol

218 "Samuel Adams Quotes from 1748-1775." Revolutionary War and Beyond, (n.d.). https://www.revolutionary-war-and-beyond.com/samuel-adams-quotes-1.html

219 Anon. National Advisory Commission on Civil Disorders, Report. Rockville, MD: National Institute of Justice, 1967. https://www.ojp.gov/ncjrs/virtual-library/abstracts/national-advisory-commission-civil-disorders-report

220 Anon. BlackPast, B. *(1967) National Advisory Commission on Civil Disorders (The Kerner Report)*. New York: Bantam Books, 1967. Posted by BlackPast.org on January 21, 2007. https://www.blackpast.org/african-american-history/national-advisory-commission-civil-disorders-kerner-report-1967/

221 Goodwin, Morgan Taylor. "Racial Battle Fatigue: What is it and What are the Symptoms?" *Medium*, December 7, 2018. https://medium.com/racial-battle-fatigue/racial-battle-fatigue-what-is-it-and-what-are-the-symptoms-84f79f49ee1e

222 Caldwell, Britt. "White women are the most dangerous upholders of white supremacy in Silicon Valley, and holding them accountable could cost you your career,

your community, and your sanity." *Medium*, April 24, 2021. https://brittwcaldwell. medium.com/white-women-are-the-most-dangerous-upholders-of-white-supremacy-in-silicon-valley-and-holding-ee62b2ec1bc1

223 Golding, Shenequa. "Maintaining Professionalism In The Age of Black Death Is . . . . A Lot." *Codeblack*, June 2, 2020. https://www.codeblack.com/2020/06/02/maintaining-professionalism-in-the-age-of-black-death-is-a-lot/

224 S. Danielle. "All The Supremacists Are White, All of the Patriarchy Are Men, But You're Probably A Gatekeeper." Raising an Advocate, Mamdemics, December 7, 2018. http://mamademics.com/supremacists-white-patriarchy-men-youre-gatekeeper/

225 "MLK: The Other America." *The Martin Luther King, Jr. Center for Nonviolent Social Change.* July 2, 2015. https://www.youtube.com/watch?v=dOWDtDUKz-U

226 Hill, Evan, Ainara Tiefenthäler, Christiaan Triebert, Drew Jordan, Haley Willis, and Robin Stein. "How George Floyd Was Killed in Police Custody." *The New York Times.* June 1, 2020. https://www.nytimes.com/2020/05/31/us/george-floyd-investigation.html

227 Hassan, Adeel. "What We Know About the Killing of Andrew Brown Jr. In North Carolina." *The New York Times*, April 28, 2021. https://www.nytimes.com/2021/04/28/us/andrew-brown-jr-shooting-north-carolina.html

228 "What to Know About the Death of Daunte Wright." *The New York Times*, April 23, 2021. https://www.nytimes.com/article/daunte-wright-death-minnesota.html

229 Miller, Joshua Rhett. "Ex-DA surrenders after charge in Ahmaud Arbery murder case." *New York Post*, September 8, 2021. https://nypost.com/2021/09/08/ex-da-surrenders-after-charge-in-ahmaud-arbery-murder-case/

230 "Ohio Wal-Mart surveillance video shows police shooting and killing John Crawford III." *The Washington Post*, September 25, 2014. https://www.washington-post.com/news/post-nation/wp/2014/09/25/ohio-wal-mart-surveillance-video-shows-police-shooting-and-killing-john-crawford-iii/

231 Smith, Mitch. "Minnesota Officer Acquitted in Killing of Philando Castile." *The New York Times*, June 16, 2017. https://www.nytimes.com/2017/06/16/us/police-shooting-trial-philando-castile.html

232 "New Ferguson Video Adds Wrinkle to Michael Brown Case." *The New York Times*, March 11, 2017. https://www.nytimes.com/2017/03/11/us/michael-brown-ferguson-police-shooting-video.html?.?mc=aud_dev&ad-keywords=auddevgate&gclid=CjwKCAjwvuGJBhB1EiwACU1Aic3YwB6sLIbS-XRYXvWpzKKohkaBJcdSF1t7qsjwPHaEGgwf03h3jhoCcSAQAvD_BwE&gclsrc=aw.ds

233 Romo, Vanessa. "Justice Department Declines To Prosecute Cleveland Officers In Death Of Tamir Rice." *NPR*, December 29, 2020. https://www.npr.org/2020/12/29/951277146/justice-department-declines-to-prosecute-cleveland-officers-who-killed-tamir-rice

234 Swan, Rachel. "Family of Oscar Grant demands murder charges for second BART officer." *San Francisco Chronicle*, December 11, 2020. https://www.sfchronicle.com/bayarea/article/Family-of-Oscar-Grant-demands-murder-charges-for-15792854.php

235 Getachew, Yaphet, Laure C. Zephyrin, Melinda K. Adams. Arnav Shah, Corinne Lewis, and Michelle M. Doty. "Beyond the Case Count: Wide-Ranging Disparities COVID-19 in U.S." *Commonwealth Fund*, September, 2020. https://doi.org/10.26099/gjcn-1z31

236 Beauchamp, Keith. *The Untold Story of EMMETT LUIS TILL*. Think Films, August 17, 2005. Posted by Mamie Till Mobley, YouTube, November 19, 2012. https://www.youtube.com/watch?v=bvijYSJtkQk

237 "Scottsboro Boys." History.com, February 22, 2018. https://www.history.com/topics/great-depression/scottsboro-boys

238 "The Groveland Four." *PBS*. (n.d.). https://www.pbs.org/show/groveland-four/

239 Duvernay, Ava. "When They See Us: A Learning Companion." Array 101, Participant Media. (n.d.). https://www.wtsu101.org

240 Rendón Laura I. *Sentipensante (Sensing/Thinking) Pedagogy: Educating For Wholeness, Social Justice and Liberation*. New York: Stylus Publishing, LLC, 2023.

241 Wilson, Shawn. *Research Is Ceremony: Indigenous Research Methods*. Canada: Fernwood Publishing, 2008.

242 Smith, Linda Tuhiwai. *Decolonizing methodologies: research and indigenous peoples by Linda Tuhiwai Smith,* 1st ed. New York: Bloomsbury Publishing, 2021.

243 Givens, Jarvis R. *Fugitive Pedagogy: Carter G. Woodson and the Art of Black Teaching*. Cambridge: Harvard University Press, 2021.

244 Woodson, Carter G. *The Negro In Our History*. United States: Associated Publishers, 1922.

245 Battiste, Marie. *Decolonizing Education: Nourishing the Learning Spirit*. Purich Publishing Limited, 2015.

246 McLean, Helen V. "Psychodynamic Factors in Racial Relations." *The Annals of the American Academy of Political and Social Science* 244 (1946): 159–166. http://www.jstor.org/stable/1024578

247 "Existing While Black." *HuffPost*. Interactive Report, (n.d.). https://www.huffpost.com/interactives/existing-while-black

248 Cragg, Nelson, Daniel Stamm, Janicza Bravo, Craig William Macneill, and Ti West, dirs. *Them*. Amazon Studios, Prime Video, 2021. https://www.amazon.com/THEM-Season-1/dp/B08XXDRJKH

249 "What is Genocide?" Holocaust Encyclopedia, United States Holocaust Memorial Museum, (n.d.). https://encyclopedia.ushmm.org/content/en/article/what-is-genocide

250 "Haldeman Diaries." Search Results, Richard Nixon Presidential Library and Museum. (n.d.). https://search.archives.gov/search?affiliate=nixon-library&page=3&query=haldeman+diaries&sort_by=&utf8=%E2%9C%93

251 Press, T. A. "Haldeman Diary Shows Nixon Was Wary of Black people and Jews." *The New York Times*, 1994, May 18. https://www.nytimes.com/1994/05/18/us/haldeman-diary-shows-nixon-was-wary-of-Black people-and-jews.html

252 Morley, Jefferson. *Snow-Storm in August: Washington City, Francis Scott Key, and the Forgotten Race Riot of 1835*. New York: Random House, 2012.

253 The Rise and Fall of Jim Crow, episode 2, "Fighting Back." Directed by Bill Jersey and Richard Wormser, aired October 1, 2022, in broadcast syndication, *PBS*, 2016, YouTube. https://www.youtube.com/watch?v=utwE5ZPd7Gk

254 WFTV News Media. *The Ocoee Massacre: A Documentary Film.* Florida: Cox Media. Aired November 1, 2020, WFTV, WFTV Now, and WFTV.com. Posted by WFTV Channel 9, YouTube, November 2, 2020. https://www.youtube.com/watch?v=HA0CLxHeH6Y

255 Hezakya Newz & Films. *The Purge: "1917 East St. Louis Massacre."* YouTube, February 10, 2019. https://www.youtube.com/watch?v=Y2AMjfIgtX0

256 *Black Wall Street*. In Search of History, History Channel. Posted by The Blackest Panther, YouTube, July 13, 2016. https://www.youtube.com/watch?v=oJbF9SGB3Yk

257 "Bill Moyers Journal Rosedale: The Way It Is." Posted by Lashunda Hodges, YouTube, January 1, 2018. https://www.youtube.com/watch?v=Dv0n1xfNf1E

258 Ed Schmitt. (2017, April 18). *Segregation Northern Style.* https://www.youtube.com/watch?v=jnnjS4ivBJI

259 Dutton, Jack. "Disabled black man dragged out of car by police." *Newsweek*, October 8, 2021. https://www.newsweek.com/clifford-owensby-disabled-black-man-dragged-car-police-1636908

260 Greene, Jack P. *Pursuits of Happiness: The Social Development of Early Modern British Colonies and the Formation of American Culture.* The University of North Carolina Press, 2003

261 Bertrand, Marianne, and Sendhil Mullainathan. "Are Emily and Greg More Employable than Lakisha and Jamal? A Field Experiment on Labor Market Discrimination" (Working Paper No. 9873; Working Paper Series). National Bureau of Economic Research, 2003. https://doi.org/10.3386/w9873

262 Roberts, Dorothy. *Killing the Black Body: Race, Reproduction, and the Meaning of Liberty.* Read by Shayna Small. New York: Random House Audio, 2020. Audible Audio ed., 14 hr., 38 min. https://www.amazon.com/Killing-Black-Body-Reproduction-Meaning/dp/B088P8HXZJ/ref=sr_1_2?gclid=Cj0KCQiA7oyNBhDiARIsADtGRZYzsqo-jCOIGSQrhaUEjAMsLYyA017hfn5uG5eQWrmhj-PNw8xvvKKsaAuf0EALw_wc-B&hvadid=481141661642&hvdev=c&hvlocphy=9032063&hvnetw=g&hvqm-t=e&hvrand=2519613703099201969&hvtargid=kwd-1029467580408&hy-dadcr=7466_9611873&keywords=killing+the+black+body+book&qid=1638130599&sr=8-2

263 "Civil Rights Cases | Law Cases [1883]." Encyclopedia Britannica, (n.d.). https://www.britannica.com/topic/Civil-Rights-Cases

264 "Civil Rights Cases, 109 U.S. 3 (1883)." Justia Law, (n.d.). https://supreme.justia.com/cases/federal/us/109/3/

265 "109 US 3 "The Civil Rights Cases" United States v. Stanley." OpenJurist, (n.d.). https://openjurist.org/109/us/3

266 "Kyle Rittenhouse, American Vigilante". *The New Yorker*, July 5, 2021. https://www.newyorker.com/magazine/2021/07/05/kyle-rittenhouse-american-vigilante

267 "Trump welcomes Kyle Rittenhouse at Mar-a-Lago days after Kenosha acquittal." *The Palm Beach Post*, November 24, 2021. https://www.palmbeachpost.com/story/news/2021/11/24/rittenhouse-visits-donald-trump-mar-lago-florida-after-tucker-carlson-interview/8747551002/

268 "Colin in Black and White." *Rotten Tomatoes*. (n.d.). https://www.rottentomatoes.com/tv/colin_in_black_and_white

269 Northup, Solomon. *12 Years a Slave.* Auburn: Derby and Miller, 1853.

270 Bennett Jr, Lerone. *Forced into Glory: Abraham Lincoln's White Dream.* Johnson Publishing Company, Inc., 2000. https://www.amazon.com/Forced-into-Glory-Abraham-Lincolns/dp/0874850851/ref=sr_1_1?crid=1HLWX2DWT5PKP&keywords=-forced+into+glory&qid=1638449053&s=books&sprefix=forced+into+%2Cstrip-books%2C213&sr=1-1

271 blacklikevanilla. "BALDWIN'S NIGGER: A 1969 Conversation with James Baldwin and Dick Gregory." *Black Like Vanilla*, 2020, January 10. http://blacklikevanilla.com/baldwins-nigger-a-1969-conversation-with-james-baldwin-and-dick-gregory/

272 "James Baldwin: Speech on Civil Rights." *Alexander Street, a ProQuest Company.* (n.d.). https://search.alexanderstreet.com/preview/work/bibliographic_ entity%7Cvideo_work%7C2787207

273 "Du Bois Center Fellows Favorite Du Bois Quotes." W.E.B. Du Bois Center, November 2020. http://duboiscenter.library.umass.edu/du-bois-quotes/

274 ABC News. "Georgetown law professor fired after Zoom conversation made public." GMA, YouTube, March 12, 2021. https://www.youtube.com/watch?v=R33C7FrsJYc

275 Corcoran, John. "I was a teacher for 17 years, but I couldn't read or write." *BBC News*, April 14, 2018. https://www.bbc.com/news/stories-43700153

276 "Disparities in the Distribution of Paycheck Protection Program Funds Between Majority-White Neighborhoods and Neighborhoods of Color in California." Latino Policy & Politics Initiative, University of California Los Angeles, December 17, 2020. https://latino.ucla.edu/research/disparities-ppp-neighborhoods-california/

277 "Hundreds of billions of dollars in PPP loans marred by racial inequity." *Reveal*, May 1, 2021. http://revealnews.org/article/rampant-racial-disparities-plagued-how-billions-of-dollars-in-ppp-loans-were-distributed-in-the-u-s/

278 "Peoria Speech, October 16, 1854." Lincoln Home, National Park Service. (n.d.). https://www.nps.gov/liho/learn/historyculture/peoriaspeech.htm

279 "The Lincoln-Douglas Debates 4th Debate Part I." Teaching American History, (n.d.). https://teachingamericanhistory.org/document/the-lincoln-douglas-debates-4th-debate-part-i/

280 "Sumptuary Laws and Taxes, Colonial." Dictionary of American History, Encyclopedia.com, August 15, 2024. https://www.encyclopedia.com/history/dictionaries-thesauruses-pictures-and-press-releases/sumptuary-laws-and-taxes-colonial

281 Fede, Andrew T. *Homicide Justified: The Legality of Killing Slaves in the United States and the Atlantic World.* University of Georgia Press, 2017.

282 Smith, W. A., Allen, W. R., & Danley, L. L. "'Assume the Position . . . You Fit the Description'": Psychosocial Experiences and Racial Battle Fatigue Among African

American Male College Students." *American Behavioral Scientist* 51, no. 4 (2007): 551–578.

283 Smith, William A., Jalil Bishop Mustaffa, Chantal M. Jones, Tommy J. Curry, and Walter R. Allen. "'You make me wanna holler and throw up both my hands!': campus culture, Black misandric microaggressions, and racial battle fatigue." *International Journal of Qualitative Studies in Education* 29, no. 9 (2016): 1189–1209.

284 Solarte-Erlacher, Marisol. "Racial Battle Fatigue, Microaggressions, and your Wellbeing." Marisol Erlacher, Blog Post, 2020. http://www.marisolerlacher.com/blog/racialbattlefatigue

285 Williams, David R. "Everyday Discrimination Scale." Harvard University, (n.d.). https://scholar.harvard.edu/davidrwilliams/node/32397

286 Cobb, Jelani, and Matthew Guariglia, eds. *The Essential Kerner Commission Report.* New York: Liveright, 2021.

287 Vile, John R. "United States v. Cruikshank." Free Speech Center at Middle Tennessee State University, September 7, 2024. https://www.mtsu.edu/first-amendment/article/58/united-states-v-cruikshank

288 "Pace v. Alabama, 106 U.S. 583 (1883)." Justia Law, (n.d.). from https://supreme.justia.com/cases/federal/us/106/583/

289 "United States v. Harris, 106 U.S. 629 (1883)." Justia Law, (n.d.). https://supreme.justia.com/cases/federal/us/106/629/

290 "United States v. Harris and others." Legal Information Institute, (n.d.). https://www.law.cornell.edu/supremecourt/text/106/629

291 Grant, Madison, and Henry Fairfield Osborn. *The passing of the great race; or, The racial basis of European history* (4th rev. ed.). New York: Scribner, 1922. http://archive.org/details/passingofgreatra00granuoft

292 "Virginia Health Bulletin: The New Virginia Law to Preserve Racial Integrity, March 1924." *Document Bank of Virginia*, (n.d.). https://edu.lva.virginia.gov/dbva/items/show/226

293 "Buck v. Bell, Superintendent of State Colony Epileptics and Feeble Minded." Legal Information Institute, Cornell Law School, 1927. https://www.law.cornell.edu/supremecourt/text/274/200

294 "WOULD CHECK BIRTH OF ALL DEFECTIVES; Dr. Woods Hutchinson Says Hope of the Race Is in Negative Eugenics." *The New York Times*, September 21, 1912. https://www.nytimes.com/1912/09/21/archives/would-check-birth-of-all-defectives-dr-woods-hutchinson-says-hope.html

295 News 19 WLTX. "Lindsey Graham questions Ketanji Brown Jackson at Supreme Court hearing." YouTube, March 22, 2022. https://www.youtube.com/watch?v=0mQboKg7xBY

296 PBS NewsHour. "WATCH: Sen. Cory Booker questions Jackson in Supreme Court confirmation hearings." YouTube, March 22, 2022. https://www.youtube.com/watch?v=C32oMd22DTI

297 PBS NewsHour. "WATCH: Sen. Josh Hawley questions Jackson in Supreme Court confirmation hearings." YouTube, March 22, 2022. https://www.youtube.com/watch?v=IoNujxJtKV4

298 PBS NewsHour. "WATCH: Sen. Marsha Blackburn presses Ketanji Brown Jackson about Roe v. Wade." YouTube, March 22, 2022. https://www.youtube.com/watch?v=vQMbBxsIwqc

299 PBS NewsHour. "WATCH: Sen. Mike Lee questions Jackson in Supreme Court confirmation hearings." YouTube, March 22, 2022. https://www.youtube.com/watch?v=73LdnKf7W20

300 PBS NewsHour. "WATCH: Sen. Ted Cruz questions Ketanji Brown Jackson on sentencing for child pornography cases." YouTube, March 22, 2022. https://www.youtube.com/watch?v=YLEZGsk_g0o

301 Wilson, Amos N. *The Falsification of Afrikan Consciousness: Eurocentric History, Psychiatry and the Politics of White Supremacy*. New York: Afrikan World Infosystems, 1993.

302 On the Shoulders of Giants. (2022, February 20). *The Failure of the Education System Pt 2 Dr. Amos Wilson*. https://www.youtube.com/watch?v=Q-Qas_Icii0

303 On the Shoulders of Giants. (2022, February 26). *The Failure of the Education System Pt 4 Dr. Amos Wilson*. https://www.youtube.com/watch?v=vlnPxNEpPz8

304 Carew, Topper, Clarke, John H., Sadauki, Owusu, and Seale, Bobby. *Say Brother: The Influence of Malcolm X (1974)*. https://www.youtube.com/watch?v=ruwLj5H0W34

305 Yette, Samuel F. *The Choice: The Issue of Black Survival in America*. New York: G.P. Putnam's Sons, 1971. http://archive.org/details/choiceissueofbla00yett

306 "Amos N. Wilson | The Psychology of Co-operative Economics." Posted by AfricanThinkingChannel, on YouTube, June 1, 2014. https://www.youtube.com/watch?v=n7kigZJninU

307 Bardaglio, Peter W. "Rape and the Law in the Old South: 'Calculated to excite Indignation in every heart.'" *The Journal of Southern History* 60, no. 4 (1994): 749–772. https://doi.org/10.2307/2211066

308 HIll, Anita Faye and Emma Jordan. *Race, Gender and Power in America*. Oxford: Oxford University Press (1995). Accessed through *Washington Post*. https://www.washingtonpost.com/wp-srv/style/longterm/books/chap1/race.htm

309 Andersen, Margaret L., and Patricia Hill Collins. *Race, Class, & Gender: An Anthology* (8th edition). Wadsworth Publishing, 2012.

310 Johnson, Paul. *A History of the American People*. Great Britain: Weidenfeld & Nicolson, 1999.

311 "Andrew Johnson: Highest Number of Slaves Owned: 8." Understanding Prejudice Project, (n.d.). https://secure.understandingprejudice.org/slavery/presinfo.php?president=17

312 "Extract from Thomas Jefferson to John Wayles Eppes, 30 June 1820 [Quote]." Jefferson Quotes & Family Letters, (n.d.). https://tjrs.monticello.org/letter/380

313 Matthews, Dylan. "Woodrow Wilson was extremely racist—Even by the standards of his time." *Vox*, November 20, 2015. https://www.vox.com/policy-and-politics/2015/11/20/9766896/woodrow-wilson-racist

314 Klaas, Brian. "Opinion | Looking back at Andrew Johnson—The president most like Trump." *The Washington Post*, July 9, 2018. https://www.washingtonpost.com/news/democracy-post/wp/2018/07/09/looking-back-at-andrew-johnson-the-president-most-like-trump/

315 "Thomas Jefferson's Racism, 1788." *The American Yawp Reader*, (n.d.). https://www.americanyawp.com/reader/the-early-republic/thomas-jefferson-notes-on-the-state-of-virginia-1788/

316 Molloy, Tim. "How C. Delores Tucker Became the Most-Hated Woman in Hip-Hop (Podcast)." *The Wrap*, November 17, 2018. https://www.thewrap.com/how-c-de-lores-tucker-suge-knight-tupac-became-the-most-hated-woman-in-hip-hop-podcast/

317 *2Pac (Ft. K-Ci & JoJo) – How Do U Want It.* (n.d.). https://genius.com/2pac-how-do-u-want-it-lyrics

318 Johnson, Roy S. "50 years ago Relf sisters were sterilized against their wishes; now Alabama, apologize, write a check." AL.com, June 12, 2022. https://www.al.com/opinion/2022/06/50-years-ago-relf-sisters-were-sterilized-against-their-wishes-now-alabama-apologize-write-a-check.html

319 Hitler, Adolf. *Mein Kampf*. London: The Paternoster Library, 1935.

320 Hitler, Adolf. "The Primacy of Race." *Mein Kampf*. (n.d.). http://www.history-muse.net/readings/HITLERMeinKampf.htm.

321 Markfield, Miriam H. (n.d.). *A More Perfect Union: Eugenics in America*. https://www.naela.org/NewsJournalOnline/NewsJournalOnline/Journal_Articles/2019/Spring2018Contents.aspx

322 Black, Edwin. "The Horrifying American Roots of Nazi Eugenics." *History News Network*, September, 2003. https://historynewsnetwork.org/article/1796

323 Black, Edwin. "Hitler's debt to America." *The Guardian*, February 6, 2004. https://www.theguardian.com/uk/2004/feb/06/race.usa

324 Grant, Nicole. "White Supremacy and the Alien Land Laws of Washington States." The Seattle Civil Rights & Labor History Project, The Civil Rights and Labor History Consortium, 2007. https://depts.washington.edu/civilr/alien_land_laws.htm

325 National Endowment for the Humanities. *The Seattle star. [volume] (Seattle, Wash.) 1899-1947, April 10, 1905, Night Edition, Image 5.*

326 Luo, Michael. "The Forgotten History of the Campaign to Purge Chinese from America" *The New Yorker*, April 22, 2021. https://www.newyorker.com/news/daily-comment/the-forgotten-history-of-the-purging-of-chinese-from-america

327 "The Immigration Act of 1924 (The Johnson-Reed Act." Milestones: 1921-1936, United States Office of the Historian, (n.d.). https://history.state.gov/milestones/1921-1936/immigration-act

328 Fredrickson, George M. *The Black Image in the White Mind: The Debate on Afro-American Character and Destiny, 1817-1914*, 2nd ed. Connecticut: Wesleyan University Press, 1971. ACLS Humanities E-Book.

329 Nash, Gary B. *Great Fear: Race in the Mind of America*. United States: Holt, Rinehart and Winston, 1970.

330 Burris, Alexandria. "Black homeowner had a white friend stand in for third appraisal. Her home value doubled." *The Indianapolis Star*, May 31, 2021. https://www.indystar.com/story/money/2021/05/13/indianapolis-black-homeowner-home-appraisal-discrimination-fair-housing-center-central-indiana/4936571001/

331 Hepler, Lauren. "'Present-day redlining': A Black homeowner says her Oakland property was undervalued by $400K." *San Francisco Chronicle*, July 23, 2021. https://www.sfchronicle.com/eastbay/article/Present-day-redlining-A-Black-homeowner-16335987.php

332 Hepler, Lauren. "A Black couple 'erased themselves' from their home to see if the appraised value would go up. It did—By nearly $500,000." *San Francisco Chronicle*, December 3, 2021. https://www.sfchronicle.com/bayarea/article/Black-Marin-City-couple-sues-appraiser-for-16672840.php

333 Hepler, Lauren. "After concerns of racism in home appraisals, what will it take to fix the $156 billion racial housing gap?" *San Francisco Chronicle*, January 23, 2022. https://www.sfchronicle.com/bayarea/article/After-concerns-of-racism-in-home-appraisals-what-16795222.php

334 Kamin, Debra. "Black Homeowners Face Discrimination in Appraisals." *The New York Times*, August 25, 2025. https://www.nytimes.com/2020/08/25/realestate/blacks-minorities-appraisals-discrimination.html

335 Shakur, Tupac. "Troublesome '96 Lyrics." Genius Lyrics, (n.d.). https://genius.com/2pac-troublesome-96-lyrics

336 Howard, Sage. "Having A Baby Made Me Rethink Black Excellence." *HuffPost,* July 19, 2022. https://www.huffpost.com/entry/black-excellence-pregnant-baby_n_62ce-c335e4b0eef119c0e128

337 Mitchell, Koritha. *From Slave Cabins to the White House: Homemade Citizenship in African American Culture* (1st ed.). Champaign: University of Illinois Press, 2020.

338 Mitchell, Koritha. *Living with Lynching: African American Lynching Plays, Performance, and Citizenship, 1890-1930* (1st ed.). Champaign: University of Illinois Press, 2011.

339 Mitchell, Koritha. "Identifying White Mediocrity and Know-Your-Place Aggression: A Form of Self-Care." *African American Review* 51, no. 4 (2018): 253–262. https://doi.org/10.1353/afa.2018.0045

340 Shakur, Tupac. "Keep Ya Head Up." Released in 1993, Track 3 on *Strictly 4 My N.I.G.G.A.Z.* . . Interscope Record, compact disc. (n.d.). https://genius.com/2pac-keep-ya-head-up-lyrics

341 Wright, Bobby E. "White Psychopathology and Black Mentacide" (n.d.), YouTube, 1:08:06, https://www.youtube.com/watch?v=e6bGlvsTR1U

342 Armour, Jody David. *N*gga Theory: Race, Language, Unequal Justice, and the Law,* read by the author. California: Los Angeles Review of Books, 2021. Audible audio ed., 11 hr., 53 min.

343 Bean, Robert Bennett. "Some racial peculiarities of the Negro brain." *American Journal of Anatomy* 5, no. 4 (1906): 353–432. https://doi.org/10.1002/aja.1000050402

344 "Clipped From The Washington Herald." *The Washington Herald*, September 3, 1915.

345 Well, Samuel R. "New physiognomy, or, Signs of character, as manifested through temperament and external forms, and especially in 'the human face divine.'" New York: Fowler & Wells Co., 1894. Digital Collections—National Library of Medicine, Medicine in the Americas, 1610-1920 Collection. https://collections.nlm.nih.gov/catalog/nlm:nlmuid-101619594-bk

346 Wilson, Amos N. *Black-On-Black Violence: The Psychodynamics of Black Self-Annihilation in Service of White Domination.* New York: Afrikan World Infosystems, 1990.

347 Wilson, Amos N. *The Psychology of Self-Hatred and Self-Defeat: Towards a Reclamation of the Afrikan Mind.* New York: Afrikan World Ecosystems, 2019.

348 Wilson, Amos N. *Blueprint for Black Power: A Moral, Political, and Economic Imperative for the Twenty-First Century.* New York: Afrikan World Infosystems, 1998.

349 "Amos N. Wilson: Special Education: Its Special Agenda Unhooded." Posted by African Thinking Channel on YouTube, May 25, 2015. https://www.youtube.com/watch?v=3QQA6ObBcRo

350 Beinecke Rare Book & Manuscript Library. Yale University, accessed March 1, 2017. https://floridalynchings.wordpress.com/wp-content/uploads/2014/04/the-lynching-of-reuban-stacey.pdf

351 The Daily Assignment (Director). (2022, March 26). *Say Brother The Influence of Malcolm X with Dr. John Henrik Clarke 1974.* https://www.youtube.com/watch?v=A2tTTf9kixM

352 King, Dante D. *THE 400-YEAR HOLOCAUST: White America's Legal, Psychopathic, and Sociopathic Black Genocide - and the Revolt Against Critical Race Theory.* Lulu Self Publishing, 2021.

353 Mossburb, Cheri, Romine, Taylor, and Yan, Holly. "LA City Councilmember Nury Martinez resigns from office, two days after stepping down from leadership post." Crime + Justice, *CNN*, October 13, 2022. https://www.cnn.com/2022/10/12/us/la-city-council-crisis-reform-expansion/index.html

354 Rodriguz, Joe Fitzgerald. "'A Slap in the Face': SFUSD Students Respond to Ann Hsu's Racist Comments." News, *KQED*, August 12, 2022. https://www.kqed.org/news/11922072/a-slap-in-the-face-sfusd-students-respond-to-ann-hsus-racist-comments

355 Schaub, Jeffrey. *London Breed continues support for disgraced SF School Board member, Ann Hsu.* (KCBS Radio: On-Demand, July 25, 2022), 1 min., 23 sec. https://omny.fm/shows/kcbsam-on-demand/london-breed-continues-support-for-disgraced-sf-sc

356 Tucker, Jill. "Mayor Breed backs recall of three San Francisco school board members: 'Our kids must come first.'" *San Francisco Chronicle*, February 15, 2022. https://www.sfchronicle.com/sf/article/Mayor-Breed-backs-recall-of-three-San-Francisco-16607126.php

357 "Tyre Nichols' death: Up to 20 hours of footage relating to deadly beating yet to be released, prosecutor says." *CNN*, February 2, 2023. https://www.cnn.com/2023/02/02/us/tyre-nichols-investigation-thursday/index.html

358 "'It's Really Hard To Figure Out': Ketanji Brown Jackson Questions Lawyers On Affirmative Action." Posted by Forbes Breaking News on YouTube, November 1, 2022. https://www.youtube.com/watch?v=qsuVB4aoufA

359 "Oral Argument - Audio: Students for Fair Admissions v. Univeristy of NC." Oral Arguments, Supreme Court of the United States, October 31, 2022. https://www.supremecourt.gov/oral_arguments/audio/2022/21-707

360 Anderson, Claud. *Detroit Black Journal*. Detroit PBS, 1995. https://www.youtube.com/watch?v=kuNv6MUYXbk

361 Anderson, Claud. *Black Labor, White Wealth: The Search for Power and Economic Justice*. Maryland: Powernomics Corporation of America, Inc., 1994.

362 "Read the full Trump-E. Jean Carroll verdict text here." *CBS News*, May 9, 2023. https://www.cbsnews.com/news/read-the-full-trump-e-jean-carroll-verdict-text-here/

363 Montague, Zach. "Affirmative Action: Rejection of Affirmative Action Draws Strong Reactions From Right and Left." *The New York Times*, June 29, 2023 https://www.nytimes.com/live/2023/06/29/us/affirmative-action-supreme-court

364 "Criminal Violence, Criminal Justice, by Charles E. Silberman." *Commentary Magazine*, January 1, 1979. https://www.commentary.org/articles/james-wilson/criminal-violence-criminal-justice-by-charles-e-silberman/

365 Shakur, Tupac. "How Do U Want It Lyrics." Genius Lyrics, (n.d.). https://genius.com/2pac-how-do-u-want-it-lyrics

366 Feinstein, Rachel A. *When Rape Was Legal: The Untold History of Sexual Violence during Slavery*. London: Routledge, 2018.

367 Jacobs, Harriet A. *Incidents in the Life of a Slave Girl, Written by Herself*. Project Gutenberg eBook [eBook #11030], 2004. https://www.gutenberg.org/ebooks/11030

368 Smithers, Gregory D. *Slave Breeding: Sex, Violence, and Memory in African American History* (Reprint edition). Gainesville: University Press of Florida, 2013.

369 Helmore, E. "10-year-old rape victim forced to travel from Ohio to Indiana for abortion." *The Guardian*, July 3, 2022. https://www.theguardian.com/us-news/2022/jul/03/ohio-indiana-abortion-rape-victim

370 Alter, Charlotte. "She Wasn't Able to Get an Abortion. Now She's a Mom. Soon She'll Start 7th Grade." *Time*, August 14, 2023. https://time.com/6303701/a-rape-in-mississippi/

371 Medina, Jennifer. "Lori Loughlin and Felicity Huffman: 1 Scandal, 2 Actresses, Diverging Paths." *The New York Times*, April 10, 2019. https://www.nytimes.com/2019/04/10/us/lori-loughlin-felicity-huffman-admissions-scandal.html

372 "What Is a Shared Psychotic Disorder?" *WebMD*, May 15, 2023. https://www.webmd.com/schizophrenia/shared-psychotic-disorder

373 "Psychological Projection: Dealing With Undesirable Emotions." EverydayHealth.com, November 15, 2017. https://www.everydayhealth.com/emotional-health/psychological-projection-dealing-with-undesirable-emotions/

374 Walker-Barnes, Chanequa. "Pathological Whiteness: Diagnosing the Hidden Wound." TedTalk, TheoEd, (n.d.). https://www.theoed.com/pathological-whiteness

375 Sinclair, Charlene and Kim, Claire Jean. "Colorlines Live: Asian Americans in an Anti-Black World." June 13, 2023. Livestreamed. YouTube, 58:44. https://www.youtube.com/watch?v=h5rrNVLbcyQ

376 Hoffman, Frederick Ludwig, and Irving Fisher. *Race Traits And Tendencies Of The American Negro And Appreciation And Interest* (Volume XI). United States: American Economic Association, 1896.

377 Morris, Charles. *The Aryan Race: Its Origins and Its Achievements*. Chicago: S.C. Griggs, 1888.

378 Lohr, Steve. "Occupational Segregation Drives Persistent Inequality, Study Says." *The New York Times*, September 4, 2023. https://www.nytimes.com/2023/09/04/business/black-workers-education-segregation.html

379 Jardina, Ashley, Peter Q. Blair, Justin Heck, and Papia Debroy. "The Limits of Educational Attainment in Mitigating Occupational Segregation Between Black and White Workers" (Working Paper 31641). National Bureau of Economic Research, 2023. https://doi.org/10.3386/w31641

380 McLaurin, Melton. *Celia, a Slave*. Read by Mia Ellis. California: Tantor Audio, 2022. Audible audio ed., 6hr., 51 min.

381 Nelson, Joshua Q. "44 states introduced bills, took steps to restrict teaching CRT or how teachers discuss racism, sexism: Report." Education, *Fox News*, May 4, 2023. https://www.foxnews.com/media/44-states-introduced-bills-took-steps-restrict-teaching-crt-how-teachers-discuss-racism-sexism-report

382 Kennedy, John. "DeSantis signs into law 'Stop WOKE Act' to restrict race discussions in Florida." Policy and Politics, *Tallahassee Democrat*, April 22, 2022. https://www.tallahassee.com/story/news/politics/2022/04/22/florida-governor-desantis-stop-woke-act-race-bill-law-sign-discussions-republicans/7403239001/

383 Yousif, Nadine. "Ron DeSantis government bans new advanced African American history course." *BBC News*, January 20, 2023. https://www.bbc.com/news/world-us-canada-64348902

384 Migdon, Brooke. "What is DeSantis's 'Stop WOKE Act'?" Changing America, Respect, Diversity+Inclusion, *The Hill*. August 19, 2022. https://thehill.com/changing-america/respect/diversity-inclusion/3608241-what-is-desantiss-stop-woke-act/

385 Kim, Claire Jean. "The Racial Triangulation of Asian Americans." *Politics & Society* 27, no. 1 (1999): 105-138. https://doi.org/10.1177/0032329299027001005

386 Black, Edwin. *IBM and the Holocaust: The Strategic Alliance Between Nazi Germany and America's Most Powerful Corporation-Expanded Edition* (2nd edition). United States: Dialog Press, 2012.

387 Paoletti, Gabe. "7 Popular Brands That Owe Some Of Their Current Success To Their Nazi Ties." All That's Interesting.com, October 7, 2017. https://allthatsinteresting.com/major-brands-nazi-collaborators

388 "Village of Euclid v. Ambler Realty Co., 272 U.S. 365 (1926)." Justia Law, (n.d.). https://supreme.justia.com/cases/federal/us/272/365/

389 Nelson, Robert K. "Mapping Inequality: Redlining in New Deal America." University of Richmond, (n.d.). https://dsl.richmond.edu/panorama/redlining/

390 "Black History Month: Oakland Physician Stood Up for Housing Rights." *East Bay Express | Oakland, Berkeley & Alameda*, February 6, 2019. https://eastbayexpress.com/black-history-month-oakland-physician-stood-up-for-housing-rights-1/

391 *Dr_Buckingham*. (n.d.). https://www.docspopuli.org/articles/Dr_Buckingham.html

392 "Dr. Dewitt Buckingham." *Oakland Tribune*, 7, July 19, 1954.

393 "Dr. Dewitt Buckingham." *Oakland Tribune*, 21, August 20, 1954.

394 Blackmen Speak, dir. *DeWitt Buckingham & Black Men Speak provide inspiration, hope, life experience, and musical encouragement to the CASRA Fall Conference members 10 27 28 2011 The Power of Connection in a Time of Change.* YouTube, October 28, 2011. https://www.youtube.com/watch?v=O7slSytd5q8

395 Bella, Timothy. "Florida school 'segregated' Black students for talk on test scores, parents say." *Washington Post*, August 23, 2023. https://www.washingtonpost.com/education/2023/08/23/florida-black-students-assembly-test-scores/

396 Ahmed, Issam. "Harvard study finds implicit racial bias highest among white people." Social Sciences, Phys.Org, May 22, 2023. https://phys.org/news/2023-05-harvard-implicit-racial-bias-highest.html

397 "The Nuremberg Race Laws." Holocaust Encyclopedia, United States Holocaust Memorial Museum, June 2, 2021. https://encyclopedia.ushmm.org/content/en/article/the-nuremberg-race-laws

398 "At Iowa rally, Trump doubles down on comments about immigrants poisoning the nation's blood." *PBS NewsHour,* December 20, 2023. https://www.pbs.org/newshour/politics/at-iowa-rally-trump-doubles-down-on-comments-about-immigrants-poisoning-the-nations-blood

399 "Trump doubles down on immigrant 'blood' remark, says he 'never read Mein Kampf.'" *NBC News*, December 20, 2023. https://www.nbcnews.com/politics/donald-trump/trump-doubles-immigrant-blood-remark-says-never-read-mein-kampf-rcna130535

400 "'Married to Medicine' star Dr. Jackie slammed for saying black women "cry wolf" about pregnancy pains." *New York Post*, December 20, 2023. https://pagesix.com/2023/12/20/entertainment/married-to-medicine-star-dr-jackie-slammed-for-saying-black-women-cry-wolf-about-pregnancy-pains/

401 "Really?! 'Married to Medicine' Star Dr. Jackie Called Pregnant Black Women the D-Word." *The Root,* December 21, 2023. https://www.theroot.com/really-married-to-medicine-star-dr-jackie-slammed-fo-1851117353

402 Jordan, Winthrop D. *White Over Black*. Chapel Hill: University of North Carolina Press, 2012. https://uncpress.org/book/9780807871416/white-over-black/

403 "Governor Ron DeSantis Suspends State Attorney Monique Worrell for Neglect of Duty and Incompetence." Ron DeSantis: 46th Governor of Florida. August 9, 2023. https://www.flgov.com/2023/08/09/governor-ron-desantis-suspends-state-attorney-monique-worrell-for-neglect-of-duty-and-incompetence/

404 Lacy, Akela. "Georgia Supreme Court Blocks GOP Attack on Trump Prosecutor." The Intercept, November 28, 2023. https://theintercept.com/2023/11/28/georgia-district-attorney- fani-willis/

405 Gamble, Justin. "North Carolina Supreme Court justice files lawsuit over state investigation into her comments about diversity." *CNN*, September 4, 2023. https://www.cnn.com/2023/09/04/us/anita-earls-lawsuit-diversity-statements-reaj/index.html

406 Blow, Charles M. "Opinion | The Persecution of Harvard's Claudine Gay." *The New York Times*, January 4, 2023. https://www.nytimes.com/2024/01/03/opinion/harvard-claudine-gay-politics.html

407 "The cost of silence: Dr. Nakita Mortimer's tragic story." KevinMD.com., October 20, 2023. https://www.kevinmd.com/2023/10/the-cost-of-silence-dr-nakita-mortimers-tragic-story.html

408 Williams, Quintessa. "Lincoln University Community Calls For President's Termination Amid Dr. Bonnie Bailey's Passing." *HBCU Buzz*, January 11, 2024. https://hbcubuzz.com/2024/01/lincoln-university-community-calls-for-presidents-termination-amid-dr-bonnie-baileys-passing/

409 "Obituaries in Nashville, TN." *The Tennessean*. (n.d.). https://tennessean.com/ten263517

410 "President JoAnne A. Epps." Office of the President, Temple University, (n.d.). https://president.temple.edu/university-leadership/past-presidents/president-joanne-epps

411 "Remembering President JoAnne A. Epps." *Temple Now*, September 22, 2023. https://news.temple.edu/news/2023-09-22/remembering-president-joanne-epps

412 "Vol State Announces Loss of Fourth President, Dr. Orinthia Montague." Volunteer State Community College, (n.d.). https://www.volstate.edu/news/vol-state-announces-loss-fourth-president-dr-orinthia-montague

413 Herrnstein, Richard and Charles A. Murray. *The Bell Curve: Intelligence and Class Structure in American Life*. New York: Simon & Schuster, 1994.

414 "The Blinding of Issac Woodard." American Experience, PBS, YouTube, May 14, 2024. https://www.youtube.com/watch?v=80GKeyIqDW0

415 Warring, Elizabeth. "The YWCA Speech, Reaction, and 'Meet the Press' Interview." Champions of Civil and Human Rights in South Carolina, January 17, 1950. https://digital.library.sc.edu/exhibits/champions/volume-1-2/part-5/elizabeth-mrs-j-waties-waring/